A READER IN
PLANNING THEORY

A READER IN PLANNING THEORY

Edited by

ANDREAS FALUDI Dipl-Ing, Dr techn

Formerly Principal Lecturer in Planning Theory, Oxford Polytechnic

PERGAMON PRESS

Member of Maxwell Macmillan Pergamon Publishing Corporation

OXFORD · NEW YORK · BEIJING · FRANKFURT
SÃO PAULO · SYDNEY · TOKYO · TORONTO

U.K.	Pergamon Press plc, Headington Hill Hall, Oxford OX3 0BW, England
U.S.A.	Pergamon Press Inc., Maxwell House, Fairview Park, Elmsford, NY 10523, U.S.A.
PEOPLE'S REPUBLIC OF CHINA	Pergamon Press, Room 4037, Qianmen Hotel, Beijing, People's Republic of China
FEDERAL REPUBLIC OF GERMANY	Pergamon Press GmbH, Hammerweg 6, D-6242 Kronberg, Federal Republic of Germany
BRAZIL	Pergamon Editora Ltda, Rua Eça de Queiros, 346, CEP 04011, Paraiso, São Paulo, Brazil
AUSTRALIA	Pergamon Press Australia Pty Ltd, P.O. Box 544, Potts Point, N.S.W. 2011, Australia
JAPAN	Pergamon Press, 5th Floor, Matsuoka Central Building, 1-7-1 Nishishinjuku, Shinjuku-ku, Tokyo 160, Japan
CANADA	Pergamon Press Canada Ltd., Suite No. 271, 253 College Street, Toronto, Ontario, Canada M5T 1R5

Copyright © 1973 Andreas Faludi

First edition 1973
Reprinted 1974, 1976, 1978 (twice), 1983, 1984, 1986, 1988, 1991

Library of Congress Cataloging in Publication Data

Faludi, Andreas, comp.
A reader in planning theory.
(Urban and regional planning series, v. 5)
1. Regional planning—Addresses, essays, lectures.
2. Cities and towns—Planning 1945- —Addresses,
essays, lectures.   I. Title.   II. Series.
HT391.F27   309.2′12′01   72-11536

ISBN 0-08-017066-8 (Hardcover)
ISBN 0-08-017067-6 (Flexicover)

Printed in Great Britain by BPCC Wheatons Ltd, Exeter

Contents

Foreword

THE introduction to Part I explains why this reader contains contributions to a theory *of* planning rather than to theory *in* planning. Beyond this broad distinction based on theoretical argument, there are practical considerations which I have had to make. This foreword addresses itself to these secondary factors contributing to my choices.

The literature from which I have drawn comes largely from the United States, is partly social science-based, and not very easily accessible to planners on this side of the Atlantic. The main sources are the volumes of *Journal of the American Institute of Planners* published at a time when the journal was not so widely read abroad as it appears to be now. This applies in particular to the United Kingdom where, following a deliberate decision on the part of the then Town Planning Institute to press for expansion of planning education, a great number of planning schools have been set up recently. A majority of these are located in relatively new institutions of higher education. They tend to lack adequate library facilities, quite apart from the fact that back volumes of the *Journal of the American Institute of Planners* are impossible to obtain, apart from reprints which, however, are not available of the most interesting volumes.

Other material which is less accessible to planning students and practitioners than the ordinary literary diet on which they feed has also been included. It is hoped that this will stimulate them to compare their own practices with American planning. Not only is the American planning literature rich in intellectual stimuli and easily accessible from the point of view of language, it may also provide occasion for reflecting on current developments on one's own doorstep. The Americans have, for instance, been through debates concerning the role of the planner which the now Royal Town Planning Institute set into motion in late 1971. The fact that this debate has so far not produced any appreciation of a parallel development occurring only a few years before makes one wonder whether British planners ever read at all much of what is written outside the United Kingdom.

In making the selection, I have made no special effort to include papers under two topics which are currently much in fashion: *social planning* and *public participation*. Social planning is, in my submission, a misnomer. On a certain level, planning in the public sector may always be regarded as "social" in that it is geared towards the achievement of social ends—whatever that may mean! Practically, even the planning of private corporations has a strong "social" element. They, too, require internal adjustment of ends similar to the socio-political process and they, too, have to adapt to their social environment.

In this sense, the concept of social planning is too inclusive to be useful. Social planning is simply co-terminous with planning. The adjective "social" merely signals an (albeit laudable) intention of taking the social dimension of this activity seriously. Where there is more implied, i.e. where "social" refers to a substantive area of concern, it would therefore be desirable to specify this area—for instance, social welfare planning, the planning of social facilities, etc. But then, this type of planning is by definition included under the general concept of planning theory advanced in this reader.

As regards public participation, there are salient differences between the United States and other countries. In the United Kingdom, for instance, public participation is an innovation, not only in the field of planning, but generally in the field of public policy-making. In the United States, with its much less elaborate system of local government, and with considerably less favourable attitudes towards government generally, there has always been citizen participation in the various functions of local government.

There has not been therefore the same enthusiasm for participation as an innovation as there is in Britain, but much more concern for its abuses in terms of certain sections of the community dominating at the expense of others. Here, the *planner as an advocate* trying to rectify the imbalance of access to technical information and expert skills between wealthy sections of the community on the one hand and ethnic minorities and the poor on the other is a much more significant concept than participation *per se*.

This shows that participation—like so many other concepts—means different things to different people, thus underlining one of the objectives guiding the selection of entries: that planning itself ought to be understood as a rational problem-solving strategy employed in a particular social and institutional context. Advocacy planning, instead of participation generally, has therefore been included as the significant development occurring at the time and in the environment from which this reader mainly draws.

Acknowledgements

MY INTEREST in planning theory goes back to 1967/8 when I spent one year as a British Council Scholar. I am very grateful to Maurice Broady, then Senior Lecturer at the University of Southampton and now Professor of Social Administration at University College, Swansea, for having introduced me to this field and for providing me with intellectual stimuli which have influenced my thinking ever since.

I have also had the benefit of direct contacts with distinguished American scholars during a summer school organized by the American–Yugoslav Project at Ljubljana in 1969, and of the ensuing personal contacts and friendships. My thanks are therefore due to the Theodor Körner–Stiftungsfonds zur Förderung von Wissenschaft und Kunst for giving me an award for attending this most stimulating school.

Last but not least my colleagues amongst staff and students of the Department of Town Planning of the Oxford Polytechnic have been congenial critics and a sympathetic audience and thus contributed to my intellectual development over the past four years.

I have received encouragement and valuable help from the Editorial Board of Pergamon's Urban and Regional Planning Series, and in particular from its Chairman, George Chadwick, Professor of Town and Country Planning at the University of Newcastle; the Editor of this series, Mrs. Peggy Ducker, has also assisted in many ways.

My wife has helped by sharing the many worries, excitements and chores of the life which we have chosen for ourselves, and by being a congenial companion. More specifically, she has taken care of the bibliographical side of things—drawing on the extensive support system which she has built up for me over the years.

The various drafts have been typed by Mrs. Heather Jones in her usual meticulous way for which I owe her my thanks.

Acknowledgement is due to publishers, editors and authors of the papers included. The detailed credits are given in a footnote accompanying each paper. My special thanks go to Mrs. Ruth Glass for reworking her paper for publication in this volume, to Professor E. C. Banfield for correcting the misprints in the original version of his paper, to Professor John Friedmann for an extensive correspondence relating to this reader, and for the valuable advice which I have received, and to Professor Dr. Rolf-Richard Grauhan for his assistance in translating his paper from German.

While every attempt has been made to trace copyright holders, in one or two cases this has not proved possible and the editor and publishers would be glad to hear from any additional copyright holders of material in this reader.

Woodstock   ANDREAS FALUDI

PART I

WHAT IS PLANNING THEORY?

Introduction

IN THIS introductory section, I shall set out to demonstrate that there is a useful distinction to be drawn between theory *in* planning and theory *of* planning, and why this reader concentrates on the latter. Also, I make a further distinction between *normative* and *positive* or behavioural theory of planning, and how this affects the material included. Finally, as an introduction to an important paper devoted to this topic, I shall review essays considering the question of what is planning theory.

THEORY IN PLANNING VERSUS THEORY OF PLANNING

Planning is the application of scientific method—however crude—to policy-making.[1] What this means is that conscious efforts are made to increase the validity of policies in terms of the present and anticipated future of the environment. What it does not mean is that planners take over in the field of politics.

Validity is an attribute of the process by which decisions are made. This process involves advisers, as the suppliers of scientific intelligence, and decision-makers. Advisers and decision-makers interact, thus forming a planning agency. Planning is what planning agencies do, i.e. bring scien-

---

[1] Definitions given for systems analysis (Quade, 1968) and operational research (Beer, 1966) are the same as that of planning given above. This underlines one of the points to be made about planning theory, i.e. the generality of the phenomenon planning, and hence its wide applicability.

tific advice to bear on decisions concerning policies during an interactive process involving the roles of advisers and decision-makers.

The relationship between decision-makers and their advisers is often presented as that between master and servant: managers employ operational researchers (Beer, 1966), military staffs employ systems analysts (Quade, 1968), planning committees employ planners. The assumption, each time, is quite clearly that of the adviser coming into the game *at the pleasure* of the decision-maker.

There is nothing inherently wrong with being employed to help. The question for the adviser is only whether the process by which he and his decision-making master arrive at decisions is valid, or whether their relationship distorts this process. He might ask questions like: Does he pay regard to the evidence which I submit? Does the decision-maker provide me with adequate guidance on the problems which he wants solved? Are the reasons for his making a decision valid in their own terms? These are reasonable questions to ask for somebody concerned with the validity of the process which he is engaged in.

The point is that decision-makers, like other people, do not like their actions and their motives being questioned, and certainly not by their advisers, who are supposed to help *them*. Advisers in many fields have therefore had occasion to complain about their masters. Having trained minds, they have gone beyond grumbling and asked that simple question which is at the heart of all scientific investigation: *Why?* Upon which they have concluded that their own relationship with their masters (in short, the planning agency) must become the object of reflection, theoretical understanding and, ultimately, transformation so that planning shall become more valid. They have moved from considering the role of their own type of scientific theory *in* planning to the theory *of* planning.

Rather than talking specifically about planners and politicians, I have couched this argument in general terms. This is because there is evidence for the generality of this phenomenon of advisers becoming interested in the way in which their advice reaches fruition. That town planners are concerning themselves with the theory of planning in these terms will be documented in this reader. But social workers are doing the same, especially now that they are reorganizing their departments (Kogan and Terry, 1971; Foren and Brown, 1971). Similarly, operational researchers have taken a look at planning in private enterprise (e.g. Beer, 1966; Ackoff, 1969) and in public authorities (Friend and Jessop, 1969). The extent to which their findings and prescriptions are similar, and the degree to which the different fields of planning begin to influence each other, suggest that planning is a general approach to decision-making and is not tied to the activities of any profession or department of government.

There are other reasons for making the distinction between theory of planning and theory in planning. One lies in the differences between *form* and *content*. A theory on which a policy is based may be perfectly valid in itself, and the policy still be invalid. Thus, some models may be a perfect way of allocating residential activities. Yet policies based on them sometimes run into difficulties because a local amenity group puts up a successful fight against expansion of their village. The conclusion which the model builder must draw from this is that the way in which what he should do has been determined in the first instance has been invalid, or that the politician is not really representative of his constituency. These are questions concerning precisely the form of the planning process, and not the content of planning policies.

The second reason why the distinction between theory in planning and theory of planning ought to be made is that there are unfortunate consequences in *not* making it. J. Brian McLoughlin (1969), in his book on the "systems approach" to urban and regional planning, advances a view of planning theory based in location theory, i.e. what I call theory *in* planning. But, quite clearly, he also makes pronouncements as regards the theory *of* planning. For instance, he suggests that the planning process must have a "shape" which is isomorphic to the process by which human beings transform their environment. In this way, the whole theory of planning becomes a corollary to theory in planning. The attention given to it is thereby reduced so that McLoughlin has been criticized—quite rightly as I think—for putting forward a simplistic view of the actual processes by which decisions are made (Silvester, 1971, 1972).

I hasten to say that,I hope the distinction which I propose will not result in separation. There are hopeful signs that both sides are drawing closer together. Recent views of urban systems picture them as socio-technical complexes with their institutional part including planning agencies. Proponents of theory of planning, on the other hand, begin to take into account what Bolan, in the last paper included in this selection (see pp. 371–94), calls the "issue attributes". These reflect our knowledge concerning the environment and hence the state of theory *in* planning, for example whether this leads to reliable predictions or whether there is a great element of uncertainty in predictions derived from it. It is perfectly conceivable, therefore, to envisage one type of planning theory forming an envelope to the other, and there is no *a priori* way of saying which would contain which. It is only that, currently, urban and regional planners still neglect the theory of planning, seeing it as somewhat ephemeral instead of the basis of what they are doing. It is this neglect which this reader should rectify.

NORMATIVE VERSUS POSITIVE THEORIES OF PLANNING

As regards theory of planning, the distinction has been drawn between normative and behavioural approaches, first of all to the study of decision-making in management (Cyert and March, 1959; Dyckman, 1961). It is a distinction made in the planning study by Daland and Parker (1962), and recently also in the study of "policy formation" by Bauer (1968). The distinction is analogous to that between (normative) political theory and (positive) political science: normative theory is concerned with how planners ought to proceed rationally. Behavioural approaches focus more on the limitations which they are up against in trying to fulfil their programme of rational action. (See Bolan's paper, in particular p. 373.)

Obviously, normative and positive theory of planning have some bearing on each other. In the first instance one might say that empirical findings modify prescriptions. Thus, Lindblom and his collaborators maintain that since in actual fact planning never proceeds rationally, rational-comprehensive planning is not a suitable normative concept (Dahl and Lindblom, 1953; Braybrooke and Lindblom, 1963; Lindblom, 1965, see also pp. 151–69).

But Banfield (see p. 149) draws the opposite conclusion from finding that organizations do not engage in rational planning. For him, what remains is precisely the validity of rationality as a normative ideal! Yet, surely this must mean that some form of progress towards this ideal is conceivable. It is precisely in the analysis of the conditions under which such progress may take place that behavioural approaches to the study of planning may help.

Closely related to this idea is that of turning the opposing ideals of rational-comprehensive and piecemeal planning into empirical concepts. Thus, Madge (1968) suggests: ". . . 'total' and 'piecemeal' theories are the poles between which actual ideologies of social planning vary."

Similarly, Kahn (1969), in a recent collection of *Studies in Social Policy and Planning*, observes: "In the United States . . . the distinction between the incremental and the comprehensive is quantitative and not qualitative."

I have myself moved into this direction in some of my own writing, devising "dimensions of planning behaviour", one of them being precisely that of the rational versus the piecemeal mode of planning (Faludi, 1970, 1971).

Generally, the existence of concepts and instruments for relating theory to empirical reality, i.e. of a positive theory of planning, is seen as a sign of *maturity* of an area of intellectual pursuit. Admitting that most of the material included remains on the level of normative theory therefore means admitting to lack of sophistication of the theory of planning. Thus, most of the papers in Parts II and III are more prescriptive than descriptive. Even where Banfield and Lindblom draw on the empirical study of planning, all that they provide are generalizations which, furthermore, relate primarily to what they have to say about the rational planning process as an ideal. The most clearly empirical study in these sections is Altshuler's essay (see pp. 193–209).

Part IV of this reader is somewhere between a normative and a descriptive orientation. It is full of empirical references, though mostly at the level of tentative observations. Use is made of the body of literature which is available in organizational behaviour, though interest is still with what planning ought to be.

It is only in Part V that the positive theory of planning dominates. Here, the poverty of this field becomes evident in the extremely narrow range of literature on which one can draw. Besides, what is presented are frameworks for empirical research, not results. The great amount of effort that would be needed to obtain such results makes it questionable whether a behavioural approach would really be the answer to that most pressing problem of theory of planning: to provide a basis for improvements to planning procedures and planning agencies, or what has been called *meta-planning* (Wilson, 1969).

Clearly for a long time to come such meta-planning will have to rely on a theory of planning devoid of adequate empirical backing. Besides, assuming even all the requisite research effort being spent, the significance of a positive theory may simply be that of elucidating what the obstacles in the way of achieving *alternative* ideals are, not which ideal to choose. Thus, finding interdependencies between what many individuals in society do may be construed as supporting the idea of common action, or as a regrettable limitation on individual freedom to be reckoned with, depending on one's normative assumptions. The world-as-it-is does simply not provide a final clue as to how we should wish to see it!

FRAMEWORKS FOR THE STUDY OF THEORY OF PLANNING

There has been surprisingly little written on what planning theory is or ought to be. Even in the *Journal of the American Institute of Planners* papers considering its nature and scope are far and few between. Significantly, most of them have arisen out of the effort of academics to present to their students reasonably coherent frameworks for understanding planning. Having a corps of academics reflecting upon the nature of its activity, and thereby going beyond practice, is an asset for a profession like planning, a fact which is sometimes forgotten by its practitioners. All too often, the latter tend to see the planning schools as training camps for professionals in their own image. However, as Kaplan (1964) says, theorizing has novel responses as its behavioural correlate. The academic study of planning thus provides stimuli for innovation, an observation which can certainly be made of American planning.

Theory has already loomed large in Perloff's essay on planning education published after the closure of the famous Chicago School (Perloff, 1957). Benjamin A. Handler's seminar report "What is planning theory?" (1957) is another example of the concern of academics for developing this field. In recent years, Henry C. Hightower's (1970) review of the teaching of planning theory is highly instructive of the level of sophistication which has apparently been reached during the sixties, though he still reports lack of consensus on the subject-matter and the approaches to be taken.

Throughout the years, one or the other framework for "theory of planning" has been offered such as Lawrence L. Haworth's "An institutional theory of the city and planning" published during the same year (1957) as

Handler's report on that seminar at the University of Michigan. Handler's own contribution appended to that report, arguing for basing planning theory in economic theory, is another example. But of the papers building on the academic teaching of planning theory, Paul Davidoff and Thomas A. Reiner's "A choice theory of planning" has gained the highest reputation of all.

This is a normative theory of planning. On the basis of a series of postulates derived from economic analysis, and of philosophical assumptions concerning the purpose of planning, they suggest how the planner ought to proceed. Particularly noteworthy is their treatment of facts and values in goal-setting.

Davidoff and Reiner were subsequently challenged by John Dakin (1963). Points of contention were whether a theory of choice coming from economic theory was adequate to cover all aspects of planning, whether planning should aim at proceeding in a fully rational manner, whether the time was ripe for developing a general theory of planning such as the two authors had demanded, and whether theory ought to be so general as to explain planning under whichever political ideology.

Dakin insisted, for instance, that the role of intuition and experience should be acknowledged and that too much explicitness had its dangers. Davidoff and Reiner (1963) retorted by saying that ". . . intuition or experience unsupported by reason are weak reeds on which to rest".

They linked this with their belief in the essentially democratic nature of scientific planning, thus also answering the point about planning under different ideologies: properly conceived, it is *not* the servant of whichever power cares to employ planning. Scientific planning requires democracy: ". . . because of the need for value determination in science (in regard, for example, to the criteria and measures to be employed), a scientific decision model must resemble a democratic decision model."

Davidoff and Reiner put forward an elegant argument. However, some comments are still needed. These concern basic assumptions and the conclusions which they draw from them. It is evident that they take the position of *methodological individualism*, i.e. the doctrine ". . . that facts about society and social phenomena are to be explained in terms of facts about individuals" (Lukes, 1970).

For instance, they answer Dakin's point: "The question of whether or not planning is to be regarded as effective is probably not a choice within society, but only as between one society and another. The cultural pattern of our society decides for us that planning is an effective kind of behaviour" in a way which shows their methodological assumptions saying that a "... social decision emerges as human beings ... decide ..." (Davidoff and Reiner, 1963). Thus, they in effect deny theoretical status to such collective concepts as cultural pattern. One is reminded of Durkheim's argument concerning the existence of "social facts", and the split in the social sciences which this has caused ever since.

With their refusal to grant theoretical status to concepts like cultural pattern goes their distaste for anything like the public interest. They clearly build on a pluralist model of society. Indeed, in their paper they use the concept of advocacy, around which Davidoff would eventually write his seminal paper on "Advocacy and pluralism in planning" included later in this reader (see pp. 277–96).

Their assumptions lead them to conclusions with important consequences for planning theory. Their theory can only prescribe how planners ought to operate, it does not explain planning: "We did not intend to present a law of the way planning has, does, or will operate. We do not believe there can be such a law, any more than a single theory of health or justice" (Davidoff and Reiner, 1963).

Apparently, planning itself, when referring to what planners generally do, is suspect as a concept because of the methodological connotations which this has. It is not a foregone conclusion, however, that methodological individualism and pluralist models of society are the only acceptable assumptions on which to base planning theory. I subscribe to Kaplan's (1964) principle that each level of analysis should be granted autonomy of inquiry. Papers included under "positive theory of planning" in Part V show that other writers have thought it perfectly conceivable to make pronouncements concerning the way in which planning operates, thus taking a position opposed to Davidoff and Reiner's.

REFERENCES

Part I

Ackoff, R. L. (1969) *Corporate Planning*, John Wiley, New York.
Bauer, R. A. (1968) The study of policy formation: an introduction, *The Study of Policy Formation* (edited by Bauer, R. A. and Gergen, K. J.) Collier–Macmillan, London.

BEER, S. (1966) *Decision and Control*, John Wiley, New York.

BRAYBROOKE, D. and LINDBLOM, C. E. (1963) *A Strategy for Decision-Policy Evaluation as a Social Process*, The Free Press, Glencoe, Illinois.

CYERT, R. M. and MARCH, J. G. (1959) "A behavioural theory of organisational objectives", *Modern Organization Theory* (edited by HAIRE, M.), John Wiley, New York.

DAHL, A. and LINDBLOM, C. E. (1953) *Politics, Economics and Welfare*, Harper, New York.

DAKIN, J. (1963) "An evaluation of the 'choice' theory of planning", *Journal of the American Institute of Planners*, Vol. 29, pp. 19–27.

DALAND, R. T. and PARKER, J. A. (1962) "Roles of the planner in urban development, *Urban Growth Dynamics* (edited by CHAPIN, F. S. and WEISS, F. S.), John Wiley, New York.

DAVIDOFF, P. and REINER, T. A. (1963) "A reply to Dakin", *Journal of the American Institute of Planners*, Vol. 29, pp. 27–28.

DYCKMAN, J. W. (1961) "Planning and decision theory", *Journal of the American Institute of Planners*, Vol. 27, pp. 335–45.

FALUDI, A. (1970) "The planning environment and the meaning of 'planning' ", *Regional Studies*, Vol. 4, pp. 1–9.

FALUDI, A. (1971) "Towards a three-dimensional model of planning behaviour", *Environment and Planning*, Vol. 3, pp. 253–66.

FOREN, R. and BROWN, M. J. (1971) *Planning for Service*, Charles Knight, London.

FRIEND, J. K. and JESSOP, W. N. (1969) *Local Government and Strategic Choice*, Tavistock Publications, London.

HANDLER, B. A. (1957) "What is planning theory?", *Journal of the American Institute of Planners*, Vol. 23, pp. 144–50.

HIGHTOWER, H. C. (1970) "Planning theory in contemporary professional education", *Journal of the American Institute of Planners*, Vol. 35, pp. 326–9.

KAHN, A. J. (1969) *Studies in Social Policy and Planning*, Russell Sage Foundation, New York.

KAPLAN, A. (1964) *The Conduct of Inquiry: Methodology for Behavioural Science*, Chandler, Pennsylvania.

KOGAN, M. and TERRY, J. (1971) *The Organisation of a Social Service Department: A Blue-Print*, Bookstall Publications, London.

LINDBLOM, C. E. (1965) *The Intelligence of Democracy*, The Free Press, New York.

LUKES, S. (1970) "Methodological individualism reconsidered", *Sociological Theory and Philosophical Analysis* (edited by EMMET, D. and MACINTYRE, A.), Macmillan, London.

MADGE, C. (1968) "Planning, social", *International Encyclopedia of the Social Sciences*, Vol. 9, pp. 125–9.

McLOUGHLIN, B. J. (1969) *Urban and Regional Planning A Systems Approach*, Faber & Faber, London.

PERLOFF, H. S. (1957) *Education for Planning—City State and Regional*, John Hopkins, Baltimore.

QUADE, E. S. (1968) Introduction, *Systems Analysis and Policy Planning* (edited by QUADE, E. S. and BOUCHER, W. I.), Elsevier, New York.

SILVESTER, M. (1971) "Zur Kritik des Systemansatzes bei der Planung", *Stadtbauwelt*, Heft 32, S. 296–300.

SILVESTER, M. (1972) "The contribution of the systems approach to planning", *The Systems View of Planning* (Authors: DIMITRIOU, B., FALUDI, A., McDOUGALL, G., SILVESTER, M.), Oxford Working Papers in Planning Education and Research, No. 9.

WILSON, A. G. (1969) *Forecasting Planning*, Centre for Environmental Studies, London.

A Choice Theory of Planning*

Paul Davidoff and Thomas A. Reiner

PLANNING is a set of procedures. The theory we present rests on this belief. We will analyze the implications of this assertion and then identify the steps comprising these procedures. Further, we will show the bearing of these steps on behavior in fields where planning, as we define it, is practiced. What we have to say applies equally well to such diverse endeavors as urban land use planning, national economic planning, business planning, and others, for the same steps are followed no matter what the substantive or geographic focus.[1]

Planning Defined

We define planning as a process for determining appropriate future action through a sequence of choices. We use *determining* in two senses: *finding out* and *assuring*. Since appropriate implies a criterion for making judgments concerning preferred states, it follows that planning incorporates a notion of goals. *Action* embodies specifics, and so we face the question of relating general ends and particular means. We further note from the definition that *action* is the eventual outcome of planning efforts, and, thus, a theory of planning must be directed to problems of effectuation.

The choices which constitute the planning process are made at three levels: first, the selection of ends and criteria; second, the identification of a set of alternatives consistent with these general prescriptives, and the selection of a desired alternative; and, third, guidance of action toward

* Reprinted by permission of the *Journal of the American Institute of Planners*, Vol. 28, May 1962.
[1] However, the substantive is important and gives a particular instance of planning its special character. We leave a discussion of this point to another time, and focus in this paper on the ground common to all types of planning.

determined ends. Each of these choices requires the exercise of judgment; judgment permeates planning.[2] We will show the need for and some means of rendering judgments explicitly and with reason.[3]

Having introduced the definitional base, we now turn to three sets of propositions that are prerequisites for our planning theory. The first set refers to the subject-matter of planning and the environment in which it takes place, and is offered as postulates depicting the world-as-it-is. The second set of propositions describes the purposes for which planning is employed. We infer the purposes of planning, as defined above, from the uses to which it is put in dealing with the conditions set forth in the first set of propositions. The third set identifies elements which in their inter-relation compose the planning act and distinguish it from other forms of behavior. This set is derived from consideration of planning's purposes and the environmental postulates.

The Environment Surrounding Planning

The following set of postulates, describing aspects of the world-as-it-is, rests in part on axioms that have been found helpful in economic theory. The remaining postulates in this set also are statements on which there is general agreement.

1. Individuals have preferences and behave in accordance with them.[4] Actors are to some extent able to order their preferences. Different objects of preference, for any actor, may substitute for or complement each other.[5] Preferences express comparisons between wants: these wants have several features. An actor never experiences complete satisfaction of all his wants. Further, man finds that enjoyment brought on by addition to those goods and services already held pales with possession of increasing amounts.

---

[2] The judgment basis of decision-making in general is analyzed by Churchman [7]. Numbers in brackets refer to the Bibliography at the end of this article.

[3] We are concerned with the problem, so trenchantly posed by Haar [13], that a major task confronting the planner is to see that he acts in a nonarbitrary manner, administratively as well as conceptually. We develop in these pages a theory of non-arbitrary planning.

[4] Preferences are not absolute, yet they can be measured with tools of probability analysis.

[5] An individual's consumption of fuel would rise with purchase of a car: gas and autos are complementary goods. Use of public transit facilities will decline with the acquisition of a car: these are substitutable entities.

This is the familiar notion of diminishing marginal utility. To say that man is able to order his preferences among all alternatives is an exaggeration. For example, "poverty of desires" may limit his preference field. This problem becomes even more acute where alternative future goal situations are to be compared.

2. **Actors vary in their preferences.** The fact that men do not appraise things similarly complicates the allocation problem in society. It does so in two ways: the aggregation of individual preferences is sometimes a highly complex matter.[6] Second, there is considerable dispute whether there is any group interest or common welfare other than the sum of individual preferences.[7] It is often possible, however, to group the individuals with similar preference patterns. Such, for example, is the practice of economic determinists as well as of social analysts accustomed to draw conclusions from observation of manifest behavior.

3. **Goods are produced and services, including labor, are performed** subject to the constraint that diminishing returns set in at a given level. Beyond a certain point, "another buck just doesn't give as big a bang as it used to". This idea corresponds, on the supply side, to the notion on the demand side of diminishing marginal utility from goods and services.

4. **Resources are scarce and consequently output is limited.** Factors which go into the production of goods and services are, at any one point in time, limited in supply. This is the essence of the problem of priorities; we cannot achieve all things that need doing, or are desirable, at any one time.

5. **The entity for which planning is undertaken**—be it a production unit or a metropolitan area—will typically consist of interrelated parts generally in flux. Any action has consequences that add additional reverberations to such a system. To describe this condition we use terms such as "network effect", "organic structure", or "the need for coordination".

6. **Man operates with imperfect knowledge.** He also is often illogical (by formal canons), as where his preferences are not transitive,[8] or where

---

[6] This is the aggregation paradox analyzed by Arrow [2]. See also Baumol [5], ch. 13.

[7] Meyerson and Banfield [20], pp. 322–9, present the contending viewpoints.

[8] The transitivity assumption appears in various deductive systems. A transitive preference scheme will posit that where an individual prefers X to Y, and Y to Z, he also prefers X to Z.

his several values, at least at the levels at which he perceives them, are in conflict with each other. Thus, his abilities to calculate and control are ever limited. Severe, too, is conflict between demands for immediate action and for non-arbitrary decision. Kaplan [16] has well illustrated this predicament. "We are playing a game in a taxi with the meter running; even though we may possess a theory of the game, the cost of computing the optimal strategy may be too great." Man will doubtlessly continue to operate somewhere in the realm of bounded rationality, rather than reach perfect rationality.[9]

Planning's Purposes

Given these postulates, which describe the environment in which planning takes place, we move on to discuss why the planning act is undertaken. Ultimate purposes cannot be appraised from within a system: there is need to rely on outside criteria to evaluate such ends. We shall limit our discussion to presentation of objectives implicit in planning endeavors.

We refer to ultimate objectives of planning (external purposes), not to substantive matters (internal purposes) such as urban renewal, harmonious land use relations, or most profitable output. What reasons might institutions have for calling on planners to help them achieve their specific objectives?

Planning has been employed for a number of reasons, any one of which can serve independently or in combination with others as the objective of planning. Critics of the direction, efficacy, and value of contemporary planning should recognize the possibility of such a variety of perspectives; they might then see that the means in question are appraised differently for different purposes.

Three classes of objectives seem to exist. The first is efficiency and rational action; the second is market aid or replacement; and the third may be labeled change or widening choice.

1. *Efficiency and rational action.* In a world of scarcity there is a need to conserve resources and also to allocate them in an efficient manner. Planning is seen as a means of reducing waste or producing the greatest return

---

[9] For example, Schoeffler's [24] is a model of full rationality: Simon's [26] model postulates "satisficing," a more limited concept of rationality.

from employment of resources, although the line between these is not always clear. The distinction may rest on the amount of control that is exercised.[10] Definitions of waste or of optimum allocation hinge on assessment of wants. As we postulated above, different clients have different patterns of preference. Therefore the efficient utilization of resources would be that which satisfied the particular preferences of individual actors—as such preferences are determined and aggregated in a manner accepted in a given society. Efficiency thus is measured in terms of the purpose it serves.

Rationality is sometimes conceived as (a) referring to increasing the reasonableness of decisions, and sometimes as (b) involving full knowledge of the system in question. In the former sense (a) the task of planning may be to provide information to decision-makers, and, in certain cases, to the clients and the public at large about what presently exists and what may be expected in the future under alternative conditions. With this information the actors can better satisfy their own wants. The latter concept of rationality (b) is far more demanding of planning, for it requires identification of the best of all alternatives evaluated with reference to all ends at stake. The alternative thus selected as optimal implies, and is implied by, an efficient course of action.

2. *Market aid or replacement.* Planning would be of little, if any, use for an environment where an open, fully competitive market (either political or economic) operated perfectly. Such a market would imply that both buyers and sellers knew fully the relative worth over time of the items and services they sought and possessed, bought and sold, and of all the alternatives they had. Such a market would also require free entry and each participant's having, as it were, a single vote, with no party exercising monopolistic control over any segment of the market. Although such a market system does not exist, it remains a goal for some purpose: particularly as a model for optimum allocation of sets of goods and services in

---

[10] Waste itself involves notions of efficiency or optimum output per input. Efficiency, waste, and optimizing are interrelated; fruitful discussion of their relation depends on the particular model or ideal employed. Thus these terms take on one meaning in a competitive market model and quite another in a model which has, underlying, an objective that investments not be retired until their physical usefulness has been exhausted.

response to preferences of participants. Planning may be desired precisely in order to bring the society a few steps closer to such a goal. On the other hand, certain critics deny the possibility of a working competitive market. Their objective is to replace an imperfectly operating market system with some other scheme for distribution of scarce resources in response to claims upon them. Seen from this perspective, planning is to serve a new and controlling system of pricing and distribution.

Either of these objectives seizes on planning as a vehicle which collects, analyzes, and publicizes information (such as forecasts and assessment of third-party costs and benefits) required to make reasoned decisions. Those who favor the use of planning to make the market operate effectively do not see planning as a direct agent of change, but rather as providing the factual basis that will permit various value alternatives to be confronted and tested. Those who seek a market substitute view the planning act as more directly responsible for change. In this view planning becomes a "directive" method that will in itself yield rational order; the planner's task is enlarged to include examining value alternatives and, in some instances, suggesting particular courses of action.

3. *Change or widening of choice.* Given scarcities, social and individual choices must be made about the manner in which resources are to be allocated: how, when, to whom, to what purpose, and in what combination. The pure democratic ethic posits that no one has the wisdom or ability to make decisions for the society or for another individual; choice-making is left to the individual or to a majority of the individual voters.

In today's world, the inadequacy of this position is self-evident. Individuals increasingly delegate decision-making powers to legislative bodies; legislatures delegate to administrative and executive hands. This is specifically clear in the public realm; analogous conditions prevail in industry and in other institutions. Delegation often decreases individual opportunity to choose, but this decrease has limits; the decision-maker can both question and inform the individual client about the issues at hand. The planning process can be specifically employed to widen and to publicize the range of choice of future conditions or goals, as well as of means. This function may be extended to include opening opportunities where choice can be exercised. Lack of techniques and of willingness often holds back urban planners in this realm.

Widening of choice may overlap objectives of rational action. Those choices between alternatives that are central to the rational decision-making model clearly cannot be made in the absence of knowledge about such alternatives. The chooser must be informed of the range of choices and of the implications of each of the choices open. This suggests that the planner ought to render explicit the implications of proposals.

Planning can serve as a vehicle for the portrayal of utopian solutions. As distinct from plans expressing incremental improvements or even large-scale modifications along familiar lines, utopian plans show courses of action or end states involving fundamental change in values or environmental reconstruction. The utopian plan may open choice in several ways. It may give meaning to an old value by placing it in an unfamiliar setting. It may spell out the implications of total commitment to one or more values. It may shake belief in the *status quo* and suggest possibility of change and the directions this may take.[11]

A belief in the possibility of effective planning rests on the assumption that man controls his destiny: either by affecting the rate and direction of ongoing change or by initiating such motion. Planning is often relied on to achieve such control. Many of the reform features of city planning can be traced to a conviction that it is possible to improve man's conditions or to arrest decline.

Planning Characteristics

We next consider those elements which, in their interrelations, characterize the planning act. Though we wish to use these elements to distinguish planning from other forms of behavior, we recognize the considerable overlap between such fields as operations research, decision-making, or problem-solving, and planning.

We suggest the following as necessary components of the planning act.

1. *The achievement of ends.* Our definition of planning incorporates a concept of a purposive process keyed to preferred, ordered ends. Such ends may be directions or rates of change, as well as terminal states. Means

[11] On the relations between utopias and urban planning, see: Dahl and Lindblom [9], pp. 86–88; Meyerson [19]; Reiner [22]; and Riesman [23].

are not proposed for their own sake, but as instruments to accomplish these. The ends are not given, irrevocable, but are subject to analysis.

2. *Exercise of choice.* Planning is behavior which sees—at many levels—values formulated, means established, and alternatives selected. Our definition of planning stresses exercise of choice as its characteristic intellectual act.

3. *Orientation to the future.* Time is a valued and depletable resource consumed in effecting any end. Planning, an end-directed process, is therefore future oriented. Each of the ultimate objectives of planning implies a need in the present for information about the future. Estimates of future states are also important for what they imply for present behavior; thus, points are identified where control is required if ends are to be achieved. Moreover, planning involves assigning costs to deferred goal satisfaction and to losses arising from postponed actions. The task of calculating interest rates thus implicitly incorporates planning.

4. *Action.* Planning is employed to bring about results. It is a step in an ends-means chain leading to that which is desired.

5. *Comprehensiveness.* Planning serves to relate the components of a system. In order to allow decision-makers to choose rationally among alternative programs, the planner must detail fully the ramifications of proposals. In a world of imperfect knowledge this requirement must be balanced with that of action.

The Planning Process

As he faces these realities and concerns, and as he strives to identify appropriate courses of action, the planner engages in choice at three fundamental levels. These jointly constitute the process of planning. They are: *value formulation, means identification,* and *effectuation.* They are the necessary and sufficient steps constituting planning. We believe each represents an analytically useful category, for associated with each step are distinct methods of operation and problems of theory.

VALUE FORMULATION

Fact and Value

Our analysis of the value-formulation process and of the planner's responsibilities in dealing with values has as its basis the philosophical distinction between fact and value.

A fact is a descriptive statement involving definitions and postulates, and a relationship. It is an assertion of the truth of the relationship. "X is Y" is one characteristic form of a factual statement.

Values may be expressed as moral statements, or as statements of preference, of criteria, or of ends—more particularly goals. For our purposes, each of these can be related to, or transformed into, any of the others. Moral statements take the form of "X ought to Y", or, in terms more familiar to urban planners, "metropolitan areas ought to be surrounded by greenbelts". Statements of preference take the form "X is preferred to Y", or, "I would rather live in a single-family detached house than in a multifamily dwelling". Statements of ends or goals take the form "X is the end state sought", or, "Our goal in housing is the re-creation of New York as the first major city of the world without a slum". Criteria statements take the form, "when confronted with a choice between X and Y, apply rule M", or "when choosing between possible urban renewal sites, select the one with the highest reuse potential".

We further maintain that a given nondefinitional assertion would belong either to the category of facts or that of values and that any discourse could be divided in this manner. There are, on the one hand, uses, tests, and criticisms singularly appropriate to values and, on the other, those singularly appropriate to facts.[12]

Yet fact and value are closely related. The separation of fact and value in itself requires certain assumptions and possibly violation of the dictates of reason.[13] Let us consider some of the ways in which fact and value may be related.

1. Factual statements and their analysis invariably reflect the values of

---

[12] The position presented thus far rests on logical positivism, see: Ayer [3] and Carnap [6].

[13] In the last analysis, judgment, choice, and values enter into any verification. On this point, see Churchman [7], chaps. 4–6.

their makers; if only in the importance attached to them or the sequence in which they are studied.[14]

2. Our personal experiences show that our values are colored by our understanding of facts.[15]

3. We can make factual assertions about values: for example, their distribution in a given group. Conversely, one can make value assertions about facts, as does the city planner who desires to counter the fact of public apathy about a public program.

Verification of facts and verification of values, nevertheless, involve different techniques. The definition of a fact requires the possibility of disproving the assertion. Further, the true measures of facts lie on a probabilistic continuum; we cannot be absolutely certain of any assertion. Disconfirming and verifying value statements are highly complex issues that are by no means resolved. How then can the imperative of a value statement be tested? Disagreement on a value position cannot be resolved by recourse to facts.[16] We can speak of verification of values only in terms of their consistency with values of a higher level. Eventually, however, there must be reference to ultimate values which are essentially assumed and asserted as postulates.

The many goals within a system of values can be viewed in terms of their interrelations, although we can at times conveniently focus on individual goals. Considering an individual goal as a part, rather than as the entirety, of a system of ends has important analytic consequences. One goal may appear as superior to an alternative goal when both are measured against a higher value; however, the alternative may appear as a better means of satisfying a system-wide set of ends. This suggests that goals can be compared in terms of both their intrinsic and their instrumental worth. Values exist in a hierarchy. The hierarchical relation of values provides a means for whatever testing of values is possible. A value may be tested, that is, understood and its reasonableness assessed, by specifying values of a lower level it subsumes and by comparing it with other lower-level values as a means to achieve values of a higher level. We emphasize that a given value may be viewed both as a means and an end.

[14] See, for example, Merton [18] and Myrdal [21].

[15] Stevenson [29] gives one formulation of this problem.

[16] This position has been developed by a large number of contemporary philosophers: in particular we find support in Churchman [7].

The planner, as an agent of his clients, has the task of assisting them in understanding the range of the possible in the future and of revealing open choices. He does this in two ways—one involving facts and the other, values. The planner deals with facts to predict the nature of the future. Such predictions take account of a variety of different factors in the environment as well as likely effects of alternative controls. Such predictions permit comparison with conditions that are desired. Knowledge of gaps between desired and predicted conditions may suggest the nature of further controls needed.

The planner deals with values to discover which future conditions are presently desired and which may be desired by future clients. The environment desired for the future is, *in the first instance*, purely a matter of values. There is nothing in the factual side of the planner's work which, *in the first instance*, can reveal to him the desired nature of the future. But once a particular set of values concerning the future is posited, knowledge of facts is needed to determine the relative weight of a particular value. For example, value *X* might be preferred in the first instance, but subsequent knowledge of the costs of achieving *X* might lead to heightened consideration of another value. We agree with Kaplan [16] who has written of the importance of "confronting values with facts" in order to make "valuation realistic".

Constraints should be imposed only after choices are expressed. All too often planners first predict the nature of the future, then help set in motion programs that fulfill this prophecy, and thus limit men's aspirations. Planners should not let such predictions about the future limit the range of choice, for controls can alter the future and can make predicted outcomes improbable. However, evidence revealed through prediction can suggest undesirable aspects of a given course of control. Thus, prediction and control are complementary.

We would prefer to see planning operate under the assumption that all things are possible, given the willingness to meet their costs. Only when the client of the planner reveals that the costs are excessive should the future condition be excluded from consideration. If this procedure is followed, the planner's client remains in control.

Responsibility

Although we propose that the planner become vitally involved with values, we must make clear our belief that the planner should act with a keen sense of responsibility. He cannot, as an agent of his clients, impose his own ideas of what is right or wrong. We do not wish to see the planner's influence on decisions limited, but we would argue strongly that the planner's role in dealing with values must be constrained so that he acts as a responsible agent.

If an ultimate objective of planning is to widen choice, and the opportunity to choose, then the planner has the obligation not to limit choice arbitrarily. If an ultimate objective of planning is efficiency, then the planner cannot afford prematurely to dismiss any set of means. An examination of current goal-setting practice would show that planners as a rule fail to reject explicitly alternatives not included within their final plans. Thus, a proposed master plan contains a list of goals, but not a list of rejected goals. Further, such plans seldom indicate why the accepted goals were selected. If the planner is to be permitted to reject alternatives it must be because he has some knowledge or skill that provides a rational basis for such acts of rejection. This basis can be provided only by the values of the clients. Our contention rests on the thesis that goals are value statements, that value statements are not objectively verifiable, and, therefore, that the planner, by himself, cannot reasonably accept or reject goals for the public. This is crucial: we maintain that neither the planner's technical competence nor his wisdom entitles him to ascribe or dictate values to his immediate or ultimate clients. This view is in keeping with the democratic prescriptive that public decision-making and action should reflect the will of the client; a concept which rejects the notion that planners or other technicians are endowed with the ability to divine either the client's will or a public will.[17]

Clients

It is not for the planner to make the final decision transforming values into policy commitments. His role is to identify distribution of values

---

[17] Another reason for interest in clients' values is that their assessment permits prediction of aggregate private decisions and behavior, and thus leads to more effective planning.

among people, and how values are weighed against each other. To do this, the planner must determine relevant client groups. We can speak of two general classes: the immediate client, or the planner's employer; and the ultimate clients, those affected by the proposals.

The values sought are the clients; we reject the notion that individuals express the values of an institution, or what has been called the organismic view of the public interest. Values are personal; institutions do not hold values and purported expressions of institutional will cannot be proved or disproved. An institution does not have a will separate from that of its members; otherwise, man is the ward of that which he can master and control. Institutions exist to serve man. It is important to state our position explicitly (although ours is not an uncommon one) because of its meaning for the planning process we describe. It implies that the planner should not search for the "interest" of the entity for which he works, be it Philadelphia, General Motors, or the United States.

The planner therefore must take a preliminary step: the identification of his clients. Often, terms of employment prescribe the reference group for the planner's activity. But in public planning, with intervening administrative and legislative levels, to identify clients is a difficult task, and one that is often sidestepped.[18] The failure properly to identify relevant clients lies at the bottom of many of the current difficulties of the urban renewal program.[19]

In some situations the planner's perspective is limited to the values given by his immediate client, for his employer may exclude the planner from what might be deemed a political area. When the planner is permitted (or, as is frequently the case, asked and urged) to study the larger client group, serious problems confront him. What type of information should be elicited from the clients? Should the planner study the values of a random sample of the population, or should he classify the relevant population and then sample the different groups, or should he otherwise assign values to these aggregations? If he has chosen the second course, the planner will be required to establish explicit criteria for the definition of groups.

---

[18] Likewise, is management or the stockholder the immediate client in a corporate planning situation? See *Dodge* vs. *Ford Motor Co.*, 204 Mich. 459, 170 N.W. 688. See also, operation research literature, viz. Churchman, Ackoff, and Arnoff [8], chap. 1.

[19] As documented by Gans [12] and Seeley [25].

One such criterion should be to aggregate individuals expected to have similar cost-benefit expectations.

Clients might thus be grouped according to income, race, age, occupational characteristics, location, or by roles in various institutions. Any one individual might fall in several or all such categories. Just as we deny an institutional will, neither shall we find a group interest. That which expresses the values of a majority of a group need neither represent that class's permanent view nor the views of each member.

Analysis of Values

Let us now identify what information about the values of clients should be sought and analyzed. Values are not self-evident, simple entities, but, though complex, neither do they defy analysis. The planner should consider values from two perspectives: first, as the clients' internal states of valuation: second, externally, as the entities which are valued. It is easy to slip into a position where internal and external values are not distinguished, where the preference structure of an individual is not separated analytically from the commodities, services, or conditions which are the objects of his preference. We may find that for some purposes value analysis should concentrate on the internal states, such as those previously discussed, while, for other purposes, study can more fruitfully focus on the external. As one proceeds from more general to more specific values, the external elements seem more evident, dominant, and measurable.

To lend substance to our discussion of internal states, let us focus on values such as health, wealth, and power,[20] which might be considered values at a middle range of generality. These values should be considered in the following ways.

1. For a given value: how widely is it held? What is its spread and distribution in the institution and amongst client groups?

2. What is the intensity of the value? Techniques of measurement are not sharply developed here. The only meaningful intensity scale may be

---

[20] We sidestep the question of the selection of these values; they are taken from Lasswell and Kaplan [17] who offered these as part of a plausible value system.

one measuring overt behavior, for example, migration. It may also be desirable to distinguish between those values held in private and those shared as when attitudes are publicly voiced or voted. The planner might be particularly concerned with identifying conditions under which privately held values become public. This is related to whether a value is strongly held by an individual, or whether he is amenable to changing it.

3. Does the individual believe he can or cannot influence the achievement or a goal?

What are the characteristics of the external value entities? The stock of such things as wealth or health that an individual possesses at any one time, in combination with his internal values, provides a significant basis for planning analysis. An individual's well-being is measured by:

(a) his absolute stock of valued entities;

(b) divergence of his stock from his own goals (his aspirations); and

(c) divergence of the stock of valued entities from a level set by others (this is the familiar notion of standards).

The difference noted in (b) and (c) need not be equal.[21] For purposes of analysis, information on both gaps is desirable. A criterion for planning action would give a directive to narrow either the subjective gap, the objective gap, or some combination.

Valued entities can be measured in several ways. First, regarding the amount held or desired: is possession a 'yes-no' phenomenon, does it exist in discrete lumps, or is it measured along a continuum?[22] Second, how easily is the valued item transferred from person to person?[23] Third, along the continuum which measures the individual or social origin of a value: is the valued entity internalized, or is it other-directed?[24] Fourth,

---

[21] For example, the political theorist asks: Can freedom be measured objectively, or is it purely a subjective state? Or, in the urban planner's world: How is adequacy of municipal services to be measured?

[22] Survival might be in the first category, days at work without interruptions due to illness in the second, and degree of health in the third.

[23] Wealth has low transfer costs, whereas health or rectitude have high costs of transfer.

[24] Thus, affection may be totally other-directed, whereas, depending on market conditions and assumptions, wealth is only partly so. Health is largely internalized, although not exclusively so: subjective well-being reflects knowledge of others' states, and identification of well-being hinges partly on publicly held criteria.

measurement of valued objects also must embody recognition that some are not subject to restrictions of finiteness.[25]

Planning analysis of an entire value system would lead to portrayal of value hierarchies. It is by study of such structures and by defining the levels therein that it is possible to identify, reduce, or even eliminate the inconsistencies in pursuit of a system of goals. With knowledge of the hierarchy, the planner can better pinpoint specific means.

Ideally, for purposes of planning analysis, value hierarchies should be formulated to provide criteria for specific action or inaction in all cases. We recognize that this sets a highly demanding requirement, for it must account for discord and inconsistencies within and among people. Yet, there are at least three processes the planner may employ to resolve value conflict and efficiently attain plural goals. First, assigning exchange prices to several goals permits their joint pursuit. Second, posing alternatives, analyzing ramifications, and disseminating information contribute to effective bargaining between proponents of contending values. Third, rendering value meanings explicit provides common grounds for appraisal.

Though the planner tries to formulate unitary hierarchies, these may not be attainable, and, in any case, are not desirable in their monolithically consistent form. For there is virtue in highlighting conflict of values and goals: a richer, if only temporary, synthesis grows out of advocacy.

Evaluation of Values

Although a value statement cannot be verified by empirical data, it can be referred to other value statements in the hierarchical structure. Furthermore, implications of values can be detailed to permit greater understanding of their meanings. The process of rendering a value explicit also reveals the way in which the value may be transformed into a goal statement. Let us illustrate the different ways of treating a value by reference

[25] Wealth would be quite finite, given a particular technological and capital context, a pricing system, and a fixed time period. Health may be finite, but only within some of its definitions. It is harder to assign such ceilings to affection (if, however, this were to be measured in sociometric terms, there is a ceiling, a very high one, on interaction possibilities). Justice or skill would seem to defy notions of a maximum, although it may be possible to set a minimum. Finiteness is related to depletability. Thus, commodities constituting wealth are generally consumed in use, while skills grow with exercise.

to a currently popular aim: "It is desirable to maintain the level of investment in, and the output from, centrally located business districts." The transformation of this statement into a planning goal is: "The preservation of the C.B.D." For purposes of analysis, we might begin by defining the key terms in either the moral statement or the goal statement. For example, what is meant by the term "preserve"?[26] Next we would seek the reasons underlying the goal. We could ask what benefits and costs would arise under each alternative. Or, we might observe that the value was related to others.[27] In sum, the process of explaining the possible reasons underlying a value and the possible effects of its pursuit would permit more intelligent choices between such a value and other similarly treated values.

The final product of the value formulation stage of planning should be alternative sets of objectively measurable goals and criteria. Objective measures are prescribed first because they limit the possibility of abuse through arbitrary decision. Second, if an objective of planning action is to achieve ends, then the ends selected must be achievable. Some ends may be unattainable because of their generality, vagueness, or ambiguity. We do not assert that such ends do not have importance in value formulation, but an objectively measurable end must be deduced from them if a specific direction is to be given to planning means. Criteria are employed for choosing the best means to achieve stated ends. Only where criteria are stated in objective form can alternative means be reliably compared, with assurance that the means selected are directed toward the same goals.

We have suggested that value formulation yields alternative sets of goals. This requirement is supported by the following reasoning. We plan in a world of limited knowledge, a world in which facts are probabilistic and values debatable. Under such circumstances "correct" decisions do not

[26] In speaking of preserving a C.B.D., is the implication that the C.B.D.'s activity should be maintained at its current level, or at its current level relative to a certain region as a whole? Or, does "preserve" mean that the older business district should be maintained as a central focus for particular functions: trade, exchange, recreation, etc.?

[27] Preservation of the C.B.D. may be sought in order to enlarge the assessment base so as to permit reduction of taxes. Or, it may be sought out of the belief that scale factors operate which require a central complex as a necessary condition for provision of desired facilities. Both these hypotheses are subject to evaluation and the validity of the initial goal (preserve the C.B.D.) may thus be tested.

exist. The merit of a decision can only be appraised by values held individually or in a collectivity, but such values, as we have pointed out, are not verifiable. In such a situation, the goal for decision-making should be increasing the degree of assurance (of decision-makers and clients) that the choice made was at least as reasonable or more reasonable than any other alternative. This goal is best attained by bringing to bear on every decision the greatest amount of relevant information concerning the ramifications of all alternatives.

In general, if the planner is not to make final decisions (and even where he is delegated the power to make such decisions), alternative possibilities should be explicitly scrutinized. We object strenuously to the current practice in urban planning of excluding all but the selected alternatives from consideration.[28] Even if the planner prefers a single alternative, a preference we believe he should assert as strongly as desired and permitted, he has the obligation to detail objectively and explicitly the meaning and implication of each alternative. We recognize that the planner must exercise judgment as to which alternatives should be considered as possibilities. But this can be done discreetly through explication of the criteria he employs.

Time Perspective of Plans

We have espoused widening clients' choices. The planner, to do so, must offer value alternatives not currently given great weight in society. The planner should be called upon to present tentative objectives—new, radical, or even absurd alternatives. This involves creative and utopian thought and design. The planner can engage in such thought; possibilities for significant societal change are great (although the immediate willingness may be lacking). Significant planned change generally takes a long time. For this reason, a long-range plan should embody consideration of alternatives which set forth values of a higher level and include some which are distinctly different from those currently approved.

A short-term plan on the other hand will suffer from constraints of time and from necessity for action. This being true, it should focus on purposes

---

[28] Attempts to display alternatives prove worthless where there is a failure to compare the relative costs and benefits of the posed alternatives.

which are fairly certain to receive political approval. The short-range plan must include consideration of values which have been approved and given expression in past programs, for in part it is a plan showing an efficient way of moving into the immediate future. The preparation of the short-term plan thus calls for identification and analysis of currently pursued goals (as they may be found, for example, in explicit or implicit form in budgets and other public documents). Goals in opposition to the accepted ones, when held by those with significant power, must also be given attention.

A middle-range plan (perhaps for a five-year period) provides an opportunity to mesh the extreme points of view regarding societal change which are expressed in the other two plans. Estimates of future conditions can be made with greater assurance than in the long-range plan. There is more accurate knowledge of what may occur under different controlled situations. Alternatives posed in such a five-year plan should be those carrying some commitment to implementation, as opposed to mere intention (such as might set the criterion for inclusion in the long-range plan).

For each of the three plans, a number of methods are available to the planner seeking to identify possible values and value groupings. These methods include: market analyses, public opinion polls, anthropological surveys, public hearings, interviews with informed leaders, press-content analyses, and studies of current and past laws, of administrative behavior, and of budgets. Singly, and more so in combination, these are superior to reliance on planners' intuition or guesswork.

In each plan, the importance of placing value formulation first cannot be overstated, though there is great reluctance in urban planning to start with a search for ends. Even where goal selection is placed first, there is a tendency to underplay this and to return to familiar territory—"survey and analysis."[29] We do not understand the logic that supports ventures in research before the objectives of the research have been defined.[30] Such emphasis on research is premised on an ill-founded belief that knowledge of facts will give rise to appropriate goals or value judgments. Facts by

---

[29] There is one legitimate and necessary exception: survey and analysis of client values. Study of their shape, incidence, and intensity makes a valid starting point for planning studies.

[30] A practical reason to delay research studies is to avoid unnecessary or unproductive studies. Planning agencies, as is painfully known, are the repositories of many unutilized surveys.

themselves will not suggest what would be good or what should be preferred. To illustrate this point, a factual survey of housing conditions in a given area would not give rise to a value judgment or a goal in the absence of an attitude about the way people ought to live in residential structures.

Values are inescapable elements of any rational decision-making process or of any exercise of choice. Since choice permeates the whole planning sequence, a clear notion of ends pursued lies at the heart of the planner's task, and the definition of these ends thus must be given primacy in the planning process.

MEANS IDENTIFICATION

In the next stage of the planning process, ends are converted into means. The crucial question is: how to proceed, by nonarbitrary steps, from a general objective to a specific program? We stress that the hierarchy of means be deduced logically from ends.

The process of means identification commences once an attempt is made to identify an instrument to a stated end. It terminates when all the alternative means have been appraised in terms of their costs and benefits (as calculated by criteria referring to all relevant goals) and, in certain cases, where the power is delegated, a particular implementing means is chosen to be the desired alternative to achieve the stated purpose. The identification of a best alternative implies a need for operational criteria for such choices.[31]

The most general end and the most specific means represent extreme points along a continuum. The task of deducing from a value the tools for its implementation is not a one-step operation. A particular program may serve either as a means or as an end, depending on its relation to other values, programs, or tasks, and depending on the perspectives of the relevant individuals.

Methods for the identification of means conveniently fall into two

---

[31] We distinguish decision-making from planning: the former is usually restricted to choices among given alternatives, whereas we see the latter as a process incorporating the formulation of ends, as well as ways of identifying and expanding the universe of alternatives. On decision-making literature see the recent article by Dyckman [11].

categories. The first is the identification of a universe of alternate means consistent with the value. The alternatives identified would be those which were conditions sufficient for achievement of the goal. This is the deductive element of the model, a task which may take the form of identifying all the feasible alternatives, or a finite number, or possibly only one for comparison with existing conditions. The choice depends on the planner's skills, technical as well as creative. At this point, we are not familiar with any rigorous techniques, either in the natural or the social sciences or in philosophy, which would enable us to identify the full set of possible alternatives to the achievement of an end.[32]

Certain steps might be taken to reduce the number of alternatives to be considered, such as the aggregation, into a few representative alternatives, of all the alternatives constituting a continuum or series of continua. Where alternatives refer to policies in a short-range perspective, a useful approach is review and evaluation of the set of programs currently in use, at several levels of operation and in various combinations.

The second task in means identification is the weighing of alternatives identified in the first step. Two types of weights are involved. One refers to the degree to which a given means satisfies the end sought. The other is a probability score: an estimate of the likelihood that the end will be associated with the means employed. At this point, the planner must pay close heed to the subtleties and complexities of causal, producer-product, and correlation relationships.[33] Using criteria developed in the value formulation stage, such weights are attached to each alternative. One alternative may then be identified as superior to others: that is, optimal by preestablished criteria. However, this last step should be taken only if an explicit delegation of power has been made. In all cases there is a clear

---

[32] The one exception might be some classes of programming: given a set of restrictive constraints, all feasible solutions are implicitly identified. However, two types of problems arise with programming. Programming is not operational or even relevant to many aspects of planning. More important, the approach requires that explicit constraints be set: there often is loss in precisely that flexibility needed for meaningful expansion of the set of alternatives. For a review of programming literature, see Stevens [28]. An excellent recent introduction to this topic will be found in Baumol [5], chap. 5.

[33] For definition and discussion of these terms, see, for example, Ackoff [1], pp. 65–68.

responsibility to reveal to the decision-maker the grounds for selecting the particular alternative.

Legal procedures adopted in our society reject the thesis that ends justify any means; furthermore, means vary in their effects on different client groups. Hence, the process of means identification is politically charged and must be resolved without arbitrariness. The technician has an important role to play in assessing the impact of alternative means. However, the tasks of adopting criteria for evaluation (during the value-formulation stage) and determining finally the appropriate alternatives are not his, unless these functions have been expressly delegated.

The technician should make explicit to the clients all the information he can muster as to hypothetical consequences resulting from adoption of each of the means considered. Two classes of verifiable, nonarbitrary planning techniques are relevant in this regard. These may be labeled "optimizing" studies, and "comparative impact" analyses. The former would select the best solution out of all possible courses of action, given a criterion of "best" and given explicit constraints. The optimizing study itself would identify all alternatives; these do not have to be determined beforehand. Linear programming is such a technique.

Comparative impact analyses have a more modest aim: weighing already identified alternatives subject to some criteria. The simplest form is comparison between the effects of a single improvement, as against maintenance of the *status quo*. An input-output study is an example, provided a rule is added which allows assessment of the merits of the consequent states. Other examples are comparative cost and cost-benefit studies.

At the moment, our means-identification skills are limited. Nevertheless, we can state standards for such endeavors, whether conducted in contemporary handicraft manner or using more sophisticated techniques which may develop.

1. We seek to identify a set of means so related to the given purpose as to include the one that is "best". Thus, the set of alternatives identified by a means-identification effort must not omit one (identified by some other method than that used) clearly superior to the one selected.

2. The alternatives identified must possess certain features of measurability. There must be "success indicators", which, at a later stage, make it possible to assess the effectiveness of means programs.

3. Means identification should be consistent. That is, alternatives

selected as optimal in the pursuit of a goal should be consistent with the alternatives employed in pursuit of another goal, or least inconsistent with achievement of other goals.

4. Finally, we seek to develop mean-identification methods that are manageable, ones that do not burden us with irrelevant and excessive alternatives. Analysis must be possible, and also productive to actors constrained by time.

EFFECTUATION

In effectuation, the third step in the planning process, the planner guides previously selected means toward attainment of goals adopted in the first stage. Effectuation is concerned with administration of programs and with control; it has been discussed at great length, and from various points of view, in administration theory. We limit our discussion to those aspects of effectuation so essential or peculiar to the planning process that a theory of planning requires their consideration.

There is some question whether concern with effectuation belongs in a theory of planning for it can be held that planning ceases with identification of means and is not concerned with their application. This position implies a cleavage separating policy and administration. Such separation assumes that, once commitments are secured to accomplish intended objectives, policy making terminates and administrators carry out the programs. Contemporary administrative thought has strongly undercut this. distinction between policy and administration[34] by showing, for example, how administration of a program can lead to unwanted results. Thus, we pose for the planner the role of an overseer, one who aids policy makers by observing the direction programs are given and by suggesting means for redirecting these toward their intended goals. If circumstances are unusual and significant, unanticipated consequences are likely to occur, the planner will suggest immediate reconsideration of goals or means. There are several reasons why the undesired and unanticipated may arise:

1. Administrators consciously or unconsciously redirect programs. This is not surprising where, typically, several bureaucratic levels are involved in implementing an objective. Each of these levels may involve a separate

[34] For a review of this issue, see Simon [27].

set of actors with unique interpretations of facts, ends, and personal responsibilities.

2. Programmatic means are general and in their application to specific areas or individuals may cause injustice. A whole program may be jeopardized where such injustice is sufficiently grave.[35] Variance procedures, for example, represent explicit recognition of the need to apply equity in certain specific circumstances, yet variables may cumulatively thwart program ends.

3. Not every consequence can be predicted. If (previously) unanticipated events do arise (or are later predicted) they may have significant impact. In some cases the impact will lead to pressures sufficient to alter goals or to introduce new controls.

In serving as an overseer of programs the planner's role is analogous to a feedback control mechanism. The ultimate recipient of information is the policy maker, but in some circumstances the planner may be delegated the task of redirecting a program's administration so that it stays on course. Another significant aspect of the planner's feedback role is the storing of information regarding client reaction to programs and to total or partial achievement of various goals. In this fashion the planner performs a value formulation task, understanding contemporary reaction to the world as it is. This coincidence of value formulation and effectuation stages suggest the ongoing nature of the planning process.

Aspects of effectuation actually commence with agreement on goals and criteria in the value formulation stage: in urban planning, for example, with publication of the first part of a master plan. The function we see for the master plan is to set forth basic accepted policies, the goals and criteria of the government. The master plan need not contain details of programs derived during the means-identification stage. But it must include the criteria necessary to control exercise of administrative discretion.

We conceive of the master plan as an amendable document, one that reflects the political consensus at a given moment as to desired change over the short-, middle-, and long-range periods. The master plan serves as an instrument for evaluating and overseeing the use of controls and functions as a yardstick against which progress toward goals can be

---

[35] The relocation problems arising from urban renewal programs are examples in point.

measured. Ideally, all the controls employed to effectuate a plan could be deduced from the criteria set forth in the master plan, but specific control need not be part of the master plan. The task and methods of deducing controls from the master plan belong to the means-identification stage. Languages such as "in accordance with a comprehensive plan" would mean "deducible from" such a plan.

We have reserved our consideration of controls until this discussion of effectuation because of their importance for action. However, values as to the nature of controls and the criteria to guide their use are formulated in the earlier stages of the planning process. There are many forms of control from which to choose: those that are directed (such as ones relying on immediate impact on identified clients) as well as those that are automatic (as those that depend on the operation of a free market). Both directed and automatic controls may be imposed by strict regulations or by more subtle means, such as influence or prediction posed to fulfill itself. In our society the Constitution and the positive and common laws embody values governing use of controls. Controls may be exercised from many points within a system.[36]

The planner should establish for his clients' consideration alternative criteria in reference to controls. One set of criteria might deal with the location and character of controls and of the planning function. Such a set would resolve for a particular institution the question of whether controls and planning functions should be centralized or decentralized.[37] Still another set of criteria might deal with relations between controller and controlled. Thus, for example, where individual freedom was highly valued the criterion might be: the control employed should be one which achieves the desired end with the least restriction of the prevailing rights of individuals. Other criteria in this set might answer such questions as:

1. What consideration, if any, should be given to those proximately affected by a control? Should there be compensation?

2. Should the accepted limits of control be a function of the purposes it seeks to achieve? Under which circumstances do ends justify means?

3. What rights will be afforded individuals to question or contest

[36] For a thorough study of types, costs, benefits, and other aspects of controls, see Dahl and Lindblom [9].

[37] This question has been debated by a number of urban planners: Bassett [4], Walker [31], Howard [15], Tugwell and Banfield [30], and also Dunham [10].

particular controls ? For example, what should be the content and requirements of a public hearing, or under what circumstances could the consti-
tutionality of legislation or legality of administrative discretion be
challenged ?

The planner, however, does not have total authority and is himself
subject to many constraints. Within any institution, forces, some rational,
some irrational, are at work affecting decisions; only some of these are
subject to the controls developed by the planner. Planning calculations
are set against those arising out of market processes and are either
challenged or relied upon by power groups with their own interests.
Furthermore, a given planning agency often coexists with others responsible
for parts or the whole planning process. Thus, a city planning department
may work in co-operation (or conflict) with planning divisions of other
departments. In a pluralistic society this is inevitable and acts to limit the
planner's activities. But, again, it also can contribute to that higher synthesis we saw arising from conflict of ideas and values.

CONCLUSIONS

The theory presented in this paper has numerous implications both for
the education of planners and for the role planners play in public affairs,
industry, welfare organizations, and other areas. It is our conviction that
contemporary urban planning education has been excessively directed to
substantive areas and has failed to focus on any unique skills or responsibilities of the planner. Such planning education has emphasized understanding of subject-matter: cities, regions, facilities, housing, land use,
zoning, transportation, and others. In fact, the student has had thrust
upon him a growing list of courses and is perennially in danger of becoming a Jack-of-all-trades (almost all, but never enough), and a master of
none. In a few years on the job he sinks into an uninspired and intellectually blunted administrator-generalist or public relations semiexpert.
Planning education, until now, has paid little or no attention to methods
for determining ends and relating ends to means. And although some tools
of effectuation are studied, their relation to a planning process is largely
neglected. The very obvious shortcomings of current master plans reflect
both the bias and the inadequacy of their formulators' training.

The back issues of this and other planning journals are replete with self-conscious consideration of the urban planner's role as a professional. Planners frequently assert their status of a profession and so implicitly claim a distinct body of knowledge and procedures. Is this claim premature ?

It has been our intent to set forth a theory of planning complete in the sense that it defines the field, its purpose, its methods, and the constraints imposed on it by its surrounding environment. Though we do not contend that planning is a task which any one individual can perform in its entirety, we do believe that a curriculum can be developed to prepare each planner to engage in the process and analyses described. There would have to be much reliance on skills and accumulated knowledge in related social sciences, law, ethics, statistics, and applied mathematics. We also believe there is possibility for fruitful exploitation of the common ground between planning and such new fields as operations research and decision theory. However, it should be noted that operations researchers, in their quest for optimal processes, have shown relatively little interest in formulating goal alternatives, and that decision-making theory has largely focused on ways to make the best choice from among given alternatives in response to set criteria. The task we have outlined for planning clearly transcends these in scope.

Attempts are currently under way in a number of universities to teach aspects of planning theory. However, no school has, as yet, focused on planning methods. Our conclusions suggest that, at least for the present, departments of planning should be separated from departments of subject-matter, for example, urbanism, regionalism, welfare programs, industry. Planners should be trained to apply their methods to a variety of subject areas, though any given institution may have to limit its scope to one or a few such areas. We do not mean to suggest, though, that a planner's education should ignore study in subject areas. Rather, we urge that such areas become the testing ground for the application of planning.

Our colleague Britton Harris recently wrote in these pages [14] that "at least for the moment there can be no theory of city planning which is wholly divorced from a theory of cities, and hence no wholly general theory of planning as such". We have taken up his call for reaction to this thesis, and hope that the discussion will continue. We have arrived at a different conclusion. In the long run, we would assert that procedures and substance cannot be treated separately. For the present, the need is great for widespread attention to planning method.

BIBLIOGRAPHY

1. ACKOFF, RUSSELL L. *The Design of Social Research*, University of Chicago Press, Chicago, 1953.
2. ARROW, KENNETH J. "A difficulty in the concept of social welfare", *Journal of Political Economy*, Vol. LVIII, No. 4 (August 1950), pp. 328–46.
3. AYER, ALFRED J., *Language, Truth and Logic*, Dover Publications, Inc., New York, 2nd ed., 1946.
4. BASSETT, EDWARD M., *The Master Plan*, The Russell Sage Foundation, New York, 1938.
5. BAUMOL, WILLIAM J., *Economic Theory and Operations Analysis*, Prentice-Hall, Inc., Englewood Cliffs, N.J., 1961.
6. CARNAP, RUDOLF, "Logical positivism", in MORTON WHITE (ed.), *The Age of Analysis: 20th Century Philosophers*, Mentor Books, New York, 1955, pp. 203–25.
7. CHURCHMAN, C. WEST, *Prediction and Optimal Decision*, Prentice-Hall, Inc., Englewood Cliffs, N.J., 1961.
8. CHURCHMAN, C. WEST, RUSSELL L. ACKOFF and E. LEONARD ARNOFF, *Introduction to Operations Research*, New York, John Wiley & Sons, Inc., 1957.
9. DAHL, ROBERT A. and CHARLES E. LINDBLOM, *Politics, Economics, and Welfare*, Harper & Brothers, New York, 1953.
10. DUNHAM, ALLISON. "City planning: an analysis of the content of the master plan", *The Journal of Law & Economics*, Vol. I (October 1958), pp. 170–86.
11. DYCKMAN, JOHN W., "Planning and decision theory", *Journal of the American Institute of Planners*, Vol. XXVII, No. 4 (November 1961), pp. 335–45.
12. GANS, HERBERT, "The human implications of current redevelopment and relocation planning", *Journal of the American Institute of Planners*, Vol. XXV, No. 1 (February 1959), pp. 15–25.
13. HAAR, CHARLES M., "The Master Plan: an inquiry in dialogue form", *Journal of the American Institute of Planners*, Vol. XXV, No. 3 (August 1959), pp. 133–42.
14. HARRIS, BRITTON, "Plan or projection", *Journal of the American Institute of Planners*, Vol. XXVI, No. 4 (November 1960), pp. 265–72.
15. HOWARD, JOHN T., "In defense of planning commissions", *Journal of the American Institute of Planners*, Vol. XVII, No. 2 (Spring 1951), pp. 89–94.
16. KAPLAN, ABRAHAM, "On the strategy of social planning", "a report submitted to the Social Planning Group of the Planning Board of Puerto Rico, September 10, 1958", mimeographed.
17. LASSWELL, HAROLD D. and ABRAHAM KAPLAN, *Power and Society*, Yale University Press, New Haven, 1950.
18. MERTON, ROBERT K., "The role of applied social science in the formation of policy", *Philosophy of Science*, Vol. XVI, No. 3 (July 1949), pp. 161–81.
19. MEYERSON, MARTIN, "Utopian tradition and the planning of cities," *Dædalus*, Vol. XC, No. 1 (Winter 1961), pp. 180–93.
20. MEYERSON, MARTIN and EDWARD C. BANFIELD, *Politics, Planning and the Public Interest*, The Free Press, Glencoe, Ill., 1955.
21. MYRDAL, GUNNAR, *Value in Social Theory*, Harper & Brothers, New York, 1958.
22. REINER, THOMAS A., *The Place of the Ideal Community in Urban Planning*, University of Pennsylvania Press, Philadelphia, 1962 (in press).

23. RIESMAN, DAVID, "Some observations on community plans and utopia", *The Yale Law Journal*, Vol. LVII (December 1947), pp. 173–200; reprinted in *Individualism Reconsidered*, The Free Press, Glencoe, Ill., 1954.
24. SCHOEFFLER, SIDNEY, "Toward a general definition of rational action", *Kyklos*, Vol. VII, No. 3 (1954), pp. 245–73; reprinted in *The Failure of Economics*, Harvard University Press, Cambridge, Massachusetts, 1955: Appendix A.
25. SEELEY, JOHN R., "The slum: Its nature, use and users", *Journal of the American Institute of Planners*, Vol. XXV, No. 1 (February 1959), pp. 7–14.
26. SIMON, HERBERT A., "A behavioral model of rational choice", *Quarterly Journal of Economics*, Vol. LXIX, No. 1 (February 1955), pp. 99–118; reprinted in *Models of Man*, John Wiley & Sons, Inc., New York, 1957; ch. 14.
27. SIMON, HERBERT A., *Administrative Behavior*, Macmillan, New York, rev. ed., 1956.
28. STEVENS, BENJAMIN H., "A review of the literature on linear methods and models for spatial analysis", *Journal of the American Institute of Planners*, Vol. XXVI, No. 3 (August 1960), pp. 253–9.
29. STEVENSON, CHARLES L., *Ethics and Language*, Yale University Press, New Haven, 1953.
30. TUGWELL, REXFORD G. and EDWARD C. BANFIELD, Book Review of Walker's "The planning function in urban government", *Journal of the American Institute of Planners*, Vol. XVII, No. 1 (Winter 1951), pp. 46–49.
31. WALKER, ROBERT A., *The Planning Function in Urban Government*, 2nd ed., University of Chicago Press, Chicago, 1950.

THE IDEA OF PLANNING

Introduction

PLANNERS, like other professionals, habitually reassure themselves of the importance of what they are doing. There exists a plethora of statements concerning the idea of planning, and any selection aspiring to represent the multitude of viewpoints would make a separate volume. The three papers included have been selected to document *change* in the idea of planning. Its direction is away from a concern purely with the *physical* environment and towards intentionally *rational, comprehensive* planning; away from a primarily *practice-orientated* profession towards greater reliance on *theoretical understanding*; and away from the domination of planning by *architects* and *engineers* towards opening its ranks to various disciplines, notably in the *social sciences*. This change occurred first in the United States, but it is now almost universal.

With respect to this phenomenon, the three papers take up different positions. Ruth Glass and Donald L. Foley give a critical historical and institutional analysis of British planning more than a decade after the spate of post-war planning legislation. Criticisms similar to these stimulated changes taking place, initially in the United States. Melvin Webber's paper in turn was written when the situation there was ripe for new ideas to come to fruition. It is consequently much more "positive" and imbued with considerable optimism.

THE CRITICS OF TRADITIONAL PLANNING

Ruth Glass's paper foreshadows the concern with social problems, and in particular with questions of distributive justice occurring in the United States and also increasingly elsewhere. It deplores the division between *social, economic* and *physical* planning and castigates town planners for their mechanistic mode of thought and their conservatism masquerading as utopian commitment. But beyond this now familiar charge, her paper is a prime example of how any critical analysis of planning soon turns on the planning institutions themselves, a point made in the introduction to Part I.

Here, she addresses herself to the role of scientific intelligence in a practical activity such as planning, thus making an early contribution towards *planning theory*. For instance, in her analysis of the doctrines of British planning, and of vested interest building up, one is reminded of Stafford Beer's (1966) identification of barriers in the way of integration between science and management. The fact that analogies may be drawn between her arguments and those made by a distinguished operational research practitioner underlines one of the points which she makes, i.e. that there is a common element to all planning.

The paper also expands on differences between the United States and Great Britain. Drawing valid inferences from the usually more advanced American experience depends on the correct appreciation of the divergence between assumptions underlying institutions on both sides of the Atlantic. Her paper advances understanding by demonstrating how the traditional trust in public authority, heightened by the feeling of "togetherness" during and immediately after the war, has impeded criticism of British planning. Such trust is in contradistinction to America, where mistrust in government is deeply engrained in national culture.

Nobody can be more aware of such differences than Americans observing the British scene. Like Foley in his paper, they are mostly puzzled by what they see and their interest is aroused. Many American academic teachers of planning have spent sabbatical leaves in Britain. The fruits of such opportunity for the leisurely pursuit of intellectual curiosity are a host of very interesting studies of British planning which the British planning profession itself would be hard put to equal.

Foley's paper is a complement to Ruth Glass's critique. He analyses how three not fully compatible elements in the ideology of British town planning provided it with an appeal to a wide range of actual and potential supporters. The paper also points out that the ambiguities between these divergent strands of thought led to abandoning the ideal of comprehensiveness in favour of expedience and the much more innocuous concern for amenity and the environment generally. Reminding planners of their original claim, it argues that the rational-comprehensive ideal can only be approximated by amalgamating the *social sciences* with planning in *theory building* including theories of planning in the terms of this reader.

CHANGE IN AMERICAN PLANNING

What had seemed extravagant in Britain soon became established fact in the United States: the orientation of planning towards the *social sciences*. This resulted not in the least from some astonishing achievements in terms of physical development of American post-war planning. With the help of federal funds, which in turn had attracted much private investment, urban renewal had transformed many of the city centres. But the inter-relationship between physical structure and the social fabric of a city had also resulted in tremendous dislocation of ethnic minorities and the poor. Foremost among the critics of urban renewal were social scientists like Herbert J. Gans (1965) and Martin Anderson (1964). With the character-istic openness to *criticisms* which distinguishes so many Americans, the new awareness of social problems resulting from planning policies led to a great deal of soul-searching in the profession. This, together with the recognition of increasing technological and methodological intricacy, resulted in efforts to widen the scope of the profession.

Predictably, there was conflict between those who wanted to continue attacking social problems in an indirect manner, i.e. by tampering with the physical fabric of cities, and those who wanted to make more direct approaches unhindered by the traditional definition of "physical" planning. The issue around which this conflict developed was that of deleting those words printed in italics in the following passage from Article II of the constitution of the American Institute of Planners. It describes the planning professional's sphere of activity as: ". . . the planning of the unified development of urban communities and their environs and of states, regions, and the nation, as *expressed through determination of the comprehensive arrangements of land uses and the land occupancy and regulation thereof*" (see Davidoff's paper in particular p. 293).

The issue was resolved in 1967: a planner is somebody who shows: ". . . devotion to the public interest and mastery of the principles and techniques employed in the comprehensive planning process" (Scott, 1969).

Melvin Webber's paper played a significant part in this conflict. Commissioned by the American Institute of Planners in 1963, it constituted a statement of the philosophy of comprehensive planning as it dominated the thinking of many American planners. It was congenial to the concept of the city primarily as a social system, but one inhabiting physical artefacts. Being a "political" document addressed to an audience which had an inherently optimistic intellectual make-up, at a time when optimism was rather more justified than a few years later, it was full of enthusiasm, exhorting planners to take up the *challenge* of comprehensive planning. Whether this optimism is defensible in principle, i.e. whether comprehensive planning is something planners ought to be aiming for, is a question which the papers in the following section discuss.

REFERENCES

Part II

ANDERSON, M. (1964) *The Federal Bulldozer: A Critical Analysis of Urban Renewal 1941–1962*, M.I.T. Press.

BEER, S. (1966) *Decision and Control*, John Wiley, New York.

GANS, H. J. (1965) *The Urban Villagers: Group and Class in Life of Italian-Americans*, The Free Press, Glencoe.

SCOTT, M. (1969) *American City Planning*, University of California Press, Los Angeles.

The Evaluation of Planning:
Some Sociological Considerations*

Ruth Glass

IN DISCUSSING urban development in various parts of the world, we are always asked to consider Western experience of "planning". Yet the term is usually a misnomer. The relevant British experience is chiefly in the field of "town and country" planning; the American in the field of "city planning". It is these branches of planning, therefore, to which I shall have to refer here. But I am doing so reluctantly: it would be preferable to use the term "planning" in the purist sense, on the assumption that all aspects—economic, social, physical, national, regional and local planning —have to be regarded jointly as parts of the same enterprise. (The adjectives, though of some technical use, tend to obscure the essential unity of the concept.)

For several reasons I would like to outline some of the distinctive features of Western planning which are rarely made explicit—with special reference to British experience, but keeping also some comparisons with the United States in mind. The discussion will be especially concerned with "evaluation"—not least because it is in the appraisal of planning principles and processes that the main contribution of sociology to planning can and should be made.

This is not to say that it is the prerogative of sociologists to evaluate

* This paper is a slightly abbreviated version of an article published in the *International Social Science Journal*, Vol. XI, No. 3, 1959. It was originally submitted, on behalf of the International Sociological Association, to the United Nations Seminar on Regional Planning, held in Tokyo from 28 July to 8 August 1958. The paper was written in December 1957. Two small insertions were made in February 1959.

social policy and administration, that they can do so unaided, or that they are as yet fully capable of doing so. Nor does it mean that most of them have a burning desire to do such work. But it is undoubtedly an essential part of their professional responsibilities to make the attempt; and it is unlikely that it will be carried on in a systematic fashion without them.

Of course, sociologists can also give "technical assistance" in territorial planning. Their technical role in this field, however, is in turn largely determined by the scope and content of planning policies, and indeed by the interpretation of the concept of planning itself. (If the social sciences play no part in developing these concepts—if city planning, for example, is thought of merely as "civic design"—there appears to be hardly any need for the collection and analysis of demographic and sociological data.) By and large sociological considerations in planning are, therefore, synonymous with studies of value judgements, and studies for the purpose of developing and applying criteria of appraisal.

STUDIES FOR THE PURPOSE OF EVALUATION

Types of Study

Such studies would have to be continuous—a series rather than a single enterprise—and they would have to have several branches. These are:

1. The social history of those ideas which are implicit or explicit in planning policies. An awareness of their content and genesis is essential for making the planning process self-conscious, and for preventing such concepts from becoming *idées fixes*.

2. An investigation of the factual evidence for, and of socio-economic changes relevant to, particular planning principles, and also to plans for particular areas. (Continuous investigations are needed, for example, to test those planning principles which relate to the distribution of urban settlements by type and size. Among such studies are those of the structure of population and industries; of the location and use of services and amenities; of journeys to work, and of their cost in terms of time and money; and of the pattern of communications—that is, of transport and of linkage between different land-uses and activities.)

3. Studies of planning administration. (For example; case studies of

the division of functions between and within planning authorities; of the process of formulating policies, of their application in practice; and, in particular, studies of the criteria used in making decisions.)

4. Empirical examinations of the results of planning. (For instance, studies of changes in industrial structure, and of planned communities.)

However diverse such studies would be, in their various ways they would all be concerned with the same main question: as, by definition, planning is a comprehensive and a rational process, it is necessary to find out to what extent it has already, and can acquire, these attributes in practice. Of course, the answers can never be expected to be entirely positive and optimistic. As there are conflicting interests and aspirations in society, and in the minds of individuals, and as the moods of different decades exist simultaneously, there are bound to be conflicting value judgements, and *a priori* policies, many of which are experimental and have to await, or may never obtain, objective justification. Moreover, as a mechanical giant super-brain has not yet been invented which could correlate all aspects of planning, anticipate the manifold implications, and thus issue millions of coherent detailed decisions, administrative processes are bound to be competitive and frequently incompatible. Definitions of "planning" which give it an almost divine aura of comprehension and comprehensiveness must therefore remain in the realm of fiction.

Nevertheless, it is by no means a naïve and academic exercise to ask—and to search—for reason and compatibility in planning policies and processes. Unless that is done, planning makes no sense. Like the social sciences, planning is based on the assumption that there are powerful common denominators of needs and aims in society—in other words, that the public interest can be defined and pursued in terms of consistent social policies, though it is highly complex and not the sum total of simultaneously overt interests. This assumption (which has to leave a wide loophole for arbitrariness) has to be tested constantly. Without such tests the area of unreason and incompatibility cannot be narrowed.

Lack of Examples

However, the appropriate questions have not been asked in a systematic fashion with reference to British planning, nor have they been asked in the United States. (I do not know a single example of a coherent series of studies concerned with the evaluation of planning policies and processes in Britain or the United States, though there are fragments which confirm the need for such continuous research.)[1]

These fragments show, moreover, that the obligation to carry out studies of this kind has to be written into the planning legislation, as was in fact demanded by the three classic British planning reports—the Barlow, Scott and Uthwatt reports—which prepared the ground for the establishment of the present British system of land-use planning. (Some of their important recommendations—those concerning the structure of the central planning authority and its research functions—have, however, not been followed.)[2]

Scattered efforts of appraisal are no substitute. They cannot be patched together to make a coherent whole, and even their individual value is rather small. Though that is a truism, especially in planning, it still needs to be repeated: even when it becomes strikingly obvious in practice, its implications tend to be ignored. This happened, for instance, in an official investigation in Britain—that of the "Committee on Administrative Tribunals and Enquiries", which made one of the rare attempts to evaluate administrative procedures. (In this case it was mainly an appraisal of the safeguards for equity in those procedures which have, or appear to have, quasi-judicial functions.) The Committee could not possibly obtain the complete evidence which it needed to fulfil its obligations according to its terms of reference. Many aspects remained obscure because the statutes do not require that a central record of administrative decisions be kept as a matter of routine.[3] Occasionally, the absence of data made it impossible

---

[1] Among such fragmentary examples in Britain are the following official reports: *Report of the Committee on Qualifications of Planners* (the Schuster report), Cmd. 8059, London, H.M.S.O., 1950; the evidence and the *Report of the Committee on Administrative Tribunals and Enquiries* (the Franks Committee), Cmd. 218, London, H.M.S.O., 1957. There are also accounts by observers: e.g. Orlans, H., *Stevenage: A Sociological Study of a New Town*, London, 1952. Of special value in this context is a historical study: Ashworth, W., *The Genesis of Modern British Town Planning*, London, 1954.

[2] *Royal Commission on the Distribution of the Industrial Population: Report*, Cmd. 6153, London, H.M.S.O., 1940. (The Barlow report.) *Report of the Committee on Land Utilisation in Rural Areas*, Cmd. 6378, London, H.M.S.O., 1942. (The Scott report.) *Expert Committee on Compensation and Betterment. Final report*, Cmd. 6386, London, H.M.S.O., 1942. (The Uthwatt report.)

[3] This was true especially in the field of town and country planning, though some improvements in record-keeping have been made since 1958.

for the Committee to ask pertinent questions, and when such questions were asked, the need for data was admitted, only to be immediately forgotten. And that again is to be expected: unless an administrative system is set up from the start so as to be "self-conscious" in its operations, it will resist subsequent sporadic attempts to introduce analytical devices.

Obligatory and Independent Studies

Though independent inquiries are also needed, they cannot take the place of administrative self-awareness. While the administrator is bound to be rather complacent, at least in public, about the work of his organization, and while he is also preoccupied with the obstructions—economic, political, social and bureaucratic—by which he is surrounded in the execution of policies, the independent observer tends to use criteria of appraisal which fit an ideal, not an actual society. His criticisms could, therefore, do more harm than good: they might be discredited as being unrealistic, and will thus harden the administrator's resistance to such criticisms, in particular, and to research, in general. In that way, the distance between the insider and the outsider becomes even greater, and the chances of their co-operating—as they should in genuine studies of evaluation—become more remote.

BRITISH EXPERIENCE

The lack of self-awareness in the British planning system is the defect of a virtue—or rather of a series of virtues. Though these positive and negative aspects are due to a particular historical combination of circumstances, they are relevant to the consideration of planning efforts elsewhere.

The Public Interest

First and foremost, there is comparatively little scepticism or even curiosity about the system because it has been established by common consent, in recognition of the public interest. This recognition, in turn, had grown up in response to the early-nineteenth-century experience of *laissez-faire* industrial and urban developments. While for several decades such developments drove the "two nations" further apart—indeed the "classes" did not regard the "masses" as human beings like themselves—

it became increasingly obvious that society could not live with such deep cleavages: the danger of revolt, and of contagious disease and social disorganization could not be ignored. "Some . . . measures are urgently called for, as claims of humanity and justice to great multitudes of our fellow men, and as necessary not less for the welfare of the poor than the safety of property and the security of the rich."[4] So gradually a sense of mutual responsibility began to develop, and with it the awareness that the communal interest has precedence over private interests—the acceptance, that is, of state control in many fields of economic and social activity. Undoubtedly, urbanization as such contributed to the rather early acceptance of state regulations, which was noticeable already during the mid-nineteenth century. The very fact of living in so small, densely populated, highly urbanized a country provided constant object lessons of social interdependence.

There was thus already a well-established ideological background for "socialization" (in both senses of the term) when the Second World War and the immediate post-war period made the concept of the public interest more acceptable than before. The war effort demanded economic planning; reconstruction demanded environmental planning. We need, said the Uthwatt report, "co-ordinated planning as a whole compared with the confused development in the past in an isolated and regional manner".[5] At the time, both political parties supported this view, and they were not ahead of public opinion. Planning was no longer mainly thought of as a code of regulations to repair the damage of *laissez-faire* and to prevent further damage in odd patches, but as the instrument of the welfare state. It was during those years that the legislation was passed, and the administrative machine established for the control of the distribution of industry and for the system of town and country planning. (The main features of the latter were: the preparation of local development plans under central, ministerial supervision; the control of "development", as defined by the Act, in terms of land-use and buildings; and the nationalization of development rights and values.[6])

[4] United Kingdom, *Report of the Select Committee on the Health of Towns*, London, H.M.S.O., 1840, pp. xiv, xv.

[5] *Uthwatt Report*, 1942, *op. cit.*, para. 11, p. 7.

[6] However, subsequently, the most important element of the system was discarded: development rights were denationalized. (See note 7.)

Unfortunately, however, the various aspects of planning were separated. Economic planning was split up into various branches, and physical planning was set apart as yet another one. While one Ministry deals with a major aspect of economic planning—location of industry, another Ministry is entrusted with town and country planning. (But the term "planning" is no longer included in its title.)

Since the forties, British society has again become more sharply stratified; the recognition of national purposes and needs has faded; and the controls themselves have become feeble.[7] And yet the memory of common consent by which the planning system was set up is still sufficiently strong to prevent any major controversy and stocktaking. There are debates, of course, but mainly on peripheral matters of procedure and technique. Any mistakes that were made at the beginning in the organization of planning—such as the administrative separation of various planning functions, and the lack of provision for research in the planning process—have thus become stabilized. And that is the case, too, because these mistakes are not strikingly obvious—especially not to a public that has an innate trust in public authority.

Trust in Public Authority

This trust, again, is a matter of tradition. The overwhelming need for reform during the nineteenth century and thereafter could be met only by the development of new social and political institutions—in particular, by public authorities with well-defined standards of competence and morality. The new planning authorities, central and local, have been grafted on the established pattern. Though they may thus be slow in adapting themselves to new roles and conditions, they have also inherited

---

[7] A case in point was the increasingly ambivalent attitude to the principle of the nationalization of development rights, which was established by the Town and Country Planning Act of 1947 in accordance with the recommendations of the Uthwatt report. Legislation introduced in 1958 (since this paper was written) has virtually abolished this crucial principle—with the result that there has been, since then, a predictable unchecked spiralling of land values; and in effect a return to *laissez-faire*, though nominally the machinery for plan-making and development control still exists.

the old virtues.[8] So far (until the late fifties) they have continued to deserve the confidence of the public. And so long as the administrative machine works without undue friction, there seems to be not much point in taking it apart to examine its components.

The Planning Profession

There is yet another reason why there is little drive to do so, and this, too, is paradoxically a positive one: it is the rapid growth and stabilization of the planning profession. Just as the system for town and country planning was created with efficiency, so the consequent great demand for planners—to work both inside and outside public authorities—was met, apparently, with swift success. As a result, the improvised features—both of the system and of the profession—have become permanent. By virtue of becoming an established institution and an established profession respectively, both have acquired vested interests in maintaining themselves unchanged—vested interests which reinforce one another. Neither the institution nor the profession has those built-in controls of scepticism which make it possible to remain young. Altogether, planning has become respectable far too easily and far too quickly.

The new planning profession is an amalgam of several old ones. The

---

[8] The fact that new planning functions are being performed within long-established, rather conservative institutions has certain obvious disadvantages. For instance, as a result, these functions were split up, and are being carried out separately by different government departments, and by local authorities whose boundaries are not necessarily appropriate for such purposes, and which naturally resent proposals to change their frontiers. Moreover, the tradition of *ad hoc* empiricism in British public administration does not offer a suitable ideological environment for twentieth-century planning. Again, the administrative machinery for land-use planning lacks devices for self-analysis, and thus appears to have insufficient safeguards against administrative discretion—mainly because, like other public services, this machinery was built on the assumption that Parliament supplies such devices and safeguards adequately. But Parliament can hardly do so in an age of increasingly complex state responsibility. Nevertheless, at least in Britain, there are also distinct advantages in giving the new planning functions to established government agencies: indeed, it often seems that the advantages outweigh the disadvantages. That was the conclusion which we reached after our own comparison of the planning work of new agencies—the New Town Development Corporations—and that of established institutions, the counties and county boroughs, which were then the local planning authorities. The new agencies seem to have the defects of the old ones often in an accentuated form, and without the compensating virtues.

demand for planners brought about by the Town and Country Planning Acts of the forties was met almost entirely by recruits from three disciplines —architecture, engineering and surveying—which for long have had high professional standards and strong organizations of their own. And the demand was met, of course, also by administrators whose traditional code of conduct is such that they achieve an identification with the institution which they serve: throughout their working day, their only individuality is that of the posts they occupy.[9]

In their new role as planners, people from these various well-established disciplines tend to group themselves according to their old alignments. Previous professional distances are maintained—the antipathy between administrative and technical civil servants, for example, and that between architects and engineers. And this happens partly by force of habit—each of these groups has a specific approach and craftsmanship—but also just because these groups, though diverse, have certain traits in common: those which make for exclusiveness. They are all specialists; and apart from some sections among the architects who are rather heterogeneous, they all tend to be conservative in their professional outlook, particularly in guarding their specialization. In their own fields, they are all used to a mechanistic mode of thought—to a fairly straightforward sequence of cause and effect, in terms of a limited number of material factors. They have no problems of boundaries: their areas are well defined, and so are their terms of reference. (It is their job, for instance, to find out *how* a given number of houses for a given group of people should be designed, but not to ask *why* that should be done.) They thus have no urge to establish

---

[9] This is, of course, a characteristic feature of the British Civil Service, in keeping with the ethos of the British "Public School". The official is simply a member of a team. And though at first sight such depersonalization is rather forbidding, on closer acquaintance, and especially after comparison with other manners of officialdom, its values are apparent. It is this depersonalization which makes the system systematic; it creates an overt, comprehensible and thus fairly tolerable bureaucracy: it minimizes "the insolence of office". Because the role of the individual is neutralized, a clear-cut division of functions and responsibilities is achieved. (And incidentally, it is this depersonalization, too, which explains why after office hours the British civil servant is often a rather eccentric man.) Of course, such a system has its defects, one of which is its resistance to innovation. A representative of a new discipline or technique appears as an individual; his post is not yet depersonalized, and his function is, therefore, only very slowly and grudgingly accepted.

new relationships, nor to question the reasons for instructions which are comfortably explicit. And when there are imponderables—as there are especially in architecture—intuition, subjective tastes and judgements have to be applied; without them, there could be no creative design.

Thus the loose federation of various branches of technology and the arts which is called the planning profession is likely to remain just that—a separate profession in name, but not in terms of a distinct individual identity. Resistance to change is implicit in its make-up and has become accentuated by the mere fact of its existence: the common interest in the maintenance of the profession is the strongest bond that holds it together (though each branch tends to think of planning as a new professional label added to its own previous one). Of course, there are other links as well: the shared loyalty to an institution or to a place, for example, and the common experience of frequent frustrations. But the ideal of international planning literature—the kind of "teamwork" that is a truly collaborative effort of as many disciplines as ones care to name, the social and natural sciences with their various acquaintances from the technical and artistic fields, directed by a super-planner—that ideal is still very remote from reality.

And it is indeed unrealistic. There is the danger that such a vision (especially that of the planner as a superman, with qualities of strength, wisdom and goodness resembling those of an archangel) might well lead to vague eclecticism. British town and country planning has the distinct advantage that it is comparatively free from that.[10] The members of the profession are craftsmen in their own right. The difficulty is that it is mainly technology and the arts which are represented in the profession: the social sciences are likely to remain outside so long as central government maintains the administrative division between different aspects of planning—social, economic and physical. There is, moreover, too early and too narrow a specialization in the disciplines from which planners are now recruited; and these disciplines are not taught so as to produce scientific curiosity and a scientific attitude. Postgraduate education in town and country planning as such comes too late, and cannot be sufficiently exten-

---

[10] One official report, however, the *Schuster Report, op. cit.*, gave a superman definition of a planner.

sive, to modify previous habits of thought significantly.[11] British planning does not suffer from a lack of angels; it needs devils.

History of Planning Ideas

It needs them—and through them an injection of scientific empiricism, expressed in terms of theoretical critique as well as modest fact-finding— also because so many of the concepts which are implicit or explicit in British land-use planning have *a prioristic* and utopian origins. They are the idea of nineteenth-century reformers, and especially those of the utopian writers, who saw social conditions and relationships in terms of black and white, and in terms of straightforward interactions. They believed firmly that environment directly determines human character and social structure—and that their recipes for the reform of environment (such as industrial villages and garden cities) had universal validity and would assure that men everywhere live happily ever after. They were confident, moreover, of the power of rational persuasion and of a steady sequence of social progress. And as the diagnosis appeared to be so simple, and the cure so obvious, there seemed to be no need for systematic inquiry.[12]

Since then, society has become more complex, and the prospect of social change far more ambiguous, and yet the old ideas have been maintained and have become fixed prejudices. Though several movements contributed to town planning, and traces of the old divisions still remain, it is the ideol-

---

[11] The social sciences still play only a very small part in the curriculum of most planning schools in Britain, and indeed an even smaller part in the curriculum of architectural, engineering and surveying education. Moreover, a good deal of postgraduate education in town and country planning is part-time. It is often taken by people who are already in jobs, who tend to consider their postgraduate course as a strictly vocational one, and who enter it primarily so as to obtain promotion. For this purpose, close acquaintance with the social sciences is by no means regarded as an advantage. Of course, there are many reasons for the separation between the social sciences and planning. The social sciences, too, are to blame: the frigidity is mutual.

[12] The "utopians" appear to have been unaware of, and they were certainly not influenced by, the distinguished social studies carried out by many of their contemporaries. There is no sign of recognition of the work of Charles Booth and the Webbs, for example, in the writings of Ebenezer Howard and his successors.

ogy of the utopians which has become predominant.[13] It is they who are
the "super-ego" of current planning thought—not only in Britain, but also
in many other parts of the world which have imported British planning
notions. The anti-urban bias in town planning has to be attributed to their
influence. The love for formula-making is due to them, and so are the
strong anti-sociological tendencies, visible particularly in ideas such as
those of the neighbourhood unit and the garden city, which are imbued
with nostalgic ideas about the virtues of the small-scale, "balanced" and
self-contained community. It is because the utopians have provided
planners with their own home-made sociology that there has been a
persistent separation between town planning and the social sciences in
Britain. The utopian version of "sociology"—mechanistic, romantic and so
happily definite in its conclusions—is one which appeals especially to the
disciplines represented in the planning profession.

The Victorians, and the utopian writers especially, were afraid of bigness
in all its forms—be it a large city or a large organization. The big city—
crowded, ugly and unhealthy, a panorama of class conflict, the image of the
growing power of the working class—was seen throughout the nineteenth
century and well into the twentieth century as an "aggregate of masses,
our conceptions of which clothe themselves in terms that express something portentous and fearful". It was seen as "a danger to security and
all pleasant things".[14] It appeared to be, and indeed it was, a threat to the
established social order.

---

[13] The various nineteenth-century movements which led to subsequent efforts
for town planning went separate ways. Among them was that for public health,
led by Chadwick and his supporters who conducted pioneer investigations; the
campaigns for the housing of the working classes and for municipal reform:
and the movement for social regeneration which I have referred to as the utopian
movement in the text because this adjective gives the best brief clue to its main
characteristics. It was sponsored by the writers of utopias and by the advocates of
community experiments (such as Robert Owen, James Silk Buckingham, J. Minter
Morgan, the Reverend H. Solly and William Morris) and by those who, in fact,
created model communities—Sir Titus Salt at Saltaire, the Cadburys at Bournville,
the Levers at Port Sunlight, Ebenezer Howard at Welwyn and Letchworth. Though
an apparently motley group working at different points of time from the early
nineteenth century to the early twentieth century, they were homogeneous in terms of
their main ideas, especially of those which have been influential in town planning.

[14] W. Cooke Taylor, *Notes of a Tour in the Manufacturing Districts of Lancashire*,
London, 1842, p. 6. And: C. F. G. Masterman, "The English City" in *England: a
Nation*, being the papers of the Patriot's Club, London, 1904, p. 61. Victorian and
Edwardian literature is studded with statements of this kind.

So Chalmers, the Scottish theologian writing in the early nineteenth century, for example, already put forward his "principle of locality"— the division of the city—in order to dispel this menace. It should be remembered, said Chalmers, "how much it serves to divide and to weaken the force of popular violence, when the vast and overgrown city is broken down into separate parochial jurisdictions . . . where the people, instead of all looking one way . . . and forming into a combined array of hostile feeling and prejudice . . . are habituated to look several ways to that nearer and more interesting regime by which they are respectively surrounded." Thus can the "unmanageable mass", which would otherwise "form into one impetuous and overwhelming surge against the reigning authority", be "penetrated and split up into fragments . . .".[15]

To split up the "mass" was the main motive behind all those interrelated ideas of town design, which were later elaborated, and which are intended to remove, or at least to camouflage, urban characteristics—such as ideas about density (the lower the better), decentralization, new towns, neighbourhood units.

Ambivalence

A good deal of ambivalence in viewing social change is implicit in all these notions. And it has been the persistence of this ambivalence which has been of more consequence than the persistence of the particular ideas as such. Ambivalence explains many of the uncertainties in British planning; it has contributed greatly to the lack of self-awareness both in the system and in the profession. The utopians thought that environmental changes could prevent those major social changes of which they were afraid: they believed that an exodus from the town to the countryside, and the splitting up of the city into villages, would prevent social upheaval. They recommended that changes should be made for the sake of preservation; indeed, for the purpose of returning to the past—an idealized, unhistoric past. And like the nineteenth-century writers, their twentieth-century ideological heirs, too, have felt safe in "looking backward", though this is not supposed to be the attitude of planners.

Nevertheless, town planning was advocated as a device for getting the

---

[15] T. Chalmers, *The Christian and Civic Economy of Large Towns*, 3 vols., Glasgow, 1821–6, Vol. 2, pp. 39–40.

best of all worlds: individualism and socialism; town and country; past and future; preservation and change.[16] In other words, the planners promised the people that they could have their cake and eat it.

This is an attractive doctrine: it presents so many different faces that it hardly seems to require scrutiny. It appeals to conservatives and socialists alike. This streak of ambivalence has certainly helped the British planning system in winning consent.

Of course, there were other more solid reasons for setting up the system as well, and though there were divisions, the community of interests was not entirely illusory. It was, moreover, just because so many of the planning ideas were old that they were so widely accepted during the 1940s. For better and for worse, they had percolated through all strata of society: the anti-urban attitudes of the upper class, for example, had been followed by the suburban drift of the middle class, and then by that of some sections of the working class. There had been sufficient time to make Victorian and Edwardian ideas popular, but not yet enough time for contrary views to develop, and to be advocated by opinion leaders.[17]

Moreover, the experience of the inter-war and war years had given new point to ideas which had been put forward earlier in a different context and with different motives. The experience of the depression revealed the vulnerability to unemployment of areas with highly specialized heavy industry, and the consequent need for planned distribution of population and industry. The growth of giant conurbations; the threat to agricultural land and productivity resulting from urban sprawl; the congestion of communications caused by the pushing of new motor transport along an

---

[16] The "garden city" especially, as outlined by Ebenezer Howard, was intended to be such a compromise device. And it is this ideology which is still the dominant one in British land-use planning.

[17] During the last few years, there has been a perceptible change. Attitudes towards urbanism are beginning to be modified, though so far only by rather small, but potentially influential minorities. Some sections of the middle and upper classes are becoming increasingly aware of the disadvantages of suburban and ex-urban existence—and particularly of the hardships of long journeys to work. Employers in the central metropolitan area experience considerable problems of labour recruitment and retention. Last, but not least, many architects and some planners, too, rebel against "subtopia" for aesthetic reasons. Though—or perhaps just because—the advocacy of these new views is occasionally vociferous, it is rather vague: as yet there have been no comprehensive statement of the socio-economic arguments for a departure from the still prevailing nineteenth-century anti-urban bias.

old road system; strategic considerations in an age of air warfare—all these and many other aspects contributed to the recognition of the same need. And they also led to the view (expressed with modifications by the Barlow report which dealt with the matter) that the growth of cities must be controlled.[18] In the elaboration and later application of this view, however, the previous utopian conditioning for it played a large part; the notion became exaggerated, was once again cherished as a dogma and adorned with sentimental nineteenth-century embroidery. Once again planners found it convenient to borrow their models of the future from a past ideology.

The Conservative Outlook

Such borrowing is inevitable and quite useful when it reflects a due respect for continuity. But when it is done dogmatically, without investigation of past premises in the light of actual and potential conditions and values, it can get planning into a muddle. It might, and indeed it has, led planners to underestimate the people's capacity to accept change, and even their desire for change. It has thus also led to an overemphasis on "preservation" as the aim of planning at the expense of "change", although —if that tendency is carried too far—"planning" makes no sense. Planning for the *status quo* is a contradiction in terms.

Planning policy and administration have been conservative in their outlook, apparently on the assumption that the public has the same attitude. Indeed, it often seems that planners believe—"the people, that is us". The lack of self-consciousness in the system and in the profession—and with it the lack of evaluation, in general, and the divorce between social research and social policy, in particular—all this contributes to the persistence, indeed to the hardening, of this belief. As planning has not kept in step with the realistic observation of contemporary society— and there is in any case far too little observation of this kind—planners (and many sociologists, too) continue to think of "the people" as their own

[18] As the report said: ". . . mere size need not in itself be a disadvantage, but it is size without system, chaotic growth without the adoption of proper principles alike for social well-being and for industry, that are to be avoided." *Barlow Report, op. cit.*, p. 155, para. 325.

particular mirror images.[19] The diversity of needs, wants and aspirations in society is obscured, policy-makers and administrators can quite happily continue to regard their own subjective preferences as objective, universal ones.

Bias

But if there is too facile an identification of particular interests with the public interest, planning operations are bound to become biased in favour of particular groups. When conflicts of interests are ignored or glossed over, they are likely to become sharper: they can then hardly be resolved. It is then not possible to agree to differ.[20] And when that happens, policies tend to be vague—they are then policies in name only, without giving adequate guidance—and the criteria of planning control, too, tend to be feeble, leaving too wide a margin for subjective interpretation.

Such hazards are illustrated in the practical experience of the British planning system every day. Increasingly there are criticisms, aimed so far not against the system as such, but against the uncertainty of its direction (though, if such objections are not met, they can easily develop into opposition to "planning" itself). As yet, it is not state control to which people object, but inexplicitness in the exercise of control—especially in giving reasons for decisions.

And this uncertainty and vagueness is paradoxically due to the fact that the planning system and the profession are far too sure of themselves:

[19] In particular, the current tendency in the social sciences towards "micro-sociology" does little to remove, and indeed helps to reinforce, such misconceptions. *Ad hoc* studies of small groups, or of subtle inter-personal relationships, carried out without reference to the social universe to which such groups belong, are bound to be inconclusive and misleading.

[20] If the ambivalence in the dual aims of the British planning system—the aims of preservation and change—had been clearly recognized from the outset, these would probably be nowadays far less at cross-purposes with one another. Again, if the opposed notions of the two major political parties in giving the planning system bi-partisan support had been spelled out, there would be less confusion nowadays both within each party and also in inter-party debates. There would then have been a better chance of resolving, instead of perpetuating, the conflict. Spurious cleavages arise, moreover, because the existence of the significant ones is so much taken for granted that they are not made explicit. But in the long run, this can hardly work. If "planning" promises all things to all men, it will satisfy very few indeed.

land-use planning has become a technical doctrine which does not recognize its ambivalence, nor does it consider its limitations. It is, therefore, expressed in terms of far too meticulous standards (with reference to density, for example) on the one hand, and in terms of rather obscure notions (such as that of "amenity") on the other. Apparent precision and ambiguity often appear side by side: though rigid "standards" are applied, decisions are worded so as to avoid generalizations. The maxim is: "each case should be treated on its own merits." But one does not like to be told, for instance, that one cannot convert one's house into two flats, thus increasing its occupancy from three persons to six, because that would raise the density above the maximum permitted for that street, though of course the woman next door could take in lodgers, or have babies, without asking for planning permission. Nor does it make sense if one is refused permission to build a house of contemporary design in a neighbourhood of mock-Tudor houses—on the grounds that the building of the new house would be "contrary to the amenities of the area".[21]

There might be bias in such decisions. But if there is, it does not necessarily occur because planners are influenced by the personal pressure of the applicant rather than by the merits of his case. In that respect, British central and local authorities have been so far usually beyond reproach. (Indeed, it is in part their genuine tradition of fairness which explains why neither they nor the public have been more alert in looking out for bias, whatever its cause.) When there is prejudice, it tends to be impersonal—quite often the by-product of parochialism. There are arbitrary features in planning thought and technique—not least because the outlook is so narrow.[22]

[21] These are examples of actual cases—of adverse decisions by local planning authorities against which the applicant appealed to the Minister (who has the last word whenever there is a disagreement between the local planning authority and a would-be developer). The attitude expressed by the planning authority in these particular cases is by no means atypical: similar examples have often been found in our studies of development control.

[22] Our case studies of planning administration indicate that the larger planning authorities are more objective (and thus less arbitrary) in their considerations and decisions than the smaller ones. There is a definite advance in sense and sensibility as one moves from the rural to the urban areas, and from local to central authorities. Such variations are, in turn, related to the degree of political consciousness of the various authorities. Party politics help in getting a wider horizon, and thus in diminishing arbitrariness.

If it were not so, planners might realize that they could well afford to be more tolerant. Sometimes, as in the density case just referred to, they seem to be unaware of the facts of life, and thus do not recognize, for example, that it is impossible to control population density as precisely as they are attempting to do. They are making their job more difficult than it needs to be: it is through unnecessarily meticulous standards and controls that many frictions are created between the planners and the planned.

A study of adverse decisions in British development control has shown that such avoidable spurious disagreements are no less frequent than serious conflicts of interests. And with common sense even the latter could be more often reconciled if only their existence were admitted. There is so much undeniable social interdependence in a small country like Britain. In matters of land-use, especially, it still happens that opposed factions reach the same conclusions, though for different reasons, when an issue is clearly presented.[23]

Doctrinaire Planning

There may be still a potential community of interests in British planning. But nowadays, it is mainly the remembrance of a period of exceptional unanimity, and also the trust in public authority, which keep the system going. There are signs that both the memory and the confidence are wearing thin. Increasingly it seems that the system is becoming so disjointed and conservative as to acquire a vested interest in the maintenance of the *status quo*. And as its positive purposes are being pushed into the background, its restrictive features are becoming predominant. When planning is doctrinaire, it is also autocratic. Arbitrary administrative decisions follow from arbitrary value judgments. There is a danger that the planning

---

[23] This happened, for instance, when the then Minister of Housing and Local Government made amendments to the Development Plan of the London County Council. The Labour Party (the majority party) and the Conservative Party on the Council united in their opposition to certain amendments, though for different motives, and not simply for the reason of asserting the authority of London local government versus central government.

system will forget its *raison d'être*—the rational and just pursuit of the public interest.[24]

SUMMARY

It is just because British land-use planning is in many respects rather advanced, that it provides an example of the need for appraisal—and in particular, of the lack of evaluation, and of its causes and consequences. Although the British system is by no means exceptional in being rather complacent, there are specific reasons for the lack of self-criticism in British institutions. And of course these show also, once again, that the resemblance between planning efforts in different parts of the world is mainly a semantic one. There is hardly any likeness, for example, between British and American "planning".

The British planning system, set up to be "comprehensive, continuous and consistent", is in fact split up into separate branches—economic and physical—and inclined to become highly opportunistic. Nevertheless, it is still at least nominally devoted to the pursuit of the public interest, and it is on that assumption that the system has won common consent. But the concept of state control in the public interest, crucial to the definition of planning in Britain, is absent in the United States. There, the term refers almost exclusively to "city planning". And the so-called planning operations are frankly designed in the interests of particular groups, and often almost equally frank in their prejudices against others. Whatever the reasons for such overt favouritism, the important point in the present context is that it is taken for granted as a matter of course: it would still be politically unwise in Britain; it is politically proper in the United States. While the British still have an innate trust in public authority, the Americans have a deep-seated mistrust: they would, therefore, much rather have

[24] Indeed, this danger has become far more pronounced during 1958 (that is, since this paper was written). And this should be kept in mind, too, in reading the summary. When I wrote the paper in December 1957, the differences between American and British planning were still striking, and even now (at the proof stage) in February 1959, they still exist. But there are signs of an increasing "Americanization" of British planning—in other words, of a rapidly growing indifference to the public interest. If this trend persists, within the next few years the differences between American and British "planning" ideology and practice, which are indicated in the following pages, will hardly any longer be significant.

"planning" in the market place than the concentration of planning power in a monolithic system of public authorities.

Thus "city planning" in the United States consists of a lot of disparate activities (for instance, those which we would call civic design, estate management and public relations) and it is carried out by a whole host of separate organizations—public, semi-public and private—even within one city. The Americans, therefore, talk of the need to "co-ordinate planning", while in the British view planning is supposed to imply co-ordination (though it may not be effective).[25]

There are different levels of consciousness in the activities which are, called "planning" in both countries—a consciousness of purposes (that is of social policy) however much it has become dimmed in Britain; a consciousness of process and technique in the United States. And perhaps more can be learned even from the lack of self-awareness of the British in the planning field than from the highly developed technical self-scrutiny of the Americans. For in "planning", in the idealized British sense, it is not possible to dissociate the question of *how* something is done from the question *why* it should be done, and for *whom*. Investigations of the first question only, on its own, are therefore hardly relevant.[26]

---

[25] Although there are, of course, difficulties of co-ordination in Britain, by comparison with the United States, Britain still has a statutory and administrative system of planning that is straightforward and closely knit; and it is in charge of government, local and central.

[26] The British and American purposes and practice of planning are so dissimilar that, as a result, questions and concepts in the evaluation of planning are also entirely different in the two countries. The British still consider planning as an instrument of social policy, and thus have premises for value judgements. These premises exist, and with them also some criteria of evaluation, though both need to be elaborated and developed. And it is because this is not done, because there is such a lack of self-awareness, that the major value premises themselves are increasingly becoming ambivalent. The Americans, on the other hand, appear to have no such basic value premises for their city planning activities. (Even the ideal of "the city beautiful"—a sufficiently neutral concept—is no longer a general one, and the ideal of "efficiency" can, of course, be variously interpreted in the interests of different groups.) And yet the Americans engage in a great deal of appraisal—of techniques of design, analysis, research, administration, decision-making. In that respect, they are ahead of the British, and they often carry out such studies in a highly skilled manner. The only trouble is that hardly any of this "evaluation" is concerned with values; that is, with the social purposes of planning: in that respect, there is a vacuum. Indeed, it would be very hard to fill it since even the value hypotheses hardly as yet exist in planning activities. Thus American studies of decision-making, for example, are usually concerned with the content of decisions only in so

As there is so little similarity in the "planning" efforts of different parts of the world, the lessons which one country can learn from another are often indirect rather than direct. Technical principles and methods (in particular, administrative ones) should not be imported without due regard to the ideas on which they are based, nor should such ideas be recommended without knowledge of their origin and context.

But it is this precisely which is so often done. There have been several elements in the doctrine of British land-use planning which have been influential in many parts of the world—irrespective of whether they fit into the new environment or not. Notions on the design and subdivision of towns, and on the limitation of their size, have been widely exported, and with them also the anti-urban bias which is implicit in them. And though some of these ideas (that of the neighbourhood unit, for example) have travelled back and forth from Europe to America and have been modified on these trips, they have remained essentially unchanged, and are still being applied in a standardized form in varying cultures and situations. Their acceptance is in part undoubtedly due to the prestige of British planning, but it may also be due to the fact that planners everywhere (and for that matter, all human beings) search for formulae and therefore tend to be uncritical in copying those which make pretty pictures.

Such copying is hardly advisable. Many of the widely accepted ideas, and the value judgements which they reflect, are the result of a particular process of historical conditioning: they would, therefore, not be appropriate to planning in other parts of the world. Nor would the counter-proposals which are increasingly being put forward—often in as doctrinaire a manner as the original notions—be necessarily acceptable.[27] As the old principles were dogmatic, and are still being advocated with stubborn persistence by the old guard of planners, the opposition to them also has to be fierce and is often equally exaggerated. When the followers of Ebenezer Howard

---

far as this is relevant to the study of the process. However, even on the strictly technical and administrative side, the operations of "city planning" have inevitably distinct disadvantages if they are divorced from social policy and the pursuit of the public interest. Thus the British have attained greater skill than the Americans in matters such as plan-making and associated activities.

[27] For instance, the arguments advanced in current controversies for vertical versus horizontal building (and high-density development) would not be applicable to developing countries, although the controversies as such would be of some interest.

and Le Corbusier argue against one another, they tend to speak with the same fanaticism, though they use a different vocabulary. Both the old and the new notions belong to the same specific history of thought: they are not generally applicable.

This history, however, is of general interest. It shows, for example, how strongly the images of urbanism and of civic design are influenced by the class structure of the city. If that had been more clearly recognized, there might have been fewer adverse practical and ideological consequences. The twentieth-century British city does not, at present, evoke conscious fears of revolution. But until recently the neglect of cities, and the flight from them, have continued; and so the old ideas, too, inspired by the old fears, have lingered on. There have thus been few positive features and positive concepts of urbanism which could serve as examples to other parts of the world.

Nevertheless, there have been concrete lessons. One of them points to the obscurantism in planning jargon. Indeed, there should be a good deal of caution in its use: it contributes to the mystique of planning. It spreads the illusion that there are likenesses where none exist, and—as with all jargon—it tends to be used as a substitute for thought.

This is apparent, for example, in the addiction to the fashionable term "regional planning". There are inevitably endless variations in the definition of a "region"—within and across national boundaries. The "region" is a rather arbitrary entity, subject to the vantage point of the observer, and the particular purposes which the definition is intended to serve. In planning to date, the region is usually an area with functional interconnections, and/or with noticeable geographical boundaries. (Again a region—like a river valley—might be delimited because it is the object of a common plan for environmental transformation—introduced, for instance, by a large power scheme.) But whatever the area and characteristics of a region, it is essentially a technical and administrative subdivision, and one which cannot remain fixed. Like other such subdivisions, it should be devised in the interest of national planning (and perhaps eventually of international planning). It is when "regional planning" is elevated to form a school or doctrine of its own, that its inherent dependence on national planning can easily be forgotten: it can then in fact be used to prevent national planning.

Thus the common terminology can easily hide both the differences and the gaps in ideology. But it is undoubtedly the ideology of planning, far more than techniques of design and administration, which needs to be considered and advanced. Planning without social policy does not make sense, and social policy without systematic thought and research is liable to become meaningless and eventually unacceptable.

In considering the planning activities of different countries, it is thus their respective ideologies, in particular, which should be compared. And wherever a scheme for the evaluation of planning is devised, there is one field of study which is indispensable—that of the social influences in the history and trends of planning ideas.

Yet more important still than any blueprints for research in aid of the evaluation of planning is the conditioning for self-awareness and self-criticism in the planning process. The system and the profession should be constituted so as to be inclined to assess their work, to welcome appraisal, and to be receptive to its findings. And this is not a theoretical prescription: it can be translated into practical recommendations.

As British experience has shown, sporadic efforts of evaluation are bound to be inadequate. But it would be perfectly feasible to build analytical devices into the administrative system: to establish, for instance, a continuous record of its operations, and thus to provide the necessary series of data. Moreover, a certain proportion of development funds should be set aside for studies devoted to the appraisal of policies, processes, techniques and results. Again the education for, and recruitment to, the planning profession should be sufficiently broad to counteract the entrenchment of vested interests in dogma and officialdom.

It is perhaps in these respects that the social sciences could make their most useful contribution. They have acquired some sophistication in examining social change; they are accustomed to consider intricate relationships; it is their professional responsibility to focus attention on social policy, to pursue a vision of social progress, to question the *status quo*. In so far as they themselves remain alert and sceptical, they could help to advance self-consciousness in planning.

British Town Planning: One Ideology or Three?*

Donald L. Foley

BRITISH town planning in rising to the status of a relatively important governmental activity and the town planning profession in its accompanying emergence have rather amazingly succeeded in pulling together markedly diverse threads of influence. Out of all of this something of an underlying rationale, a web of generally accepted basic ideas and propositions bearing the essential earmarks of an ideology, has crystallized. But careful observation also suggests that this is not merely a single ideology. Rather, it may be said to comprise three ideologies, deftly interwoven. These are at once complementary, competitive, and, in some measure, even conflicting. They may be drawn upon simultaneously or one at a time. And they may be drawn upon in various "mixes", that is, with varying relative emphasis on each.

It is the purpose of the present article to summarize and to analyse these respective sub-ideologies of contemporary British town planning. We shall also touch upon the institutional context within which they have evolved. In particular, we shall discuss the interrelations among the three. Our concluding questions focus on this phenomenon of alternative ideologies as an adaptive mechanism by which a newly institutionalized activity may steer its way amidst uncertain and often antagonistic surroundings and on the latent internal strains with which an activity relying upon such alternative ideologies must cope.

IDEOLOGY AND PUBLIC POLICY

Before dealing with the substantive features of British town planning

* Reprinted by permission of the *British Journal of Sociology*, Vol. 11, 1960.

ideology and its contextual setting, it may be appropriate very briefly to identify something of the nature and functions of an ideology in a governmental-professional activity such as town planning and to discuss how the ideology of town planning relates to the public policy of town planning.

The ideology of town planning provides a philosophic basis for the activity. It indicates the main goals and approaches. The ideology provides a basic operating rationale. In simplified terms it defines the situation for its participants, particularly specifying the main kinds of problems that the activity is to tackle and the major types of solutions, and the spirit of their application. It characteristically includes a defensive tone, providing the simple replies to criticism or attacks. While town planning also has been developing a sub-culture that specifies in richer detail the behaviour to be expected in varied situations, the ideology stresses the major ideas and approaches.

An ideology tends to build around seemingly self-evident truths and values and, in turn, to bestow a self-justifying tone to its main propositions and chains of reasoning. While the ideology may well contain highly rational arguments, it is characteristically ultra-rational in its overall spirit. It becomes comfortable and protective; and in this way contributes to the emotional security of the participant and to his self-confidence in carrying out the activity. While the ideology thus provides an essential kind of consensus supporting the activity, its self-evident and self-justifying nature may also contribute to a smug and traditional outlook and discourage a healthy self-awareness and sceptical re-examination.

In so far as town planning is a governmental function, the ideology provides a broad and attractive rationale for winning over and maintaining the allegiance of political leaders, appointed officials and citizens. As we shall develop further below, ambivalence or ambiguity in the ideology may materially enhance its chances of appealing to a greater spread of persons and groups.[1] Town planning, for example, has needed the full support from both the more conservative and the more radical.

A final function of the ideology could be to provide the rudiments of what Greenwood has termed "practice theory", a systematic set of proposi-

---

[1] We express our indebtedness to Ruth Glass' discussion of ambivalence in British planning in "The evaluation of planning: some sociological considerations", *International Social Science Journal*, Vol. XI, no. 3 (1959), pp. 402–3.

tions upon the basis of which the professional may practice.[2] This theory seeks to identify goal-values, to state the means by which these goals are to be attained, and self-consciously to submit to scientific study such of the constituent propositions as can be empirically tested. We shall refer at the close of this article to the central place such a practice theory might play for British town planning.

In theory, the ideology provides the spirit or rationale behind the activity. As a basis for consensus the ideology embraces those ideas and propositions which are so self-evident that they may be carried within the culture, so to speak, and at no point systematically reduced to official, written form. Further, one can envisage competing ideologies, although some particular configuration of these may be recognized as in general ascendancy during any given period. Public policy, on the other hand, results from the political process and guides governmental administration. It strives for a clarity in a legal sense, tends to emphasize means and procedures, and carries all the moderation and ambiguity characteristic of the political compromises to which policy must inevitably be subjected. Public policy strives for consistency, so that the full and subtle competition among alternative ideologies may be masked in the attempt to provide *a* policy. And phrases like "in the public interest" may take the place of fuller substantive reasoning which is implicit in the ideology(ies).

In actuality and with respect to British town planning, the distinction is by no means so clear. Policy may express ideology to a considerable degree, and in literate Britain this is undoubtedly the case. It thus follows that the term, ideology, in the rest of the article inevitably includes a considerable element of public policy. But we seek to identify some steps in the ideological reasoning not necessarily fully indicated in public policy statements.

THE INSTITUTIONAL CONTEXT OF BRITISH TOWN PLANNING

British town planning, in attempting to assimilate diverse streams of interests and outlook—ranging from reform to design to practical admini-

---

[2] Ernest Greenwood, in the *Social Service Review*.

stration—has a complex setting and history.[3] We shall here single out some of the most significant of these contextual features, so that we may more meaningfully depict below the salient features distinguishing contemporary British town planning ideology. A fuller interpretation of the interplay between the context and the ideology awaits subsequent treatment.

Britain, first of all, is highly urbanized; is provided with serious urban physical environmental problems, brought about by the industrial revolution and aggravated by subsequent congestion obsolescence; and is faced with great difficulties in resolving conflicting demands for highly limited supplies of land. Evolving particularly from a public concern for improving environmental health, which has also embraced housing, sanitation, and other measures, town planning has carried a distinctly ameliorative tone. The idea has been to make towns more healthy and less grim.

In the best British tradition for government acting to protect the public interest in achieving this amelioration, great trust has been placed in their officials.[4] More discretion is given to British officials, both elected and appointed, than is the case in America. This is with full confidence that the official will use the discretion fully in the public interest. This is carried out with considerable traditional anonymity and often without any full, open public disclosure as to the exact full facts and reasoning bearing on the case. This also takes place within a setting in which the central government holds the final policy responsibility and the final administrative authority, but local authorities are expected to take much of the initiative in carrying out policy.

Central government has a major responsibility for policy formulation in regard to town planning. The precise role of the higher civil servant of the administrative class in all of this is difficult for a foreign observer to ascertain with accuracy, but as guardians of the continuity and consistency of policy they are in a key position to codify an official version of ideology. This is not to belittle the final authority of the Ministers, of Cabinet and of Parliament in setting the tone for policy; it is to suggest that the higher civil servants as professional amateurs do have a distinctive

[3] See particularly William Ashworth, *The Genesis of Modern Town Planning*, London: Routledge & Kegan Paul, 1954.

[4] On the reliance on administrative discretion in Britain, see Peter Self, "Town planning in the United States and Britain: I. Law and organization", *Town Planning Review*, Vol. 25 (Oct. 1954), pp. 167–70.

responsibility for evolving and defending the full web of official pronouncements that collectively amount to policy.[5]

But, as informed participants have time and time again emphasized, town planning proceeds so much from the bottom upwards in Britain that policy is often more fully expressed in reactions by the central government to specific proposals or decisions by local authorities—in the examination of development plans proposals, in passing on planning appeals, in suggestions during informal conferences, etc.—than in advance, general policy statements by the central government. There is a sort of sidling sideways into policy rather than full and advance head-on assertion of policy.[6] This reflects the traditional and subtle relations between central and local government.

Very relevant to an understanding of British town planning is the degree to which municipalization and nationalization have been carried, and, more specifically, which particular activities have been brought under governmental operation. Housing and the redevelopment of obsolete areas have, for example, become very important local government responsibilities. Because of the important governmental proportion of all new capital investment, the task of town planning in Britain has been relatively heavily concerned with seeking to co-ordinate and to make fully public just where and when these governmental projects will take place. In addition, of course, town planning must provide a policy framework within which private development may proceed. The relative importance of the private investment sector has been noticeably on the increase in the past half dozen years.

Whether or not this is in line with the British traditions for working things out through compromise and for welcoming a set of countervailing powers as the best practical guarantee of democracy, several professions have from the start been relied upon for carrying out town planning and,

[5] Cf. Lena M. Jeger's point that pressure groups particularly concentrate on influencing the Ministerial bureaucracies, in reviewing Harry Eckstein's *Pressure Group Politics* in *The Guardian*, 3 March 1960.

[6] That policy does not get stated fully, openly, consistently, and in advance is stressed by J. A. G. Griffith in his oral evidence and by Ruth Glass and J. A. G. Griffith in their written memorandum, "Minutes of Evidence taken before the Committee on Administrative Tribunals and Inquiries, Twenty-First Day, Friday, 20th July, 1956", esp. paragraphs 17–19, 39–65, 5050–8.

hence, in helping to chart the very institutional nature of town planning as an activity.[7] The formal recognition of town planning as a profession was brought about by the combined efforts of the architect, the chartered surveyor and the engineer. In addition, lawyers and, in lesser degree, geographers and economists, have been involved. Some important differences in emphasis characterize these various professions, although they have sought to work together as "teams".

Town planning has come to be distinguished, on the one hand, from regional planning and, on the other, from country (or rural) planning. There has been no open recognition of metropolitan or conurban planning per se. (In the course of this particular paper we are using the term, town planning, as sufficiently generic to embrace urban and metropolitan planning, but where we most definitely refer to regional planning it is so stated.)

The very distinctive influence of the British garden city movement, evolving into a broader decentralist new town movement, must be recognized. This movement, pre-dating town planning proper and adapting its own philosophy and propagandist efforts to take into account emerging conditions, was ready with a substantive philosophy congenial to British values and proved amazingly influential in shaping fundamental aspects of town planning ideology.

The impact of the decade of the 1940s deserves particular emphasis. Starting with the important policy recommendations of the Barlow Commission, following with the serious bomb damage and with national involvement and deprivation in the course of the war, and culminating in a revolutionary set of legislative acts and administrative regulations, this period wrapped into a compressed time an entire "New Deal" for planning. Exceedingly varied streams of concern were pulled together into a single set of policy leads. These combined idealism and pragmatic resolution to provide the means of getting on with the job. They included the important advisory plans from which, particularly for Greater London, the central government abstracted and approved the substantive policy which essentially still remains in effect.

---

[7] For expressions of outlooks by the various professional groups having direct jurisdictional division, or overlap, with town planning see *Report of the Committee on Qualifications of Planners* (London: H.M.S.O., 1950), Cmd. 8059, esp. pp. 32–42.

THE MAIN ELEMENTS OF TOWN PLANNING IDEOLOGY

It is our purpose to focus on the substantive features of town planning ideology, rather than the procedural, and on the degree to which a particular social philosophy of city life and of urban spatial arrangement is included. We shall therefore merely mention certain components of the ideology, so that we may devote our full attention to three further substantive elements.

It is fully accepted in principle that it is the function of British government to safeguard the public interest by providing a civic approach to land planning.[8] This flows from the general recognition that present conditions of overcrowded, physically mean, and spatially sprawling conurbations constitute a distinct threat to healthy and civilized life. That this conflicts at many points with a traditional British sense of independence has posed great difficulties as to the exact guise in which planning, while admittedly needed in general, would be acceptable in specific terms. But the die has been cast, and town planning, however unpopular in its stereotyped negative and petty regulative form, is now part and parcel of British government.

British land planning carries distinctly economic and fiscal maxims interwoven with the substantive. These speak out on behalf of the public interest by insisting that public improvements return clear benefits to the community, in both service and, as possible, fiscal terms; that social costs be minimized; and that increases in land values resulting from planning policy shall be equitably distributed, preferably for use by the government in connection with further planned projects.[9] There is a distinct suspicion that speculative development is not in the public interest; and that particular land owners should not capriciously gain as by-products of public improvements or controls while the costs of these are borne by other citizens. This question of how to get needed improvements accomplished in the most economic manner has ramified into most policy questions. Garden cities or new towns, for example, have found considerable justification on an economic basis.

[8] R. Glass stresses the British governmental tradition for safeguarding the public interest. See *op. cit.*, esp. pp. 405–7.

[9] Nathaniel Lichfield, *Economics of Planned Development*, London: Estates Gazette, 1956.

Town planning is recognized as part of a broader governmental activity by which needed capital improvements are to be publicly provided. The relation between town planning and municipalized housing is particularly striking. Similarly, the relation between rebuilding, whether of obsolete or bombed areas, and town planning are intricate and mutually influential on the respective activities. Town planning has by now come to provide a British local governmental mechanism by which the location and priority of most important capital improvement projects are discussed and decided, and, correspondingly, it has had built into it all of the frustrations that go with full political debate and with the give and take of various local council committees and departments. This all stands in considerable contrast to the more advisory character of most of the city planning activity in the United States.

So much for these important features. We shall accept these without further discussion as we diagnose in greater detail what town planning in Britain aims to accomplish, particularly as to the kinds or qualities of towns and urban life it seeks. We are suggesting three substantive propositions as stating, in compressed form, the main ideologies of British town planning. As we stated in our introductory paragraph, these propositions are at once complementary and competitive. We shall first present them in rather general terms, discussing some implications of the relative importance attached to each. We shall then look at the second and third in greater detail, in separate sections below.

1. *Town planning's main task is to reconcile competing claims for the use of limited land so as to provide a consistent, balanced and orderly arrangement of land uses.* This is a sort of budget function, allocating land according to some sense of priorities and working for an overall spatial arrangement that best incorporates this allocation. By itself this ideological proposition carries a sense of neutrality. In political terms it conveys that nice ambiguity that proclaims that a balanced and orderly arrangement of land uses is in the public interest without committing the government to a pre-statement of just what constitutes this balanced and orderly arrangement.[10] It injects civic responsibility, but makes of town planning an umpire type of activity that, in turn, depends upon the wisdom and integrity of elected

[10] The Minister of Town and Country Planning Act, 1943, merely charged the Minister with the duty of "securing consistency and continuity in the framing and execution of a national policy with respect to the use and development of land".

and appointed officials to act in the public's best interest. It encourages considerable flexibility and adaptability. It ties in well with the central government's fiscal planning, in which commitments must be kept reasonably short-run so as to be able to adapt to new problems or conditions. It also accords well with the authoritativeness that seems to go with Ministerial decisions in Britain. If the Minister judges a planning decision to be in the public interest, that is that. Such a Ministerial judgement is not subject to further judicial overview.

This proposition recognizes that Britain has become so urbanized and hence so crowded and that the competing pressures for land have become so great that nothing short of governmental responsibility for an equitable distribution and an orderly arrangement of land uses will suffice. It reflects the distinct suspicion that the land market has not worked for the public interest, with even the more conservative interests agreeing that some fair system of land use controls are needed. But it conveys the conviction that in the best British traditions of democratic representation, fair play, balance and compromise, the control of land use be sensitive to public opinion and to normal political representation of interests. Further, it would seem to reject the idea that any long-range, inflexible, or dictatorial plan that would impose some particular set of political leaders' or of professional planners' notions of how Britons are to live could be permitted. The tradition of judging each case on its own merits seems to be congruent with this image of fair play and compromise, and this tradition has been extensively relied upon in the British system of planning controls.

2. *Town planning's central function is to provide a good (or better) physical environment; a physical environment of such good quality is essential for the promotion of a healthy and civilized life.* This ideological view gives to town planning more than a neutral, allocating function. It gives town planning something to champion. This somewhat simplified view of providing a better physical environment most certainly has its own attractions: much of town planning, for example, can then be built around the provision of designated space standards; these coupled with appropriate density controls can be treated in a technical manner in convincingly professional style. The provision of space in its various forms— whether for gardens around houses, for larger parks, for playing fields, or for greenbelts—seems to accord so happily with British values and to provide such a direct and heroic attack on the great villains of overcrowding,

congestion, and physical blight that it is readily accepted as an activity of self-evident merit and one with a direct emotional appeal. Similarly, the reconstruction of decrepit structures provides convincing symbolic evidence that "we are not just sitting around; we are doing something about our problems". If this can be accompanied by the conviction that new housing will help to rid us of juvenile delinquency, etc., why so much more desirable will the construction seem.

But focusing on a better physical environment also puts town planning in something of a dilemma. Either town planning conceives of this physical environment as sufficiently an end in itself, as a quality to be strived for, while the social-spatial patterns of urban living work themselves out through other mechanisms than town planning: for example, through the market mechanism, through the perpetuation of traditional community patterns, or as the resultant of varied pubiic policies not in themselves necessarily co-ordinated to the point of qualifying as planning. Or town planning openly accepts the better physical environment as merely an intermediate goal in which case the critical question must also be asked: intermediate to what further social goals? As soon as this question gets seriously asked the search for a more complete rationale pushes one rapidly beyond physical planning per se. This leads us to a consideration of the third major view of town planning's function.

3. *Town planning, as part of a broader social programme, is responsible for providing the physical basis for better urban community life; the main ideals toward which town planning is to strive are (a) the provision of low-density residential areas (b) the fostering of local community life and (c) the control of conurban growth.* This ideological view accepts, and seems to relate town planning to, the conviction that small, or at the most middle-sized, communities of houses with gardens are to be encouraged. It sees the continued growth of the very large city clusters or conurbations as a distinct threat to various British-held values. Accordingly, town planning, while also including a responsibilities for allocating land and improving the physical environment, has as its major challenge the mastery over current urban growth and expansion trends in the interest of preserving or re-creating towns and town life.

From this general philosophy, these propositions derive: the further growth of conurbations and larger towns shall be carefully controlled, and this requires controls to prevent vertical growth or crowding on the land (hence, density controls), controls of horizontal spreads or sprawl (hence, greenbelts), and controls over employment concentration (particularly on industrial employment to date). Local residential communities shall be promoted wherever reconstruction or new peripheral building provide opportunities; within conurbations, these may be neighbourhood units or larger community sectors; outside of conurbations they may be new towns or deliberately expanded smaller towns; these local communities shall be reasonably self-contained and, in so far as possible, socially balanced; they shall contain a full array of community facilities, with good, safe internal access to these facilities; work places shall be provided in or near these communities so as to provide reasonably short trips to work, to relieve the congestion arising from too many long commuting trips within a conurbation, and to provide a sense of balance to the community so that it is not a mere dormitory.

This view can be effectively carried through only if regional and national planning are vigorously fostered as fully complementary to town planning in its more restricted sense.

IMPROVED PHYSICAL ENVIRONMENT AS A GOAL

It may be worth a little fuller examination of the ideological implications of, and support for, the idea of improving the town's physical environment, that we have just identified as the second component philosophic approach in town planning today. Certainly of initial importance is its happy position as an intermediate point of view; it avoids some of the lack of purpose and commitment implicit in the first, neutralist approach, and in providing this possibility of commitment it gains a greater power of attracting support and of providing a sense that one is really working for something worthwhile if engaged in town planning. And yet it seems to avoid the complexities of this being openly an activity involving social planning; it preserves a sort of fiction that this is merely physical planning.

Ideologically the idea of focusing on the physical environment is reasonably simple. For one is able to operate on the assumption that improving the environment is followed by fairly direct and common-sense benefits. Physical environment determinism has always had a fascinating attractiveness. Its products or intermediate ends are readily graspable. A key higher (non-technical) civil servant in a Ministry dealing with town planning is alleged to have asserted some years ago that the greenbelt was the one goal he could readily understand and work toward with conviction!

In a country where a well educated, middle-class elite is induced to take upon itself so much responsibility for concerning itself with public policy, it is undoubtedly a congenial task to insist on a better physical environment as a condition for maintaining civilized living. The empirical evidence as to whether this enlightened middle-class view of what is best for people corresponds with the broad range of citizen reactions is far less clear.

There is also a distinct symbolism in seeking to control and modify the physical environment. It provides wide scope for the notions that individualism has been carried too far and that what we need is a civic architecture, a truly public sense of community arrangement. In this view, for example, the provision of public recreation space is to be given higher priority than the provision of private recreation space because the public space better symbolizes collective needs and a community attack on them. The symbolism of controlling the physical environment also involves the interest in maintaining some semblance of control over things we have been attached to in a world in which so much change seemed quite out of our control and, if anything, imposed by a combination of forces with which we felt ill-equipped to deal. Therefore, as if employing a sort of sympathetic magic, we may hold on to what we can (and to what by definition cannot talk back!).

The plan itself is an important form of expression. There is no question but that the plan carries its own aesthetics and that plan-preparation indulges in its own brand of tidying up. Putting enough green space on the map, "cleaning out" some of the mixed uses, and articulating a clear line between different uses and between town and country—these all must provide a particular satisfaction to certain kinds of persons. How little we really know about this! Similarly, reactions to a plan as being too dictatorial or too utopian may also be involved. In recent years there has been a distinct reaction, apparently, against the broad, advisory plans, linked with architects by some other professionals and some active laymen.

It is clear, too, that emphasis on the physical environment per se may play directly into the hands of certain preservationist and conservationist groups or spokesmen. It is very possible that a minority of influential preservationists can overbalance a much larger group who are not concerned or who want to see certain changes approved.

One of the most relied-upon concepts in British town planning is "amenity". This refers to a quality of pleasantness in the physical environment that is widely accepted as a goal. This, on examination, ranges from an essentially negative restriction against nuisances to a distinctly positive notion of visual delight.[11] The preservationists may find a covering rationale in the guise of amenity. Or amenity may cloak the argument of the architectural proponent of contemporary design. Amenity characteristically carries a respect for urbanity in towns, and a firm defence of the village and the countryside in the country. One sometimes gets the feeling that the British have quite self-consciously sought to protect themselves against the pragmatic inventiveness (or, in contemporary Subtopia, a mundane flatness?) of their own designs by entrusting matters to a bureaucratic Keeper of Amenity.

In their emphasis on space standards, on articulation (clearly allocating each kind of use or traffic movement to a purposely designed space), good micro-environment (at a neighbourhood or estate level) British town planning is not greatly different in spirit from American city planning. Some of the British standards are more generous than American (particularly considering the financial challenge that these standards mean for an austere British national budget); some are less generous. Some principles of site planning, shopping centre design, etc., have bounced back and forth across the Atlantic.

TOWN PLANNING AS PART OF BROADER SOCIAL POLICY

In so far as British town planning has evolved so as to give support to, and in turn be guided by, a philosophy as to what kind of towns and town life are being sought, we may identify a set of interlocking propositions which are mutually consistent and which contain a distinct sense of justification. To what extent these propositions are fully sensitive to British values and well approved by those residents affected by them is extremely difficult for a foreign observer to know. The fact that the

[11] See chap. 10, "Amenity", *Town and Country Planning, 1943–1951* (London: H.M.S.O., 1951), Cmd. 8204, pp. 138–54.

policies expressing these ideas must gain and maintain political support is in their favour as being representative. And the fact that clear alternative ideas are not more openly and cogently promoted, attests to the legitimate triumph (even if rather by default) of those ideas that are ascendent. But are alternative ideas being sufficiently encouraged and are alternatives examined and analysed?

The propositions that go to comprise this social ideology are not completely separate from certain propositions that could be part of the second view. For example, the stress on keeping town as town and country as country, and preventing their uncontrolled fusion (the threat here being termed "sprawl"), can be interpreted either in more strictly physical environmental terms, albeit with some symbolic concern for the town as a social unit, or in more social terms, in the sense that maintaining a limit to town expansion makes for a more compact town or conurbation, and consequently and purposefully, this makes for a greater amount of social interaction and a greater social psychological sense of identification with the community.

The social ideology that has emerged is essentially this: the best community life is to be provided in small, reasonably low-density communities. Building upon the traditional form and social organization of the village, an image of desirable community life is held up as an ideal. This does not insist that communities be only villages. It accepts the existence and continuing importance of large cities, but seeks to introduce into their further growth or their rebuilding a local-community social and physical environment as a town planning goal. For further growth the answer is new towns or the deliberate and controlled expansion of certain already existing small towns. For rebuilding within the larger city, neighbourhood units and communities (each embracing several neighbourhood units) are to be worked toward.

This social ideology also places great stress on providing every family with immediate access to their own garden. This is a very deep-seated and emotion-laden conviction. Without doubt it reflects values that are very much a distinctive part of British culture. For what proportion of British families it would seem to be so important a value that even some other values, such as accessibility to work or to the central urban areas, would be sacrificed in its favour it is more difficult to know.

The notions of the small community and of the small dwelling with garden seem to reflect a British value on smallness and a corresponding suspicion of large size. Running throughout the British social ideology of cities upon which town planning had drawn is the distinct and strong suspicion that great cities do not provide really decent living places for the bulk of their populations. Hence the ideological strength and support in working to control this great threat of pathological overgrowth and of the unnatural resort of high-rise apartment structures. At stake is nothing less than the threat that through uncontrolled physical development, desired social and environmental characteristics of communities will be lost.

From this idea of providing low-density residential development in small communities, it follows that densities must be held down. And in order to hold down the size of towns and conurbations, and simultaneously to prevent lateral expansion of the town into the countryside, greenbelts are introduced around the towns. We now begin to see the degree to which the controls interlock. For density controls plus greenbelt controls serve to control a conurbation's population size. Density controls also provide space within the conurbation. Greenbelt controls also provide a pleasant visual break and a recreation space. Then the further idea of overspill comes in. For in thinning out overcrowded central areas or in holding down residential densities throughout the conurbation, large blocs of residents need to be decanted. The idea is deliberately to guide this excess population out to new towns or expanded older towns. The new towns are to be located beyond the greenbelt, far enough to discourage commuting (although not render it impossible). Thus the new town philosophy becomes an integrated part of a controlled-size policy and a greenbelt policy.

Generally correlated with these policies is a national policy seeking to guide industrial employment from the larger congested conurbations, particularly Greater London, to those sections of the country where unemployment has been a serious problem. For most conurbations this has added yet another means of holding down population, by restricting employment opportunities. (For conurbations such as Liverpool where unemployment has been chronic, the situation is somewhat different, for relieving unemployment comes first, even though this may add some employment and hence ultimately some incentive for greater population.)

These policies that deal with the size of an entire conurbation and that serve to redistribute population as among regions fall within the province of national or regional planning, but become taken as social policy "givens" by town planners. This institutional division as between regional and town planning is reinforced by the distinction between social policy and physical planning. The town planning professionals, in thinking of themselves as technicians, may sometimes be disinclined to think it within their province to venture too far into the realms of the social and/or regional.

New towns in their larger inception were clearly a matter of regional planning spelled out, in point of history, as national policy. It is only the internal arrangement of new towns that is more literally town planning. In their strong support of new towns and of planned decentralization, the Town and Country Planning Association and its leader and spokesman, (Sir) Frederic Osborn, were particularly influential in the critical, formative period of the late 1930s and early and mid 1940s. As in their earlier initial impact on town planning in the decade preceding World War I, they were ready in this period of great expansion during World War II, with a philosophy that defined the ills and prescribed a ready, practicable solution. That the new towns took hold and worked reflects both the dramatic impact of such large-scale, new construction and the favourable image of a new start on an urban physical environment and a new small city.

Less perhaps needs to be said about the reliance upon neighbourhood unit concept in town planning.[12] This was in part borrowed from American city planning. Like the new town it provides a strong emotional appeal for those convinced that the city is too impersonal and complex, for it suggests the creation of small social units in the place of undifferentiated bigness. Local communities containing several neighbourhood units have also been suggested or designated. These have provided a locale for a major secondary school, for more specialized shopping, etc. Such planned local communities are also envisaged as being socially balanced, although how large or small a unit is to be in balance is not as clearly pronounced.

The most outstanding social philosophic support for this third ideological view is that provided by Lewis Mumford. His *Culture of Cities*, published in 1938 (with a cheaper English edition reprinted in 1940) provided something of a Bible. This was followed by Mumford's influential wartime

---

[12] See earlier discussions: D. V. Glass, "The application of social research", *British Journal of Sociology*, Vol. I (March 1950), esp. pp. 17–23; Leo Kuper "Social science research and the planning of urban neighbourhoods", *Social Forces*, Vol. 29 (March 1951), pp. 237–43; N. Dennis, "The popularity of the neighbourhood community idea", *Sociological Review*, Vol. 6 (Dec. 1958), pp. 191–206.

essay, *The Social Foundations of Post-War Building*, published in 1943 under the auspices of the Town and Country Planning Association and given wide distribution.

An invidious comparison as between British and continental towns is sometimes undertaken. Rasmussen, a Danish architect-town planner, in his book in the mid-thirties on London, openly lauds the openness and pleasantness of London, and asserts that the English have quite clearly been on the right tracks in contrast to most European countries.[13] Some English proponents of higher density are conceived as holding continental views. One English reaction to the vocal minority arguing for higher densities in the centre of the great British towns is that this reflects an interest in maintaining labour-class solidarity. Another reaction is that the architect-planners have become enraptured with the visual possibilities of high-rise structures and they want to try them out. Neither of these reactions takes account of the further alternative: that rebuilding parts of London or other large British cities to reasonably high densities may permit a certain segment of the population who are so inclined the opportunity to live nearer their work and nearer to the city centre. But one can see the defensive character of the low-density ideology vigorously disparaging any proposals for higher residential densities.

IDEOLOGICAL AMBIVALENCE AS AN ADAPTIVE MECHANISM

It is fascinating to conjecture just how many different images of town planning the evolving activity of town planning has needed to take into account and to seek to assimilate. Clearly, town planning in its formative period could not afford to hew too narrowly to any preconceived, rigid line. In order to get political support, to attract capable professionals, and to live up to the idea of comprehensive planning, it gathered in a welter of programmes and ideas. In part, no doubt, this was strategically imperative. It was either gather in, or be gathered in by one or another of the ring of activities and professions on every hand.

But in this process, town planning came to accept and gradually to build around certain basic ideological propositions that while not too openly in

[13] Steen Eiler Rasmussen, *London: The Unique City*, London: Jonathan Cape, 1937.

conflict were not completely congruent. It is characteristic of such a process⟩ aided as it was by the political character of the determination of its major policies, that something of a web of propositions would come to be accepted without their internal inconsistencies or strains being highlighted or reduced.

The identification in this article of three such sub-ideologies inevitably reflects a degree of selectivity. Others could, and with justification, plead the case for somewhat different classifications of ideological views. Hence, we must immediately warn against the reification of our particular conceptions. But perhaps our particular division does serve to suggest something of the fascinating paradox of town planning's basic philosophic support. It should be clear, for example, that in some ways the three ideological components blur into each other. The first and the second, landuse and physical environmental foci, do not appear incompatible, and they both steer clear of some of the greater complexities of social goals and programmes. Nor are the second and third sub-ideologies, in themselves, difficult to reconcile. They both stress goals of improving the physical environment, with the second rather concentrating on the desirability of a good environment as a social goal in itself, and the other more consciously viewing the good environment as an intermediate goal directed toward bringing about certain further goals as to the character of community life. The greatest step is from the neutralism of the first to the social advocacy of the third. But even this is not so inconsistent if one assumes that any sense of balance in the first upon which priorities may be based must inevitably depend upon some social philosophy, and that such a philosophy could in fact encompass various of the considerations also suggested more fully under the second or the third sub-ideologies.

Let us look at several examples of the kinds of problems that the coexistence of the alternative-supplementary ideological views help town planning to overcome. The first problem is how town planning can promote a firm social image of the communities to be achieved on the one hand, and, as is expected in a democratic framework, not presume to dictate just how people are to live, on the other. It does this by having parallel ideologies that provide, respectively, each kind of support. This helps to get over the difficult judge and advocate conflict that rather plagues the Ministry of Housing and Local Government. The first part of the ideology just openly calls for responding to those pressures for land that seem to reflect the greatest needs as expressed through political pressures combined with a civic sense of balance as between these needs. The second and third parts of the ideology support certain qualities of community environment toward which development should be directed.

British observers, and no doubt correctly, see American city planning as less mature in its social policy. When they express fear of the Americanization of British town planning they are deploring the possibility that British planning may become even more neutral and accepting of going trends.[14] And yet beyond a certain point British citizens, like their American counterparts, are not willing to put too much power into the hands of a town planning activity to "dictate" certain social environmental qualities as goals.

The simultaneous availability of alternative ideologies has helped to ensure political support from all quarters. In so far as Labour has sought to provide better urban environment they have tended to want to have privileges and social segregation lessened. The Labour Party's leaders have been strong advocates of the socially mixed local community or neighbourhood unit, just as, for example, they have been prone to support comprehensive schools. The Conservative government, in its national policies, has tended during the past decade to pursue certain of the somewhat more strictly environmental goals with zest (the greenbelt policy, for example, was greatly strengthened under Duncan Sandy's ministry) while lessening government's sense of responsibility for the fullest implementations of other social-policy features of town planning. Peter Self and other informed observers have reported considerable dropping away in its advocacy of social purposes previously emphasized and a corresponding rise in stressing its umpire role on the part of the Ministry of Housing and Local Government.[15]

Then there has been the problem of achieving the kind of comprehensiveness that one might readily expect of full-fledged town planning in the face of serious institutional restraints. These restraints occur at both local and central governmental levels, and mainly reflect the fact that a series of functional areas had already been carved out and distributed to government departments, committees or Ministries, as the case may be,

[14] R. Glass, *op. cit.*, footnote 1, p. 407.
[15] P. Self, *Cities in Flood: The Problems of Urban Growth*, London: Faber and Faber, Ltd., 1957, pp. 172–4.

long before town planning really came on to the scene. So how much is to be relinquished to town planning (or to national planning, if we conceive of the full national parallel)? First, town planning is given a certain umpire role with respect to land use allocation and arrangement, but virtually excluding some uses and needs by central government, and by statutory undertakers. Next, working toward designated qualities of physical environment, e.g. space and amenity, is conceded as a legitimate function. And finally certain approaches to community (and particularly residential) development are assumed by town planning. The tie-in here is historical, stemming from town planning's early interest in garden-city and suburban developments. From this evolved town planning's particular interest in residential site planning. This all amounts really to a way of defining "comprehensive" so as not to embrace too much more than the town planner has actually come to have jurisdiction over.

There has also been the not inconsiderable problem of the adaptation of an infant profession in a world in which surrounding professions have their claims well staked out. The profession has sought to attract and maintain the interest of architect-planners, engineer-planners and chartered surveyor-planners, as well as the interests of architects, engineers, chartered surveyors, lawyers, landscape architects, economists, geographers, etc. And we must not overlook the idea of training and giving experience to young men and women who will think of themselves as just town planners. Given this situation, the different major parts of the ideology provide somewhat different handles by which these various professionals may grasp, and contribute to, the field. The chartered surveyors, for example, may be a little more prone to seeing the problem as one of land allocation, and hence a particular case of broader allocation dealt with by economics. The engineers have perhaps seen the environmental problem, while also applying criteria of economic efficiency. The architects, rather conservative with respect to many political matters, have tended to be more liberal as to town planning's social policy. While they have sought to provide a better environment, they have sought in their own design-conscious way what social patterns one should be working toward and how physical plans can further such patterns.

For the professionals the breakdown of the ideology into parts also helps to resolve two other interrelated problems. One is how the professional as a technician can deal effectively with very broad social policy questions.

The other is how town planning and the town planner in pursuing what is conceived to be physical planning can grapple with the full social philosophic implications of what they do. How, they wonder, do they keep from being social planners?

THE STRAIN OF IDEOLOGICAL INCONSISTENCY

But this legitimization of town planning as an activity and a profession has been achieved only at considerable cost. Britain now has a system of town planning that is fairly well entrenched. But built into that system are certain inconsistencies. In so far as these inconsistencies are recognized as compromises, a spirit of self-awareness pervades, and an effort is underway gradually to rectify them—these would represent a healthy situation. But should these inconsistencies become too thoroughly imbedded in the ideology of the chances for self-conscious efforts to work for a coherent rationale may become ever more remote.

Some of the substantive strains which flow from the simultaneous acceptance of sub-ideologies that contain elements of inconsistency have already been identified. While trying to avoid any undue repetition of these, we do want to summarize in one place the major inconsistencies and latent conflicts.

Perhaps the major strain is the continuing attempt to be both judge and advocate. This has been given considerable discussion from legal and administrative points of view, and some modifications have recently been introduced reflecting the recommendations of the Franks Committee.[16] But the strain runs right down to town planning's philosophic roots. Is it to be preponderantly a mechanism by which elected and appointed public officials, acting responsibly and sensitively in the public interest, allocate amounts and favoured locations of land to competing demanding users and work toward a semblance of orderly development? This tends to make of town planning an activity rather different from the run of governmental activities, each with a substantive sphere to promote and to regulate. Or is it to be rather more of an activity dedicated to the provision of a physical environment that fully reflects and carries out a social policy as to the kinds of communities being sought? This would make of town planning a community-developing activity far more parallel in scope to public health or social service.

[16] The Committee on Administrative Tribunals and Inquiries.

This is, in effect, the strain between sub-ideology number one and sub-ideology number three. We have already alluded to it, and have suggested that in the formative period to date both ideologies have been accepted and have been relied upon in such mixture as best fitted circumstances and outlooks.

No full and satisfactory theory has been evolved and applied to town planning that bridges the two ideological positions. Perhaps the closest has been that suggested by Lichfield when he proposes that town planning should seek to minimize social costs and that it should work for a balance as between private and social costs.[17] This is in the spirit of various attempts throughout the world to apply economic analysis to questions of policy choice. The difficulties in this mode of comparative analysis have by no means been resolved. But it does represent the idea that a comparative analysis of costs and benefits, including social costs and benefits, may help to bring into the open the respective favourable and unfavourable features of alternative policies. It is worth asking whether sociologists may not themselves be able to introduce modes of comparative analysis as between alternative community patterns so as to throw more tested understanding into the storehouse of knowledge upon which town planners should be able to draw.

Short of a full comparative analysis of alternatives, town planning will presumably continue to be badly split as between judging among competing claims to land, each case only too much on its own merits and working to promote positively conceived community environments.

Town planning has lacked a full and sophisticated understanding of the social implications of improving the physical environment. This is so around the world, and is by no means a distinctive British problem. What seems so serious to an American observer is the seeming lack of awareness in Britain that here is an intellectual problem of significant proportions and that any fully developed rationale supporting town planning awaits successful assaults on this problem. And the complexity of the problem is belied by the simplistic reasoning that has become part of town planning's ideology. The strain here is between a rather full acceptance of sub-ideology number two that accepts improvement of the physical environment as a goal while not fully relating this to sub-ideology number three

[17] "In short . . . land planning aims at a reduction in costs, both private and social costs which is in accord with current social conscience." *Op. cit.*, p. 277.

that supports particular qualities of community life and environment as goals. Phrased somewhat differently, town planning has tried to hedge as between physical planning and social planning, has developed something of an ideological basis for doing this, and has thus never more fully faced up to its responsibility for catalysing social goals and fully analysing what physical environmental improvements most realistically facilitated these social goals.

Not unrelated to this is the profession's self-image as technical. This naturally reflects the idea that its allied professions of architecture, engineering, etc. are also technical. And, as we suggested above, it helps to perpetuate the beliefs that such professionals are competent to deal with physical planning matters but that social policy is rather a different matter, and that while the professionals can operate as technical advisers the most important policy is made by elected officials with administrative officer assistance. In fact, at the central governmental level in Britain, the technical officer has become once removed from the elected officers, with the administrative officers as liaison. But this image of providing technical advice seems to bely the inherently broad nature of town planning. Town planning does not seem to be fully recognized as an intermediate sort of activity as between broader governmental policy determination and the more precise design of specific buildings or other projects. As such it is, by definition, involved with social and political goals and it would seem appropriate for the town planning profession to revise its self-image accordingly. This could still preserve the appropriate relation between elected officials and civil servants, but it might enable the town planner to modify his "technical" and hence self-restrained role by strengthening the rather broader conception of the scope upon which his advice or recommendations might be offered. Correspondingly, this places great responsibility on the professional town planner.

There appears to be a further serious strain between the notion of long-range policy and plans and the ideas of flexible, short-range planning and project formulation. While in one sense this is a procedural or methodological difference, it also has substantive implications. If a long-range policy is to be put forth and implemented, this calls for a sense of goals and a philosophy (even if, as conservatively conceived, this is not much more than to perpetuate present land use patterns). Once this is established, it may then be desirable to sacrifice some short-run gains in the interests of greater gains over the long haul. But there is another, rather political or administrative view of planning that sees planning as a problem-solving and an adapting-to-new-circumstances activity. One can treat each new case on its own merits, so to speak, and do this with integrity provided one has a current "line" to follow. This allows the line to shift, subtly perhaps, to adapt to changing conditions, to Treasury control, to a new Minister, etc. Our reaction is that a flexible, administrative view of planning has rather taken over in the past decade or so from an earlier architectural, schematic advisory-plan view. This suggests that at the very time that town planning was seemingly being so solidified, it was in effect being somewhat reshaped from the inside.

Finally, we wish to stress the institutional restraints and inroads that have been made on town planning in contrast to the myth of its comprehensiveness. This has perhaps been one of the toughest sacrifices town planning had to make in order to be allowed to come as far as it has. A most serious segment that has never been given fully to town planning is highway and transport planning. Nor has regional or national planning been put into effect sufficiently to guarantee systematic, positive regional policies and controls.

SOCIAL SCIENTIFIC RESEARCH AND TOWN PLANNING IDEOLOGY

Town planners and sociologists might well combine efforts in looking in at town planning and in examining present town planning ideology.[18] A sociology of town planning is called for. Also needed is an open attempt to identify and to analyse the rationale (or the lack thereof) upon which current town planning practice is based; and as necessary, to explore what modifications or clarifications in this rationale might be advisable. This would, in short, be a form of theory building, but presumably of the practice–theory nature already mentioned and attributed to Ernest Greenwood.

Now theory building, it would seem, is not a respectable activity in

---

[18] For as R. Glass puts it, ". . . it is undoubtedly the ideology of planning, far more than techniques of design and administration, which needs to be considered and developed. Planning without social policy does not make sense, and social policy without social theory and research is liable to become meaningless and eventually unacceptable." *Op. cit.*, p. 408.

Britain. But if ever there were a challenge, it is precisely in bringing the intimate sense of the problems and the direct knowledge of the practice as provided by the professional together with the conceptualizing and theory-testing experience of the social scientist. Town planning as an activity is inevitably supported by various chains of reasoning. These deserve to be fully brought into the open. Then for each chain, it is essential that the links be separately exhibited. Some of these links are propositions which with some ingenuity may be statable in hypothesis form and submitted to the empirical testing of social research.

Comprehensive Planning and Social Responsibility: Toward an AIP Consensus on the Profession's Roles and Purposes*

Melvin M. Webber

I. A TIME FOR RE-EXAMINATION

The period of postwar prosperity has launched what appears to be a golden age in city planning. Keynoters at professional meetings have been proclaiming the coming-of-age to ever-larger audiences of men who are themselves struck by their sudden popularity and by their marks on the city's skyline. Never before have we been accorded such status as we now enjoy; never have so many governmental and civic leaders been so openly dependent upon our counsel; never has the American city planning movement been in a position to influence the welfare of so many Americans so profoundly. And yet, never has the path of righteousness been less clearly marked out.

Dating from 1909, when the first National Conference on City Planning was called to consider the problems of population congestion, the city planning movement has been fueled by deep-rooted concerns for the conditions of urban life. The plight of the immigrant groups, crowding into the big-city tenements, provoked a wave of social reform in search of

Author's Note: The lively responses provoked by the conference draft of this essay assure me that it touches upon some sensitive issues that are of deep concern to a great many planners. I have no illusions about the adequacy of the present formulation, especially today when so much careful rethinking is in process and when developments in theory and method are accumulating so rapidly. But I do hope that it can serve as a useful foil for a new round of deliberation on the profession's emerging roles and purposes.

I have profited from the many comments that were volunteered on the conference draft, and especially from the detailed criticisms by Paul Davidoff, Herbert J. Gans, Frederick O'R. Hayes, Morton Hoppenfeld, Roger Montgomery, Janet Reiner, Van Beuren Stanbery, and my colleagues at Resources for the Future: Joseph L. Fisher, Jerome W. Milliman, Harvey S. Perloff, and Lowdon Wingo, Jr.

* Reprinted by permission of the *Journal of the American Institute of Planners*, Vol. 29, November 1963.

effective means for attacking poverty and for accelerating social mobility. A sense of crisis and personal mission marked those early beginnings of the city planning, housing, social welfare, public health, and the related helping professions; but by now, despite the persistence of immigrant poverty and despair, these have been considerably calmed. The natural course of professionalization has taken its toll, by turning many would-be missionaries into security-conscious bureaucrats. But, potentially more important than that, the processes of professionalization are also establishing the channels through which the findings of the social sciences are being fed into practice settings. One result of the expanding flow of knowledge is the transformation of many do-gooders into good-doers, as Meyerson once phrased it. Another result is the introduction of a crop of new doubts about our traditional approaches to human betterment.

For generations it had been generally understood that the physical environment was a major determinant of social behavior and a direct contributor to individuals' welfare. Having accepted professional responsibility for the physical environment, the city planner was thus accorded a key role as agent of human welfare; the clearly prescribed therapy for the various social pathologies was improvement of the physical setting. If only well-designed and well-sited houses, playgrounds, and community facilities could be substituted for the crowded and dilapidated housing and neighborhoods of the city's slums, then the incidence of crime, delinquency, narcotics addiction, alcoholism, broken homes, and mental illness would tumble. Acculturation of ethnic, racial, and other minority groups to the American, middle-class, urban ways-of-life but awaited their introduction to the American, middle-class, physical environment.

As the findings of systematic research into the relations between social-and-physical aspects of environments and social behavior have been accumulating, however, what were once stable pillars of understanding are melting down to folklore, heartfelt wishes, and, more typically, partial truths embedded within complex networks of causes. The simple one-to-one cause-and-effect links that once tied houses and neighborhoods to behavior and welfare are coming to be seen as but strands in highly complex webs that, in turn, are woven by the intricate and subtle relations that mark social, psychic, economic, and political systems. The simple clarity of the city planning profession's role is thus being dimmed by the clouds of complexity, diversity, and the resulting uncertainty that seem to be the inevitable consequences of scientific inquiry and of the deeper understanding that inquiry brings.

But simultaneously, while social scientists are questioning city planning's central doctrine of physical environmental determinism, other critics are decrying the powerful consequences that are alleged to follow in the wake of recent physical developments. On the one hand the suburban housing tracts are accused of spawning a generation of deprived children, who are being reared by neurotic, coffee-addicted mothers in a matriarchal society from which traffic-stressed fathers and most other dissimilar people are all but excluded. On the other hand, central city redevelopment is charged with dispossessing lower-income groups of their preferred habitats, inflicting psychic disturbance, and destroying their social communities. In turn, the design of the new high-rise housing is indicted for breeding a new, sterile, culturally disinherited species.

It is very appropriate, then, in the midst of these seemingly conflicting contentions, that we should again seek to re-examine our roles as agents in the service of the city's people. We may quite properly ask ourselves again, what are our purposes? In what ways can we, who hold such large responsibility for the physical city, so conduct our affairs as to positively affect the lives of its residents?

II. TO EXTEND ACCESS TO OPPORTUNITY

The city planner's responsibilities relate primarily to the physical and locational aspects of development within a local government's jurisdiction. Although this focus of attention derives in part from the idea of environmental determinism and in part from the belief that paramount values are intrinsic to the physical city, his activities have been directed to these features of the city for important instrumental reasons as well.

Local governments are charged with building certain large and costly public works which, once constructed, are likely to exert powerful and continuing influences upon locational choices made in the private sector of the urban economy. In turn, some of these choices may contribute to changes in the social-psychic-economic-political environments within which people live, and they may therefore bear at least indirect influences upon their welfare. Decisions on these investments therefore demand the most deliberate efforts to improve rationality—to help assure *one*, that the distribution of the benefits and the costs among the city's publics is consciously intended and democratically warranted, *two*, that levels and priorities of investments are so staged as to induce the desired repercussions in the private markets, and *three*, that public resources are used for those projects and programs promising the highest social payoffs.

Although it is true that we have overestimated the roles that buildings play in shaping social behavior, it is none the less also true that some aspects of the physical environment can bring appreciable direct benefits to the city's residents. Imaginative and carefully designed buildings, streets, and open spaces are in themselves direct rewards of an advanced society; and the visual qualities of the physical environment warrant considerably more attention than they have been receiving. The beautiful city remains a goal we have yet to achieve.

Decent, sanitary, and spacious housing is itself one of the salient attributes of the good life, and our effort to accomplish the Congressional objective of "a decent home and a suitable living environment for every American family" properly remains a high-priority goal to which our profession is dedicated. Similarly, the range of facilities that municipalities construct—as accommodations for the various health, education, recreation, and other human-service agencies—necessarily affect the qualities of the services rendered; and, as inseparable aspects of the services, these facilities can contribute to full lives for the beneficiaries.

But the locational arrangements of facilities and activities bear upon the qualities of urban living in more subtle ways, too. The urban settlement has always stood at the center of civilization—the place at which the largest varieties of goods, services, and ideas are produced and distributed, and, therefore, where the most, and the most diverse, human interaction occurs. Here is where the individual is able most readily to tap the accumulated riches of the culture. This is because bare physical distance works as a barrier to human interaction. As its unique and most important commodity, the city offers reduced distances between partners to a friendship, and between sellers and buyers, employers and employed, informers and informed, helpers and helped. Metropolitan areas have flourished in our age precisely because that type of spatial arrangement has expanded people's opportunities to find fruitful associations with others.

Having been assigned responsibility for guiding land use patterns, we seek, then, to induce those patterns that will effectively increase accessibility to the diverse opportunities for productive social intercourse that are latent in an advanced civilization.

Recent improvements in transportation, combined with recent increases in incomes and other familiar changes, have made it possible for many families and firms to gain spacious quarters in the amiable outlying areas, while they simultaneously endeavor to maintain accessibility to expanding varieties of activities and sources of learning. In this time of rapid suburban development, we are striving, through further improvements in transportation and communication, to help these groups reconcile their new-found locational freedom with their growing capacities to pursue diverse interests with persons who are spatially removed.

Some classes of business and industrial establishments continue to depend upon the external economies offered by concentrated business districts, while the society as a whole continues to depend upon the flow of information and ideas that concentrated centres have traditionally fostered. With mounting sensitivity to these economic and cultural imperatives, we are trying to encourage the formation of new centres of various types and sizes and to redevelop and stabilize existing centers as the communication foci of a large-scale urban society.

For some segments of the lower-income populations, locational in-accessibility to employment opportunities, when compounded with skill deficiences and with discriminatory practices, erects an additional handi-cap which acts to further depress earning capacities. Especially for Negroes seeking work in the suburbanizing manufacturing and wholesaling industries, exclusion from the suburban housing market couples with deficient outbound commuter service to make these growing job opportunities relatively inaccessible, while opportunities near their central-city homes are contracting. Thus, the spatial relationships of residences and employment-places for the various classes of employees and jobs remain a central issue for the profession; here, improved land-use patterns and transportation systems can directly help to raise the levels of human welfare. Housing stocks in the lower and lower-middle price ranges need to be expanded in all parts of the metropolitan areas; the filtering process needs to be accelerated; the entire metropolitan housing market needs to be opened to those who are now excluded by reason of race, religion, or national origin; and transportation systems need to be developed that can serve all groups within the region.

But while physical accessibility is a necessary condition for realizing latent opportunities, it is not the sufficient condition. Differences in social status and race, shortage of job opportunities, inadequate education, low income, and personal inadequacy are likely to be far more serious obstructions to the social and economic mobility that leads to the rewards of the society. Especially for the 16 to 25 per cent of Americans who have yet to achieve a minimum acceptable standard of living, a multi-frontal attack on inaccessibility is necessary.

We face the prospect of continuing underemployment in some regions of the nation, and accelerated automation of industrial and clerical processes is culminating many of the least-skilled jobs at the very time when the postwar babies are swelling the labor force. The chronic despair of so many central-city residents is accentuating their plight; for, when expectations for betterment are low, so too are aspirations. And thus, job shortages, sense of personal insufficiency, poor performance in school, deficient cognitive, occupational, and social skills, rejection by the larger society, and a range of other disabling conditions resonate upon each other in self-perpetuating waves.

America must demonstrate that cultural deprivation and the life of the slum need not be the permanent condition for any of her people. By opening new opportunities for learning new skills and for earning a better living, we can help those who are dependent upon outside supports to gain the self-respect and the dignity they have been denied. Especially for Negroes, Puerto Ricans, and Mexican-Americans, who are encountering the most numerous obstacles along the paths of social mobility, we must demonstrate that America's affluence can be as accessible as it was to the European immigrants who preceded them in our urban centers. Especially for them, the city must become the school for learning the means of earning the city's riches.

But it is not only the residents of slum and deteriorating areas whom we seek to serve. Our expanding aged populations, relieved of their roles as productive members of the society, must find new ways of contributing their skills and knowledge for the welfare of others and, more important, for recapturing their own sense of personal pride and dignity. The large-scale housing projects for the aged, removed from the lifestream of the larger community, are not likely to contribute to these ends. And so, we are searching for new housing arrangements and new social programs to help them remain active members of the communities in which they live. Similarly, the middle-class majority groups, although usually self-supporting, none the less require a wide variety of governmental services and facilities that will further expand their opportunities for self-improvement and for creative contributions to the welfare of the total community.

For all these groups, there are probably no more direct routes to human betterment than improvements in the educational systems and stimulation of the regional economies. No other public activities are likely to be more effective in equipping individuals for self-dependency and growth.

Although the locations of physical facilities for schools and economic activities are certainly of but secondary importance to their successes, they are none the less contributive. The physical planner does indeed have a significant role to play in pursuing the larger social purposes, but his greatest potential contribution will be realized only if he can accurately appraise the relative effectiveness of the various servicing and facilities-building programs in which he has a hand.

III. TO INTEGRATE LARGER WHOLES

We are coming to comprehend the city as an extremely complex social system, only some aspects of which are expressed as physical buildings or as locational arrangements. As the parallel, we are coming to understand that each aspect lies in a reciprocal causal relation to all others, such that each is defined by, and has meaning only with respect to, its *relations* to all others.

As one result of this broadened conception of the city system, we can no longer speak of the physical city versus the social city or the economic city or the political city or the intellectual city. We can no longer dissociate a physical building, for example, from the social meanings that it carries for its users and viewers or from the social and economic functions of the activities that are conducted within it. If distinguishable at all, the distinction is that of constituent components, as with metals comprising an alloy.

With improved understanding of economic and social systems, the idea of "capital" is being extended beyond "things" to encompass the human, intellectual, and organizational resources as well. The skills and capacities of our populations, the accumulated knowledge and wisdom of the culture, and the ways in which we organize ourselves for the joint conduct of our affairs, all contribute to our productive capacities and wealth in ways that are inseparable from those of the physical equipment and natural resources we use.

Planning for the locational and physical aspects of our cities must therefore be conducted in concert with planning for all other programs that governmental and non-governmental agencies conduct. Public capital-improvement programs and budgets must allocate financial and other resources among all constructing and serving activities, in an effort to create the most effective programmatic mix of facilities and services of the various types.

As the minimum condition necessary to this task, each municipal agency should be expected to trace out the probable and significant consequences that its programs would have upon the aspects of the city that other agencies focus upon. In this way, each agency would be better informed about the likely conditions in the future and hence better able to make rational recommendations of its own. But mere exchange of good forecasts is not enough.

All proposed programs must be subjected to systematic valuation, if intelligent choices are to be made among them. The new sophistication developing in benefit-cost analysis is beginning to make it possible to appraise a heterogeneous array of proposals against a common set of criteria. Such a valuative method would permit comparisons of the relative social payoffs that might accrue from pursuing one bundle of policies versus another; for example, in assessing the likely returns from alternative social-welfare programs, alternative economic-development programs, and alternative public-works projects. Similarly, it would permit economic public investments to be made by identifying more effective and less costly program packages that might be substituted for less effective and more costly ones.

With improved capacities to forecast probable consequences and to assess probable payoffs, planners in the various governmental agencies should be more effective investment counsellors to their legislatures. Improved data systems will permit planners continuously to meter the states of affairs of the various population groups, the economy, the municipal fisc, the physical plant, and other aspects of the city. Improved theory, describing and explaining the processes of city life and city growth, will permit us more sensitively to identify those crucial points of public intervention that are appropriate to accomplishing specified objectives. The newly developing decision models—which rely upon the new data, the new theory, and, equally, upon the goal hypotheses of politicians and planners—are already permitting us to simulate what would happen *if* given policies were adopted, and thus to pretest the relative effectiveness of alternative courses of action in accomplishing stated ends.

But none of these is sufficient. Improving capacity for rationality must be joined with improving wisdom—there is no other name. It is *here* that the road forks, the one route leading to technocratic control by elites, the other to guided expansion of individual freedom. That map has often been misread to place the fork at junctions that are sometimes labeled "art" and "science" or sometimes as "intuition" and "reason". But we now know that those signposts are false, that those who would be planners must thereby be artists-scientists—no less than that the so-called artist is thereby rigorous analyst of the real world and that the so-called scientist is thereby imaginative and perceptive innovator. Whatever his professional affiliation, the governmental planner may boast that proud title only if he is at once insightful critic, informed analyst, and ingenious designer of action programs, in turn aimed by images of social betterment that are built of reason and wisdom.

There is cause for much optimism in all these respects. Now, for the first time in democratic society, we are acquiring the conceptual and the technical competence to undertake comprehensive policies planning Now that we are learning how to predict systematically the kinds, scales, and distributions of benefits and costs that various public programs generate, we can more effectively and more wisely integrate the programs of the various agencies into mutually reinforcing program bundles. Now, when so many thoughtful and creative minds are being turned to the big urban-policy issues, the rate of social invention is increasing. If it were possible to gain consensus on objectives, we would be more likely than ever before to succeed in our efforts to attain them.

Of course, ideal solutions to problems, full identification of probable consequences, and faultless evaluation of alternative actions are all patently impossible. We will always lack perfect knowledge; mature judgment will always be too scarce; and the limitations of human intellectual capacities will never permit adequate comprehension of the urban system's complexities. The best will always elude us; only the better can ever be found.

Even so, the better is seldom self-evident; for the city's many publics rarely hold mutually compatible objectives. Some students of urban politics have been describing the city as a jungle in which overlapping interest groups of all sorts compete avidly for favor and advantage in pursuing their separate ends. Because the rewards and penalties of the political game are so large, few are willing, voluntarily, to sacrifice personal gain for even the most studied and judicious image of a "public welfare". The recent spate of studies on decision-making in city councils reveal a persistent unwillingness of elected officials openly to confront hotly contested issues, preferring to deal with them covertly or to regard them as "technical matters" for professional staffs to decide.

In pursuit of their respective images of the public welfare and of democratic decision-making, the professionals in city hall have been seeking to change the rules of that political game. A major ploy in this effort is simply to supply better information and better analysis and then to open the information channels to public view; for with reduction of ignorance and secrecy goes a reduction in special advantage. Similarly, by publicly exposing probable social consequences of legislative actions, legislators are less likely to respond insensibly and less likely to retreat from political responsibility through the "technical matter" route. And, when confronted with fuller information of market conditions and governmental plans, the private investor is less dependent upon special advantage, for he will often find his private interest really is compatible with the public interest.

Among the more powerful of the interest groups affecting governmental policies are the professional staffs within municipal government, who hold vested interests in their own brands of programs and projects. Each tends to see the road to social betterment through the biasing lenses of its own profession's filters, and each therefore competes with the others for the limited financial resources they must divide. Physical planners are no less guilty of this sort of professional partiality than are their colleagues in public health, education, law enforcement, or engineering. But there are many hopeful signs suggesting that this narrow perception is giving way to a more holistic view of the policy-making task.

Professional staffs are now working together with a commonality of interests that may be unprecedented. The current beginnings of local social planning councils and inter-agency coordinating committees reflect a growing search for the social consequences that really matter, and a growing recognition that the web of inter-dependencies inexorably unites them all. In some cities collaboration is already being supplanted by co-ordination, and in a few leading cities systematic integration of programs is being attempted. Despite the inevitable rigidities of municipal bureaucracy, some agencies *are* searching for higher-level optima to which their own programs might contribute.

Much more than local integration of plans will be necessary, however. Many state and federal programs operate as indirect, and frequently unintended, influences upon the choices and the opportunities that are opened to people in cities and metropolitan areas. The capital-gains provisions of the federal and state income-tax laws, the mortgage-insurance programs of the V.A. and the F.H.A., the Federal Reserve System's controls on rediscount rates, the changes in accessibility affected by transportation and communication facilities and rates, the federal water and power projects, the allocation of defense contracts, and numerous other actions of non-local governments modify locational market conditions to which individual firms and households respond. Although the effects of these indirect controls may be more difficult to predict, they are surely more influential in shaping urban-settlement and land-use patterns than are some of the more direct land-use controls.

The construction and grant programs of federal and state agencies—in education, health, transportation, housing, economic development, urban renewal, delinquency control, and related fields—still lack the integration that would permit common ends to be sought. The ideas of the workable program and the community renewal program need to be extended substantively, as ways of raising the quality standards for local planning and as further means of assuring that the many interacting local, state, and federal activities are effectively fitted together.

City planners are likely to be key members in the new partnerships among professionals and politicians at the several governmental levels. The planners have long occupied a uniquely important position in local government, having been the custodians of the holistic view and the utopian tradition. The profession's history has been distinguished by a restless concern for those intangible attributes of the city that are too easily neglected in the day-to-day concentration on short-run problems and partial solutions. The city planners who have earned our highest respect are those whose visions of betterment became epidemic in their communities, raising civic aspirations and forcing solutions of specific problems to be sought within the larger and longer-term policy frameworks they helped establish.

As men who have specialized in the general, the truly effective city planners have functioned as catalysts for synthesizing the developmental plans prepared by the more specialized groups in government. By bringing representatives of public and private agencies together, they have helped to create new amalgams that better reflect both the separate and the mutual goals of the various participants. Individual plans for components have thus been reframed to accord with criteria established by the plans for the next-larger systems of components that, in turn, conform to more comprehensive over-views of the future and of the community's objectives.

Thus, for example, community housing policy is now typically treated as an integral aspect of over-all community social-welfare and land-use policies. Highway and transit facilities, only recently regarded by the transportation engineers as devices for satisfying traffic demand, are now treated as both servers and shapers of the larger land-use and accessibility relationships. In urban renewal the focus of attention is being expanded from the decaying slum buildings to include the larger life environments of the disadvantaged occupants. In turn, this is leading to more enlightened programs in community development, to individualized approaches to human development, and to more humane procedures for family relocation.

In these and numerous other ways, the city planner's realistic idealism, his orientation to the whole city, and his focus upon future conditions have placed him in a position of intellectual leadership. With increasing numbers and varieties of skilled specialists now entering the city's employ, the city planner's outlook will become increasingly important, and his educational mission more difficult. But simultaneously, with improved understanding of the relationships among the various aspects of the city, rational integration will become increasingly possible.

Of course, we claim no monopoly on knowledge, foresight, or wisdom in the urban field. Many of the functions that city planner's have traditionally performed are now being assumed by others who are better equipped to conduct specific studies, to lead specific programs, and to integrate them with others. In the presence of increasingly sophisticated theory and method, the planner's conventional reliance upon personal experience and private intuition is unlikely to be accepted as readily as it was in the past. Unless he can keep apace of the intellectual developments in urban theory and planning method, it is quite possible that his integrative roles will be largely assumed by some new group of planners, oriented to more comprehensive wholes, while the city planner becomes a specialist in land use, community facilities, and urban design. In this respect the future is indeterminate, but the profession has no jurisdictional claims to protect. We do stand prepared, though, to participate actively in these endeavors and to represent a human purpose and a holistic approach to the city's problems and opportunities which, we are persuaded, are most likely to increase the welfare of the people, who, as Henry Churchill succinctly put it, *are* the city.

IV. TO EXPAND FREEDOM IN A PLURALISTIC SOCIETY

As the comprehensiveness of municipal planning expands and as operating programs become more effectively integrated, the sheer efficiency and inflexibility of it all may inadvertently reduce the range of some citizens' choices. Unlike unorganized or ineffective series of separate programs, the mutual reinforcements of an all-out, co-ordinated effort can build a rolling momentum, which, should it be poorly designed, could seriously hurt some people before the course of action could be redirected.

This could be especially troublesome for the minority racial and ethnic groups whose value systems and behavior differ greatly from those of the middle-class professionals who design the programs intended to help them. We, in the several welfare professions, have frequently assumed that our ways are best ways, that our aspirations are or should be their aspirations, that a neighborhood designed to suit us is just the type that would best suit them.

There is now a growing appreciation, though, that cultural diversity is an intrinsic characteristic of our society, and we are coming to accept this kind of pluralism as a societal goal deliberately to be pursued. As one of its paramount functions, then, planning in a democratic society is being seen as a process by which the community seeks to increase the individual's opportunities to choose for himself—including the freedom to consume the society's produce and the freedom to choose to be different.

During the course of our history, the nation has learned that we cannot rely upon either chance or unseen hands to assure widened choice and abundance for all. Expanding freedom requires deliberate governmental actions, designed both to extend and to restrict individuals' liberties, as the contextual circumstances demand. To the end of expanding freedom and increasing the nation's wealth, a variety of controls that restrict individuals' liberties have by now been firmly established in custom and in law. Among the more notable are the anti-trust laws that seek to avoid the concentration of power in too few hands and to increase productivity; the regulations of the various public-utility commissions that establish prices and set rules of conduct; the pure food and drug laws that seek to protect consumers from the errors or the wiles of the industry; and the various municipal regulations designed to improve health and increase safety. Any restriction of liberties is of course fraught with hazard, for it is too easy either to invoke the doctrine of majority rule in usurping individual rights or to invoke the doctrine of individual rights in limiting majority freedom. A number of guiding principles are clear, however.

1. Certain regulations may be justified as means of forestalling *social costs*, that is, preventing one person from imposing hardships upon others without compensating them for their losses. If the spill-over effects of an individual's actions are likely to harm others, those actions may be prohibited, thus converting potential social costs into private costs to be borne by the actor. Or, if it is not possible to avoid the actions, he may be required to pay the persons who suffer the costs, again requiring that the actor bear the burden. (This is, of course, the prime justification for nuisance-control zoning, pollution-control legislation, and, indeed, the fundamental proposition underlying the police power.)

2. Some regulations and public programs find their justification in explicit political decisions to *redistribute income* among the populations. In matters of this kind the polity is sovereign; and income-redistribution decisions may be based upon purely moral grounds, so long as due process is respected. (Examples of income-redistributive measures are by now plentiful. They include public housing, public education, aid to dependent children, recreational programs, and the property and income taxes that finance them.)

Each of these two circumstances involves transfers of costs, benefits, or prerogatives from some individuals to others, with governmental agencies serving as coercive brokers to the transactions. Total wealth of the community is not necessarily affected by these transfers. Other types of governmental activities, however, do seek to increase the total wealth.

3. Under special circumstances *all individuals profit by yielding certain of their rights* to a central authority, because the total returns to the community are thereby increased, and each person's share can be greater. This is in the nature of an economic game in which all players are winners. (Examples here include popular allegiance to a governmental system of legislatures, executives, and courts, whose stability is prerequisite to individual security and freedom; the universal acceptance of the traffic signal's authority, which assures time savings and greater safety to all; and the assignment to governments of exclusive production rights for the "collective goods", such as national defense and city streets that, by their very nature, are available to everybody if they are supplied at all.)

4. In a similar way, tax-supported *information services* serve to foster increased productivity by increasing opportunities for making more rational private decisions, by stabilizing investment expectations, and by raising aspiration levels concerning the community's development. (Examples are the federal censuses and the new state and metropolitan data-reporting systems that serve to inform all interested members of the community about the current states of affairs; and governmental declarations of intent, as expressed in city plans and budgets, that aid private persons and groups in their efforts to anticipate future conditions, and that may encourage them to conform to collective aims.)

Having been closely associated with zoning regulations and land-clearance procedures, we are well aware of the vices that can be committed under the general-welfare sanctions. These controls have too often dispossessed some individuals of their property rights in the name of majority benefits, and they have too often been used as instruments of political power to further the private ends of some groups at the expense of others. Zoning and redevelopment programs carry unavoidable income-redistribution features that make them particularly susceptible to favored application and make them extremely difficult to apply equitably. As one reflection, large-lot zoning and exacting building codes in suburban municipalities have recently been used as tools for social discrimination and as unnecessary constraints upon individual freedom. Some aspects of urban redevelopment programs have been similarly criticized for the hurts they have imposed upon groups they have displaced.

We would prefer that these and other controls be applied with greater restraint and with greater sensitivity to the question of who benefits and who sacrifices. To accomplish the larger society's purposes, we look to the gradual reduction of controls on individual choice when benefits cannot be explicitly demonstrated and warranted. To this end, we seek ordinance revisions favoring greater permissiveness and greater flexibility for individual actions.

Although we recognize the necessity to centralize certain kinds of decisions in government, a major purpose in setting these decisions should be to expand the possibilities for decentralized decisions—to increase the number of options that are thereby opened to individual persons. Through explicitly goal-directed investments in public-service programs and in public works, governments can help expand the volume and the diversity of the society's produce and, in turn, can help increase individuals' capacities selectively to consume it.

The history of public education in America reveals a model for other governmental programs to emulate, for here the over-riding purpose has been to give, rather than to take—to open, rather than to foreclose choices. Those who have been successfully served by our public schools have been better equipped to support themselves and have been less dependent upon social welfare services than are their less fortunate neighbors. In turn, they are able to contribute to and then consume the growing varieties of goods, services, and ideas that prophesy the eventual elimination of poverty from the nation.

Since we are a long way from achieving equal opportunity, however, our plans must account for wide variations in degrees of freedom and in capacities to consume. Poverty and the deprivations of racial minority groups persist as the most pressing social issues confronting municipal governments. They call for an all-out reappraisal of programmatic priorities and for imaginative new programs aimed, above all, at increasing a sense of personal dignity and at fostering positive images of self and group.

Many of our present municipal programs are proving inadequate to this need. Lower-income families, who must budget larger proportions of their earnings for rent, are typically more eager to find cheap housing than they are in getting the modern housing facilities that middle-income families enjoy. Similarly, they must place higher priorities on developing low-cost transit service to employment places than they put on the amenities of open space and recreational facilities that others are seeking. Enforced relocation into higher-priced but superior housing is not likely to improve their standards of living if it requires reductions in the food budget. Declines in transit service, which may be tolerable for those who can afford automobiles, can be severely damaging for those who cannot.

Family- and youth-guidance services, occupational retraining programs, empathetic teachers and compatible school curricula, professionalization of low-skilled service jobs, inexpensive health services, the removal of racial bars, and increased employment opportunities are certain to be more immediately helpful to the city's underprivileged groups than are many of the community facilities that now absorb large proportions of municipal budgets. Although many of these activities do not fall within the city planner's areas of special competence, he is nonetheless a key agent in setting municipal-investment priorities; and he is thus in a position to guide municipal policies toward the issues that really matter.

Our purpose is to find those wealth-increasing approaches that will benefit *all* members of the society. Where such consummate returns are not possible, we seek to design those minimum controls that will avoid abuses by forestalling probabilities of individuals or groups harming others. Where income-redistribution effects are either unavoidable or publicly intended, we would have the gains go to those most in need of help. And when sacrifices must be made, especially when they must be made by those least able to sustain them, we would have them accompanied by commensurate payments.

City planning is moving through a period of rapid change—some have called it a revolution, so dramatic is the transformation likely to be. The major sign is a growing sophistication. The main prospect is a large increase in the profession's effectiveness. The chief stimulant has been the injection of a large body of theory and method that has been accumulating in the social and behavioral sciences over the decades and which, until recently, the profession had been largely immune to. Now, the problems of urbanization are attracting the attention of men from all the arts, humanities, and social sciences; and they are allying themselves with the urban-policy professions in what is fast becoming a saturation of talent into urban policy-making.

The infusion of new blood into the planning profession has brought with it a growing appreciation of the organizational complexities marking the societal systems that the city mirrors. Concomitantly, attention is being redirected from the form of the city to the processes that relate the inter-dependent aspects of the city one to the other. And, in turn, with improved understanding of how the city-system works, our capacities for effective intervention and willful change are improving rapidly. But effectiveness and will can come to nothing if they are not guided by wisdom. Worse, the damages wrought can be severe, the more because the levers of con-temporary government sweep wide arcs.

The contemporary planners inherit a proud tradition of service, an egalitarian ethic, and a pragmatic orientation to betterment that are as old as the early social reform movements that spawned the profession. The caretaker of the idea of progress during the long years when it lay in disrepute in respectable quarters, the planner is now being wooed as the Cinderella of the urban ball. The resulting marriage of the social sciences and the planning profession holds out the promise that a new level of intelligence will be merged with noble purpose, in confronting the prob-lems and the opportunities of the day. And then, the payoffs of this new partnership will come, if they are to come at all, in imaginative social inventions that will increase the city's riches, while distributing them to all the city's people.

TOWARDS COMPREHENSIVE PLANNING?

Introduction

IN THIS section, the debate which has developed around the *possibility* and *desirability* of comprehensive planning will be documented. The principals in this debate are planners exploring the implications of their claim for rationality of their procedures on the one hand and social scientists on the other.

About the two camps, two observations can be made. First, what distinguishes planners and their critics in these days of growing sophistication, at least in the élite of the planning profession, is less their intellectual calibre and more their temperament. Planners are *optimistic* whilst social scientists are reared on *scepticism*.

The second observation concerns the alternative assumptions about the nature of society which proponents and opponents of comprehensive planning tend to make, the latter more consciously than the former. The critics of comprehensive planning see society as a collection of individuals and groups, a view which is often described as *pluralistic* or even atomistic (Etzioni, 1968). Proponents of comprehensive planning, on the other hand, are more inclined to see society as an *organic whole*, something which is, in a metaphorical way, more real than the collection of individuals which it embraces. The distinction between these views has profound influence on key-concepts of comprehensive planning like the public interest, as Altshuler's paper will demonstrate.

RATIONAL-COMPREHENSIVE PLANNING
EXPLORED

If there has ever been a classic planning study, then Meyerson and Banfield's *Politics, Planning and the Public Interest—the Case of Public*

Housing in Chicago (1955) qualifies for this designation. The first two papers in this section have been written by the two co-authors of this book, and they evolve around a common interest they have in the meaning of planning as a help to rational choice.

As regards the context of their joint study, there are two streams of development in early American planning which were described by Perloff (1957) in a background study to his famous book on *Education for Planning*. One stream going back to the earliest days of the "City Beautiful" movement advocated long-range "comprehensive" or "master" plans to be drawn up by independent, non-political planning commissions. This was, and to some extent still is, a popular device for taking certain functions of government "out of politics". The Chicago Housing Authority, on which Meyerson and Banfield wrote, was of this kind.

However, during the depression attitudes towards local government shifted. For one, *public planning* became less of an anathema. Parallel to this, there was a growing interest in efficiency in government, while the first rudimentary cost accounting techniques were being developed such as the capital budget. This trend has continued ever since, especially with efforts to avert a post-war depression giving an added incentive for public spending. In the same way as in Britain, planning was seen by its proponents as becoming "positive", i.e. capable of actively promoting social ends on a broad front thus expanding the scope of *comprehensive planning* beyond the physical master plan:

> Planning . . . has helped to bring to the forefront, and into the consciousness of governments and of the general public, the importance and desirability of being concerned . . . with relationships among people, physical objects, and ecological forces; of trying to see things wholly, of setting goals and trying to figure out the best way of achieving them . . . a dynamic relationship has developed between city planning as an idea and an activity, on the one side, and, on the other, the broadening popular view of municipal government responsibility and the more widespread acceptance of the need for consciously working towards an improved urban environment. (Perloff, 1957.)

Meyerson's paper presents practical proposals for implementing "positive" planning, whilst retaining the idea of a *comprehensive plan*. At the same time, he makes a claim for planners to play a central role in urban government. But, whilst the professional context of his paper has been forgotten (American planners have largely given up their attempt to achieve full professionalization), the proposal for a *middle-range bridge* is one of the most influential ones ever to be made in the pages of the *Journal of the American Institute of Planners*. The *Community Renewal Program* under the Housing Act of 1959 introduced this continuous, intermediate planning function (Scott, 1969).

Possibly as a result of his earlier collaboration with Banfield, Meyerson recognizes that traditional comprehensive planning has never really been effective, because of the lack of relevant information and guidance to decision-makers concerning immediate implications of long-term plans. He also recognizes the roles of *politics* and the *market* as powerful forces with which planning must reckon, and to which planning is subordinate, though perhaps more so in the United States than elsewhere. Yet, as against the sceptic Banfield, Meyerson retains his optimism: decision-makers need information which planning can provide; planning can act as a local "G2", as a "lubricant" of the market.[1]

Meyerson's concern was therefore with making comprehensive planning meaningful in terms of the guidance which it offered to *actual* decision-making, a point also made by Daland and Parker (1962) on the basis of their empirical studies of planners in operation. His proposals were for introducing an intermediate form of plan, and one is reminded of action area plans which were devised for a similar reason in Britain only a few years afterwards. For the rest, he advocates changes to the institutions of planning and the functions which they should fulfil.

His concern was markedly less with method than with basic ideas. The criteria of rational planning as outlined by Banfield were still too far from what could systematically be achieved. Even cost benefit analysis was still in its infancy, and had mostly been applied to individual projects only: Lichfield's application of cost benefit analysis to urban planning was not to become known in America until 1960 (Lichfield, 1960).

As regards the model of the *rational planning process*, Banfield can probably claim to have stated it first in the planning literature, though he

---

[1] There is an ambiguity in the position of those who merely wish to facilitate the operations of the market by disseminating information. Since attending to available information, and even more so acting on such information, depends on a certain amount of slack in resource-utilization, powerful groups are more likely to benefit than others. This observation has been made by Bićanić (1967) concerning the advantages which the French monopolies have gained from participating in the activities of the French National Plan, and more recently by Brian J. Styles (1971) concerning public participation in planning.

evidently draws a lot from works in administrative theory and decision-making flourishing during that decade. The present paper written a few years after publication of their joint book contains an almost identical statement and draws heavily in other ways on the Chicago study. Since then, planning and public administration have drawn closer together, not only in practice, but also as regards their theoretical foundation.

What becomes evident for the first time in Banfield's paper is the wide gap between the *ideal* of rational-comprehensive planning, and the *reality* of organizational choice. Having stated what rational decision-making would mean, Banfield finds scores of reasons why organizations do *not* engage in it, and everybody who has ever tried making a rational choice in an only slightly complex situation will recognize some of his own frustrations in the list he gives. It is only as a *normative* model that the rational planning process has any meaning at all.

THE CHALLENGE TO RATIONAL-COMPREHENSIVE PLANNING

Lindblom denies the validity of rational-comprehensive planning even as an ideal. His paper on "muddling through" gives a very good summary of the intellectual programme which he has stood for ever since he started investigating decision-making.

Lindblom's thesis must be seen against the background of a decade of advances in the theory of decision-making documented by Dyckman (1961). These had generated considerable optimism about improvements to planning and policy-making, an optimism which caught up with city planners at around the turn of the decade. There were originally only a few strands of sceptical thought which Lindblom once summarized in a joint paper with Hirschman (Hirschman and Lindblom, 1962).

To the best of my knowledge, there has never been a cogent refutation of Lindblom's thesis from a planner though, to be sure, it has been criticized in other circles (Dror, 1968; Etzioni, 1968; see also pp. 217–29). But even in his short paper included here, one can detect several of the characteristics of his thinking: To start with, there are simple *flaws* in his argument. Then, there are not so much faults as *ambiguities*. Finally he commits the sin of mixing, in an inadmissible manner, *factual* and *normative* arguments which, however, makes what he says deceptively obvious:

decision-makers do not, cannot, and as a matter of fact have no chance of ever being able to, decide in ways outlined by the rational-comprehensive model. Why therefore stick to it?

The flaws in Lindblom's argument are that he completely replaces validity as a criterion for decisions with agreement, that he absurdly magnifies theory, and that he identifies rational-comprehensive with another form of planning which I shall call blueprint planning.

Let me begin by pointing out Lindblom's extreme *scepticism* regarding the possibility of basing decisions on valid knowledge. He argues for replacing the search for knowledge as a basis for decisions by political or market choices. This argument is related to what he feels to be the only criterion of a good decision, i.e. agreement. Now, surely, some measure of agreement is an important pre-condition of decision-making, but it is wrong to say that it ought to *replace* valid knowledge. Policy-makers who disregard such knowledge are liable to be unsuccessful in terms of achieving what they want to achieve, no matter whether they have reached agreement on policies or not.

Here, the examples which Lindblom quotes are misleading. They are examples showing why different interest groups agree to the same policy for *different* ends. But examples most pertinent to this question would be those of agreement reached for *conflicting* ends. Assuming that the agreed policy is one which is relevant to both ends, disappointment with its results is bound to follow, at least to one of the partners to this agreement. He will presumably think in retrospect that it might have been a good idea to analyse the relationship of this policy with his own ends—despite what Lindblom suggests.

Let me hasten to say that I do not claim that planning policies could ever be based on analytical knowledge *alone*. The commitment to implement policies, and—as Grauhan (see pp. 297–316) argues in his paper—the willingness to take risks, must supplement knowledge in policy-making, especially where no valid knowledge is available. Knowledge and political agreement are both important, and neither can be neglected without detriment to success in planning and policy-making.

Turning to his distinction between the "root" method relying on theory and the "branch" method relying on successive comparisons, one must point out that he magnifies *theory* to superhuman proportions. "Successive comparison" means to construct theory. The difference between this and what Lindblom calls theory is one of the scope of investigations. This, however, is a pragmatic question and does certainly not amount to an *a priori* distinction between decision-making approaches.

Not only does Lindblom misrepresent "theory", he also identifies the rational-comprehensive approach, wrongly in my opinion, with "blueprint planning". Blueprint planning is a form of planning which determines every detail of the solution to a problem, and only then proceeds unswervingly towards implementing the plan. As Popper (1961), Kaplan (1963) and others have pointed out, it is the mark of totalitarian regimes.[2]

But there is nothing in the rational method itself which suggests that it must proceed in this fashion—except for the linearity of its presentation. There is every possibility of changing direction during the implementation of policies, of going back to objectives, of redefining the range of alternatives considered. Indeed, taking into account Lindblom's own argument, it may be more practicable to enter the process at the stage of considering feasible policies, and only at this stage to analyse the underlying objectives subsequently investigating more alternatives designed to achieve the same objectives—or an amended range of objectives for that matter!

Whilst these are comments on errors which Lindblom makes, there are also ambiguities in his argument. There are at least five in this one paper: the cautious language which he uses; his tendency to represent dominant trends as unqualified facts and limitations on problem-solving as absolute barriers; a lack of precision at the fundamental point of his argument: agreement; and his cavalier treatment of long-range planning.

His cautious language, to start with, allows one to imply that there are exceptions to the rule of muddling through being a superior strategy. Thus, he says that ". . . when compared to the root method, the branch method *often* looks far superior . . .", and elsewhere that the latter: ". . . will be superior to any other decision-making method available for complex problems *in many circumstances* . . .".[3]

[2] In *A Strategy of Decision*, Braybrooke and Lindblom (1963) refer to Popper as a strand of anti-synoptic thought, quoting his argument against utopian engineering (Popper, 1961). Yet, there is nothing in Popper's writing which may be interpreted against using knowledge, or searching for knowledge. He only argues against taking its validity for granted and therefore not allowing for the possibility of action based on such knowledge failing. This is process planning and not muddling through.

[3] Italics mine.

Yet, if he qualifies his statements in this way, whilst putting incremental decision-making forward as a normative model, then it is incumbent upon him to explain the circumstances under which it does *not* apply.

Add to this Lindblom's tendency of representing what are quite possibly dominant tendencies as statements of fact: "Policy does not move in leaps and bounds . . ." is one of them. Here, Etzioni counters Lindblom by saying that more fundamental decisions are made than Lindblom states (see p. 221). In a similar way, Melvin Webber (1965) has argued, with Great Britain and Puerto Rico in mind, that regardless of Lindblom's persuasiveness we know that governments *are* able to take big investment leaps.

Lindblom also repeatedly represents human capacities for problem-solving as absolute barriers of rational choice. Yet, surely, they can only be relative! Otherwise, no forms of problem-solving would be feasible, not even a limited comparison between incremental alternatives. From here, it is only one step to asking to what *degree* human limitations constitute barriers to rationality, and how these can be overcome, removed, circum-vented, or simply pushed a little bit further, questions which his defeatist attitude does not allow Lindblom to ask.

He is also ambiguous on the point on which much of his argument rests, i.e. on the lack of agreement about ends. He describes prior overall agree-ment as virtually impossible to achieve such that rational-comprehensive decision-making becomes impracticable as a strategy. Yet he thinks it is perfectly in order to talk about *groups* continuously adjusting their interests to each other. How do *they* arrive at what their interest is? Is there a co-herent, identifiable group interest? True, Lindblom ends his paper by suggesting that even institutions representing one grouping might benefit from fragmenting their decision-making but, by talking about a group interest, he still implies that diverse views can be summed up in some coherent fashion. Why, then, should this be *a priori* impossible for larger entities?[4]

There is finally the very cursory treatment which Lindblom gives to long-run considerations. He says that "muddling through" does not necessarily neglect long-run considerations and objectives, thus shifting

[4] A "group interest" is as much an abstraction as the "public interest", or even the interest of an individual is, as Etzioni (1968) points out. See on this also Bauer (1968) and Cyert and March (1959).

from the level of factual to analytical statements which is in contradistinction to the rest of his paper. Surely, since he makes such an effort to find
out what decision-makers do in *actual fact*, it may have befitted him to say
whether long-run interests *are* neglected in "muddling through" or not.
With "muddling through" relying so heavily on agreement as a measure of
success, it is at least reasonable to suppose that there will not in effect be
enough groups with the altruistic attitude of defending long-term against
short-term objectives: expedience is one of the marks of pluralist politics,
as its defenders point out themselves (see Altshuler, pp. 183–209; see on
this point also Etzioni's discussion of Lindblom's thesis on p. 220).

Now this is another example of the basic problem of Lindblom's way
of arguing: the habit of mixing *normative* with *factual* statements. A great
deal of the evidence which he puts forward belongs to what has been
described as a "positive" theory of planning. Yet his conclusions fall
into the province of a "normative" theory of planning. He presents
prescriptions for how planners *ought* to proceed.

To be sure, the findings of a positive theory of planning may have
relevance for normative theory. If, for instance, a normative theory of
planning would state that *any* departure from its prescriptions constituted
evidence for inaptitude on part of the planner, i.e. if it implicitly imposed
sanctions for not achieving what—and here I agree with Lindblom—
cannot be achieved, then his findings would change such a theory. But
from what he says it does not follow that rational-comprehensive planning
ought not to be striven for. Such a conclusion only follows from an entirely
different and only vaguely stated assumption which he makes, i.e. that of
the extension of the market choice model to public policy choices. This
assumption may be, as Broady (1968), Etzioni (1968; see also p. 220),
and others have pointed out, a reflection of the particular institutional
context of America.

Planning theory is therfore well advised to study Lindblom's writing,
especially his competent review of behavioural studies of planning,
whilst remaining circumspect about his prescriptions. The behavioural
element ought to be incorporated, thus allowing planning theory to provide models which are feasible yet more optimistic than Lindblom's, such
as Etzioni's "mixed scanning" strategy (see pp. 217–29).

OPTIMISM IN THE MID-SIXTIES

The next three papers of this section were written in the mid-sixties almost a decade after Meyerson's bid for combining city planning with rational guidance to policy-makers. Robinson's and Friedmann's papers show some considerable optimism concerning the possibility of actually fulfilling this promise.

It is significant for this optimism that Robinson's paper has, for instance, been published as part of a symposium on "The New Urban Planning". It relays how Meyerson's plea, and the introduction of the Community Renewal Program, have led to a spate of activities representing considerable moves towards comprehensive planning, thus incidentally showing that improvements are possible despite Lindblom's scathing comments.

Robinson's hopes derive mainly from improvements to the *techniques* and the *technology* of planning which have occurred in the years following 1956. His proposal is that of extending the logic of the Community Renewal Program to what he calls Community Development Programming representing a complete programme of rational policy-making proceeding by continuously analysing action proposals in the light of human goals, pursuing their inter-relationship, and monitoring their implementation.

Some of Robinson's comments relating to the institutional structure of planning foreshadow Friedmann's reply to Altshuler. This is where, with the advantage of hindsight, one is able to identify a shortcoming, not so much of this particular paper but of the whole rationalistic view of policy-making. As many planners before have done, Robinson treats institutional structure (and with it ideas concerning political organisation) as the *dependent* variable which ought to adapt to new approaches to planning as the independent variable. Thus, Community Development Programming should have an "appeal to managers and controllers in city government", presumably because of the increase in effective power which it would afford. Yet this increase has itself political significance, and this requires careful consideration.

Political scientists like Wildavsky (1968) and Altshuler have since reasserted the supremacy of politics over the rationalism of planners, though the latter more forcefully in his book than in his paper included in this section: ". . . the city planner like almost everyone in American politics controls so little of his environment that unquestioning acceptance of its major features is a condition of its own success" (Altshuler, 1965).

In his paper, Altshuler is more concerned with the concept of the *public interest* and the way it appears to be singularly unsuited to provide guidance in decision-making. There is, in particular, no public interest outside of what the political process, as it is at the present, defines it to be. Since the political process is fragmented—witness the great number of special purpose agencies, and of ethnic and other groups making their presence felt—Altshuler's concept of the public interest is also fragmented.[5]

Despite his critical stance, Altshuler shows different intellectual temperament from Lindblom. He is much more careful in establishing what the precise implications of his findings are. In particular, he does not advocate a model of his own, at least not in the explicit form as Lindblom. The conclusion which he allows himself to draw is an indication of areas of weakness in planning theory, not a prescription for what planners ought to do.

Nevertheless, Altshuler's careful refutation of his contemporary planners' claim for comprehensiveness must not go completely unquestioned. He assumes, first of all, that little or no knowledge concerning interdependencies between different areas of policy-making is available, and secondly that "co-ordination" should not be divorced from operational activities. Yet, as regards interdependencies, the lack of precision in their measurement to which he alludes is surely a matter of *degree*. There is some information available concerning "externalities" which can provide guidance for policy choices though, to be sure, no decisions can be made without additional guidance from politicians.

As regards the planner's co-ordinative role, Altshuler puts the case for a mixed staff-line function invoking the authority of nobody less than Winston Churchill and also Chester Barnard. The alternative of having separate staff planning-units as a safeguard against "Gresham's Law of Planning" (routine activity tends to drive out non-routine activity) has been argued by Simon (1960). Thus, it is not a foregone conclusion that planners should necessarily get involved in operational activities—and

---

[5] It is important to see his comments firmly against the background of *American* politics. There may be alternative ways of defining the public interest as Altshuler himself observes in his book. Even in America, there are different "patterns of influence"—see Mann (1964); for the implications for planning see Rabinovitz (1969).

thus forfeit their claim for impartial representation of the public interest, as Altshuler concludes.

The possibility of identifiable interdependencies between different areas of public policy, and of a differentiation between staff- and line-functions, are clearly implied in Friedmann's reply to Altshuler. He differentiates between policies and programme planning, with the first providing at least a loose framework for the second. Among the tools of policies planning there are capital budgets and development plans which may both be seen as a sort of resource budget. The idea is also implied of these plans and programmes as an interlocking system of intentions, predictions and resource allocations spaced out over different time horizons similar to the scheme proposed by Friedmann in his extensive essay on "Planning as a vocation" (Friedmann, 1966/7).

What is strikingly evident in Friedmann's short paper is the optimism which he, much like many other planners, shows and which is in sharp contrast to the scepticism of social scientist-critics of planning. In Friedmann's case this optimism is tempered by his thorough acquaintance not only with the current American social science literature, but also with its antecedents in European philosophy. Despite all this, and despite long and varied experiences of planning under difficult circumstances, his belief in rational action is basically unbroken.

This may be an optimism which is hard to justify with respect to American planning. All too often, the essential co-ordination and consultation within and between institutions of government may simply not take place. An even more fundamental problem is the deep fragmentation and dissent which have been afflicting the very fabric of American social life since these papers were written. Consequently, very little has been heard about rational-comprehensive planning in America since the mid-sixties.

I do not think that this can be regarded as conclusive evidence against rational-comprehensive planning. It may simply be that it is too far from what is possible in the particularly difficult circumstances of the United States. Even there, there are some recent indications for a renewed interest in comprehensive planning, though possibly more on the regional level, and a step or two removed from the turmoil of the cities. Referring to the Appalachian Regional Commission, Rothblatt answers Lindblom in 1971: ". . . rational-comprehensive planning . . . is . . . an ideal which can . . . be approximated in the real world . . ." (Rothblatt, 1971).

In the cities, too, and possibly in parallel to the rediscovery of the virtues of accountable rather than instant government documented in the next section, expertise, if not comprehensive planning, comes to be valued once again (Mitchell *et al.*, 1970). Perhaps the tables are turning, now that black people begin to assert themselves having gained some measure of political power. Perhaps, the factual and analytical element of policy-making will come to be recognized not to replace the value- and political-element, but to complement and augment it by increasing awareness and by extending political choice.

Also, if comprehensive planning may have been somewhat less of a focus of interest in the United States recently, then it is certainly in vogue in Great Britain. There is a great deal of interest now in planning not only in its physical sense—the subject of traditional British *town and country planning*—but also as an instrument of rational policy-making, a development which shows signs of assimulating and improving upon American experiences.[6]

Finally, ways exist of coping with those limitations on problem-solving capacity on which, amongst others, the critics of rational-comprehensive planning build their case. This argument is made brilliantly by Etzioni in the last paper of this section where he proposes "mixed-scanning" as a *planning strategy* incorporating elements of both the rational-comprehensive and the incrementalist approach to decision-making. This article brings in a nutshell what Etzioni has to say on these approaches in his profound study on *The Active Society* (Etzioni, 1968).

Mixed-scanning provides a description of and a prescription for effective action. As a strategy, it is well adapted to the psychology of human beings (see, for example, Miller *et al.*, 1960; Miller, 1968). It also includes the acceptance of elements of *risk* which action involves and thus complements a view of man as stamping his image on an uncertain world, transforming himself during the process and deriving the impetus for yet more *learning* and *growth* from the unintended consequences of his actions.

---

[6] Americans are sometimes amazed by the confidence of British planners. See Donald A. Kruekeberg's review of Friend and Jessop (1969) in the *Journal of the American Institute of Planners*, January 1970. Conversely, British planners seem to be more successful in adopting advanced techniques such as Planning Programming Budgeting than the Americans, a comment which Tony Eddison made at the conference on "The Future of Planning Education" in Oxford in April 1971.

It is my opinion that mixed-scanning is one of the most important things that have happened to planning theory in the recent past, and that planners and planning theorists will have to devote their attention not only to this concept but also to the whole framework devised by Etzioni around it (see, for example, Chadwick, 1971; Faludi, 1971, 1972; Friedmann, 1969, 1971).

REFERENCES

Part III

ALTSHULER, A. A. (1965) *The City Planning Process*, Cornell University Press, Ithaca, New York.

BAUER, R. A. (1968) "The study of policy formation. an introduction", *The Study of Policy Formation* (edited by BAUER, R. A. and GERGEN, K. J.), Collier–Macmillan, London.

BIĆANIĆ, R. (1967) *Problems of Planning—East and West*, Mouton, The Hague.

BRAYBROOKE, D. and LINDBLOM, C. E. (1963) *A Strategy of Decision: Policy Evaluation as a Social Process*, The Free Press, Glencoe, Illinois.

BROADY, M. (1968) "From planning techniques to a theory of planning", *SCUPAD Bulletin*, Vol. 4, pp. 74–80.

CHADWICK, G. (1971) *A Systems View of Planning*, Pergamon Press, Oxford.

CYERT, R. M. and MARCH, J. G. (1959) "A behavioral theory of organisational objectives", *Modern Organization Theory* (edited by HAIRE, M.), John Wiley, New York.

DALAND, R. T. and PARKER, J. A. (1962) "Roles of the planner in urban development", *Urban Growth Dynamics* (edited by CHAPIN, F. S. and WEISS, F. S.), John Wiley, New York.

DROR, Y. (1968) *Public Policymaking Reexamined*, Chandler, Pennsylvania.

DYCKMAN, J. W. (1961) "Planning and decision theory", *Journal of the American Institute of Planners*, Vol. 27, pp. 335–45.

ETZIONI, A. (1968) *The Active Society*, Collier–Macmillan, London.

FALUDI, A. (1971) "Towards a three-dimensional model of planning behaviour", *Environment and Planning*, Vol. 3, pp. 253–66.

FALUDI, A. (1972) "Teaching the planning process", *Journal of the Royal Town Planning Institute*, Vol. 58, pp. 111–14.

FRIEDMANN, J. (1966/7) "Planning as a vocation", *Plan Canada*, Vol. 6, pp. 99–124; Vol. 7, pp. 8–26.

FRIEDMANN, J. (1969) "Notes on societal action", *Journal of the American Institute of Planners*, Vol. 35, pp. 311–18.

FRIEDMANN, J. (1971) "The future of comprehensive urban planning: a critique", *Public Administration Review*, Vol. 31, pp. 315–26.

FRIEND, J. K. and JESSOP, W. N. (1969) *Local Government and Strategic Choice*, Tavistock Publications.

HIRSCHMAN, A. O. and LINDBLOM, C. E. (1962) "Economic development, research and development-policy making: some converging views", *Behavioral Science*, Vol. 7, pp. 211–22, and in *Systems Thinking* (edited by EMERY, F. E.), Penguin, Harmondsworth, 1969.

KAPLAN, A. (1963) *American Ethics and Public Policy*, Oxford University Press, New York.

KAPLAN, M. (1969) "Advocacy and the urban poor", *Journal of the American Institute of Planners*, Vol. 35, pp. 96–104.

LICHFIELD, N. (1960) "Cost benefit analysis in city planning", *Journal of the American Institute of Planners*, Vol. 26, pp. 273–9.

MANN, L. D. (1964) "Studies in community decision-making", *Journal of the American Institute of Planners*, Vol. 30, pp. 58–65.

MEYERSON, M. and BANFIELD, E. (1955) *Politics, Planning and the Public Interest*, The Free Press, Glencoe.

MILLER, G. A., GALANTER, E. and PRIBHAN, K. H. (1960) *Plans and the Structure of Behavior*, Holt, Rinehart & Winston Inc., New York.

MILLER, G. A. (1968) *The Psychology of Communication*, Penguin, Harmondsworth.

MITCHELL, M. L., MANN, L. C. II and JAYSON, R. F. (1970) "The case for environmental planning education in black schools", *Journal of the American Institute of Planners*, Vol. 36, pp. 279–84.

PERLOFF, H. S. (1957) *Education for Planning—City, State and Regional*, John Hopkins, Baltimore.

POPPER, K. (1961) *The Poverty of Historicism*, Routledge & Kegan Paul, London.

RABINOVITZ, F. F. (1969) *City Politics and Planning*, Atherton Press, New York.

ROTHBLATT, D. (1971) "Rational planning reexamined", *Journal of the American Institute of Planners*, Vol. 37, pp. 26–36.

SCOTT, M. (1969) *American City Planning*, University of California Press, Los Angeles.

SIMON, H. A. (1960) *The New Science of Management Decision*, Harper, New York.

STYLES, B. J. (1971) "Public participation—a reconsideration", *Journal of the Town Planning Institute*, Vol. 57, pp. 163–7.

WEBBER, M. M. (1965) "The role of intelligence systems in urban systems planning", *Journal of the American Institute of Planners*, Vol. 31, pp. 289–96.

WILDAVSKY, A. (1968) "The political economy of efficiency: cost-benefit analysis, systems analysis, and program budgeting", *Planning Programming Budgeting: a Systems Approach to Management* (edited by LYDEN, F. I. and MILLER, E. G.), Markham, Chicago.

Building the Middle-range Bridge for Comprehensive Planning*

Martin Meyerson

WHEN De Tocqueville visited here a hundred years ago, he commented that whenever two Americans got together, they formed an organization. In recent years, it has become fashionable for European observers to laugh about our tendency to elaborate on organization—now, these observers say, whenever two Americans doing the same sort of work get together, they form a profession.

PROFESSIONALIZATION

The social scientists have also focussed on this tendency to professionalize. They have analyzed certain general procedures followed by all emerging professional groups. Their analyses amount to a recital of the natural history of professionalization. First, persons of imagination and vision, and a profound dissatisfaction with the world as they see it, outline the scope of new problems and propose new approaches to these problems. These are persons trained in other disciplines, often diverse disciplines; they are people of broad interests and an ability to dramatize problems and inspire others. Whatever literature is produced is polemic, general, devoted to portrayal of problems, and clamors for the attention of a citizenry already perplexed and vexed by other matters.

As more and more recognition is given to the importance of the newly discovered problems, limited funds are made available for exploring or solving these problems. More people are attracted as lay enthusiasts or as practitioners in the field; organizations are set up; conferences are held. Schools are established to give specialized training; the course of instruc-

* Reprinted by permission of the *Journal of the American Institute of Planners*, Vol. 22, No. 2, 1956.

tion grows longer and longer. A unique vocabulary is developed; non-professionals cannot talk it. A literature geared to specific problems emerges; nonprofessionals find it complex and dull. Soon people begin to think in terms of "careers" as well as in terms of solving problems. Salaries, job classifications, personnel qualifications, specialization within the field become important. Attempts are made to broaden functions and responsibilities, to grow bigger and bigger, to be imperialistic in scope and numbers. More and more efforts are made to make the activity expert, technical, scientific—and beyond the ken of nonprofessionals. This culminates in licensing or registration to keep out pretenders. By this time, the profession has "institutionalized"; its members acquire the power of reproduction—that is, it is the present professionals not the market situation who determine what standards must be met by new entrants.

Despite the gibes of some European observers and despite the implied gibes of the social scientists, I think our American tendency to professionalize on the whole is a good one. By being self-conscious about our work activities we do try to develop our methods and body of knowledge and to improve our competence. The danger lies in the stage when we become too rigid, when we are no longer capable of absorbing new ideas or going in new directions, or willing to discuss our problems with people in other fields. However, planning is too new an activity to be that institutionalized. We are in the expansionist, imperialistic stage, and who am I to go counter to the natural history of our emerging profession?

Therefore, I want to speak today as an imperialist for city planning. I want to speak today about expansion—about increasing our numbers, multiplying our budgets, strengthening our effectiveness, expanding our functions, and, of course, raising our salaries.

EXPANDING FUNCTIONS

I shall focus on expanded city planning functions and responsibilities which if not performed by planning agencies may very well be performed by other agencies of local government. However, I believe planning agencies are not only best equipped to perform these functions, but their own effectiveness will be enormously increased by doing so.

However, we might well ask if increasing our scope of operations will not be done by sacrificing preparation of long-range plans. Do not the administration of zoning and subdivision control already rob us of time and energy to devote to long-range planning? Of course they do. Yet they are also ways in which planning is translated effectively into daily changes of urban development.

For background to some of the additional functions I want to discuss, let me wear two hats. One is my hat at ACTION—the American Council to Improve Our Neighborhoods. The other is my hat as city planning professor. Wearing ACTION's hat, my responsibilities during the past year and more have required me to travel to many parts of the country, and to talk with many of the people who made the key decisions which shape our cities and towns. These are the mayors, the city managers, the heads of operating municipal departments, the homebuilders, the merchants and industrialists, the civic leaders. Their decisions are the decisions that set the stage for the decisions of the everyday citizen—his choices on where he lives, his kind of work, the activities he and his family will have an opportunity to participate in. And I was struck by the fact that the mayor and the merchant, the head of the renewal agency and the homebuilder are at a loss to find the specific framework to provide them with the kinds of guidance they need to make rational decisions.

As I talked with these people, it was very encouraging to me to find the respect in which they hold the city planner and to recognize it as a tribute to the responsible growth of our profession. However, their respect is rarely derived from an awareness of the importance of long-range comprehensive planning. Rather their respect is based on the project-planning accomplishments of the city planner and related officials. They speak their admiration for the highway extensions, the new zoning districts, the design of a group of public buildings, the development of a park preserve or a new terminal improvement. Partly, of course, it is because so much of our attention has necessarily gone to project-planning that little effort has been left for long-range comprehensive planning, and thus little opportunity for it to be understood, let alone for it to be vigorously supported.

Yet the framework required by the people who make some of the key decisions for both private and public community development is not provided by project-planning. Nor is the urgency of these decisions met by the kind of long-range comprehensive planning we usually do. I have concluded that a middle ground is needed. An intermediate set of planning functions must be performed on a sustained, on-going basis to provide the framework for the homebuilder who must decide how many units he should, as well as can, build next year; for the government official who must decide whether the signs of unemployment in the locality require special public action; for the appointed commissioner who has no sense of whether a particular policy which his agency might follow and obtain bonds to execute will fit in with other current city policies; for the industrialist who wants to know what specific land use changes will be made in an area within the next few years before he commits his corporation's resources; for the redevelopment agency which has no knowledge as to what the effects of previous slum-clearance projects have been and the lessons that can be learned from them.

Now changing my hat, as a professor of city planning, one of my major concerns is that we train students for the responsible posts they will hold not only this year but ten years from now. An apprenticeship might be a far superior way to a university curriculum if our main object were to prepare people for specific present jobs. What kind of a job will the planner be expected to do ten years from now? I have been trying to get some sense of this and thus of needed educational programs. I am of course talking primarily about city planning, although I believe what I am saying applies to resources planning and other kinds of planning as well. I also recognize that most city planners in the future may not work for what we regard as city planning agencies. This does not mean that they should not be trained as city planners.

Now, wearing both my hats at the same time, I wonder very much whether the impressions I have got for the need and importance of a middle-ground planning activity may not be a clue to some of the crucial functions of the profession in the years ahead, and thus a clue to planning education in the years ahead as well. The additional functions I propose are suggested not to detract from long-range planning but to make it more meaningful.

I propose that we consider whether the following middle-ground community planning functions are appropriate to our province:

1. *A Central Intelligence Function* to facilitate market operations for housing, commerce, industry and other community activities through the regular issuance of market analyses
2. *A Pulse-taking Function* to alert the community through quarterly or

other periodic reports to danger signs in blight formation, in economic changes, population movements and other shifts
3. *A Policy Clarification Function* to help frame and regularly revise
development objectives of local government
4. *A Detailed Development Plan Function* to phase specific private and
public programs as part of a comprehensive course of action covering
not more than 10 years
5. *A Feed-back Review Function* to analyze through careful research
the consequences of program and project activities as a guide to
future action

These are interrelated functions. The intelligence, pulse-taking and
review functions roughly parallel the types of measures we are learning to
utilize nationally, for example through the Council of Economic Advisers,
to encourage equilibrium and new growth in employment and investment.
On the community level, we would not want to restrict ourselves to just
economic concerns. But nationally we have developed during the last
twenty years a type of sensitivity to changes in the economy which permit
adjustments when the economy gets markedly out of balance. We have
developed a whole series of statistics and indices such as building starts,
prices of hogs, consumer credit, a type of periodic information which we
never had before. Then, if there are maladjustments in the economy
revealed through periodic checks, we may adjust the mortgage rate, place
governmental orders in areas where there is unemployment and try to take
other measures to bring about equilibrium.

The five functions I want to discuss this evening envisage a similar
role for the city planning agency—a role which brings planning and policy
closer together. They are functions which city planning agencies to some
extent fulfill already. However, they are not part of the routine view of
appropriate city planning activity.

What do these five functions mean for municipal planning?

1. *The Central Intelligence Function.* The planning agency as the local
G2 to aid the operations of the market.

The market place—the mechanism which brings together producer and
consumer, supply and demand—is the primary method under democratic
capitalism by which land and other resources are allocated to those activities by which people live, work, play and raise their families.

Market decisions are more important than governmental ones in giving substance to the design and structure of our urban communities. In our cities, for example, we see that people who desire housing accommodations are more and more choosing to live in the suburbs. These represent individual choices to satisfy individual values and fit individual circumstances. But these individual choices add up to a major shift in urban patterns—not only in housing, but in shopping and many other facilities as well. The changes in urban patterns due to market selection are so decisive and have such widespread and interlocking consequences that they almost appear as though someone had directed them. (Perhaps this is the invisible hand of the market to which Adam Smith refers.)

However, the local businessman, the industrialist and the consumer rarely have the kind of accurate enough information to make rational decisions. Currently, builders, investors, business and industrial firms have such vast unknown factors with which to deal that the risks involved either operate as brakes on activity or inflate the costs of production or financing. The consumer has to act on conjecture rather than real knowledge of choices open to him.

The city planning agency in most communities is the local unit of government best equipped to provide a market analysis function. Data would have to be obtained and analyzed continuously. Regular market reports would be issued by the planning agency. Depending on the urgency of the market decisions, some of the reports could be issued monthly, some quarterly, some semiannually, some annually. There could be special reports on the new home building market, on investment in plant, on consumer income and spending, on land and building costs. The planning agency is an appropriate one for this function, not only because it has a nucleus of people dealing with these community characteristics but also because this kind of regular and constant market analysis is crucial to the achievement of present functions of planning and some of the other ones I am discussing today.

Detailed market analysis for the city, for the metropolitan area and for subregions in this area would enable both the producer and the consumer to make more intelligent choices in respect to the location, investment, building and land utilization for industry, commerce, housing and other main facilities and activities. The political philosophy of the country rests on the market as the key means to allocate resources. If the city planning agency regularly checks and interprets the local market situation as I suggest here, it can lubricate the process of urban development and achieve many of the main objectives of city planning by facilitating intelligent individual actions.

2. *The Pulse-taking Function.* The planning agency as the watchdog for community danger signs.

It is true that most community development decisions are made through market mechanisms rather than through governmental planning mechanisms. However, one of the reasons why planning has become an accepted governmental activity is that the market has frequently exhibited such frictions and even malfunctioning that desired community ends have not been achieved. For example, a main impetus to planning came from the fact that the market was not allocating land uses in such a way as to preserve residential values during the useful life of the property. Planning was expected, through land use and other controls, to compensate for the problems—the failures—of the market.

However, planning has too often been in the position of correcting mistakes after they have happened rather than in the position of detecting and removing trouble spots before they lead to major mistakes. I therefore recommend that the planning agency submit a quarterly or other periodic report to the local chief executive alerting the community danger signs. Which neighborhoods are showing blight factors at an increased pace? Are certain transit routes losing most of their passengers? Are there signs that certain industries are about to either come in or leave the area? The planning agency should thus perpetually scan the community for indications of maladjustment. Failures of firms, increased congestion, incipient changes in land use, new demands for services might thus be detected before they gather a momentum almost impossible to stop.

To be effective the planning agency's pulse-taking report must not only alert the community to trouble spots, but must also point to remedial action. Inevitably this means a policy focus.

3. *The Policy Clarification Function.* The planning agency as an aid in framing and regularly revising development objectives of local government.

I have just suggested that the planning agency be alerted to detect any trends potentially harmful to the community. This implies that policies would be devised to halt undesirable changes and promote desired ones in the community, and that the planning agency would take some initiative in indicating the most suitable policy measures. Specific inducements to encourage private actions as well as direct public measures would be needed.

Much of the determination of community policy will evolve through the political process. In a pluralistic society such as ours, there are many conflicting values and there is, as a result, competition among goals. The competition will be expressed and settled largely through politics.

The planning agency, however, can analyze alternative policies. It can help determine what benefits can be achieved as against what costs will be incurred by different specific policies.

Politicians could be given detailed information on the advantages and disadvantages of alternative courses of action to achieve desired goals. Planners should be prepared to say to politicians—if you wish to do such and such, then such and such consequences are likely to result. The planning agency would not be usurping the task of political decision-making but it would be making clear what the implications of alternative policy decisions are, so that more meaningful policy choices can be made. The planning agency, furthermore, can serve as the instrument for making known the policy choices once they are made. The planning agency, by suggesting revisions to policymakers on the basis of changed conditions, can encourage periodic presentations of community development policy. Probably a coherent development policy statement should be consciously revealed each year through the mass media of communication.

4. *The Detailed Development Plan Function.* The planning agency as the preparer of a short-range comprehensive plan spelling out specific actions to be taken.

The gap between the developmental policies of government discussed above and a long-range master plan for the future community can be bridged by the preparation of short-run plans, of five to ten years in time span. The development plan would link measures to deal with current problems with long-range proposals to attain community goals.

For many politicians and businessmen the master plan is too generalized and too remote to seem real. For planners, on the other hand, ameliorative measures which attack symptoms rather than basic problems are too piece-meal, too hastily considered to seem worthwhile. I suggest the short-run development plan as that compromise between immediate problems and future expectations which will permit coherent policy effectuation. This type of plan preparation will require detailed, timed and localized pro-gramming of governmental policies for private as well as for public actions. Detailed cost estimates of private as well as public development, and specific administrative and legal measures to carry out the programs will have to be worked out.

Long-range comprehensive plans commonly reveal a desired state of affairs. They rarely specify the detailed courses of action needed to achieve that desired state. By their long-range nature they cannot do so. The development plan, in contrast, will indicate the specific changes in land use programmed for each year, the rate of new growth, the public facilities to be built, the structures to be removed, the private investment required, the extent and sources of public funds to be raised, the tax and other local incentives to encourage private behavior requisite to the plan. The development plan—which incidentally in a more limited form is required by law in England—would have to be acted upon each year and made an official act for the subsequent year, much as a capital budget is put into law. Revised yearly it would become the central guide to land use control, to public budgeting and to appropriate private actions to achieve directed community improvement.

5. *The Feed-back Review Function.* The planning agency as analyzer of the consequences of program and project activities in order to guide future action.

Currently, we in planning agencies have no systematic means of analyz-ing the effect of planning measures or programs of action. It is astonishing, for example, that we have never analyzed the effects of zoning. We have never studied what the effects of this interference in the land markets have been on the monopoly position of different kinds of businesses, on the costs of land, on the encouragement or discouragement of certain types of development.

I suggest that we maintain a constant feed-back of information on the intended and the unintended consequences of programs that are adopted locally. For example, if a new area is developed in the central business district with new office buildings, shopping facilities, and cultural activities, we ought to assess the unintended effects as well as the intended ones of just what happens to the older, existing sections of the central business district and to the surrounding area. Does the new development serve as catalyst and stimulator of further improvements or does it drain off activities from the remainder of the district? These kinds of questions must be asked and answered so that we can learn from our experiences and can adjust our future programming and planning.

The more such a review function is performed, the more readily it can be performed. As a body of review knowledge is built up on the parking effects of highways, on the use made of playgrounds, on whether public housing and redevelopment projects achieve their objectives, on the impact of off-street loading ordinances, the more simply can new measures be gauged.

IMPLICATIONS OF THESE FUNCTIONS FOR PLANNING AGENCIES

This may sound like a formidable range of new or at least much enlarged functions. Whether such proposals are practical depends on the situation in particular cities.

I have made a plea that we consider adding certain functions intermediate between ad hoc decisions on a subdivision plat, for example, and long-range comprehensive planning. The capital budget and program in current city planning practice comes closest to this intermediate position. Of course I believe that the functions I have suggested are ones that would be of great benefit to local government and to community development. However, the functions I mentioned could be lodged in various existing or possible municipal agencies. Assuming these functions have merit, I am convinced that the planning agency should be the appropriate niche for them. This is for us in the A.I.P. to decide, or it may be decided for us. We will not have a great deal of time in which to decide. Two cities, a large one and a moderate-sized one, both known in recent years for their good government, are establishing posts called "development coordinator". Should this responsibility not have been delegated to or assumed by city planning? It is too early to say that this is prophetic of a trend. It is not too early, however, to say that planners have the opportunity to take on the development coordination function, to extend their range from the generalized plan on the one hand and the day-to-day demands on the other to the intermediate type of sustained on-going planning activities I have suggested.

But a planning agency capable of achieving some of the functions I have suggested today will require far greater specialization than we have ever had in municipal planning. It is true also that more planners will be required by specialized agencies in transportation, housing and other fields. They will be required especially in such agencies if the functions I suggest above develop. However, the specialization will be required mostly by the planning agencies themselves to prepare detailed development plans, perpetual inventories of market characteristics and the other tasks demanded. It will require personnel with joint specialization, or more properly, people who are specialists in a particular field and generalists in planning. Joint designer-planners, statistician-planners, highway expert-planners, real property lawyer-planners, utility engineer-planners and other dually trained personnel will be necessary. Incentives will have to be provided to enable people willingly to acquire such dual background—in other words, we will have to pay them as well as offer intellectual satisfactions and the satisfactions which come from socially useful work.

But if we do extend our planning functions—and even if we merely try to fulfill our present tasks as we see them—we need a level of budget for local planning of a kind we have never seen before. The planner currently is responsible for advising on expenditures running into hundreds of millions of dollars and on programs intimately affecting the lives of thousands, or in some cases, millions, of people. Decisions of such far-reaching consequences should not be financed through sub-standard salaries, blighted budgets and penny-pinched research. It is true that planning costs our local communities in the United States between $7\frac{1}{2}$ and 10 million dollars annually. But this is insignificant when a single mile of an expressway in a single city may cost twice that much. It is unneccesary for me to point out that the total annual expenditure on city planning in the United States is less than the cost of a single public building or a fraction of the budget of my own and other academic institutions or that some of the efficiencies which can be derived from city planning in even a single city could pay for the entire cost of city planning in the country.

I do not know how much the additional functions I have suggested would cost. Costs would vary, of course, with the thoroughness of performing each function and with the size of the community. (I have completely side-stepped the issue of whether the planning agency should also attempt to administer or to oversee the short-range development plans, and if so, to what degree.) However, such planning will clearly be very costly.

My own basic premise is that good staff is essential to the performance of planning functions and good staff is expensive staff. I agree completely with the statement in the Schuster report of Great Britain that "more than ever before the planning authorities need to recruit people with first-class intellectual qualities and first-class educational attainments. Everything else that we have to say is secondary in importance to this".

It is to the credit of planning that we have been able to attract people so far through the challenge of the field rather than the remuneration offered them. However, we must recognize that just as our universities and colleges cannot well exist from the subsidy of low salaries, so planning and other governmental activities cannot sustain high quality work through the subsidy of underpaid labor. Beardsley Ruml recently advocated paying professors as much as $30,000 a year. We should hardly be expected to feel that the top jobs in planning should pay less than that.

I preambled my comments tonight with a thumbnail sketch of the natural history of all professions. Each attempts to get for itself a bigger share of the pie of responsibility, of status, of resources and of income. Just within this last week a colleague, a neighbor, and a third person whom I did not know, made the following claims in the press: The race relations expert said discrimination was America's Number One problem. The criminologist said the rising wave of juvenile crime was America's Number One problem. The third person—the psychiatric administrator—said mental health was America's Number One problem.

But these claims are not true. Naturally, you and I as city planners are convinced the Number One problem of America is the development of America's cities, their housing, their transportation and all the other elements that make them viable.

In conclusion, as an imperialist for the profession I have computed that about one-half of one per cent of municipal expenditures in the United States could result in an expenditure for planning of almost ten times what it is now. Such an expenditure I feel sure would clearly enable us to do our day-to-day jobs, to do long-range planning, and to add major substance to our work through the on-going middle-range type of comprehensive planning I have described. Since Chicago fifty years ago, we have urged others to make no little plans. Let's make no little plans for the development of our own profession in terms of resources, in terms of public support, in terms of education, and in terms of laying claim to emerging new functions.

Ends and Means in Planning*

Edward C. Banfield

THE word "planning" is given a bewildering variety of meanings. To some
it means socialism. To others the layout and design of cities. To still others
regional development schemes like TVA, measures to control the business
cycle, or "scientific management" in industry. It would be easy to over-
emphasize what these activities have in common; their differences are
certainly more striking than their similarities. Nevertheless, it may be that
there is a method of making decisions which is to some extent common to
all these fields and to others as well and that the logical structure of this
method can usefully be elaborated as a theory of planning.

Such an attempt leads at once to the action frame of reference, the
means-ends schema, and the usual model of rational choice. An actor (who
may be a person or an organization) is considered as being oriented towards
the attainment of ends. Planning is the process by which he selects a
course of action (a set of means) for the attainment of his ends. It is "good"
planning if these means are likely to attain the ends or maximize the chances
of their attainment. It is by the process of rational choice that the best
adaptation of means to ends is likely to be achieved.

In this article we propose first to develop sufficiently these common
conceptions to provide a simple theory of planning, one which is essentially
a definition. It will be descriptive in conception and will deal with how
planning would have to be done in order to achieve the fullest attainment of
the ends sought, not how it actually is done (this latter would be a theory
of the sociology of planning). We shall then discuss the argument that the

* Reprinted from the *International Social Science Journal*, Vol. XI, No. 3, 1959,
with the permission of Unesco.

139

procedures of organizations do not in fact even roughly approximate those described in the theoretical model; this argument will be illustrated with brief reference to a particular case which the author and a colleague have described elsewhere.[1] We shall then consider the question of why it is that organizations do so little planning and rational decision-making.

I

The concept of rational choice has been expounded with great rigour and subtlety.[2] Here a much simplified approach will suffice; a rational decision is one made in the following manner: (a) the decision-maker lists all the opportunities for action open to him; (b) he identifies all the consequences which would follow from the adoption of each of the possible actions; and (c) he selects the action which would be followed by the preferred set of consequences. According to this definition, no choice can ever be perfectly rational, for there are usually a very great—perhaps an infinite—number of possible actions open to the actor and the consequences of any one of them would ramify *ad infinitum*. No decision-maker could have the knowledge (or the time!) to evaluate even a small fraction of the actions open to him. It is possible, however, to be more or less systematic in the canvass of alternatives and probable consequences, so that the conception is not an entirely useless one. For practical purposes, a rational decision is one in which alternatives and consequences are considered as fully as the decision-maker, given the time and other resources available to him, can afford to consider them.

A plan (unless we depart very far from customary usage) is a decision with regard to a course of action. A course of action is a sequence of acts which are mutually related as means and are therefore viewed as a unit; it is the unit which is the plan. Planning, then, as defined here, is to be distinguished from what we may call "opportunistic decision-making", which is choosing (rationally or not) actions that are not mutually related as a single means. The rational selection of a course of action, i.e. the

---

[1] The conceptual scheme and much of the ensuing argument is set forth more elaborately in Martin Meyerson and E. C. Banfield, *Politics, Planning, and the Public Interest*, Glencoe, Ill.: The Free Press, 1955.

[2] For example, Sidney Schoeffler, *The Failures of Economics*, Cambridge, Mass.: Harvard University Press, 1955, Appendix I.

making of a rational plan, involves essentially the same procedure as any rational choice: every possible course of action must be listed, all the consequences which would follow from each course must be identified, and that course selected the consequences of which are preferred.

The process by which a plan is rationally made may conveniently be described under four main headings:

1. *Analysis of the situation.* The planner must lay down in prospect every possible course of action which would lead to the attainment of the ends sought. His task is to imagine how the actor may get from where he is to where he wants to be, but his imagination must work within certain conditions which are fixed by the situation, especially by the resources at his disposal (not merely possessions, of course, but legal and other authority, information, time, executive skill, and so on) and by the obstacles in his way. His opportunity area consists of the courses of action "really" open to him, i.e. those which he is not precluded from taking by some limiting condition. It may be, of course, that he has no opportunity area at all—that there is absolutely no way by which the ends sought may be achieved —or that the opportunity area is a very restricted one.

2. *End reduction and elaboration.* An end is an image of a future state of affairs towards which action is oriented. The formulation of the end may be extremely vague and diffuse. If so it may have to be reduced to specific or "operational" terms before it can serve as a criterion of choice in the concrete circumstances. The formulation of the end may be elliptical; in this case the planner must clearly explain the meaning in full. An end may be thought of as having both active and contextual elements. The active elements are those features of the future situation which are actively sought; the contextual are those which, while not actively sought, nevertheless cannot be sacrificed without loss. (The man who burned down his house in order to get the rats out of the cellar ignored a contextual end in his effort to achieve an active one.) The planner's task is to identify and clarify the contextual as well as the active components of the ends. If they are not fully consistent, he must also "order" them, i.e. he must discover the relative value to be attached to each under the various concrete circumstances envisaged in the courses of action or, as an economist would say, prepare an "indifference map".

3. *The design of courses of action.* Courses of action may have a more or a

less general character. At the most general level, a developing course of action implies a description of the "key" actions to be taken or the commitments to be made. These constitute the premises upon which any less general course of action is based, e.g. at the "programme" or "operations" levels. In other words, decisions of a less general character represent choices from among those alternatives which are not precluded by the more general decisions already taken. A developing course of action may be chosen arbitrarily or capriciously and a programmed course of action based upon it may then be selected with elaborate consideration of alternatives and consequences: in such a case there is "functional rationality" but "substantive irrationality".

4. *The comparative evaluation of consequences.* If the plan is to be rational, all consequences—not merely those intended by the planner—must be taken into account. To a large extent, then, good planning is a search for unintended consequences which might follow from the attainment of the active or contextual ends. The planner cannot pick and choose among the consequences of a given course of action: he must take them all, the unwanted along with the wanted, as a set. Their evaluation therefore must be in terms of the net value attached to each set. If all values could be expressed in terms of a common numerical index (e.g. prices) this would raise no great difficulties. In practice, however, the planner must somehow strike a balance between essentially unlike intangibles. He must decide, for example, whether x amount of damage to a beautiful view is justified by y amount of increase in driving safety.

II

So far the discussion has been intended to make reasonably clear what is meant by "rational planning". If we now take this definition as a yardstick and apply it to organizational behaviour in the real world we are struck at once by two facts: there is very little planning, and there is even less rationality.

In general organizations engage in opportunistic decision-making rather than in planning: rather than laying out a course of action which will lead all the way to the attainment of their ends, they extemporize, meeting each crisis as it arises. In the United States even the largest industries do not look forward more than five or ten years. In government, the American planning horizon is usually even less distant. Moreover, such plans as are made are not the outcome of a careful consideration of alternative courses of action and their probable consequences. As a rule the most important decisions—those constituting the developing course of action—are the result of accident rather than design; they are the unintended outcome of a social process rather than the conscious product of deliberation and calculation. If there is an element of rationality it is "functional" rather than "substantive".

A few years ago the writer and a colleague set out to describe how decisions were made by a large and progressive public body, the Chicago Housing Authority.[3] We knew that the housing agency was one of the best administered in the United States (my colleague, a professor of planning on leave from a university, was in fact its director of planning) and we therefore assumed that if we observed closely enough we could see how a large organization lays out alternative courses of action, evaluates their probable consequences, and so arrives at what is, in the circumstances, a rational decision. We did not expect to find that the model described above was being followed consciously or in detail, of course, but we did suppose that the course followed would roughly approximate it.

What we found was entirely different from what we anticipated. The authority might conceivably have sought to attain its end by one of various courses of action. (It might, for example, have given rental subsidies to enable people with low incomes to buy or rent housing in the market. Or it might have built small housing projects for eventual sale. Or again, following the example of the United Kingdom, it might have built new towns in the hinterland beyond the metropolis.) No major alternative to what it was doing was considered. The developing course of action—to build large slum-clearance projects—was treated as fixed, this course of action had been arrived at cumulatively, so to speak, from a number of unrelated sources: Congress had made certain decisions, the Illinois legislature certain others, the City Council certain others, and so on. Unless the housing authority was to embark upon the unpromising task of persuading all these bodies to change their minds, the development "plan" had to be taken as settled—settled on the basis of decisions made without regard to each other. "The process by which a housing programme for Chicago

[3] Martin Meyerson and E. C. Banfield, *op. cit.*

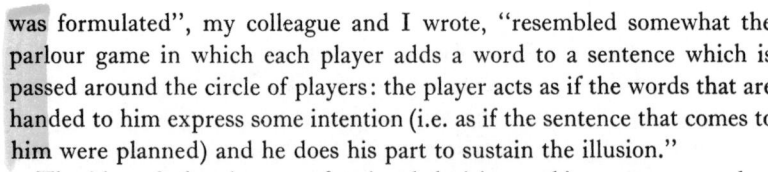

was formulated", my colleague and I wrote, "resembled somewhat the parlour game in which each player adds a word to a sentence which is passed around the circle of players: the player acts as if the words that are handed to him express some intention (i.e. as if the sentence that comes to him were planned) and he does his part to sustain the illusion."

The idea of planning, or of rational decision-making, assumes a clear and consistent set of ends. The housing authority, we found, had nothing of the kind. The law expressed the objectives of housing policy in terms so general as to be virtually meaningless and the five unpaid commissioners who exercised supervision over the "general policy" of the organization never asked themselves exactly what they were trying to accomplish. Had they done so they would doubtless have been perplexed, for the law said nothing about where, or in what manner, they were to discover which ends, or whose ends, the agency was to serve.

The agency had an end-system of a kind, but its ends were, for the most part, vague, implicit and fragmentary. Each of the commissioners—the Catholic, the Jew, the Negro, the businessman, the labour leader—had his own idea of them, or of some of them, and the professional staff had still another idea. There were a good many contradictions among such ends as were generally agreed upon. Some of these contradictions went deep into fundamental questions. For example, the authority wanted to build as much housing as possible for people with low incomes; but it also wanted to avoid furthering the spread of racial segregation. These two objectives were in conflict and there was no way of telling which should be subordinated or to what extent.

Most of the considerations which finally governed the selection of sites and of the type of projects were "political" rather than "technical". A site could not be considered for a project unless it was large enough, unless suitable foundations for high-rise construction could be sunk, and so on. But, once these minimal technical conditions were met, for the most part the remaining considerations were of a very different kind: was the site in the ward of an alderman who would support the project or oppose it?

III

Unfortunately there does not exist a body of case studies which permits of the comparisons that would be interesting—comparisons, say, between large organizations and small, public and private, single-purpose and multipurpose, American and other. Despite this lack, some general observations are possible. While the Chicago Housing Authority may be a rather extreme case, there are compelling reasons which militate against planning and rationality on the part of all organizations.

1. Organizations do not lay out courses of action because the future is highly uncertain. There are very few matters about which reliable predictions can be made for more than five years ahead. City planners, for example, can know very little about certain key variables with which they must deal: how many children, for example, will require schools or playgrounds ten years hence? Recent experience has shown how little even demographic predictions can be trusted. The Chicago Housing Authority could not possibly have anticipated before the war the problems it would have to face after it. Some people, knowing that they cannot anticipate the future but feeling that they ought to try, resolve the conflict by making plans and storing them away where they will be forgotten.

Not only do the conditions within which the planner works change rapidly, but so also do the ends for which he is planning. A public housing programme which is begun for slum clearance may, before the buildings are occupied, be primarily an instrument for the reform of race relations. It need hardly be said that the means most appropriate to one end are not likely to be most appropriate to the other.

When an organization is engaged in a game of strategy with an opponent the element of change is likely to be of special importance. The opponent tries to force change upon the organization; the organization's actions must then be a series of counter-measures. In the nature of the case these cannot be planned. To a considerable extent all organizations—and not especially those engaged in "competitive" activities—are constantly responding to change which others are endeavouring to impose upon them.

2. When it is possible to decide upon a course of action well in advance it is likely to be imprudent to do so, or at least to do so publicly (as, of course, a public agency ordinarily must). For to advertise in advance the actions that are to be taken is to invite opposition to them and to give the opposition a great advantage. This is a principle which many city planners have learned to their cost.

3. Organizations, especially public ones, do not consider fundamental alternatives because usually there are circumstances which preclude them, at least in the short run, from doing anything very different from what they

are already doing. Some of these circumstances may be the result of choices which the organization has already made; others may be externally imposed. The housing authority, for example, could not cease building its own housing projects and begin giving cash subsidies to private builders: public opinion favoured projects rather than subsidies and the agency had recruited and trained a staff which was project minded and not sub-sidy minded. The organization's commitments, and often other obstacles as well, may be liquidated over time and a new course of action initiated. But the liquidation is expensive: it may be cheaper to retain for a while an obsolescent course of action than to incur the costs of instituting a new one. If the organization could see far enough into the future it might liquidate its commitments gradually, thus making an economical transition to a new course of action. As a rule, however, it cannot anticipate very clearly or surely what it will want to do a few years hence. Moreover, if it acknowledges its doubt about the wisdom of what it is presently doing it risks giving aid and comfort to its enemies and damaging its own morale.

4. Organizations have a decided preference for present rather than future effects. One might think that public organizations, at least, would be more willing than are persons to postpone satisfactions—that, in the language of economics, they would discount the future less heavily. They do not seem to, however, and this is another reason why they do not plan ahead.

5. The reason they discount the future so heavily is, perhaps, that they must continually be preoccupied with the present necessity of maintaining what Barnard has called the "economy of incentives". That is to say, the heads of the organization are constantly under the necessity of devising a scheme of incentives by means of which they can elicit the contributions of activity required to keep it going. Any scheme of incentives is inherently unstable. It must be continually rebuilt according to the needs of the moment. "Indeed, it is so delicate and complex", says Barnard, "that rarely if ever, is the scheme of incentives determinable in advance of application."[4]

6. The end of organizational maintenance—of keeping the organization going for the sake of keeping it going—is usually more important than any substantive end. The salmon perishes in order to give birth to its young. Organizations, however, are not like salmon; they much prefer sterility to death. Given the supremacy of the end of organizational maintenance,

[4] Chester I. Barnard, *The Function of the Executive*, Cambridge, Mass.: Harvard University Press, 1938, p. 158.

opportunistic decision-making rather than planning is called for. Indeed, from the standpoint of maintenance the organization may do well to make as few long-term commitments as possible. Advantage may lie in flexibility.

7. The end-system of an organization is rarely, if ever, a clear and coherent picture of a desirable future toward which action is to be directed. Usually it is a set of vague platitudes and pious cant the function of which is to justify the existence of the organization in the eyes of its members and of outsiders. The stated ends are propaganda, not criteria to guide action. What John Dewey said in *Human Nature and Conduct* of a person applies as well to an organization: it does not shoot in order to hit a target; it sets up a target in order to facilitate the act of shooting.

8. It follows that serious reflection on the ends of the organization, and especially any attempt to state ends in precise and realistic terms, is likely to be destructive to the organization. To unify and to stir the spirit they must be stated in vague and high-sounding terms. When they are reduced to their real content they lose their magic and, worse, they become controversial. Had it attempted to formulate a set of ends relating to racial policy the Chicago Housing Authority would certainly have destroyed itself at once.

9. It follows also that organizations do not as a rule attempt to maximize the attainment of their ends or (to say the same thing in different words) to use resources efficiently. If the ultimate end is the maintenance of the organization, how indeed is "maximization" possible? The organization may endeavour to store up the largest possible quantity of reserves of a kind which may be used for its maintenance at a later time (e.g. to accumulate "good will", or the wherewithal to procure it, in advance of need). In this case there is a quantity—utility—which is being maximized. But if substantive ends are regarded, Herbert A. Simon is right in saying that organizations "satisfice" (i.e. look for a course of action that is satisfactory or good enough) rather than maximize.[5]

[5] See the discussion of this in the preface to the second edition of *Administrative Behaviour*, New York: Macmillan, 1957, pp. xxv–xxv and the references given there to Simon's more technical writings. Simon says (p. xxiv) that human beings "satisfice" because "they do not have the wit to maximize". This does not seem to be quite the right way of putting it. If the trouble is merely that they lack wit to make the necessary calculations, then they are trying to maximize and failing or, in another view of the matter, succeeding given their limitations. The point being made here, at any rate, is not that organizations lack wit but that they lack will to maximize; in other words, it is the nature of their end-system rather than their ability to compute which is here in question.

10. Laying out courses of action, clarifying ends, and evaluating alternatives are costly procedures which take time and money and cannot be carried out without the active participation of the chief executives. However great may be the resulting gain to the organization, full attention to the present crisis—assuming the supreme importance of organizational maintenance—is likely to result in far greater gain. Paradoxical as it may seem, if all costs are taken into account it may be rational to devote very little attention to alternatives and their consequences.[6]

11. Rationality, as defined above, is less likely to be found in public than in private organizations. One reason for this is that the public agency's ends often reflect compromise among essentially incompatible interests. This is not an accidental or occasional feature of public organization in a democracy. Where conflict exists and every conflicting element has to be given its due, it is almost inevitable that there be an end-system which "rides madly off in all directions".

12. Whether or not conflict is built into the end-system, the end-systems of public organizations are vastly more complex than those of private ones. Contextual ends, in particular, are far more numerous. A private builder, for example, does not concern himself with the effect of high-rise construction on birth rates and family life, but a public one must. The more complex the end-system of the organization, the harder to devise courses of action, the more consequences must be evaluated, and the greater the likelihood that some ends will be sacrificed in the endeavour to attain others. That rationality, in the sense of the definition, becomes more difficult to achieve is of course not an argument against public enterprise: perhaps private enterprise does not take enough ends into consideration.

IV

The reader may by now have come to the conclusion that since organizations are so little given to the rational adaptation of means to ends nothing is to be gained from constructing such a model of planning as that set forth above.

Certainly this would be the case if one's interest were mainly sociological. For the study of how organizations actually behave an altogether different conceptual scheme would probably be most rewarding.

[6] See Sidney Schoeffler, *op. cit.*

But if the interest is normative—if it is in describing how organizations would have to act in order to be in some sense more effective or efficient—it is hard to see how reference to such a model can be avoided or, indeed, why its lack of realism should be considered a defect. And students of administration are, after all, chiefly interested in describing organization only so that they may improve it. Their problem, then, is to find a theoretical model which, without being so far removed from reality as to be a mere plaything, is yet far enough removed to suggest how organizations may be made to function better.

It would be a contribution to the development of a suitable theory if there were a body of detailed case studies, all of them built on a common conceptual scheme so as to allow of significant analytical comparisons. It would be particularly helpful to have a full account of the workings of an organization which is so placed as to be able to encourage the fullest development of planning and rational choice: one, let us say, with a few clearly defined purposes, free of political and other conflict, blessed with a large opportunity area, and headed by persons who make a realistic attempt to be rational. How fully and clearly would such an organization explain and define its ends? How often and how elaborately would it consider alternative courses of action at the various levels of generality? How exhaustively would it inquire into probable consequences, the unintended as well as the intended? Would it perhaps carry planning and rationality beyond the point where marginal cost equals marginal return? And would it "maximize" or, to use Herbert Simon's term, would it "satisfice"?

The Science of "Muddling Through"*

Charles E. Lindblom

SUPPOSE an administrator is given responsibility for formulating policy with respect to inflation. He might start by trying to list all related values in order of importance, e.g. full employment, reasonable business profit, protection of small savings, prevention of a stock market crash. Then all possible policy outcomes could be rated as more or less efficient in attaining a maximum of these values. This would of course require a prodigious inquiry into values held by members of society and an equally prodigious set of calculations on how much of each value is equal to how much of each other value. He could then proceed to outline all possible policy alternatives. In a third step, he would undertake systematic comparison of his multitude of alternatives to determine which attains the greatest amount of values.

In comparing policies, he would take advantage of any theory available that generalized about classes of policies. In considering inflation, for example, he would compare all policies in the light of the theory of prices. Since no alternatives are beyond his investigation, he would consider strict central control and the abolition of all prices and markets on the one hand and elimination of all public controls with reliance completely on the free market on the other, both in the light of whatever theoretical generalizations he could find on such hypothetical economies.

Finally, he would try to make the choice that would in fact maximize his values.

An alternative line of attack would be to set as his principal objective,

* Reprinted by permission of the *Public Administration Review*, Spring 1959.

either explicitly or without conscious thought, the relatively simple goal of keeping prices level. This objective might be compromised or complicated by only a few other goals, such as full employment. He would in fact disregard most other social values as beyond his present interest, and he would for the moment not even attempt to rank the few values that he regarded as immediately relevant. Were he pressed, he would quickly admit that he was ignoring many related values and many possible important consequences of his policies.

As a second step, he would outline those relatively few policy alternatives that occurred to him. He would then compare them. In comparing his limited number of alternatives, most of them familiar from past controversies, he would not ordinarily find a body of theory precise enough to carry him through a comparison of their respective consequences. Instead he would rely heavily on the record of past experience with small policy steps to predict the consequences of similar steps extended into the future.

Moreover, he would find that the policy alternatives combined objectives or values in different ways. For example, one policy might offer price-level stability at the cost of some risk of unemployment; another might offer less price stability but also less risk of unemployment. Hence, the next step in his approach—the final selection—would combine into one the choice among values and the choice among instruments for reaching values. It would not, as in the first method of policy-making, approximate a more mechanical process of choosing the means that best satisfied goals that were previously clarified and ranked. Because practitioners of the second approach expect to achieve their goals only partially, they would expect to repeat endlessly the sequence just described, as conditions and aspirations changed and as accuracy of prediction improved.

BY ROOT OR BY BRANCH

For complex problems, the first of these two approaches is of course impossible. Although such an approach can be described, it cannot be practiced except for relatively simple problems and even then only in a somewhat modified form. It assumes intellectual capacities and sources of information that men simply do not possess, and it is even more absurd as an approach to policy when the time and money that can be allocated to a policy problem is limited, as is always the case. Of particular importance to public administrators is the fact that public agencies are in effect usually instructed not to practice the first method. That is to say, their prescribed functions and constraints—the politically or legally possible—restrict their attention to relatively few values and relatively few alternative policies among the countless alternatives that might be imagined. It is the second method that is practiced.

Curiously, however, the literatures of decision-making, policy formulation, planning, and public administration formalize the first approach rather than the second, leaving public administrators who handle complex decisions in the position of practicing what few preach. For emphasis I run some risk of overstatement. True enough, the literature is well aware of limits on man's capacities and of the inevitability that policies will be approached in some such style as the second. But attempts to formalize rational policy formulation—to lay out explicitly the necessary steps in the process—usually describe the first approach and not the second.[1]

The common tendency to describe policy formulation even for complex problems as though it followed the first approach has been strengthened by the attention given to, and successes enjoyed by, operations research, statistical decision theory, and systems analysis. The hallmarks of these procedures, typical of the first approach, are clarity of objective, explicitness of evaluation, a high degree of comprehensiveness of overview, and, wherever possible, quantification of values for mathematical analysis. But these advanced procedures remain largely the appropriate techniques of relatively small-scale problem-solving where the total number of variables to be considered is small and value problems restricted. Charles Hitch, head of the Economics Division of RAND Corporation, one of the leading centers for application of these techniques, has written:

> I would make the empirical generalization from my experience at RAND and elsewhere that operations research is the art of sub-optimizing, i.e. of solving some lower-level problems, and that difficulties increase and our special competence diminishes by an order of magnitude with every level of decision making we attempt to ascend. The sort of simple explicit model which operations researchers are so proficient in using can certainly reflect most of the significant factors influencing traffic control on the George Washington

---

[1] James G. March and Herbert A. Simon similarly characterize the literature. They also take some important steps, as have Simon's recent articles, to describe a less heroic model of policy-making. See *Organizations*, John Wiley & Sons, 1958, p. 137.

Bridge, but the proportion of the relevant reality which we can represent by any such model or models in studying, say, a major foreign-policy decision, appears to be almost trivial.[2]

Accordingly, I propose in this paper to clarify and formalize the second method, much neglected in the literature. This might be described as the method of *successive limited comparisons*. I will contrast it with the first approach, which might be called the rational-comprehensive method.[3] More impressionistically and briefly—and therefore generally used in this article—they could be characterized as the branch method and root method, the former continually building out from the current situation, step-by-step and by small degrees; the latter starting from fundamentals anew each time, building on the past only as experience is embodied in a theory, and always prepared to start completely from the ground up.

Let us put the characteristics of the two methods side by side in simplest terms.

Rational-Comprehensive (Root)	Successive Limited Comparisons (Branch)
1a. Clarification of values or objectives distinct from and usually prerequisite to empirical analysis of alternative policies.	1b. Selection of value goals and empirical analysis of the needed action are not distinct from one another but are closely intertwined.
2a. Policy-formulation is therefore approached through means-end analysis: first the ends are isolated, then the means to achieve them are sought.	2b. Since means and ends are not distinct, means-end analysis is often inappropriate or limited.

[2] "Operations research and national planning—a dissent", *Operations Research*, Vol. 5, p. 718 (October 1957). Hitch's dissent is from particular points made in the article to which his paper is a reply; his claim that operations research is for low-level problems is widely accepted.

For examples, of the kind of problems to which operations research is applied, see C. W. Churchman, R. L. Ackoff and E. L. Arnoff, *Introduction to Operations Research*, John Wiley & Sons, 1957; and J. F. McCloskey and J. M. Coppinger (eds.), *Operations Research for Management*, Vol. II, The Johns Hopkins Press, 1956.

[3] I am assuming that administrators often make policy and advise in the making of policy and am treating decision-making and policy-making as synonymous for purposes of this paper.

3a. The test of a "good" policy is that it can be shown to be the most appropriate means to desired ends.

3b. The test of a "good" policy is typically that various analysts find themselves directly agreeing on a policy (without their agreeing that it is the most appropriate means to an agreed objective).

4a. Analysis is comprehensive; every important relevant factor is taken into account.

4b. Analysis is drastically limited:
   (i) Important possible outcomes are neglected.
   (ii) Important alternative potential policies are neglected.
   (iii) Important affected values are neglected.

5a. Theory is often heavily relied upon.

5b. A succession of comparisons greatly reduces or eliminates reliance on theory.

Assuming that the root method is familiar and understandable, we proceed directly to clarification of its alternative by contrast. In explaining the second, we shall be describing how most administrators do in fact approach complex questions, for the root method, the "best" way as a blueprint or model, is in fact not workable for complex policy questions, and administrators are forced to use the method of successive limited comparisons.

INTERTWINING EVALUATION AND EMPIRICAL ANALYSIS (1b)

The quickest way to understand how values are handled in the method of successive limited comparisons is to see how the root method often breaks down in *its* handling of values or objectives. The idea that values should be clarified, and in advance of the examination of alternative policies, is appealing. But what happens when we attempt it for complex social problems? The first difficulty is that on many critical values or objectives, citizens disagree, congressmen disagree, and public administrators disagree. Even where a fairly specific objective is prescribed for the administrator, there remains considerable room for disagreement on sub-objectives. Consider, for example, the conflict with respect to locating public housing, described in Meyerson and Banfield's study of the Chicago

Housing Authority[4]—disagreement which occurred despite the clear objective of providing a certain number of public housing units in the city. Similarly conflicting are objectives in highway location, traffic control, minimum wage administration, development of tourist facilities in national parks, or insect control.

Administrators cannot escape these conflicts by ascertaining the majority's preference, for preferences have not been registered on most issues; indeed, there often *are* no preferences in the absence of public discussion sufficient to bring an issue to the attention of the electorate. Furthermore, there is a question of whether intensity of feeling should be considered as well as the number of persons preferring each alternative. By the impossibility of doing otherwise, administrators often are reduced to deciding policy without clarifying objectives first.

Even when an administrator resolves to follow his own values as a criterion for decisions, he often will not know how to rank them when they conflict with one another, as they usually do. Suppose, for example, that an administrator must relocate tenants living in tenements scheduled for destruction. One objective is to empty the buildings fairly promptly, another is to find suitable accommodation for persons displaced, another is to avoid friction with residents in other areas in which a large influx would be unwelcome, another is to deal with all concerned through persuasion if possible, and so on.

How does one state even to himself the relative importance of these partially conflicting values? A simple ranking of them is not enough; one needs ideally to know how much of one value is worth sacrificing for some of another value. The answer is that typically the administrator chooses—and must choose—directly among policies in which these values are combined in different ways. He cannot first clarify his values and then choose among policies.

A more subtle third point underlies both the first two. Social objectives do not always have the same relative values. One objective may be highly prized in one circumstance, another in another circumstance. If, for example, an administrator values highly both the dispatch with which his agency can carry through its projects *and* good public relations, it matters little which of the two possibly conflicting values he favors in some abstract

[4] Martin Meyerson and Edward C. Banfield, *Politics, Planning and the Public Interest*, The Free Press, 1955.

or general sense. Policy questions arise in forms which put to administrators such a question as: Given the degree to which we are or are not already achieving the values of dispatch and the values of good public relations, is it worth sacrificing a little speed for a happier clientele, or is it better to risk offending the clientele so that we can get on with our work? The answer to such a question varies with circumstances.

The value problem is, as the example shows, always a problem of adjustments at a margin. But there is no practicable way to state marginal objectives or values except in terms of particular policies. That one value is preferred to another in one decision situation does not mean that it will be preferred in another decision situation in which it can be had only at great sacrifice of another value. Attempts to rank or order values in general and abstract terms so that they do not shift from decision to decision end up by ignoring the relevant marginal preferences. The significance of this third point thus goes very far. Even if all administrators had at hand an agreed set of values, objectives, and constraints, and an agreed ranking of these values, objectives, and constraints, their marginal values in actual choice situations would be impossible to formulate.

Unable consequently to formulate the relevant values first and then choose among policies to achieve them, administrators must choose directly among alternative policies that offer different marginal combinations of values. Somewhat paradoxically, the only practicable way to disclose one's relevant marginal values even to oneself is to describe the policy one chooses to achieve them. Except roughly and vaguely, I know of no way to describe—or even to understand—what my relative evaluations are for, say, freedom and security, speed and accuracy in governmental decisions, or low taxes and better schools than to describe my preferences among specific policy choices that might be made between the alternatives in each of the pairs.

In summary, two aspects of the process by which values are actually handled can be distinguished. The first is clear: evaluation and empirical analysis are intertwined; that is, one chooses among values and among policies at one and the same time. Put a little more elaborately, one simultaneously chooses a policy to attain certain objectives and chooses the objectives themselves. The second aspect is related but distinct: the administrator focuses his attention on marginal or incremental values. Whether he is aware of it or not, he does not find general formulations of objectives very helpful and in fact makes specific marginal or incremental comparisons. Two policies, X and Y, confront him. Both promise the same degree of attainment of objectives *a, b, c, d,* and *e.* But X promises him somewhat more of *f* than does Y, while Y promises him somewhat more of *g* than does X. In choosing between them, he is in fact offered the alternative of a marginal or incremental amount of *f* at the expense of a marginal or incremental amount of *g.* The only values that are relevant to his choice are these increments by which the two policies differ; and, when he finally chooses between the two marginal values, he does so by making a choice between policies.[5]

As to whether the attempt to clarify objectives in advance of policy selection is more or less rational than the close intertwining of marginal evaluation and empirical analysis, the principal difference established is that for complex problems the first is impossible and irrelevant, and the second is both possible and relevant. The second is possible because the administrator need not try to analyze any values except the values by which alternative policies differ and need not be concerned with them except as they differ marginally. His need for information on values or objectives is drastically reduced as compared with the root method; and his capacity for grasping, comprehending, and relating values to one another is not strained beyond the breaking point.

RELATIONS BETWEEN MEANS AND ENDS (2b)

Decision-making is ordinarily formalized as a means–ends relationship: means are conceived to be evaluated and chosen in the light of ends finally selected independently of and prior to the choice of means. This is the means–ends relationship of the root method. But it follows from all that has just been said that such a means–ends relationship is possible only to the extent that values are agreed upon, are reconcilable, and are stable at the margin. Typically, therefore, such a means–ends relationship is absent from the branch method, where means and ends are simultaneously chosen.

Yet any departure from the means–ends relationship of the root method

---

[5] The line of argument is, of course, an extension of the theory of market choice, especially the theory of consumer choice, to public policy choices.

will strike some readers as inconceivable. For it will appear to them that only in such a relationship is it possible to determine whether one policy choice is better or worse than another. How can an administrator know whether he has made a wise or foolish decision if he is without prior values or objectives by which to judge his decisions? The answer to this question calls up the third distinctive difference between root and branch methods: how to decide the best policy.

THE TEST OF "GOOD" POLICY (3b)

In the root method, a decision is "correct", "good", or "rational" if it can be shown to attain some specified objective, where the objective can be specified without simply describing the decision itself. Where objectives are defined only through the marginal or incremental approach to values described above, it is still sometimes possible to test whether a policy does in fact attain the desired objectives; but a precise statement of the objectives takes the form of a description of the policy chosen or some alternative to it. To show that a policy is mistaken one cannot offer an abstract argument that important objectives are not achieved; one must instead argue that another policy is more to be preferred.

So far, the departure from customary ways of looking at problem-solving is not troublesome, for many administrators, will be quick to agree that the most effective discussion of the correctness of policy does take the form of comparison with other policies that might have been chosen. But what of the situation in which administrators cannot agree on values or objectives, either abstractly or in marginal terms? What then is the test of "good" policy? For the root method, there is no test. Agreement on objectives failing, there is no standard of "correctness". For the method of successive limited comparisons, the test is agreement on policy itself, which remains possible even when agreement on values is not.

It has been suggested that continuing agreement in Congress on the desirability of extending old-age insurance stems from liberal desires to strengthen the welfare programs of the federal government and from conservative desires to reduce union demands for private pension plans. If so, this is an excellent demonstration of the ease with which individuals of different ideologies often can agree on concrete policy. Labor mediators report a similar phenomenon: the contestants cannot agree on criteria for settling their disputes but can agree on specific proposals. Similarly, when one administrator's objective turns out to be another's means, they often can agree on policy.

Agreement on policy thus becomes the only practicable test of the policy's correctness. And for one administrator to seek to win the other over to agreement on ends as well would accomplish nothing and create quite unnecessary controversy.

If agreement directly on policy as a test for "best" policy seems a poor substitute for testing the policy against its objectives, it ought to be remembered that objectives themselves have no ultimate validity other than they are agreed upon. Hence agreement is the test of "best" policy in both methods. But where the root method requires agreement on what elements in the decision constitute objectives and on which of these objectives should be sought, the branch method falls back on agreement wherever it can be found.

In an important sense, therefore, it is not irrational for an administrator to defend a policy as good without being able to specify what it is good for.

NON-COMPREHENSIVE ANALYSIS (4b)

Ideally, rational-comprehensive analysis leaves out nothing important. But it is impossible to take everything important into consideration unless "important" is so narrowly defined that analysis is in fact quite limited. Limits on human intellectual capacities and on available information set definite limits to man's capacity to be comprehensive. In actual fact, therefore, no one can practice the rational-comprehensive method for really complex problems, and every administrator faced with a sufficiently complex problem must find ways drastically to simplify.

An administrator assisting in the formulation of agricultural economic policy cannot in the first place be competent on all possible policies. He cannot even comprehend one policy entirely. In planning a soil bank program, he cannot successfully anticipate the impact of higher or lower farm income on, say, urbanization—the possible consequent loosening of family ties, possible consequent eventual need for revisions in social security and further implications for tax problems arising out of new federal responsibilities for social security and municipal responsibilities for urban services. Nor, to follow another line of repercussions, can he work through the soil bank program's effects on prices for agricultural products in foreign markets and consequent implications for foreign markets and consequent implications for foreign relations, including those arising out of economic rivalry between the United States and the U.S.S.R.

In the method of successive limited comparisons, simplification is systematically achieved in two principal ways. First, it is achieved through limitation of policy comparisons to those policies that differ in relatively small degree from policies presently in effect. Such a limitation immediately reduces the number of alternatives to be investigated and also drastically simplifies the character of the investigation of each. For it is not necessary to undertake fundamental inquiry into an alternative and its consequences; it is necessary only to study those respects in which the proposed alternative and its consequences differ from the status quo. The empirical comparison of marginal differences among alternative policies that differ only marginally is, of course, a counterpart to the incremental or marginal comparison of values discussed above.[6]

Relevance as Well as Realism

It is a matter of common observation that in Western democracies public administrators and policy analysts in general do largely limit their analyses to incremental or marginal differences in policies that are chosen to differ only incrementally. They do not do so, however, solely because they desperately need some way to simplify their problems; they also do so in order to be relevant. Democracies change their policies almost entirely through incremental adjustments. Policy does not move in leaps and bounds.

The incremental character of political change in the United States has often been remarked. The two major political parties agree on fundamentals; they offer alternative policies to the voters only on relatively small points of difference. Both parties favor full employment, but they define it somewhat differently; both favor the development of water-power resources, but in slightly different ways; and both favor unemployment

---

[6] A more precise definition of incremental policies and a discussion of whether a change that appears "small" to one observer might be seen differently by another is to be found in my "Policy Analysis", *American Economic Review*, Vol. 48, p. 298 (June 1958).

compensation, but not the same level of benefits. Similarly, shifts of policy within a party take place largely through a series of relatively small changes, as can be seen in their only gradual acceptance of the idea of governmental responsibility for support of the unemployed, a change in party positions beginning in the early thirties and culminating in a sense in the Employment Act of 1946.

Party behavior is in turn rooted in public attitudes, and political theorists cannot conceive of democracy's surviving in the United States in the absence of fundamental agreement on potentially disruptive issues, with consequent limitation of policy debates to relatively small differences in policy.

Since the policies ignored by the administrator are politically impossible and so irrelevant, the simplification of analysis achieved by concentrating on policies that differ only incrementally is not a capricious kind of simplification. In addition, it can be argued that, given the limits on knowledge within which policy-makers are confined, simplifying by limiting the focus to small variations from present policy makes the most of available knowledge. Because policies being considered are like present and past policies, the administrator can obtain information and claim some insight. Non-incremental policy proposals are therefore typically not only politically irrelevant but also unpredictable in their consequences.

The second method of simplification of analysis is the practice of ignoring important possible consequences of possible policies, as well as the values attached to the neglected consequences. If this appears to disclose a shocking shortcoming of successive limited comparisons, it can be replied that, even if the exclusions are random, policies may nevertheless be more intelligently formulated than through futile attempts to achieve a comprehensiveness beyond human capacity. Actually, however, the exclusions, seeming arbitrary or random from one point of view, need be neither.

Achieving a Degree of Comprehensiveness

Suppose that each value neglected by one policy-making agency were a major concern of at least one other agency. In that case, a helpful division of labor would be achieved, and no agency need find its task beyond its capacities. The shortcomings of such a system would be that one agency might destroy a value either before another agency could be activated to safeguard it or in spite of another agency's efforts. But the possibility that important values may be lost is present in any form of organization, even where agencies attempt to comprehend in planning more than is humanly possible.

The virtue of such a hypothetical division of labor is that every important interest or value has its watchdog. And these watchdogs can protect the interests in their jurisdiction in two quite different ways: first, by redressing damages done by other agencies; and second, by anticipating and heading off injury before it occurs.

In a society like that of the United States in which individuals are free to combine to pursue almost any possible common interest they might have and in which government agencies are sensitive to the pressures of these groups, the system described is approximated. Almost every interest has its watchdog. Without claiming that every interest has a sufficiently powerful watchdog, it can be argued that our system often can assure a more comprehensive regard for the values of the whole society than any attempt at intellectual comprehensiveness.

In the United States, for example, no part of government attempts a comprehensive overview of policy on income distribution. A policy nevertheless evolves, and one responding to a wide variety of interests. A process of mutual adjustment among farm groups, labor unions, municipalities and school boards, tax authorities, and government agencies with responsibilities in the fields of housing, health, highways, national parks, fire, and police accomplishes a distribution of income in which particular income problems neglected at one point in the decision processes become central at another point.

Mutual adjustment is more pervasive than the explicit forms it takes in negotiation between groups; it persists through the mutual impacts of groups upon each other even where they are not in communication. For all the imperfections and latent dangers in this ubiquitous process of mutual adjustment, it will often accomplish an adaptation of policies to a wider range of interests than could be done by one group centrally.

Note, too, how the incremental pattern of policy-making fits with the multiple pressure pattern. For when decisions are only incremental—closely related to known policies, it is easier for one group to anticipate the kind of moves another might make and easier too for it to make correction for injury already accomplished.[7]

Even partisanship and narrowness, to use pejorative terms, will sometimes be assets to rational decision-making, for they can doubly insure that what one agency neglects, another will not; they specialize personnel to distinct points of view. The claim is valid that effective rational coordination of the federal administration, if possible to achieve at all, would require an agreed set of values[8]—if "rational" is defined as the practice of the root method of decision-making. But a high degree of administrative coordination occurs as each agency adjusts its policies to the concerns of the other agencies in the process of fragmented decision-making I have just described.

For all the apparent shortcomings of the incremental approach to policy alternatives with its arbitrary exclusion coupled with fragmentation, when compared to the root method, the branch method often looks far superior. In the root method, the inevitable exclusion of factors is accidental, unsystematic, and not defensible by an argument so far developed, while in the branch method the exclusions are deliberate, systematic and defensible. Ideally, of course, the root method does not exclude; in practice it must.

Nor does the branch method necessarily neglect long-run considerations and objectives. It is clear that important values must be omitted in considering policy, and sometimes the only way long-run objectives can be given adequate attention is through the neglect of short-run considerations. But the values omitted can be either long-run or short-run.

SUCCESSION OF COMPARISONS (5b)

The final distinctive element in the branch method is that the comparisons, together with the policy choice, proceed in a chronological series. Policy is not made once and for all; it is made and re-made endlessly. Policy-making is a process of successive approximation to some desired

---

[7] The link between the practice of the method of successive limited comparisons and mutual adjustment of interests in a highly fragmented decision-making process adds a new facet to pluralist theories of government and administration.

[8] Herbert Simon, Donald W. Smithburg, and Victor A. Thompson, *Public Administration*, Alfred A. Knopf, 1950, p. 434.

objectives in which what is desired itself continues to change under reconsideration.

Making policy is at best a very rough process. Neither social scientists, nor politicians, nor public administrators yet know enough about the social world to avoid repeated error in predicting the consequences of policy moves. A wise policy-maker consequently expects that his policies will achieve only part of what he hopes and at the same time will produce unanticipated consequences he would have preferred to avoid. If he proceeds through a *succession* of incremental changes, he avoids serious lasting mistakes in several ways.

In the first place, past sequences of policy steps have given him knowledge about the probable consequences of further similar steps. Second, he need not attempt big jumps toward his goals that would require predictions beyond his or anyone else's knowledge, because he never expects his policy to be a final resolution of a problem. His decision is only one step, one that if successful can quickly be followed by another. Third, he is in effect able to test his previous predictions as he moves on to each further step. Lastly, he often can remedy a past error fairly quickly—more quickly than if policy proceeded through more distinct steps widely spaced in time.

Compare this comparative analysis of incremental changes with the aspiration to employ theory in the root method. Man cannot think without classifying, without subsuming one experience under a more general category of experiences. The attempt to push categorization as far as possible and to find general propositions which can be applied to specific situations is what I refer to with the word "theory". Where root analysis often leans heavily on theory in this sense, the branch method does not.

The assumption of root analysts is that theory is the most systematic and economical way to bring relevant knowledge to bear on a specific problem. Granting the assumption, an unhappy fact is that we do not have adequate theory to apply to problems in any policy area, although theory is more adequate in some areas—monetary policy, for example— than in others. Comparative analysis, as in the branch method, is sometimes a systematic alternative to theory.

Suppose an administrator must choose among a small group of policies that differ only incrementally from each other and from present policy. He might aspire to "understand" each of the alternatives—for example, to know all the consequences of each aspect of each policy. If so, he would indeed require theory. In fact, however, he would usually decide, that *for policy-making purposes*, he need know, as explained above, only the consequences of each of those aspects of the policies in which they differed from one another. For this much more modest aspiration, he requires no theory (although it might be helpful, if available), for he can proceed to isolate probable differences by examining the differences in consequences associated with past differences in policies, a feasible program because he can take his observations from a long sequence of incremental changes.

For example, without a more comprehensive social theory about juvenile delinquency than scholars have yet produced, one cannot possibly understand the ways in which a variety of public policies—say on education, housing, recreation, employment, race relations, and policing—might encourage or discourage delinquency. And one needs such an understanding if he undertakes the comprehensive overview of the problem prescribed in the models of the root method. If, however, one merely wants to mobilize knowledge sufficient to assist in a choice among a small group of similar policies—alternative policies on juvenile court procedures, for example—he can do so by comparative analysis of the results of similar past policy moves.

THEORISTS AND PRACTITIONERS

This difference explains—in some cases at least—why the administrator often feels that the outside expert or academic problem-solver is sometimes not helpful and why they in turn often urge more theory on him. And it explains why an administrator often feels more confident when "flying by the seat of his pants" than when following the advice of theorists. Theorists often ask the administrator to go the long way round to the solution of his problems, in effect ask him to follow the best canons of the scientific method, when the administrator knows that the best available theory will work less well than more modest incremental comparisons. Theorists do not realize that the administrator is often in fact practicing a systematic method. It would be foolish to push this explanation too far, for sometimes practical decision-makers are pursuing neither a theoretical approach nor successive comparisons, nor any other systematic method.

It may be worth emphasizing that theory is sometimes of extremely limited helpfulness in policy-making for at least two rather different reasons. It is greedy for facts; it can be constructed only through a great collection of observations. And it is typically insufficiently precise for application to a policy process that moves through small changes. In contrast, the comparative method both economizes on the need for facts and directs the analyst's attention to just those facts that are relevant to the fine choices faced by the decision-maker.

With respect to precision of theory, economic theory serves as an example. It predicts that an economy without money or prices would in certain specified ways misallocate resources, but this finding pertains to an alternative far removed from the kind of policies on which administrators need help. On the other hand, it is not precise enough to predict the consequences of policies restricting business mergers, and this is the kind of issue on which the administrators need help. Only in relatively restricted areas does economic theory achieve sufficient precision to go far in resolving policy questions; its helpfulness in policy-making is always so limited that it requires supplementation through comparative analysis.

SUCCESSIVE COMPARISON AS A SYSTEM

Successive limited comparisons is, then, indeed a method or system; it is not a failure of method for which administrators ought to apologize. None the less, its imperfections, which have not been explored in this paper, are many. For example, the method is without a built-in safeguard for all relevant values, and it also may lead the decision-maker to overlook excellent policies for no other reason than that they are not suggested by the chain of successive policy steps leading up to the present. Hence, it ought to be said that under this method, as well as under some of the most sophisticated variants of the root method—operations research, for example —policies will continue to be as foolish as they are wise.

Why then bother to describe the method in all the above detail? Because it is in fact a common method of policy formulation, and is, for complex problems, the principal reliance of administrators as well as of other policy analysts.[9] And because it will be superior to any other decision-making

[9] Elsewhere I have explored this same method of policy formulation as practiced by academic analysts of policy ("Policy analysis", *American Economic Review*, Vol. 48, p. 298 [June, 1958]). Although it has been here presented as a method for public administrators, it is no less necessary to analysts more removed from

method available for complex problems in many circumstances, certainly superior to a futile attempt at superhuman comprehensiveness. The reaction of the public administrator to the exposition of method doubtless will be less a discovery of a new method than a better acquaintance with an old. But by becoming more conscious of their practice of this method, administrators might practice it with more skill and know when to extend or constrict its use. (That they sometimes practice it effectively and sometimes not may explain the extremes of opinion on "muddling through", which is both praised as a highly sophisticated form of problem-solving and denounced as no method at all. For I suspect that in so far as there is a system in what is known as "muddling through", this method is it.)

One of the noteworthy incidental consequences of clarification of the method is the light it throws on the suspicion an administrator sometimes entertains that a consultant or adviser is not speaking relevantly and responsibly when in fact by all ordinary objective evidence he is. The trouble lies in the fact that most of us approach policy problems within a framework given by our view of a chain of successive policy choices made up to the present. One's thinking about appropriate policies with respect, say, to urban traffic control is greatly influenced by one's knowledge of the incremental steps taken up to the present. An administrator enjoys an intimate knowledge of his past sequences that "outsiders" do not share, and his thinking and that of the "outsider" will consequently be different in ways that may puzzle both. Both may appear to be talking intelligently, yet each may find the other unsatisfactory. The relevance of the policy chain of succession is even more clear when an American tries to discuss, say, antitrust policy with a Swiss, for the chains of policy in the two countries are strikingly different and the two individuals consequently have organized their knowledge in quite different ways.

---

immediate policy questions, despite their tendencies to describe their own analytical efforts as though they were the rational-comprehensive method with an especially heavy use of theory. Similarly, this same method is inevitably resorted to in personal problem-solving, where means and ends are sometimes impossible to separate, where aspirations or objectives undergo constant development, and where drastic simplification of the complexity of the real world is urgent if problems are to be solved in the time that can be given to them. To an economist accustomed to dealing with the marginal or incremental concept in market processes, the central idea in the method is that both evaluation and empirical analysis are incremental. Accordingly I have referred to the method elsewhere as "the incremental method".

If this phenomenon is a barrier to communication, an understanding of it promises an enrichment of intellectual interaction in policy formulation. Once the source of difference is understood, it will sometimes be stimulating for an administrator to seek out a policy analyst whose recent experience is with a policy chain different from his own.

This raises again a question only briefly discussed above on the merits of like-mindedness among government administrators. While much of organization theory argues the virtues of common values and agreed organizational objectives, for complex problems in which the root method is inapplicable, agencies will want among their own personnel two types of diversification: administrators whose thinking is organized by reference to policy chains other than those familiar to most members of the organization and, even more commonly, administrators whose professional or personal values or interests create diversity of view (perhaps coming from different specialties, social classes, geographical areas) so that, even within a single agency, decision-making can be fragmented and parts of the agency can serve as watchdogs for other parts.

Beyond the Middle-range Planning Bridge*

Ira M. Robinson

IN THE keynote speech delivered to the annual meeting of the American Institute of Planners in 1956, Martin Meyerson called on city planning agencies to add certain intermediate functions to the traditional long- and short-range ones.[1] He called for a bridge between decisions on projects and decisions on long-range, comprehensive plans. His proposal of additional middle-range responsibilities for city planning was directed primarily toward the alleviation of what he saw to be its chief contemporary deficiencies:

1. Failure to provide current and meaningful information to support rational and coherent private and public action.
2. Failure to translate the remote, goal-oriented master plan into meaningful and operative goal-action statements for decision-making within and without the government.
3. Failure to induce the kind of forward planning at the operating departmental level that would lead to eventual accomplishment of previously adopted long-range goals and policies.

Author's note. For some of the ideas expressed in this paper, the author has benefitted from innumerable discussions with various members of the Arthur D. Little staff who were involved with him in the San Francisco Community Renewal Program, particularly Tom Kingsley and George Williams. He has also benefitted from a continuing dialogue with Melvin M. Webber, extending over some three years, on the subject-matter of this paper. However, none of these persons is responsible for the author's views.

* Reprinted by permission of the *Journal of the American Institute of Planners*, Vol. 31, November 1965.

[1] Later reprinted as "Building the middle-range bridge for comprehensive planning", *A.I.P. Journal*, Vol. XXII (Spring 1956), pp. 58–64.

4. Failure to evaluate the intended and unintended consequences of previously implemented actions.

It is almost a decade now since this formulation was presented. In the intervening period the city-planning profession has been slowly building this middle-range bridge, although, to be sure, most agencies still go about their business as usual. Major footings for the bridge are being provided by the federal Community Renewal Program (CRP), which appeared in 1959 as an amendment to the 1949 Housing Act. The seemingly innocuous amendment was presented in only one small paragraph, which seemed to remain almost unnoticed for about two years. Then a few cities took a closer look at its provisions; interest began to grow, and a few applications for federal grants were submitted to the HHFA. In the past several years there has been a spurt of interest in this program, and today it is being used by about 125 cities, including many of the largest ones.

In a few cities the CRP has been recognized for what it is; a major new approach to urban renewal and a radical new departure for city planning. The amendment was the stimulus for a new wave of innovations in the urban renewal process. More significantly, it has resulted in a re-examination of many traditional city-planning approaches and methods that we had to take for granted, and it has introduced new and powerful techniques potentially useful for urban analysis and planning in general.

In response to the deficiencies of traditional master plans, a number of central cities have undertaken to prepare CRP's that are marked by widened substantive concerns, by shortened time-horizons, and by a focus upon programmed action. These cities have also discovered that the close inter-relationships among long-range planning, renewal, and many other governmental functions affecting the physical order of a city require a systematic evaluation of a broad spectrum of programmes undertaken by a large number of public and private agencies. The CRP staffs in these cities have designed programs of action that encompass services and facilities for social welfare, education, health, and transportation, as well as the traditional concerns of urban renewal. Some of the major staffs are investigating the feasibility of using certain sophisticated techniques developed in other fields, such as mathematical simulation models, in order to test the likely consequences of alternative public actions.

Although the success of these innovative CRP's is still to be determined (most of the plans have not yet been tested in the real world), it is hoped that they will lead to the next logical step in city planning—what I shall call *Community Development Programming.* When this happens, the city planning profession will have built a firm middle-range bridge, and the effectiveness of the agencies will be enormously increased.

The primary purposes of this paper then, are to describe some of the new "middle-range" planning approaches and methods that are being developed under various CRP's and to sketch out the key elements of the proposed Community Development Programming concept, which is derived from Meyerson's original formulation and made operational through the CRP.

I. THE MIDDLE-RANGE BRIDGE FOR COMPREHENSIVE PLANNING

Meyerson's suggested additional middle-range planning roles and functions are briefly reviewed below.

The Central Intelligence Function

The planning agency should function to aid the operations of the private market. It should facilitate market operations for housing, commerce, industry, and other community activities by regularly issuing market analyses.

His concern here was with the local businessmen, the industrialists, and the consumers who rarely have the quality of information that rational decisions require. To undertake this market-analysis function, data would have to be obtained and analyzed continuously. Regular market reports should be issued by the planning agency. Some could be issued monthly, some quarterly, some semi-annually, and some annually, depending on the urgency of the situation. There would be special reports on such items as the home-building market, investment in plants, consumer income and spending, and land and building costs.

Detailed market analysis for the city, for the metropolitan area, and for subregions in the area, should enable both the producer and the consumer to make more intelligent choices with respect to the location, investment, building, and land utilization for industry, commerce, housing, and other major facilities and activities. If the city-planning agency would regularly check and interpret the local market situation, it could thereby lubricate the natural processes of urban development and renewal. Many of the main objectives of planning can best be achieved by facilitating intelligent actions by the individual investors who are the builders of American cities.

The Pulse-taking Function

The agency should watch for community danger signs. City-planning agencies typically respond to mistakes after they have occurred, rather than anticipating trouble and avoiding it before mistakes are made. It was recommended, therefore, that the planning agency become the city's "DEW-line", constantly scanning the community and its developmental processes for indications of maladjustments and danger signs: increase of blight factors, loss of transit patronage, clues of the entry or leaving of certain industries, changes in neighborhood household composition, pointing to the need for new and special demands for services. Changes of these types might thus be detected before they gather a momentum almost impossible to stop or accommodate. A quarterly or other periodic report to the local chief executive was therefore recommended, alerting him to impending community changes. To be effective, this report would also recommend remedial action. This means a policy focus, which brings us to Meyerson's third expanded city-planning function.

The Policy-clarification Function

The planning agency should aid in framing and regularly revising development objectives and policies of its local government devised to halt undesirable changes and promote desired ones. It should take the initiative in indicating suitable policy measures. This would involve not only direct public measures, but, equally important, specific inducements to encourage preferred private actions.

The determination of community policy evolves, of course, through the political process. In our pluralistic society there are many conflicting values, resulting in partisan competition among goals, which is ultimately expressed and partially settled through politics. Meyerson saw the planning agency as facilitating this process by analyzing alternatives, and helping to determine the benefits to be achieved as against the costs incurred by various specific policies. Politicians could then have detailed information on the advantages and disadvantages of alternative policies aimed at achieving desired goals. The planning agency, without usurping the role of the politician, would thereby clarify the implications of alternative policy decisions, and help assure that more policy choices were made.

The Detailed Development Plan Function

The planning agency should prepare short-range and middle-range comprehensive plans, stating specific sequences of actions to be taken over periods of five to ten years.

These would bridge the gap between the developmental policies of government and a long-range master plan setting forth a desired future state. The development plan would link measures aimed at current problems with long-range proposals aimed at higher-order community goals. This type of plan would require detailed, timed, and localized programming of governmental policies for private and public actions. Detailed cost estimates of private and public development, and specific administrative, organizational, and legal measures to carry out the programs would also be prepared.

Long-range comprehensive plans commonly reveal a desired future state of affairs, rarely specifying detailed courses of action needed to achieve that state. By the changing nature of things, they cannot do so. The five- to ten-year development plans, in contrast, would indicate the specific changes in land use and other requisite actions programmed for each year. The development plan would be acted upon each year and made an official act for the subsequent year, much as the capital budget is adopted.

The Feedback Review Function

The planning agency should analyze the actual consequences of post-program and project activities, so that it might better guide future actions. With others, Meyerson deplored the fact that planning agencies have no systematic means of analyzing the effects of action programs (zoning is, of course, the most notorious example) and recommended that they maintain a constant feedback of information on both the intended and the unintended consequences of enacted programs.

II. THE COMMUNITY RENEWAL PROGRAM: CONCEPT AND PRACTICE

It is sufficient here to say that the underlying purpose and intent of the federal Community Renewal Program is to enable a city to analyze its overall renewal requirements and to prepare a program of actions to meet them, in consideration of the financial, administrative, and social resources available. Rather than recount the details of the concept, or describe various CRP's that have been prepared, this discussion will show how renewal planning and programming has encouraged the development of new methods and approaches applicable to each of Meyerson's middle-range planning functions.

On-going Data and Information Systems

The Urban Renewal Administration places heavy emphasis on the need for establishing procedures for continuing the community's first CRP on a current basis.[2] While the URA acknowledges that most communities will undertake a major effort in the initial preparation of the CRP, it is insistent that the continuing changes in local renewal problems and potentials be taken into account through periodic revision and review. To maintain its effectiveness, the CRP must be responsive to the changes in conditions and problems revealed by subsequent information. Continuity requires that this objective be incorporated in each city's CRP organization from its outset. This can be done, according to URA, by proper organization of staff and through the design of methods for data-gathering and reporting, as well as by making provision for periodic review and updating.[3] URA

---

[2] Housing and Home Finance Administration, Urban Renewal Administration, *CRP: Community Renewal Program Policy*, October 1963.

[3] U.R.A. suggests that this objective can best be implemented if CRP staffing arrangements and use of personnel are closely related to on-going local government processes so that the continuing and periodic work necessary to keep the CRP current can be most readily accomplished. Although special project staffs and use of consultants may be appropriate, according to the URA, to some aspects of the CRP, it does not feel that they generally can achieve continuity. It therefore recommends that either a local body be given responsibility for this function, or that a special purpose continuing body be created. Whenever possible, the URA recommends that the person in charge of the CRP should also be given responsibility for maintaining continuity.

recommends that careful design of data-gathering and presentation techniques facilitates later revisions necessary to keep the data current. This involves notation of sources, making possible later revisions and comparisons between earlier and current data aimed at measuring trends and accomplishments.

In accordance with this approach, many cities have developed systematic data and information systems as part of their CRP's. Typically, these systems are designed to perform three functions: to monitor current conditions, problems, and trends—corresponding to Meyerson's central intelligence function; (2) to prepare key indicators of change, in order to alert the community to certain maladjustments and danger signs—corresponding to his pulse-taking function; and (3) to evaluate progress of the recommended program and assess its impact as a guide to future policy—corresponding to his feedback-review function.

The New York and San Francisco CRP's may be cited as two examples of this approach. As part of its extended CRP, New York City is setting up a data system, consisting of a current file of basic pertinent facts stored on punch cards and magnetic tape to be tabulated and analyzed by machine. There are five types of data the system is expected to contain:[4] (1) information based on parcels of land, describing activities and structures; (2) information for each block in the city, describing the characteristics of its land and structures; (3) information on a small-area basis describing nonresidential activities; (4) information on a small-area basis describing population, family and household, and dwelling-unit characteristics; (5) information for various larger areas (health-service districts, boroughs, the city as a whole, or the region as a whole) to provide indicators of basic economic and social conditions such as unemployment or delinquency rates.

To make these data useful to the city's officials, it is proposed that regular staff reports be produced, summarizing the state of the city's residential areas. The state-of-the-city reports will include estimates of renewal progress and pertinent changes; they will point out newly apparent problems and opportunities in both the residential and nonresidential spheres. The kinds of information expected to be presented in these reports include:

[4] New York Department of City Planning, "Draft Amendatory Application to the Housing and Home Finance Agency for a Community Renewal Program Grant for the City of New York", March 1964.

(1) the types of residential buildings currently being constructed, demolished, or converted as a result of both public and private actions; (2) year-to-year estimates of changes in the local composition of residents, and (3) estimates of changes in the physical condition of the city's housing stock.

Similarly, the San Francisco Community Renewal Program recommends that as part of the continuing renewal planning system in city government, a state-of-San Francisco annual report be prepared, comprising similar types of information. Moreover, it recommends that a series of key indicators of change—referred to as "key symptomatic statistical indicators"—be especially monitored on a continuing basis.

The San Francisco CRP recommends that five major housing-inventory series be collected on a continuing basis and subaggregated into neighborhoods, as delineated by the CRP staff for its mathematical simulation model of the residential space market.[5] These five housing-inventory series grow out of the major structural elements incorporated in the simulation model.[6] First, permit data concerning improvements, to include all forms of remodeling that increase the value of an existing structure. Such information on a neighborhood basis will help to delineate potential neighborhood problem areas; neighborhoods naturally upgrading themselves, not needing special treatment; and neighborhoods experiencing some natural upgrading but needing some form of public encouragement.

Second, an annual collection of building permits granted for the construction of new housing. Annual comparisons of these data for the total city will provide information concerning the entire city's economic health, and also indicate the degree to which the city is reversing any trend toward housing obsolescence. Inter-area comparisons will provide the analyst with an early insight into changing relationships, as some neighborhoods raze existing structures and provide new units in their place, while other areas show little or no construction activity.

Third, an annual series on vacancies will be maintained. Fourth, a current housing-price index will be available. Fifth, efforts will be made to monitor changes in the size and composition of the city's population.

---

[5] Ira M. Robinson, Harry B. Wolfe, and Robert L. Barringer, "A simulation model for renewal programming", *A.I.P. Journal*, Vol. XXXI (May 1965), p. 128.

[6] For a further discussion of these recommended symptomatic indicators, see Arthur D. Little, Inc., *San Francisco Community Renewal Program: Analysis, Strategy, Program* (preliminary final report), April 1965, pp. 6.28–6.31.

New Methods for Testing Alternative Renewal Policies

Several CRP's have developed interesting new methods to assist in analyzing alternative renewal policies and to predict their benefits and costs. The Philadelphia CRP is noteworthy in this regard.[7] A major part of its effort is being devoted to relating broad categories of municipal investment to the different actions and specific programs of city government that can accomplish various investment objectives. The categories include investment in people (education, health, and other services), housing and the physical environment, economic development, property transportation, and general support. Concentrating initially on housing and the physical environment (ultimately it is hoped to cover all of the investment categories), the Philadelphia CRP staff has developed a programming system designed to review, analyze, and schedule the diverse activities contributing to the development of the city. This programming approach is a method for taking inventory and assessing existing programs designed to cope with development problems, determining where these programs can be applied most effectively, identifying areas of concern where existing programs are inadequate, designing new programs to meet needs, and scheduling existing and new programs over an extended time period within the city's financial limitations. This system has involved the participation of a large number of municipal agencies in evaluating their own programs by clarifying objectives, measuring past accomplishments, and estimating the requirements needed to meet various levels of achievement.

By comparing different means of accomplishing the same objective— for example, the relative effectiveness of additional expenditures for clearance of substandard houses as compared to the same expenditure for generating economic development that might increase the income of renters—Philadelphia's CRP hopes to measure and evaluate relative cost and effectiveness for alternative approaches. By developing a system that will chart progress among programs sponsored by many different agencies, the planners can assess the relations between program performance and the basic objectives of city development. By making program objectives explicit, Philadelphia policy-makers and citizens can be presented with a

[7] See Philadelphia Community Renewal Program, Technical Paper Number 4, *Community Renewal Programming*, December 1962.

manageable array of evaluated alternatives, from which they can select, combine, emphasize, or defer programs according to their preferences.

The Philadelphia method of analysis has developed a series of "program plans", again focusing initially on programs concerned with housing and the physical environment.[8] They define, in workable terms, the operations of public, semi-public, and private agencies having an impact on the city's development process. Each program plan includes: the description of the program, its objectives, the legal basis for involvement, the preconditions for effectiveness, its relationships to other programs and agencies, specific targets for accomplishment, methods of evaluating its ability to achieve the desired results, the resources required for completing the presently authorized program and the proposed one, and the current cost of the program.

Patterned after systems evaluation techniques developed by the Department of Defense, the Philadelphia CRP's programming approach promises to become a valuable addition to the analytic tools available for renewal and, ultimately, municipal programming in general.

Another approach to clarifying basic renewal policy alternatives is being used in New York City.[9] In the latter part of the first phase and the early part of the second phase of New York's CRP, five successive "rounds" of analysis are being undertaken. Each successive round adds factors or variables to the analysis. The first round, for example, evaluates the implications of a total clearance program for the city's most blighted areas, accompanied by an effort to maximize the net amount of new housing possible under current financial constraints. By round five, the goal is to prepare a renewal program that will estimate the financial resources required to achieve adjustments in the housing stock and residential environment to meet the demands of various categories of households. Intervening rounds of study are devoted to testing the value and limitations of conservation, rehabilitation, and clearance actions, estimating alternative as well as current resource constraints, matching household compositions with changes in the housing stock, and introducing needs for community facilities as well as housing.

---

[8] Community Renewal Program, Philadelphia, "Program Plans for Development Activities" (undated, mimeographed).

[9] New York Department of City Planning, *op. cit.*

The Pittsburgh and San Francisco methods to assist analysis of alternative goals, policies, programs, and plans represent a quite different approach. In these cities, formal mathematical models are being developed to simulate the workings of the city.[10] The objective is to create, with the assistance of computers, a replica of the real world which will enable alternative renewal policies and actions to be tested and their implications evaluated. The San Francisco model focuses on the workings of the private investment market in urban residential real property. By simulating the behavior of this market, the model designers hope to develop a tool for testing the effect of public actions on the workings of the private sector. In its current form, the San Francisco simulation model deals only with the residential sector; however, it is hoped that further refinements will permit the introduction of the nonresidential sector.

Pittsburgh's simulation model has as its objective the measurement of impacts of urban renewal projects and plans on a variety of key municipal indicators, such as tax returns, level of housing vacancies, and availability of employment. When completed, the model will enable the city's decision makers to compare the alternative impacts of many different urban renewal actions.

Action-program for Renewal

The ultimate purpose of the Community Renewal Program, as its title implies, is to develop a feasible comprehensive program of renewal actions, including, according to U.R.A. federally assisted urban renewal operations and other related public and private actions. The program, in accord with U.R.A.'s directives, should designate the type of renewal treatment appropriate to each area of the city, assign priorities for renewal action, set forth time-sequenced schedules of actions, and be relatively specific and definite about near-future actions, even though distant future actions must be vague.

It is apparent that the CRP action-program is similar to Meyerson's proposed five- to ten-year detailed development plan, albeit focused on physical renewal. This can perhaps best be illustrated by briefly listing

[10] For a description of these models, see: Wilbur A. Steger, "The Pittsburgh Urban Renewal Simulation model", *A.I.P. Journal*, Vol. XXXI (May 1965), pp. 144–9; and Ira M. Robinson *et al.*, "A simulation model for renewal programming", *ibid.*, pp. 126–34.

the elements included in the program of action recommended as part of the San Francisco Community Renewal Program.[11] These include:

1. A statement of housing and renewal goals for the twelve-year period 1966 through 1978.
2. A recommended set of policies or "strategies" to guide renewal action during this period, including policies for improving resident's economic and social status in blighted and nonblighted areas, as well as for improving the properties themselves.
3. A set of "potential project areas" to receive special renewal treatment during the first six-year phase of the twelve-year program, and the types of treatment appropriate for each area.
4. The types of public actions in general required in the neighborhoods that will not receive special renewal treatment, for example, capital improvements, code enforcement.
5. The kinds of private actions that are required.
6. Estimated public cost of the special renewal treatment program.
7. A set of "supporting actions" which should be undertaken by various city departments and agencies to implement the recommended program and carry out the renewal objectives.
8. Recommended techniques and administrative organization for the continuing revision of the CRP. These include provisions for the gathering and analysis of data and for revising or extending the recommended action program as progress is made toward achieving CRP objectives, or as unforeseen conditions develop that warrant program alteration.

III. THE NEXT STEP: COMMUNITY DEVELOPMENT PROGRAMMING

The CRP represents a tremendous conceptual and procedural contribution to the planning art. Its underlying approach represents a basic shift in city-planning philosophy, for it explicitly recognizes that it is not enough to "draw a picture" of the desired future city, and then try to adjust each short-range program to somehow conform to this picture. The processes of private, as well as public, actions and reactions that might produce the

[11] Arthur D. Little, Inc., *San Francisco Community Renewal Program: Analysis, Goals, Long-range Policies and Program* (Final Report), September 1965.

desired future state must be systematically traced through future time and evaluated. The CRP comprehends the city in dynamic process, rather than as a static configuration. At the very least, the CRP has been oriented to the processes of growth and change, and tries to "get inside" the workings of the real estate market subsystem.

Moreover, to help the planner understand these processes, new tools of urban analysis, including experimental simulation models, have been encouraged. It is striking that it has taken so little time to make these models operational as tools for monitoring and analyzing the various interrelations that tie the city's subsystems together.

The CRP has also stimulated city planners to recognize the importance of adequate, quantified information as an aid in monitoring conditions, changes, and trends; helping members of the private sector, such as the businessman, consumer, and home-owner to make better decisions; detecting trouble and danger signs before they become too serious; assessing the costs and benefits of alternative policies; and evaluating the impacts and consequences intended and unintended, of public and private programs.

Most important for the profession's development the CRP has encouraged city planners to recognize the need to establish planning-and-programming as a continuing process of city government, related to and integrated with the everyday operations of city departments and agencies. It has served as an instrument for organizational and administrative change in city government, aimed at bringing together the planning and effectuating agencies concerned with urban renewal. This has occurred in two ways. First, several CRP's have recommended changes in the way that urban renewal and related public actions ought to be administered and organized. An example of this is the San Francisco CRP, which recommended far-reaching changes in that city's organizational structure for code enforcement, urban renewal, and renewal and development coordination.[12] A key element in these recommendations was the appointment to the Mayor's staff of a Development Director whose responsibilities, in addition to coordinating the activities and programs of the renewal and renewal-related departments and agencies, would also include preparation of an

[12] Arthur D. Little, Inc., *San Francisco Community Renewal Program: Report on Organization and Administration for Renewal*, March 1963.

Annual Renewal Program for San Francisco for approval by the Mayor.[13] This would be done in cooperation with the city's Inter-Agency Committee on Urban Renewal and the City Planning Department.

The second way the CRP has affected organizational and administrative changes in city government is related to the organization of the CRP's themselves. In a growing number of cities, there is a developing pattern of administering the CRP that is likely to have lasting and far-reaching effects on the way that public policies and programs in urban renewal are formulated. The tendency is for control or central direction of the CRP to be organized under the chief executive, and for the policy-making role in the CRP to be carried out by a committee of leading public officials. Typically, this policy committee includes the city's urban renewal co-ordinator (where such a position exists), and the heads of the principal planning, renewal, and development agencies: city planning, redevelopment, public housing, and code enforcement.

This pattern of CRP organization and administration has emerged in cities where the initial interest in, and stimulus for, the program came from the city planning department or the renewal agency. It quickly became apparent that the broad-gauged nature of the CRP was such that it could not be administered solely by a single municipal agency.

Further, the CRP has forced urban renewal staffs and city planners to rethink certain traditional tools of renewal and city planning. They have become operationally sensitive to the effects on the quantity and quality of the city's housing exerted by federal income-tax policy, national monetary policy, local real property tax assessment policy, the state of the local economy, and incomes of different population groups, in addition to code enforcement and other traditional tools. So renewal specialists and planners, as staff of their CRP's, have found themselves in roles of policy formulators in the once-foreign fields of finance, monetary policy, social welfare, economic development, and more.

As a result, since housing is itself only instrumental to accomplishing certain higher-level social purposes, the CRP has forced planners—now equipped with improved concepts and analytic techniques—to look for

---

[13] A subsequent supplemental paper to the O & A Study, *A Survey of the Office of the Mayor*, detailed the functions and responsibilities of the proposed position of Development Director.

other kinds of public intervention to improve the condition of the city's residents. Above all, the programmatic emphasis of the CRP, combined with a new sense of the value of cost-effectiveness tests, has at last forced many of the cities' planners to understand that urban renewal programs should not be designed to help buildings. We have been often told that "buildings don't have problems, only people do". The CRP approach has forced us to understand the profundity of that seeming truism. As a result, the focus of attention is being redirected from the city's real estate to its social and economic conditions; and urban renewal and city planning show signs of shifting from the traditional concentration on land use to the conditions of urban life. The federal anti-poverty program, for example, has renewed our concern for the problems of disadvantaged minority groups in our cities. This has led several CRP's to search for social service programs and economic development programs to best serve the people living in deteriorated and near-deteriorated areas of our cities. In turn, they have been led to seek out the best program "mix" (whether it consists of physically or nonphysically focused programs, or both) for achieving a given objective.

It may be that—after several generations of search—we are now equipped to undertake comprehensive planning. If planners can take the creative and unifying ideas from the federal CRP concept, draw upon the innovative approaches and methods developed in practice, and then extend these ideas in scope, content, and functions, we may soon be establishing truly comprehensive Community Development Programming processes in city governments.

Community Development Programming would differ from the federal CRP concept in three significant respects: (1) it would be directly concerned with all aspects of the city system relevant to specific social, economic, and physical problems; (2) it would be concerned with *all* programs and activities of local government directly or indirectly affecting economic, social, and physical renewal and development; and (3) it would formally and explicitly recognize the importance of establishing community-wide programming as an on-going process of city government. The key elements of this proposed new approach to city planning are sketched below.

The Programming Process

Every department and agency of city government and most private agencies dealing in services to people have a set of policy instruments commonly called a *program* (or "program of activities") designed to meet their responsibilities. Similarly, these public and private bodies engage in *programming*, the process of selecting from among alternative programs over time and from among varying rates of investment that are financially feasible.

The proposal, a community development program, would consist of a time-phased, sequenced set of governmental policies and programs (departmental programs) for private and public action.[14] Community Development Programming (CDP) would be an on-going governmental process of formulating, maintaining, applying, reviewing, and overseeing the community development program.

Community Development Programming, to be undertaken by a central planning and programming agency of city government, would comprise the following activities:

1. Continuing identification and clarification of major city problems, drawing upon the on-going data and information system and the key symptomatic statistical indicators developed from that.

2. Continuing identification and clarification of city programs to deal with these problems, following the "program plan" reporting approach of the Philadelphia CRP.

3. Continuing collection and prediction of information, drawing upon an on-going information system and upon formal models of the city system.

4. Dissemination of the information, collected and predicted, both to the public agencies and to the public at large through an annual state-of-the-city progress report.

5. Continuing policy analysis and revision using the Philadelphia "program packages" approach and simulation models similar to those developed in Pittsburgh and San Francisco.

6. Annual determination of the objectives and targets.

---

[14] As originally envisioned by Meyerson, the Program would serve as the central guide to programming housing and renewal activities (both public and private), to land use changes, to economic and social development programs, to educational, medical services and similar programs, and to all municipal investments in general. It would cover a ten-year period, but would only be detailed for the first six years.

7. Assembly and recommendation of an annual budget for development and renewal; formulation of policy guides, and a six-year schedule of the elements of the program.
8. Annual review of the six-year program, based in part on the information fed back to the programmers, reporting the extent of success with public actions taken the previous year, and, where necessary, consequential revision of the next year's program, as well as of the following five-year program.

CDP would lead to an officially adopted policy guide and program for the development and renewal of a city, consisting of the following components:

1. Specification of the problems to be treated in the ensuing period and a detailed policy statement regarding the local government's approaches to alleviation of the problems.
2. A set of timed-objectives and operating targets to guide the city's developmental and renewal investments for the following six years —the objectives and targets to encompass economic and social, as well as the physical aspects of city life.
3. An itemized list of the specific public and private actions that will contribute to accomplishing the objectives.
4. A time-phased and costed set of public programs to be carried out by various departments and agencies over the future six-year period, including a statement of each program's objectives, the agency responsible for its execution, the foreseeable performance targets of each program, the method of evaluating performance, and costs of the program by year over the six years.
5. An adopted budget and action plan for the first year of the six-year program.

Prospects of CDP

What are the prospects for Community Development Programming in the future? Will it become standard operating procedure in all large central cities or remain just another good idea which nobody implements? It is obviously not possible to provide answers to these questions at this time. The CRP concept itself did not catch on until some two or three years after the 1959 amendment to the Housing Act. There are, however, several factors that support an optimistic view.

While it is too early to evaluate the success of the CRP's now prepared, the prospect looks promising. As it becomes a more widely accepted tool for renewal planning, the chances of moving to the next logical step, Community Development Programming, become greater.

Most important, perhaps, is the inherent logic of the concepts underlying the CRP approach, an approach compatible with the rationalistic philosophy of American city planning, characterized by the long-range view, comprehensiveness, coordination, and explicitly stated goal-structures. To this approach, held throughout most of the history of U.S. city planning, the CRP concept, and now the CDP, add the following elements: (1) the need to define alternative courses of action; (2) the examination and testing of these alternatives; (3) the explicit ranking and weighting of the consequences against the pre-established goals; (4) an awareness that the physical aspects of the city are not separable from the economic and social, and therefore must be treated in concert with them.

These new elements represent the obvious additions that are needed to make city-planning procedures and methods more compatible with the emerging theories and models of rational decision-making and problem-solving. Not all city planners are committed to rationalism, but trends in planning over the last fifty years have clearly been moving toward more, rather than less, rationality in the solution of urban problems.

Underlying the CDP approach is the concept that planning, management, and control are inseparable local government functions. The CDP therefore, should appeal to managers and controllers in city government. Increasingly, these persons are better trained and many of them know the value of research, being generally aware of the need to seek new methods for increasing efficiency and rationality. They have adopted and pioneered in new tools of public management, such as performance budgeting and its related tool, the "program budget", and electronic data-processing, techniques integral in the CDP approach. The CDP, therefore, should improve their effectiveness.

The changes in the organizational and administrative structure for renewal which have taken place in many cities, partly induced by the CRP, represent a logical first step towards establishing the kinds of institutional changes implied by a Community Development Programming process.

Once the Renewal Coordinator or Development Director has assumed responsibility for coordinating and integrating renewal functions and programs, the next logical step is to subsume under his responsibility all developmental functions as well.

Another positive factor is an increasing public awareness of urban problems and the need to find feasible solutions, and a growing recognition of the potential role of city planning in solving these problems. At the same time, there appears to be an uneasy impatience and skepticism about some of the traditional planning tools—a feeling that these methods do not face the realities of the problems which trouble the average citizen. Many of the criticisms leveled against the federal urban renewal program by citizen groups focus on an apparent lack of concern for the people living in the neighborhoods subject to renewal actions. In this respect alone, the focus of the CDP on people rather than buildings should be welcomed.

The CRP, and now the CDP, represent efforts to reunite the various professional interest groups and disciplines traditionally concerned with urban problems: the city planners, the housing and urban renewal specialists, and social scientists concerned with such urban problems as crime, delinquency, mental health, and poverty. This union between planning, renewal, and housing is taking place not because of exhortation or because it is "right" and "logical", but primarily because of the developing theories and the technical advances in urban model-building, which explicitly illuminate the interrelations among long-range planning goals and policies, renewal activities, and the housing market. Without these developments no amount of hortatory advice would bring these groups out of their separate compartments. Similarly, as new theories and models of human behavior are built, especially those relating social behavior, human development, and physical environment, we will find closer ties among the social scientists and those traditionally associated with city planning, renewal, and housing. Inevitably, these technological developments will be reflected in administrative and governmental rearrangements.

Implementation of the CDP approach in city government will require a new type of city planner, one whose training will be far different from the traditional approach of the planning schools. Fortunately, several planning schools have been moving in the right direction, emphasizing planning analysis, model building, systems analysis, social-economic processes, and so forth. While much of this work is available through other university departments, a few planning schools are introducing these areas of concentration into their own planning curricula. As more planning schools adopt these approaches, we will find an outflow of "city and regional developmental programmers", qualified for roles in central planning agencies and within the individual departments equipped to perform the functions and responsibilities implied by the CDP approach.

Finally, the prospects seem good for the legislative framework within which the CDP concepts and approach might be implemented, for it is quite likely that this expanded concept would be welcomed by federal urban renewal administrators. They have already pointed the way, recognizing that effective planning and progamming for urban renewal must be concerned with all government activities. David Grossman, until recently the federal official responsible for the CRP, wrote in this *Journal:*

> Still another issue that remains to be clarified is the extent to which a CRP should go beyond programming of urban renewal actions to include a broader spectrum of local government actions. Federal policy in this regard is quite open, recognizing that urban renewal touches on virtually all other activities of local government . . . the decision as to how far a given community will go in relating its development program to the CRP is largely in the hands of the locality itself; URA's policy insists only that adequate resources of proven ability to conduct the outlined program be assured.[15]

Among federal urban renewal administrators, there is also increasing recognition of the need to bridge social planning and physical planning. For example, the U.R.A. Administrator, William Slayton, recently told a renewal workshop panel on "The Role of Urban Renewal in the War on Poverty":

> Urban renewal . . . was clearly symptom-oriented in its conception. It was focused on real property—albeit with a revolutionary concern for people in its relocation requirements.
> In the 15 years since its inception . . . we have seen, increasingly, both the need for and the realization of rapprochement between physical and social planning, between renewal and social action. But the fully effective liaison of the two approaches has almost everywhere been frustrated by the absence of the tools to deal as effectively with the problems of human beings as with the problems of physical decay and blight.

[15] David A. Grossman, "The CRP: policy development, progress and problems" *A.I.P. Journal*, Vol. XXIX (November 1963), p. 267.

Then, addressing himself specifically to the relationship between urban renewal and the war on poverty, Mr. Slayton continued:

> . . . the dawn of a new day has come with the signing by President Johnson of the Economic Opportunity Act of 1964. The close and intimate role the urban renewal program should play in this effort is obvious . . . the prototype programs on which the community action program of the Economic Opportunity Act was largely based were undertaken in New Haven and Boston largely at the initiative of the local urban renewal agencies . . . the opportunity for a vastly more effective renewal program in partnership with community actions programs is now on our doorstep.

Many of the approaches and methods which have been developed as parts of various CRP's throughout the country, and which potentially, if not in fact, go beyond any physical or blight bias, were encouraged by the U.R.A. administration. The simulation models developed in Pittsburgh and San Francisco, and the Philadelphia "program package" approach, as examples, examine many other aspects of urban development than just blight, or even just physical property. They are capable of testing a broader range of city policies, plans, and projects than merely those oriented to physical renewal.

City planners have been accumulating some powerful new concepts and methods, in part engendered by the CRP's. The profession has acquired a new-found understanding of urban-growth processes, complementing the traditional orientation to future-state plans. There is a growing impatience in the Negro community, the city hall, and in Washington that we *do* something about the cities' problems. An increased realization that traditional city planning approaches cannot effectively deal with the real problems of our cities is forcing some agencies to increase their scope to include current issues, as well as vague futures, and people, as well as property. We may now be ready to move beyond the middle-range bridge.

The Goals of Comprehensive Planning*

Alan Altshuler

THOSE who consider themselves comprehensive planners typically claim that their most important functions are: (1) to create a master plan which can guide the deliberations of specialist planners; (2) to evaluate the proposals of specialist planners in the light of the master plan, and (3) to coordinate the planning of specialist agencies so as to ensure that their proposals reinforce each other to further the public interest. Each of these functions requires for ideal performance that the comprehensive planners understand the overall public interest, at least in connection with the subject-matter (which may be partial) of their plans; and that they possess causal knowledge which enables them to gauge the approximate net effect of proposed actions on the public interest.

COMPREHENSIVENESS AND THE PUBLIC INTEREST

This paper is concerned with some ways in which city planners have approached the first of these two requirements; that is, that they understand the public interest. Contrary to most students of planning, I consider it the more interesting one. If comprehensive planners deal with a great many more areas of public policy than specialists, their factual and causal knowledge in each area is bound to appear shallow by comparison

* Reprinted by permission of the *Journal of the American Institute of Planners*, Vol. 31, August 1965.

with the specialists in it. Their claims to comprehensiveness, therefore, if they are to be persuasive, must refer primarily to a special knowledge of the public interest.

Every government planner, no matter how specialized, must be guided by *some* conception of the public interest. Since plans are proposals of concerted action to achieve goals, each must express his conception as a goal or series of goals for his community. He will probably conceive these goals as constantly shifting rather than highly stable, as always intermediate rather than final, and as more in the nature of criteria than of concrete destinations. Community goal conceptions are likely to have these characteristics because of the limitations on collective human foresight and imagination. Nonetheless, it is impossible to plan without some sense of community goals, call them what you will. Moreover, for the planning process in any community to be democratic, and I assume in these pages that it should be, the goals must win approval from a democratic political process.

The *comprehensive* planner must assume that his community's various collective goals can somehow be measured at least roughly as to importance and welded into a single hierarchy of community objectives. In addition, he must argue that technicians like himself can prescribe courses of action to achieve those objectives without great distortion or harmful side effects of a magnitude sufficient to outweigh the gains achieved through planning. We may conceive a continuum of faith in the feasibility and desirability of comprehensive planning. The "ideal type" defender of comprehensive planning would contend that a serious effort should be made to plan the future evolution of all important economic and social patterns in detail. Other defenders would limit their support to the planning in general outline of change in particular strategic variables.

Certainly few sophisticated American defenders of planning believe that planners can achieve a total comprehensiveness of perspective on any issue. Many do believe, however, that professional planners can come closer to achieving it on numerous vital issues than other participants in the urban decision process. The primary purpose of this paper is to explore some of the foundations of this belief.

It should be noted that the explicit claims of practicing planners often suggest that a fair approximation of genuine comprehensiveness is currently attainable. By way of illustration, some case studies I wrote several years ago[1] provide evidence. They were conducted in two midwestern cities whose programs had especially good reputations among planners consulted. Let us label these cities A and B. Both had nonpartisan forms of government, weak political party organizations, and strong civil service merit systems. City A had a commission form of government; City B had a strong council-weak mayor system. City A had a population of roughly 300,000; City B, 500,000.

One case study involved the evolution of a land use plan for City A. The planning director's conception of the plan's function is described in his published introduction to it:

> The total city planning process of which land use planning is but one part, involves a continuing program of deriving, organizing, and presenting a comprehensive plan for the development and renewal of [the city] . . . The plans must be economically feasible, and must promote the common good, and at the same time [must] preserve the rights and interests of the individual.

Long discussions with every planner involved in the plan's preparation persuaded me that these words were meant literally. City planning was comprehensive and for the common good, not for any lesser objectives. Several members of the planning staff had vigorously criticized the previous planning director for offering advice freely to operating agencies without first developing, or even trying to develop, a comprehensive plan. The predecessor himself, however, had justified his recommendations in terms of their overall "effect on community life". For example, he had written in a publication on the city's proposed freeway system that, while others had considered the cost of the freeways and their effect on traffic, the City Planning Board had "special responsibilities posed by virtue of its function and status as an advisory representative citizen's group concerned with the development of all facets of the community's life".

A second case study concerned the location of a new city-county hospital in City A. In the course of a prolonged controversy, politicians turned finally to city planners to interpret the overall public interest. The City

---

[1] These case studies will shortly appear as chapters 2–5 of my book, *The City Planning Process* (Ithaca: Cornell University Press, probably late 1965). Versions of three of them have already been published separately by the Inter-University Program as "The Ancker Hospital Site Controversy", "A Land-use Plan for St. Paul", and "Locating the Intercity Freeway".

Planning Board shied from this challenge out of political prudence, but the planning staff of the city's Housing and Redevelopment Authority accepted it eagerly. Both groups of planners stated confidently in interviews that they were better equipped to recommend a wise decision than the city's consultant hospital architect, whose primary concern was how best to build a hospital. They believed that because their perspective was broader, their recommendation was very likely to be more rational.[2]

A third case study described the evolution of a central area plan for City B. The plan's primary author, with the full support of his planning director, cast its arguments in the broadest possible terms. Its operational goal was clearly a limited one: economic growth. The planner felt, however, that he had to justify the goal itself. He stressed the functions of downtown as bearer of culture, disseminator of news and ideas, haven for unique activities, supplier of taxes to support all public services, and so on. When interviewed, he emphasized that his concern was to enrich the lives of all citizens, not to line the pockets of down-town businessmen. It was merely fortuitous, he believed, that in this case the interests of property owners and those of society coincided. He admitted freely, as did all the planners in both cities, that no plan or evaluation could be entirely comprehensive. His (and their) disclaimer was perfunctory, however, as if only a minor detail were at stake. He wrote, for example, that the central area plan could not truly be termed comprehensive because: "there are and always will be elements—new aspects—yet to be studied and yet to be decided upon". He thus rejected a conception of comprehensiveness that I have termed useless; that is, that the comprehensive plan should deal with everything. In short, he admitted that the object of any decision is neces-

---

[2] The words "rational" and "wise" are often used interchangeably in evaluating public choices. This is in accord with the usage of natural law philosophers, but not with that of contemporary economic and social theorists. For the latter the term "rational" refers to the efficiency of means where ends are known. "Wisdom" refers to deep understanding and the ability to make what are considered "good" judgments on complex human issues, when goals and efficient means are not generally known.

Consequently, the planners' use of the word "rational" in the classic sense to defend their distinctly modern "expert" recommendations makes for confusion of thought. This confusion has a political function, however. It conveys the impression that expert logic or technique can produce "good" decisions on complex human issues.

sarily limited, at very least in time, but he preserved the implication that the planner's approach—that is, his goal orientation—to the object may be comprehensive.

Planners generally agree that the method of discovery of community goals can in the final analysis only be public discussion. Planners may propose alternative articulations, but goal statements can have no claim to represent community thought unless the community or its "legitimate" representatives ratifies them after serious discussion and deliberation. The primary problem in theory, then, should be to guide the vigorous discussion and to decide when it has gone on long enough. The primary problem in practice, as developed in the two cities studied, was to get any sort of discussion going at all, and then to keep it going.

The planners of City A hoped, for example, that vigorous discussion would follow publication of their land use plan. No one showed any interest in discussing it, however. The reason seemed to be that the plan's stated goals were too general. No one knew how their application would affect him in practice. Those who were not completely uninterested in the plan had learned long ago to be suspicious of "utopian" generalities. As a result, nonplanners decided with uncoordinated unanimity to ignore the plan until someone proposed specific applications of it. Only at this point, they felt, would there be anything comprehensible—whether or not comprehensive—to argue about.

The planners of City B argued that the City A planners' premises were wrong, and would have been wrong even if discussion of their plan had developed. For a discussion truly to influence the planning process, they said, it had to begin before detailed planning got under way. In their view, no one could effectively interpolate changes into a plan after it was complete without upsetting its internal harmony. If one of the goals of a plan were changed, then in theory every specific recommendation should be altered to some extent. No one had the time or intellectual energy, however, to do this when a plan had already taken definite shape. The crucial phase in the evolution of any plan, then, was the development of its first draft. Goals should be determined before this phase moved far along. They themselves tried to obtain approval for planning goals before developing their central area plan. They decided at the start that they needed a goal statement which would be both "operational" and acceptable to all "reasonable" citizens of the city. By "operational", they meant that progress toward the goal could be objectively measured, and that the broad costs, both tangible and spiritual, of striving toward it could be foreseen. Comprehensive goals, they judged, could not be operational. Therefore, reasonable men could not pass them on intelligently. It followed that goals could win intelligent public approval only if they were partial. The question was: *how* partial? Perhaps it was possible to articulate, and plan to achieve, highly general goals even if not truly comprehensive ones.

They endeavored to bring about a public discussion of essential goal options before preparing the detailed plan. Planners had applied themselves to downtown economic problems in recent years, and had developed a fairly integrated theory explaining characteristic downtown problems. Consequently, City B's planners were able to present their preferred goals with tightly reasoned arguments behind them. The parts were related and mutually reinforced. The man of affairs with a limited amount of time could quickly grasp the objectives and the main lines of reasoning on which the recommendations were based. The most general operational goal that the planners proposed was "the economic growth of downtown". They recognized that this goal was itself deceptive, however, in that it sounded noncontroversial but the measures necessary to its accomplishment could not be. In their publications on downtown planning goals, therefore, they chose to emphasize what they termed "design goals". These were in fact *types* of projects that had been tried in other cities. The planners explained the relationship between these types of proposals and the economic problems facing urban downtowns in the current period. It was possible to discuss the types of dislocation that might be expected, and so on, without bringing in specific project proposals. The discussion was a model of comprehensible argument in favor of middle range (that is, operational but still general) planning goals. It is doubtful that existing theory was (or is) sufficiently developed to support comparable justifications of goal recommendations at any other range of city planning activity.[3]

---

[3] A major reason for this, of course, is that in no urban sections but downtown do simple economic goals seem entirely adequate. Outside the United States, planners often consider them inadequate even for downtown. See, for example, the British Town and Country Planning Association's analysis of central London problems: *The Paper Economy*, London: Town and Country Planning Association, 1962.

Even in this area, however, the specific financial costs and unintended side effects that would arise on application in City B were difficult to foresee. Any intelligent discussion of planning goals had to take these (or their unpredictability) into account. For the discussion to be fully useful, the planners judged, its participants had to be willing to inform themselves about planning detail at some significant expenditure of time and effort. The discussion had to continue throughout the planning process, which itself would have peaks of activity but no final termination. Since the overall goal was partial, the discussants had to be urged to consider the full complexity of its side effects. This they could not do if they confined themselves to examination of the central economic reasoning behind the "design goals".

The first problem was how to find appropriate discussants. The comprehensive planner's search is more complicated than that of any specialist. He cannot be satisfied to consult a narrow constituency. Presumably he should understand every important goal of each of society's members. If he must deal in practice with groups rather than individuals, he should not limit himself to constellations of interest that maintain permanent formal organizations. But the planners knew of no way to approach the city's "potential" groups. These would not become actual groups unless some immediate threats activated their potential members; some potential groupings of interest that the observer might identify would not become actual even then. Even those theoretically capable of being activated, however, currently had no leaders to speak for them. The abstract discussion of goals seldom seem sufficiently immediate to spur them to organize and choose representatives. It seemed that in no other public endeavor than general goal determination was the disproportion greater between the number of groups that might reasonably become involved and the number that would.

The planners soon found that they could carry on a continuing discussion only with men whose jobs required them to spend time on the study and discussion of civic affairs. Only a few organizations in the city had such men on their payrolls. All of these fit into a few categories. Most were large downtown business firms or organizations of businessmen. A few good government groups (supported mainly by the contributions of businesses or businessmen) had representatives who took an interest in city planning, but for the most part they were in the same position as planners;

they could talk abstractly about the public interest but they could not claim any special ability to represent particular interests. The other permanent organizations in the city did not have representatives spending the bulk of their time observing civic affairs. Each had a few continuing interests (racial issues, taxes, city hiring policy, and so forth) and became politically active only when immediate threats to these arose.

Making the best of this situation, the planners tried to carry on a discussion of goals with the professional "civic affairs" representatives of downtown business. These professional discussants, however, lacked the power to commit their firms to anything. Consequently, as the discussion became more specific they became more and more noncommittal. The businessmen who had the power to commit their firms to specific courses of action had neither the time nor interest to engage in long discussions with the city planners. In a short while, even the professional discussants found that they had no time to study each tentative planning formulation with care. Thus a major difficulty was revealed (as it probably would have been in most cities). Even had the planners been able to handle all the complexity of life, they would not have found laymen willing or able to evaluate their work.

If it is so difficult to spur well-informed discussion even of such limited goals as those of the central area plan, the following question necessarily demands attention: what should be considered an adequate discussion of planning goals? Was the discussion in this case adequate even though the only participants were businessmen who took only mild interest in the discussion and were concerned only with direct economic costs and consequences? One might say that it was, because other groups could have entered the discussion to raise additional points had they wished. I was not able to find any elected officials in City B, however, who accepted this reasoning. Most were rather inarticulate about their objectives, but some were able to state their views quite precisely. Their central line of reasoning may be summarized briefly. Downtown businesses are "organizations in being". They are accustomed to watching the civic scene and searching for issues likely to affect their interests. They enter the discussion of any proposal at a very early stage and understand its potential impact on their interests relatively early. Other members of the public, however, tend to reach awareness that something is in issue and conceptualize their interests much more slowly. After the perception begins to clarify most take quite some time to organize. There is an enormous range in the amount of time, and in the degree of immediacy of a threat or opportunity, that it takes to move different groups of people with potential interest in a proposal to the threshold of organizational expression. Government never moves slowly enough or poses issues clearly enough to give everyone his say. It is fair to say that only when government moves at a snail's pace and deals with issues of rather direct and immediate impact can a significant proportion of the great multitude of interests express themselves. Therefore, democratic planning of a highly general nature is virtually impossible. No legislature or committee of interest group leaders can rationally evaluate a statement of general goals. Its members cannot, in the absence of specific project proposals and citizen reactions to them, predict how the countless measures needed to accomplish the goals will affect the overall quality of community life or the interests of their own constituents and organizations. Consequently, they are likely to prefer operating on levels where comprehension and prediction are more feasible, even if this means fragmenting policy choices rather than integrating them. In practice, this means that they will rarely commit themselves to let general and long-range goal statements guide their consideration of lower-level alternatives.

There are, no doubt, many American local politicians who would not find the preceding argument a compelling one. In localities lacking a coherent "power elite" firmly committed to a plan, however, it has a high degree of plausibility as a prescription for political survival. Its specific dictates are bound to be, at a minimum, a "project" rather than a "general planning" orientation and a disinclination to deal with controversial issues.

BASIS FOR AUTHORITY

The point was made in the previous section that truly comprehensive goals tend not to provide any basis for evaluating concrete alternatives. It is thus difficult to stir political interest in them and impossible to plan rationally in their service. Recognizing this, many contemporary planners claim to practice middle-range planning—planning for the achievement of goals that are general, but still operational.

The middle-range planning ideal clearly has much to recommend it. It permits the promise of meaningful political discussion and approval of planning goals, even if (as we have seen) the achievement may be highly elusive. From the viewpoint of the general planner, however, it has one crucial flaw. It provides no basis for the planner to claim to understand the overall public interest. Men who plan to achieve operational—even though relatively general—goals are specialists, not comprehensive planners. Consequently, they have no *obvious* theoretical basis for claiming to know better than other specialists how far each specialist goal should be pursued, and with what priority.

The case for efforts at genuinely comprehensive planning has generally rested heavily on the thought that planners can resolve conflicts among goals in expert fashion. If they cannot, if they can only articulate specialist goals, then elected officials would seem required to act as the comprehensive arbiters of conflict. If it is assumed that arbiters operate most successfully when all important considerations are presented vigorously to them, one may argue reasonably that each important cluster of operational goals should be defended by a separate agency. Philip Selznick, for instance, has contended that leaders who wish to maximize their influence should structure their organizations so that the lines of jurisdiction-dividing subunits are those along which important issues are likely to arise. His reasoning is that if issues arise within sub-units, they are likely to be decided by the sub-unit head, without the chief executive becoming aware of them. It is when sub-units themselves come into conflict that arbiters at the next higher levels are most likely to learn of issues.[4] Delegation of overall authority to arbitrate, in this view, even within the framework of highly general goal statements, is bound to transfer the substance of power from the delegator to the delegatee. If the delegator retains appellate jurisdiction he may dilute this effect. The more that he is committed to uphold the comprehensive policy vision of the delegatee, however, the less will he feel free to do so. In trying to persuade politicians to commit themselves to the policy visions of planners, defenders of comprehensive planning must contend that the politicians will benefit their constituents by doing so. To the extent that the planners themselves lack comprehensive perspectives, however, this contention becomes less and less plausible.

Beyond this, even in pursuit of their own specialist goals, planners operate in a world of whole objects, not analytical aspects. They cannot

[4] Philip Selznick, *Leadership in Administration*, Evanston: Row, Peterson, & Co., 1957.

conceive means that will further the operational goals of primary interest to them without also affecting innumerable others in uncontrolled fashion. Many planners recognize this, and try not to serve their stated operational goals exclusively. The operational goal of City B's central area plan, for example, was downtown economic growth. Its authors realized, however, that they could not reasonably ignore other goals. They wrote and spoke as though the cultural, political, spiritual, recreational and other functions of downtown could never conflict with each other or with the economic function. In practice, they were saved by their common sense; they did not press their pursuit of economic goals sufficiently far to spur public awareness of potentially serious conflicts. Conceivably, they might have listed all the significant operational goals they hoped to serve, but they would still have been left with the problem of balancing them. In short, every concrete object of planner attention is a miniature of the whole. The important analytical problems that arise in planning for an entire urban area arise also in planning any section of it.[5] Perhaps the only solution is frankly to adopt a specialist orientation, even while remaining willing to adjust specific proposals as highly distasteful side effects become apparent. It may still be plausible to maintain, however, that planners are custodians of values that somehow deserve to take precedence over the values propounded by other specialists. Let us consider the most persuasive lines of reasoning frequently advanced in support of this view.

One of the most straightforward was stated by Allison Dunham in a well-known article several years ago.[6] He claimed to have found after a survey of the planning literature that planners almost invariably believed that, at the very least, they were the officials best qualified to evaluate site proposals for every kind of facility. They based their position on the premise that planners were experts in the impact of land uses on each other. The argument, in other words, was not that planners were "wiser" than

[5] The more limited objects (e.g. neighborhoods instead of whole cities) do present somewhat different, if not lesser, problems to the comprehensive planner. Cause and effect are easier to trace on the small scene, and important differences of interest are likely to be fewer. On the other hand, if planners emphasize the common interest of each homogeneous unit, they may well accentuate the differences between units.

[6] Allison Dunham, "A legal and economic basis for city planning", *Columbia Law Review*, Vol. LVIII (May 1958), pp. 650–71.

operating agency officials, but that on certain types of issues their specialty deserved first place in the hierarchy of specialists.

On this point two queries come to mind. First, are the impacts of uses on each other regularly more important in site decisions than the intended purposes of each use? Second, can locational problems be separated meaningfully from all other problems? Let me illustrate by referring to the controversy (mentioned previously) about where in City A to locate the new city-county hospital. One powerful group was anxious to locate the hospital between the city's two largest private hospitals (which in turn were one block apart) in the downtown area. They argued that the three hospitals combined could support a great deal of expensive equipment, could attract outstanding internes and residents more easily than any one alone, and might provide the base within a few years for development of a medical school in the city. The city's planners favored a site just outside the downtown area, emphasizing the traffic congestion that would result from locating the new hospital in the immediate vicinity of the two old ones. Each side advanced other arguments as well, but these were the main ones, and for my purpose it is not necessary to judge the overall merit of either position. It is only necessary to consider the general issues which were posed: first, how much cost in traffic congestion should be accepted to obtain how much benefit to health? and second, is traffic congestion more a locational problem than building a medical center? The proponents of the three-hospital medical center argued that its benefits could be obtained only by building on the site they proposed. No others in the immediate vicinity were available. They considered the site favored by the city planners to be wholly unacceptable. The only way to argue that planners should normally be given the benefit of the doubt in disputes of this kind is to say, as Dunham did, that specialists think of the needs of their constituents, while planners think of the impact of specialist proposals on others. In this case, the constituents were sick people and hospital staff personnel, while the "others" included many of the same people, but in their other capacities: as drivers and investors, for instance. The key question is whether the "others" should have had any more presumptive right to prevail than the recognized constituents.

Another objection to this definition of planner competence is that it provides only the haziest indication of the legitimate jurisdiction of planners and of government. Just what is a locational decision? It is hardly enough to say, as planners generally have, that locational decisions are those that have an impact on surrounding property or people. Almost anything I do to my property affects my neighbor in some way. For instance, if I rent out rooms in my single-family home, I have changed the use of my land and therefore made a locational decision, by a common planning definition. Should government therefore control everything, as it already controls my right to rent out rooms? Planners deny that it should, but they have rarely asked where the cutoff point should be. They have generally been satisfied to say that government should intervene only in cases of "substantial" harm, and that common sense will prevail in interpreting the word "substantial". They may be right, but this formulation gives the citizen no theoretical guidance as to whose common sense should prevail in cases of disagreement between other decision-makers and planners.

A second persuasive line of reasoning to support the view that planners should generally prevail in such disputes is that they alone among city officials analyze city problems from an overall point of view. Operating agency officials cannot rise above their day-to-day administrative chores, and in any event their perspectives are conditioned by the narrow responsibilities of their departments. Even politicians typically devote most of their time to maintaining contacts with, and to performing errand boy services for, their constituents. In dealing with legislative proposals, they generally focus on details of immediate interest to vocal groups rather than on the overall picture. In most cities, moreover, councilmen are elected from wards; in many they work only part time at their jobs; and in some each councilman heads a city department. Only planners can devote all their time to thought about city problems at the most general level.

The most obvious criticism of this position is that freedom from operating responsibility may not be the best condition in which to make high-level decisions. Some prominent decision-makers have argued that it is a poor one. Winston Churchill, for example, has written that Stafford Cripps became restive and hypercritical of his colleagues while serving as parliamentary whip during World War II. What he needed, according to Churchill's diagnosis, was responsibility which would absorb his energies and give him a sense of the concrete issues. Those who are free from operating responsibility, concluded Churchill, tend to develop an unhelpful watchdog mentality. It is unhelpful because they usually think too abstractly to be cogent critics of complex choices among policies.[7] Similarly, Chester Barnard has written that study and reflectiveness without operating responsibility tend to lead to the treatment of things by aspects rather than wholes, to a disregard of factors which cannot be expressed precisely, and to an underestimation of the need for artistry in making concrete decisions. Because so many crucial factors cannot find expression in words, Barnard concluded, the interdependencies of social life can only be grasped intuitively. Only men of long and responsible experience are likely to acquire very much of this intuitive grasp, and therefore only such men—who will also grasp the supreme difficulty of planning in this "world of unknowns"—are qualified to plan.[8] This is unquestionably a rather mystical position, but it is no less for that a respectable and forceful one.

Barnard and Churchill agree, then, that freedom from responsibility for operating decisions is anything but fit training for planning.[9] Those

---

[7] Winston Churchill, *The Second World War*, Vol. IV: *The Hinge of Fate*, Boston: Houghton-Mifflin Co., 1950, p. 560.

Churchill was not arguing against the making of large decisions by generalists, of course. He himself was Prime Minister. Nor was he criticizing the British practice of concentrating authority within the civil service in the hands of generalists. Several points may be noted. The generalists in a British ministry exercise all formal power of decision not exercised by the minister himself. They bear responsibility as well for deciding which issues, and which specialist analyses of them, are important enough for the minister to consider. The elite corps of the generalists, the Administrative Class, are expected on entry only to think, write, and speak clearly, and to have done well in their subject of undergraduate concentration. Any subject will do, although subjects fit for "gentlemen" (i.e. men devoted to culture rather than making a living), notably the classics, have traditionally predominated. British administrators have no formal technical training for their work at all. They are platonic rather than functional leaders, but matured on responsibility rather than study. Those at the higher levels are notably unsympathetic to the ideal of general planning. They take well-known pride in deciding "each case on its merit".

Parenthetically, where city planners are employed in British ministries, they are considered technicians, capable of contributing useful advise on specialized aspects of issues, but not of being entrusted with the power to make decisions.

[8] Chester Barnard, *Organization and Management*, Cambridge: Harvard University Press, 1948, chap. 4.

[9] It should be clear that when I speak of "planning" in this article, I mean the work of determining overall policy guidelines for public activity, and means of implementing them. No single individual or agency makes such determinations alone in an American community. The recommendations of some, however, are

who accept their view are likely to believe that any one of a number of city officials may qualify better than the planning director to serve as the wise chief advisor of politicians on broad policy issues. In cities A and B, the city councils consistently acted on this belief. To the extent that they desired coordination of public works, they normally relied on their city engineers to achieve it. When the city council of B decided to separate capital budgeting from ordinary budgeting, it set up a committee composed of politicians and civic leaders. The committee was given a small staff headed by a former city councilman. Planners were shut out of the capital budgeting process entirely. When the city council of A decided that it needed a special advisor on the interstate freeway program, it appointed the incumbent city engineer, who had been about to retire. When the city engineer of B left the city government for private employ, his successor proved inadequate (in the city council's view) for the unofficial task of coordinating city public works. Within a year, the council lured him back into government, giving him the title of Development Coordinator. The city's planners believed that they should have been given the job, but they could offer no strong arguments to support their view that the engineer was less able to take the overview than they. The politician most responsible for bringing him back told me that the planners thought too abstractly and with insufficient regard to cost; whereas the engineer, though less articulate, understood the infinite, inexpressable complexity of governmental choice. In fairness to the planners, it should be added that the engineer had made his entire career in City B, looking to the city council for his raises, perquisites, and promotions. He had risen primarily because of his technical competence, to be sure, but also because the councilmen felt confident that he would not embarrass them politically and that his overriding loyalty was to themselves. The Planning Director, by contrast, had been chosen after a national search by a citizens' committee (advised by a nationally known planning consultant), had been on the local scene for two years, and had his primary base of political support outside the city government entirely. It should be mentioned that the last

---

bound to carry more weight than those of others. The crucial questions at issue in this section are (1) whether the views of planning agencies on controversial policy issues should normally be granted presumptive validity in the absence of strong evidence discrediting them; and (2) whether the training and career patterns of professional city planners equip them well for planning at the higher levels.

factor was not due to simple ineptitude on the Planning Director's part. He had chosen his strategy consciously and deliberately, judging that the city government would support effective general planning only if—and, even then, only perhaps—pressured by outside groups to do so.

A third defense that planners frequently make of their aspiration to be more than "mere" specialists is that governmental efficiency is served by having one agency keep track of everything that every city agency does, calling attention to conflicts and to means of coordinating effort for the benefit of all. The distinction between coordination and planning, however, is of practical importance only so long as planners have no power. Without power, they can as coordinators simply try to persuade groups of specialists that their respective interests will be served by improved coordination. As soon as planners begin to impose solutions or advise politicians to impose them, however, they have entered the substantive planning field. That is, they have set their perception of the public interest on substantive matters against those of the specialists who have rejected their advice. Similarly, when planners request authority to prepare a city's capital budget, they cannot justify the request on grounds of "simple efficiency", which would have to be established by the criteria of all the specialists' own goals. They must assert, at least implicitly, that they have some means of choosing among the values entrusted to each operating agency. In other words, they must claim to have goals. And the coordination of action in pursuit of substantive goals is, if it is anything, substantive planning.

One might say that the planner needs coordinative power only because some specialists stupidly or obstinately refuse to cooperate with others in the interests of "simple efficiency", even though no significant values are threatened. The specialists' answer is that no one can determine that this is the case in any particular controversy without examining it in detail. Philip Selznick has illustrated this point clearly in his analysis of the history of the Communist party.[10] The party refused to cooperate with other leftist parties in the decade before the Popular Front, despite the obvious threat of fascism. Yet this period of isolation, Selznick contends, made the party a much more valuable tool to its masters during and after the Popular Front period. During the isolation period, the "character" of the party developed

---

[10] Philip Selznick, *The Organizational Weapon*, Glencoe: The Free Press, 1960.

and became incorruptible. This extreme example illustrates a simple point: that cooperation and isolation in themselves have important effects on organizations. If an agency had claims that a measure advanced in the name of efficiency threatens important values—and any agency head who refuses the advice of the planning director will say this—no outsider can refute him until he examines the bases of his arguments in detail. If we assume that most agency heads are men of good conscience, we can likewise assume that they will have some reasons that seem genuinely sufficient to them, and that will seem so as well to at least some reasonable outsiders. In the end, no act of coordination is without its effect on other values than efficiency.

CLOSING

The purpose here is not to disparage the ideal of comprehensive planning, but rather to challenge the planning profession to reinforce its most fundamental theoretical arsenal.[11] Some of the issues raised may seem overly theoretical, and in the immediate sense perhaps they are—though to me they appeared quite close to the surface in the two cities I studied. In the long run, however, comprehensive planning and evaluation will have little effect on American cities unless their goal premises can be established in sufficiently compelling fashion (both politically and intellectually) to make politicians take notice.

[11] I have made a beginning effort at reinforcement in my article, "Reason and influence in the public service," which is scheduled to appear in a forthcoming issue of the *Public Administration Review* and as chapter 7 of my book, *The City Planning Process.*

A Response to Altshuler:
Comprehensive Planning as a Process*

John Friedmann

PROFESSOR ALTSHULER's essay is a valuable addition to the small but growing list of studies of American city planning practice.[1] The collective impact of these studies has been to shatter the received image of planning as a profession and as an institution. At the core of this image, Professor Altshuler asserts, lies the ideal of comprehensiveness. And this, he continues, "must refer primarily to a special knowledge of the public interest". The city planner views himself as the stern guardian of the public interest.[2] This particular role conception, however, often interferes with his desire to have a substantial influence over policy and program decisions. Professor Altshuler implies that the traditional self-image of planners constitutes a serious impediment to the effectiveness of planning. Thus he challenges the profession: either revise your image or resign yourselves to continued impotence. The purpose of my remarks is to take up this challenge and

* Reprinted by permission of the *Journal of the American Institute of Planners*, Vol. 31, August 1965.

[1] Martin Meyerson and Edward C. Banfield, *Politics, Planning and the Public Interest*, Glencoe: The Free Press, 1955; W. H. Brown, Jr. and C. E. Gilbert, *Planning Municipal Investments*, Philadelphia: University of Pennsylvania Press, 1961; Alan Altshuler, *The City Planning Process*, Ithaca: Cornell University Press (probably late 1965); Robert T. Daland and John A. Parker, "Roles of the planner in urban development", in Chapin and Weiss (eds.), *Urban Growth Dynamics*, New York: Wiley, 1962; Roscoe C. Martin (ed.), *Decisions in Syracuse*, Bloomington: Indiana University Press, 1961; F. F. Rabinovitz, *Politics and Planning*, On the Role of the Expert in Urban Development, unpublished Ph.D. dissertation, Department of Economics and Political Science, M.I.T., Cambridge, Mass., 1965; and Gary Greeson, *Location Decision: The Boston Common Parking Garage*, unpublished thesis, Department of City and Regional Planning, M.I.T., Cambridge, Mass., 1965.

[2] The usefulness of the concept of public interest is itself fiercely disputed. See Carl J., Friedrich (ed.), *The Public Interest*, Yearbook of the American Society for Political and Legal Philosophy, Vol. 5, New York: The Asherton Press, 1962.

suggest an image of planning that is more consonant with the institutional setting within which planning must occur.

I shall define planning as a way of managing the non-routine affairs of the city. This is a broad and loose conception that intentionally extends the scope of city planning activity beyond its present preoccupation with the physical arrangements of objects in space to all the subject concerns for which the city carries a responsibility, including:

1. Economic expansion, full employment, efficiency of governmental operations.
2. Social welfare, crime, juvenile delinquency, racial integration.
3. Education; programs and facilities.
4. Housing construction, redevelopment, neighborhood conservation.
5. Public transportation.
6. Sanitation and public health.
7. Cultural and recreational programs and facilities.
8. Control over land uses.
9. Urban design values.

Professional fields of competence have grown up around all of these concerns. It is thus no longer possible for any single person to pretend to the university of his technical abilities, nor is it possible to demonstrate that control over land uses or urban design values—the traditional areas of city planning emphasis—are the critical points of coordination. The technical expert is replacing the comprehensive planner in influencing the decisions that guide a city's development.

Actual planning experience bears out this contention. But in defense of his position, the professional city planner may argue that this fragmentation among technicians of the power to influence decision sacrifices the view of the whole which has been the traditional claim to the legitimacy of planning.

It seems to me that this assertion in defense of comprehensiveness rests on an incorrect conception of the term. Comprehensiveness in city planning refers primarily to an awareness that the city is a system of interrelated social and economic variables extending over space. To uphold the principle of comprehensiveness, therefore, it is sufficient to say, first, that functional programs must be consonant with the city-wide system of relationships; second, that the costs and benefits of these programs must be calculated on the broadest possible basis; and third, that all "relevant" variables must be considered in the design of individual programs. It follows that comprehensiveness is not a special feature of the planner's mind, a mind trained to a holistic view, but must be achieved by a process that will maximize the specialized contributions of technical experts to the solution of urban problems.

How might such a process be organized within a typical large American city? To answer this question, it is necessary to draw a distinction between policy and program planning. The former is chiefly concerned with the maintenance and achievement of *performance goals* for the city as a whole, the latter with the attainment of *achievement goals* for specific functional activities or sectors.[3] Policy planning looks toward maintaining the city as a delicately balanced socio-spatial system in a state of dynamic equilibrium. Unfortunately, we are still lacking a set of social accounts for urban units that would permit policy planners to measure the current state of the city by a few simple indices.[4] Planners are consequently unable to say when the city is performing optimally and when it is not, something that national planners, reading the indices for gross national product, employment, and related variables, find relatively easy to do for the economy. This failure to evoke a widely accepted system of urban social accounts reflects the absence of a theory of the city. Urban policy planners must therefore resort to partial equilibrium solutions as approximate measures of the total performance of the city.

Although these measures do not constitute a system, it is possible to combine them loosely into an urban development framework or *policies* plan and to derive from this plan specific *program* guidelines in all the subject areas that are of concern to the city for a period of five to ten years. Responsibility for formulating the development policies plan would rest with a Council of Urban Development Advisors attached to the office of the city's chief executive. The intention here is to duplicate at the city-scale a general planning function that is currently being carried out in most

[3] For a discussion of performance and achievement goals, see Sidney Sonenblum and Louis H. Stern, "The use of economic projections in planning", *A.I.P. Journal*, Vol. XXX, No. 2 (May 1964), p. 111.

[4] Current work on urban social accounts is summarized in Werner Z. Hirsch (ed.), *Elements of Regional Accounts*. Published for Resources of the Future, Inc. (Baltimore: The Johns Hopkins Press, 1964). Unfortunately the scope of these investigations is almost exclusively confined to economic variables.

countries at the national level and which has its counterpart in the United States in the Council of Economic Advisors. In addition to responsibility for the formulation and revision of the development policies plan, the proposed Council would:

1. Prepare an annual state of the city report.[5]
2. Engage in policy-oriented research.
3. Coordinate the statistical work of the city.
4. Establish a city-wide information system.
5. Give specific policy advice to the mayor.
6. Coordinate policy by working with task forces and special commissions that may be appointed to deal with special policy areas (the Council here might serve as a general secretariat for any staff work that needed to be done).

The medium-term program guidelines that are derived from the general premises of the development policies plan would serve as a basis for the administrative agencies of the city in designing detailed program statements. To achieve a satisfactory measure of program coordination among sectors and across geographic space, operational programs would have to be pulled together in the form of an urban capital budget and, corresponding to this budget, a development map. The effective time horizon of these two documents would be substantially less than for the development policies plan of the city, and most of the energies of planning staffs would, in fact, be devoted to the task of preparing coordinated program statements for the coming budget year, with two- or three-year projections serving as a basis for program evaluation.

Such a programming function is perhaps best centralized in the city's budget office. It could function effectively, however, only to the extent that trained programming staffs are working in each of the city's departments and specialized agencies. In coordinating sectoral programs, the budget office would be guided by the urban development plan and related policy statements that are evolved by the Council of Development Advisors. It might also attempt to initiate a formal process whereby citizen groups are brought in to advise on the functional and spatial allocations in the

---

[5] See, for example, Southwestern Pennsylvania Regional Planning Commission, *State of the Region '64*, 200 Ross Street, Pittsburgh, Pennsylvania.

budget. Towards this end, a Citizen Budget Advisory Council could be appointed on the nomination by local interest groups.

To complete the structure of planning, two more offices would need to be created at the executive level: *one*, an Office of Urban Design responsible for the physical planning aspects of capital improvement projects and the development of appropriate design criteria for controlling the visual form of the city, and *two*, an Office of Land Use Planning whose function would be to administer the city's land use plan in coordination with all other planning offices and with specific responsibility for zoning and subdivision control.

I believe that this system of planning functions—policy, program, design, and land use—organized as separate offices at the highest level of city administration would go a long way toward meeting Professor Altshuler's challenge to the planning profession. It would do so by:

1. Enlarging the scope of what is normally considered city planning to include all matters of interest and concern to the city.
2. Establishing a process of consultation and coordination that would be built directly into the decision-making structure of the city.
3. Separating within this process distinct policy and program planning functions operating on different time scales.
4. Orienting planning functions to development tasks and partial equilibrium solutions rather than to the formulation of a general equilibrium model in the form of a long-range master plan.
5. Maximizing the potential contributions of technical experts in a variety of subject fields, relying on a process of continuing, structured relationships among them to achieve the comprehensiveness which would continue to be one of the major aims of planning.

If this argument is accepted, it follows that the planning profession will need to deepen its interest in the methodology of policy and program planning and to make room in its professional curricula for the development of specialized competences in fields where only rudimentary instruction is currently provided.

Mixed-scanning:
A "Third" Approach to Decision-making*

Amitai Etzioni

IN THE concept of social decision-making, vague commitments of a normative and political nature are translated into specific commitments to one
or more specific courses of action. Since decision-making includes an
element of choice, it is the most deliberate and voluntaristic aspect of
social conduct. As such, it raises the question: To what extent can social
actors decide what their course will be, and to what extent are they compelled to follow a course set by forces beyond their control? Three conceptions of decision-making are considered here with assumptions that
give varying weights to the conscious choice of the decision-makers.

Rationalistic models tend to posit a high degree of control over the
decision-making situation on the part of the decision-maker. The incrementalist approach presents an alternative model, referred to as the art of
"muddling through", which assumes much less command over the
environment. Finally, the article outlines a third approach to social decision-
making which, in combining elements of both earlier approaches, is
neither as utopian in its assumptions as the first model nor as conservative
as the second. For reasons which will become evident, this third approach
is referred to as mixed-scanning.

THE RATIONALISTIC APPROACH

Rationalistic models are widely held conceptions about how decisions
are and ought to be made. An actor becomes aware of a problem, posits a
goal, carefully weighs alternative means, and chooses among them according to his estimates of their respective merit, with reference to the state
of affairs he prefers. Incrementalists' criticism of this approach focuses
on the disparity between the requirements of the model and the capacities

* Reprinted by permission of the *Public Administration Review*, December 1967.

of decision-makers.[1] Social decision-making centers, it is pointed out, frequently do not have a specific, agreed upon set of values that could provide the criteria for evaluating alternatives. Values, rather, are fluid and are affected by, as well as affect, the decisions made. Moreover, in actual practice, the rationalistic assumption that values and facts, means and ends, can be clearly distinguished seems inapplicable:

> . . . Public controversy . . . has surrounded the proposal to construct a branch of the Cook County Hospital on the South Side in or near the Negro area. Several questions of policy are involved in the matter, but the ones which have caused one of the few *public* debates of an issue in the Negro community concern whether, or to what extent, building such a branch would result in an all-Negro or "Jim Crow" hospital and whether such a hospital is desirable as a means of providing added medical facilities for Negro patients. Involved are both an issue of *fact* (whether the hospital would be segregated, intentionally or unintentionally, as a result of the character of the neighborhood in which it would be located) and an issue of *value* (whether even an all-Negro hospital would be preferable to no hospital at all in the area). In reality, however the, factions have aligned themselves in such a way and the debate has proceeded in such a manner that the fact issue and the value issue have been collapsed into the single question of whether to build or not to build. Those in favor of the proposal will argue that the facts do not bear out the charge of "Jim Crowism"—"the proposed site . . . is not considered to be placed in a segregated area for the exclusive use of one racial or minority group"; or "no responsible officials would try to develop a new hospital to further segregation"; or "establishing a branch hospital for the . . . more adequate care of the indigent patient load, from the facts thus presented, does not represent Jim Crowism." At the same time, these proponents argue that whatever the facts, the factual issue is secondary to the overriding consideration that "there is a here-and-now need for more hospital beds. . . . Integration may be the long-run goal, but in the short-run we need more facilities."[2]

In addition, information about consequences is, at best, fractional. Decision-makers have neither the assets nor the time to collect the information required for rational choice. While knowledge technology, especially computers, does aid in the collection and processing of information, it cannot provide for the computation required by the rationalist model. (This holds even for chess playing, let alone "real-life" decisions.) Finally, rather than being confronted with a limited universe of relevant consequences,

---

[1] See David Braybrooke and Charles E. Lindblom, *A Strategy of Decision*, New York: Free Press, 1963, pp. 48–50 and 111–43; Charles E. Lindblom, *The Intelligence of Democracy*, New York: Free Press, 1965, pp. 137–9. See also Jerome S. Bruner, Jacqueline J. Goodnow, and George A. Austin, *A Study of Thinking*, New York: John Wiley, 1956, chaps. 4–5.

[2] James Q. Wilson, *Negro Politics*, New York: Free Press, 1960, p. 189.

decision-makers face an open system of variables, a world in which all consequences cannot be surveyed.[3] A decision-maker, attempting to adhere to the tenets of a rationalistic model, will become frustrated, exhaust his resources without coming to a decision, and remain without an effective decision-making model to guide him. Rationalistic models are thus rejected as being at once unrealistic and undesirable.

THE INCREMENTALIST APPROACH

A less demanding model of decision-making has been outlined in the strategy of "disjointed incrementalism" advanced by Charles E. Lindblom and others.[4] Disjointed incrementalism seeks to adapt decision-making strategies to the limited cognitive capacities of decision-makers and to reduce the scope and cost of information collection and computation. Lindblom summarized the six primary requirements of the model in this way:[5]

1. Rather than attempting a comprehensive survey and evaluation of all alternatives, the decision-maker focuses only on those policies which differ incrementally from existing policies.
2. Only a relatively small number of policy alternatives are considered.
3. For each policy alternative, only a restricted number of "important" consequences are evaluated.
4. The problem confronting the decision-maker is continually re-defined: Incrementalism allows for countless end-means and means-ends adjustments which, in effect, make the problem more manageable.
5. Thus, there is no one decision or "right" solution but a "never-ending series of attacks" on the issues at hand through serial analyses and evaluation.

[3] See review of *A Strategy of Decision* by Kenneth J. Arrow in *Political Science Quarterly*, Vol. 79 (1964), p. 585. See also Herbert A. Simon, *Models of Man*, New York: Wiley, 1957, p. 198, and Aaron Wildavsky, *The Politics of the Budgetary Process*, Boston: Little, Brown & Co., 1964, pp. 147–52.

[4] Charles E. Lindblom, "The science of 'muddling through'", *Public Administration Review*, Vol. 19 (1959), pp. 79–99; Robert A. Dahl and Charles E. Lindblom, *Politics, Economics and Welfare*, New York: Harper & Brothers, 1953; *Strategy of Decision, op. cit.*, and *The Intelligence of Democracy, op. cit.*

[5] Lindblom, *The Intelligence of Democracy, op. cit.*, pp. 144–8.

6. As such, incremental decision-making is described as remedial, geared more to the alleviation of present, concrete social imperfections than to the promotion of future social goals.

MORPHOLOGICAL ASSUMPTIONS OF THE INCREMENTAL APPROACH

Beyond a model and a strategy of decision-making, disjointed incrementalism also posits a structure model; it is presented as the typical decision-making process of pluralistic societies, as contrasted with the master planning of totalitarian societies. Influenced by the free competition model of economics, incrementalists reject the notion that policies can be guided in terms of central institutions of a society expressing the collective "good". Policies, rather, are the outcome of a give-and-take among numerous societal "partisans". The measure of a good decision is the decision-makers' agreement about it. Poor decisions are those which exclude actors capable of affecting the projected course of action; decisions of this type tend to be blocked or modified later.

Partisan "mutual-adjustment" is held to provide for a measure of coordination of decisions among a multiplicity of decision-makers and, in effect, to compensate on the societal level for the inadequacies of the individual incremental decision-maker and for the society's inability to make decisions effectively from one center. Incremental decision-making is claimed to be both a realistic account of how the American polity and other modern democracies decide and the most effective approach to societal decision-making, i.e. both a descriptive and a normative model.

A CRITIQUE OF THE INCREMENTAL APPROACH AS A NORMATIVE MODEL

Decisions by consent among partisans without a societywide regulatory center and guiding institutions should not be viewed as the preferred approach to decision-making. In the first place, decisions so reached would, of necessity, reflect the interests of the most powerful, since partisans invariably differ in their respective power positions; demands of the underprivileged and politically unorganized would be underrepresented.

Secondly, incrementalism would tend to neglect *basic* societal innova-

tions, as it focuses on the short run and seeks no more than limited variations from past policies. While an accumulation of small steps could lead
to a significant change, there is nothing in this approach to guide the
accumulation; the steps may be circular—leading back to where they
started, or dispersed—leading in many directions at once but leading
nowhere. Boulding comments that, according to this approach, "we do
stagger through history like a drunk putting one disjointed incremental
foot after another".[6]

In addition, incrementalists seem to under-estimate *their* impact on the
decision-makers. As Dror put it: "Although Lindblom's thesis includes
a number of reservations, these are insufficient to alter its main impact as
an ideological reinforcement of the pro-inertia and anti-innovation
forces."[7]

A CONCEPTUAL AND EMPIRICAL CRITIQUE
OF INCREMENTALISM

Incrementalist strategy clearly recognizes one subset of situations to
which it does not apply—namely, "large" or fundamental decisions,[8] such
as a declaration of war. While incremental decisions greatly outnumber
fundamental ones, the latter's significance for societal decision-making is
not commensurate with their number; it is thus a mistake to relegate non-
incremental decisions to the category of exceptions. Moreover, it is often
the fundamental decisions which set the context for the numerous incremental ones. Although fundamental decisions are frequently "prepared"
by incremental ones in order that the final decision will initiate a less
abrupt change, these decisions may still be considered relatively fundamental. The incremental steps which follow cannot be understood without
them, and the preceding steps are useless unless they lead to fundamental
decisions.

Thus, while the incrementalists hold that decision-making involves a
choice between the two kinds of decision-making models, it should be
noted that (a) *most incremental decisions specify or anticipate fundamental*

[6] Kenneth E. Boulding in a review of *A Strategy of Decision* in the *American
Sociological Review*, Vol. 29 (1964), p. 931.

[7] Yehezkel Dror, "Muddling through—'science' or inertia?", *Public Administration Review*, Vol. 24 (1964), p. 155.

[8] Braybrooke and Lindblom, *A Strategy of Decision, op. cit.*, pp. 66–69.

decisions, and (b) *the cumulative value of the incremental decisions is greatly affected by the related fundamental decisions.*

Thus, it is not enough to show, as Fenno did, that Congress makes primarily marginal changes in the federal budget (a comparison of one year's budget for a federal agency with that of the preceding year showed on many occasions only a 10 per cent difference[9]), or that for long periods the defense budget does not change much in terms of its percentage of the federal budget, or that the federal budget changes little each year in terms of its percentage of the Gross National Product.[10] These incremental changes are often the unfolding of trends initiated at critical turning points at which fundamental decisions were made. The American defense budget jumped at the beginning of the Korean War in 1950 from 5 per cent of the GNP to 10.3 per cent in 1951. The fact that it stayed at about this level, ranging between 9 and 11.3 per cent of the GNP after the war ended (1954–60), did reflect incremental decisions, but these were made within the context of the decision to engage in the Korean War.[11] Fenno's own figures show almost an equal number of changes above the 20 per cent level as below it; seven changes represented an increase of 100 per cent or more and twenty-four changes increased 50 per cent or more.[12]

It is clear that, while Congress or other societal decision-making bodies do make some cumulative incremental decisions without facing the fundamental one implied, many other decisions which appear to be a series of incremental ones are, in effect, the implementation or elaboration of a fundamental decision. For example, after Congress set up a national space agency in 1958 and consented to back President Kennedy's space goals, it made "incremental" additional commitments for several years. Initially, however, a fundamental decision had been made. Congress in 1958, drawing on past experiences and on an understanding of the dynamics of incremental processes, could not have been unaware that once a fundamental commitment is made it is difficult to reverse it. While

[9] Richard Fenno, Jr., *The Power of the Purse*, Boston: Little, Brown & Co., 1966, pp. 266 ff. See also Otto A. Davis, M. A. H. Dempster, and Aaron Wildavsky, "A theory of the budgetary process", *American Political Science Review*, Vol. 60 (1966), esp. pp. 530–1.

[10] Samuel P. Huntington, quoted by Nelson E. Polsby, *Congress and the Presidency*, Englewood Cliffs, N.J.: Prentice-Hall, 1964, p. 86.

[11] *Ibid.*

[12] Fenno, *The Power of the Purse, loc. cit.*

the initial space budget was relatively small, the very act of setting up a space agency amounted to subscribing to additional budget increments in future years.[13]

Incrementalists argue that incremental decisions tend to be remedial; small steps are taken in the "right" direction, or, when it is evident the direction is "wrong", the course is altered. But if the decision-maker evaluates his incremental decisions and small steps, which he must do if he is to decide whether or not the direction is right, his judgment will be greatly affected by the evaluative criteria he applies. Here, again, we have to go outside the incremental model to ascertain the ways in which these criteria are set.

Thus, while actors make both kinds of decisions, the number and role of fundamental decisions are significantly greater than incrementalists state, and when the fundamental ones are missing, incremental decision-making amounts to drifting—action without direction. A more active approach to societal decision-making requires two sets of mechanisms: (a) high-order, fundamental policy-making processes which set basic directions and (b) incremental processes which prepare for fundamental decisions and work them out after they have been reached. This is provided by mixed-scanning.

THE MIXED-SCANNING APPROACH

Mixed-scanning provides both a realistic description of the strategy used by actors in a large variety of fields and the strategy for effective actors to follow. Let us first illustrate this approach in a simple situation and then explore its societal dimensions. Assume we are about to set up a worldwide weather observation system using weather satellites. The rationalistic approach would seek an exhaustive survey of weather conditions by using cameras capable of detailed observations and by scheduling reviews of the entire sky as often as possible. This would yield an avalanche of details, costly to analyze and likely to overwhelm our action capacities

[13] For an example involving the Supreme Court's decision on desegregation, see Martin Shapiro, "Stability and change in judicial decision-making: incrementalism or *Stare Decisis*", *Law in Transition Quarterly*, Vol. 2 (1965), pp. 134–57. See also a commentary by Bruce L. R. Smith, *American Political Science Review*, Vol. 61 (1967), esp. p. 151.

(e.g. "seeding" cloud formations that could develop into hurricanes or bring rain to arid areas). Incrementalism would focus on those areas in which similar patterns developed in the recent past and, perhaps, on a few nearby regions; it would thus ignore all formations which might deserve attention if they arose in unexpected areas.

A mixed-scanning strategy would include elements of both approaches by employing two cameras: a broad-angle camera that would cover all parts of the sky but not in great detail, and a second one which would zero in on those areas revealed by the first camera to require a more in-depth examination. While mixed-scanning might miss areas in which only a detailed camera could reveal trouble, it is less likely than incrementalism to miss obvious trouble spots in unfamiliar areas.

From an abstract viewpoint mixed-scanning provides a particular procedure for the collection of information (e.g. the surveying or "scanning" of weather conditions), a strategy about the allocation of resources (e.g. "seeding"), and—we shall see—guidelines for the relations between the two. The strategy combines a detailed ("rationalistic") examination of some sectors—which, unlike the exhaustive examination of the entire area, is feasible—with a "truncated" review of other sectors. The relative investment in the two kinds of scanning—full detail and truncated—as well as in the very act of scanning, depends on how costly it would be to miss, for example, one hurricane; the cost of additional scanning; and the amount of time it would take.

Scanning may be divided into more than two levels; there can be several levels with varying degrees of detail and coverage, though it seems most effective to include an all-encompassing level (so that no major option will be left uncovered) and a highly detailed level (so that the option selected can be explored as fully as is feasible).

The decision on how the investment of assets and time it to be allocated among the levels of scanning is, in fact, part of the strategy. The actual amount of assets and time spent depends on the total amount available and on experimentation with various interlevel combinations. Also, the amount spent is best changed over time. Effective decision-making requires that sporadically, or at set intervals, investment in encompassing (high-coverage) scanning be increased to check for far removed but "obvious" dangers and to search for better lines of approach. Annual budget reviews and the State of the Union messages provide, in principle, such occasions.

An increase in investment of this type is also effective when the actor realizes that the environment radically changes or when he sees that the early chain of increments brings no improvement in the situation or brings even a "worsening". If, at this point, the actor decides to drop the course of action, the effectiveness of his decision-making is reduced, since, through some high-coverage scanning, he may discover that a continuation of the "loss" is about to lead to a solution. (An obvious example is the selling of a declining stock if a further review reveals that the corporation is expected to improve its earning next year, after several years of decline.) Reality cannot be assumed to be structured in straight lines where each step towards a goal leads directly to another and where the accumulation of small steps in effect solves the problem. Often what from an incremental viewpoint is a step away from the goal ("worsening") may from a broader perspective be a step in the right direction, as when the temperature of a patient is allowed to rise because this will hasten his recovery. Thus mixed-scanning not only combines various levels of scanning but also provides a set of criteria for situations in which one level or another is to be emphasized.

In the exploration of mixed-scanning, it is essential to differentiate fundamental decisions from incremental ones. Fundamental decisions are made by exploring the main alternatives the actor sees in view of his conception of his goals, but—unlike what rationalism would indicate—details and specifications are omitted so that an overview is feasible. Incremental decisions are made but within the contexts set by fundamental decisions (and fundamental reviews). Thus, each of the two elements in mixed-scanning helps to reduce the effects of the particular shortcomings of the other; incrementalism reduces the unrealistic aspects of rationalism by limiting the details required in fundamental decisions, and contextuating rationalism helps to overcome the conservative slant of incrementalism by exploring longer-run alternatives. Together, empirical tests and comparative study of decision-makers would show that these elements make for a third approach which is at once more realistic and more effective than its components.

CAN DECISIONS BE EVALUATED?

The preceding discussion assumes that both the observer and the actor have a capacity to evaluate decision-making strategies and to determine which is the more effective. Incrementalists, however, argue that since values cannot be scaled and summarized, "good" decisions cannot be defined and, hence, evaluation is not possible. In contrast, it is reasonable to expect that the decision-makers, as well as the observers, can summarize their values and rank them, at least in an ordinal scale.

For example, many societal projects have one primary goal such as increasing birth control, economically desalting sea water, or reducing price inflation by one-half over a two-year period. Other goals which are also served are secondary. e.g. increasing the country's R & D sector by investing in desalting. The actor, hence, may deal with the degree to which the *primary* goal was realized and make this the central evaluative measure for a "good" policy, while noting its effects on secondary goals. When he compares projects in these terms, he, in effect, weighs the primary goal as several times as important as all the secondary goals combined. This procedure amounts to saying, "As I care very much about one goal and little about the others, if the project does not serve the first goal, it is no good and I do not have to worry about measuring and totalling up whatever other gains it may be providing for my secondary values."

When there are two or even three primary goals (e.g. teaching, therapy, and research in a university hospital), the actor can still compare projects in terms of the extent to which they realize each primary goal. He can establish that project X is good for research but not for teaching while project Y is very good for teaching but not as good for research, etc., without having to raise the additional difficulties of combining the effectiveness measures into one numerical index. In effect, he proceeds as if they had identical weights.

Finally, an informal scaling of values is not as difficult as the incrementalists imagine. Most actors are able to rank their goals to some extent (e.g. faculty is more concerned about the quality of research than the quality of teaching).

> One of the most imaginative attempts to evaluate the effectiveness of programs with hard-to-assess objectives is a method devised by David Osborn, Deputy Assistant Secretary of State for Educational and Cultural Affairs. . . . Osborn recommends a scheme of cross-multiplying the costs of the activities with a number representing the rank of its objectives on a scale. For instance, the exchange of Fulbright professors may contribute to "cultural prestige and mutual respect", "educational development", and gaining "entrée", which might be given scale numbers such as 8, 6, and 5, respectively. These numbers are then multiplied with the costs of the program, and the resulting figure is

in turn multiplied with an ingenious figure called a "country number". The latter is an attempt to get a rough measure of the importance to the U.S. of the countries with which we have cultural relations. It is arrived at by putting together in complicated ways certain key data, weighed to reflect cultural and educational matters, such as the country's population, Gross National Product, number of college students, rate of illiteracy, and so forth. The resulting numbers are then revised in the light of working experience, as when, because of its high per capita income, a certain tiny middle-eastern country turns out to be more important to the U.S. than a large eastern European one. At this point, country numbers are revised on the basis of judgment and experience, as are other numbers at other points. But those who make such visions have a basic framework to start with, a set of numbers arranged on the basis of many factors, rather than single arbitrary guesses.[14]

Thus, in evaluation as in decision-making itself, while full detailed rationalism may well be impossible, truncated reviews are feasible, and this approach may be expected to be more effective in terms of the actors' goals than "muddling through".

MORPHOLOGICAL FACTORS

The structures within which interactions among actors take place become more significant the more we recognize that the bases of decisions neither are nor can be a fully ordered set of values and an exhaustive examination of reality. In part, the strategy followed is determined neither by values nor by information but by the positions of and power relations among the decision-makers. For example, the extent to which one element of mixed-scanning is stressed as against the other is affected by the relationship between higher and lower organizational ranks. In some situations, the higher in rank, concerned only with the overall picture, are impatient with details, while lower ranks—especially experts—are more likely to focus on details. In other situations, the higher ranks, to avoid facing the overall picture, seek to bury themselves, their administration, and the public in details.

Next, the environment should be taken into account. For instance, a highly incremental approach would perhaps be adequate if the situation were more stable and the decisions made were effective from the start. This approach is expected to be less appropriate when conditions are

[14] Virginia Held, "PPBS comes to Washington", *The Public Interest*, No. 4 Summer 1966), pp. 102–15, quotation from pp. 112–13.

rapidly changing and when the initial course was wrong. Thus, there seems to be no one effective decision-making strategy in the abstract, apart from the societal environment into which it is introduced. Mixed-scanning is flexible; changes in the relative investment in scanning in general as well as among the various levels of scanning permit it to adapt to the specific situation. For example, more encompassing scanning is called for when the environment is more malleable.

Another major consideration here is the capacities of the actor. This is illustrated with regard to interagency relations by the following statement: ". . . the State Department was hopelessly behind. Its cryptographic equipment was obsolescent, which slowed communications, and it had no central situation room at all."[15] The author goes on to show how as a consequence the State Department was less able to act than was the Defense Department.

An actor with a low capacity to mobilize power to implement his decisions may do better to rely less on encompassing scanning; even if remote outcomes are anticipated, he will be able to do little about them. More generally, the greater a unit's control capacities the more encompassing scanning it can undertake, and the more such scanning, the more effective its decision-making. This points to an interesting paradox: The developing nations, with much lower control capacities than the modern ones, tend to favor much more planning, although they may have to make do with a relatively high degree of incrementalism. Yet modern pluralistic societies—which are much more able to scan and, at least in some dimensions, are much more able to control—tend to plan less.

Two different factors are involved which highlight the difference in this regard among modern societies. While all have a higher capacity to scan and some control advantages as compared to nonmodern societies, they differ sharply in their capacity to build consensus. Democracies must accept a relatively high degree of incrementalism (though not as high as developing nations) because of their greater need to gain support for new decisions from many and conflicting subsocieties, a need which reduces their capacity to follow a long-run plan. It is easier to reach consensus under noncrisis situations, on increments similar to existing policies, than to gain support for a new policy. However, the role of crises is significant; in

[15] Roger Hilsman, *To Move a Nation: The Politics of Foreign Policy in the Administration of John F. Kennedy*, Garden City, N.Y.: Doubleday & Co., 1967, p. 27.

relatively less passive democracies, crises serve to build consensus for major changes of direction which are overdue (e.g. desegregation).

Totalitarian societies, more centralist and relying on powers which are less dependent on consensus, can plan more but they tend to overshoot the mark. Unlike democracies which first seek to build up a consensus and then proceed, often doing less than necessary later than necessary, totalitarian societies, lacking the capacity for consensus-building or even for assessing the various resistances, usually try for too much too early. They are then forced to adjust their plans after initiation, with the revised policies often scaled down and involving more "consensus" than the original one. While totalitarian gross misplanning constitutes a large waste of resources, some initial overplanning and later down-scaling is as much a decision-making strategy as is disjointed incrementalism, and is the one for which totalitarian societies may be best suited.

A society more able to effectively handle its problems (one referred to elsewhere as an *active society*)[16] would require:

1. A higher capacity to build consensus than even democracies command.
2. More effective though not necessarily more numerous means of control than totalitarian societies employ (which new knowledge technology and better analysis through the social sciences may make feasible).
3. A mixed-scanning strategy which is not as rationalistic as that which the totalitarian societies attempt to pursue and not as incremental as the strategy democracies advocate.

[16] Amitai Etzioni, *The Active Society: A Theory of Societal and Political Processes*, New York: Free Press, 1968.

BUREAUCRATS, ADVOCATES, INNOVATORS

Introduction

THIS part will document the development of American thinking concerning the *institutions of planning* and the *personal qualities* of those who fill their ranks. During the sixties, this thinking has moved away from emphasizing the close liaison between planning and urban government and towards the notion of the planner as the largely self-styled champion of disadvantaged groups. Lately, this idea has in turn been questioned, not in the least by people with substantial experience in *advocacy planning*. Whilst a return to the original position is unlikely, new organizational forms for planning might be created incorporating features of traditional bureaucracy, as well as those of political institutions. Grauhan's paper concluding this section outlines one such form which is currently discussed by German planners.

PLANNING BOARD OR STAFF-FUNCTION

A certain amount of background information concerning the institutional development of American planning and, indeed, American city government, will help in understanding the issues discussed in this section.

Reference has already been made to two streams in the development of American planning. The debate between protagonists of these two schools of thought evolved precisely around the institutional form of planning: the earlier "City Beautiful" had produced the independent planning board (or planning commission) while its less beautification minded opponents favoured planning as a "staff-function" of urban government.

During the first decades of this century, most American plans were drawn up under the auspices of a planning board. This institution must be seen as part of what, in American city politics, is called the *conservative reform movement*, i.e. a movement of upper- and middle-class interests to rid city governments of political "machines" and their powerful "bosses" and to replace them by "clean" and efficient forms of government. As Meyerson and Banfield (1955) argue, the machines, though corrupt, nevertheless have been responsive to the needs of lower classes and ethnic minorities, while non-partisan forms of government—including planning boards—favour city-wide interests.

Thus, planning boards consisted of groups of respected citizens who would lend, as Nash and Durden (1964) have put it, their endorsement to the concept of planning. Pressure for such an endorsement role came from the emerging planning profession looking upon boards as allies well equipped to deal with entrenched political forces.

Critical comments on the planning board date back to the early forties. These concentrate on the lack of a clear-cut definition of its responsibilities. "(The) efforts of public agencies to operate as though they were private advocates of public policy have led them, helplessly, into the political arena. There, they have suffered the fate of early Christians among the lions." Robert A. Walker (1941) formulated the alternative as early as 1941: "Planning is one of the staff-functions and should be attached to the executive office."

From 1950 onwards, when the expanded second edition of Walker's book was published, the controversy around the planning board became a major issue in American planning thought. During the following years, most of the more convincing arguments were in favour of planning as a staff-function on grounds of political realism (Nash and Durden, 1964). Planning was seen as best located in the mainstream of urban government, and not outside it.

EXPANSION OF PLANNING AS A BUREAUCRATIC FUNCTION OF URBAN GOVERNMENT

This controversy forms the background to Dyckman's paper on "What makes planners plan?". Written in 1961, it is very characteristic of his series of "Interpretations". These were not meant to be serious pieces of research but short, rather impressionistic, exploratory papers. Inevitably, they were somewhat casual, though highly intellectual, sketches making incisive comments on contemporary American planning.

In the present paper, Dyckman anticipates expansion of the planning profession within urban government and a concomitant change in the outlook of planners from the crusader type (often associated with the conservative reform movement) to the planner having a bureaucratic function in urban government. He then asks questions concerning the influence which this development might have on new entrants into the profession which, with the benefit of hindsight, can only be called remarkable. Thus, he anticipates the battle cry of young planners of the late sixties of planners and planning being "middle-class", and their demands that planning must have a sense of mission.

His statement that, without commitment, the planner must become a tool for the powerful, and that planning is really a moral activity, reflects a point of view which he has held with great consistency throughout the years. In 1966, after publication of Davidoff's paper on advocacy planning, he reiterates that the social planner must have a theory of long-run client interest, and that he cannot afford the luxury of positivist detachment but has to educate consumers. However, as the latter-day protagonists of advocacy planning might well remember, neither he nor Davidoff for that matter have advocated replacing planners in public bureaucracies. The dilemma is not "bureaucracy or grass roots", but "What bureaucracy?" (Dyckman, 1966).

Beckman's paper has been included because it reflects very well the mood of those planners in the early sixties who have put their money on establishing planning as a function of urban government. Himself a student of public administration, and then Assistant Director for Metropolitan Areas of the influential Advisory Council on Intergovernmental Relations, he is full of the hopes of reformers in the Kennedy and Johnson administration.

Thus, Beckman's paper has a ring of optimism about it: in the preceding years, there had been a vast increase in federal spending to attack urban problems, pressure was building up to create a separate Department of Housing and Urban Development (H.U.D.), and there was a general atmosphere of faith in representative democracy and expert bureaucracy—so thoroughly shaken since. Indeed, during those years it was possible to talk about a ". . . lack of fundamental issues dividing the American people, a remarkable agreement on national goals, the abundance of natural resources, and traditions of law, order and tolerance" (Beckman, 1963).

Michael Harrington's book on *The Other America* (1962) had only just been published, and the awareness of *poverty* and the *urban crisis*, as well as the significance of the Vietnam war, had not yet grown to the major proportions which they have reached since. Lord Bryce's prophecy written as far back as 1914 was just about to become true:

> And while the outlet which the West now provides for the outflow of the great cities will have become less available, the cities will have grown immensely more populous, pauperism . . . may be more widely spread; and even if wages do not sink work will be less abundant. In fact, the chronic evils and problems of old societies and crowded countries such as we see them today in Europe, will have re-appeared on this new soil, while the demand of the multitude to have a larger share in the nation's collective wealth may well have grown more insistent. . . .[1]

Beckman's paper begins with a statement of the main theme of this section, i.e. the interplay between the planner's role and the administrative institutions of planning. He advocates a "pluralistic" model of the political process, but with strong executives engaged in implementing whatever the synthesis of various political interests might be. Here he challenges Melvin Webber in his paper on "Comprehensive planning and social responsibility" (see pp. 95–112), where the latter advocates a role for the planner which is too close to that of the politician. This leads to "conflicting identities" and to outright conflict in which the planner is "vulnerable"— a reference to the "spoilage system" in American city politics (Jacobsen and Lipman, 1959). The planner should rather serve the chief executive who, in America, often holds a political appointment.

Beckman makes a case for the planner accepting the "vital but more limited role" of a *bureaucrat*. He steers a middle course between the strongly criticized independent role of planners serving non-political planning boards and the myopic view of the planner merely as a technician. In giving his example of the way his former colleagues in the Bureau of the Budget have operated, Beckman anticipates what Grauhan has formalized in the paper concluding this section, namely how conflict within bureaucracies may result in planning agencies increasing their ability of responding creatively to challenges coming from the environment.

[1] Quoted after Carl L. Becker (1960), *Freedom and Responsibility in the American Way of Life*, Vintage Books, New York.

Still, he somehow fails to convince, perhaps because his problem of the role of the planner cannot be resolved once and for all. He glosses over the issue of the planner's orientation to the long-term future against the politician's concern with immediate gains, which may result in a real problem for planner's wanting to serve their political masters in a faithful manner. Also, his argument is very defensive, concerned as it is with protecting the planner against the upheavals of political life. Finally, the stable and high-status professional life which Beckman depicts is simply too far from the turbulent events in the American cities that have occurred in the meantime. It is with role concepts appropriate to this latter "planning environment" (Friedmann, 1967; Faludi, 1970), that the next papers are concerned with.

THE PLANNER AS A POLITICAL ACTOR

Beckman argues that the most appropriate career for a planner is that of bureaucratic official. Of the official, Max Weber says: ". . . he shall not do precisely what the politician must always and necessarily do, namely fight" (Weber, 1948).

Yet, there is a whole range of literature on planners "fighting", metaphorically speaking. Thus, Bellush and Hausknecht (1966) describe the planner's role as that of an *entrepreneur* dealing in influence instead of capital, and they show that successful urban renewal directors engage in a form of *political* activity. For the entirely different context of developing countries, Friedmann defines a very similar role for the planner as an "innovator" (Friedmann, 1964; see also pp. 345–69). Gamberg (1966) investigates planning in the political culture of some middle-sized American cities, where there is a great void in place of political influence. This planning environment is very similar to that of developing countries from where Friedmann has drawn his examples of the planner as an innovator, and Gamberg, too, finds that the planner may be a source of innovation and urges him to accept this as a challenge.

Of the papers arguing the case of the planner as engaging in political conflict, two have been selected: Rabinovitz' study on "Politics, personality and planning", concerned with the interplay of personality factors, role concepts and the institutional context of planning is the first. Davidoff's most important paper on the *planner as an advocate* is the second.

Rabinovitz argues that, in some decision-making environments, the planner must take a leading role. This is especially where influence is so fragmented amongst various interests that the successful planner has to build a "winning coalition" (Bauer, 1968) around every programme which he advocates, i.e. he must take on precisely that "broker-mediator" role which Beckmann advises him not to take. Under these circumstances, it is the role concept of "The planner as a bureaucrat" which becomes counter-productive. This is elaborated in her doctoral thesis which has -been published under the title "City Politics and Planning" (Rabinovitz, 1969) and is easily one of the gems of political science literature in the field of planning theory:

> . . . the success of planning depends in large part on the ability of existing networks of influence to adapt and change to support planning programs. Planners can make important contributions to this process not only in finding technical solutions to physical planning problems but also in creating a frame-work of support. A major part of the importance of a plan is that it can act as a mechanism for political integration. Plans have a value as symbols around which a community can be mobilised.

In her present investigation of political attitudes of planners, Rabinovitz builds on Dyckman's earlier paper and shows that, as late as 1963, planning students were still oriented mainly toward job security and a highly professional role-concept and were hostile towards political involvement. From here, she lays bare certain tensions inherent to the role concept of the planner. As a remedy, she suggests differentiating between the function of different members of the profession such that some planners in some positions would specialize for the political role of opinion-moulding, a point which has already been made by Daland and Parker (1962) on the basis of their own empirical studies.

Davidoff's paper is much more emphatic. It is a superb example of those instances where a word becomes a symbol, a banner for an emerging movement, the rallying-cry of a new generation. Davidoff himself makes reference to those whom this generation was to despise, i.e. the planning bureaucrats of the late fifties and early sixties, of whom Dyckman and Rabinovitz have written. Davidoff did not, however, envisage his advocate planner replacing the planner serving in public agencies. It is important to remember this because of what has happened since. Thus, in 1970, Keyes and Teitcher gasp that ". . . the advocacy road is becoming overcrowded with students fresh from planning schools . . . (whilst) . . . positions of importance in city government . . . are sadly bereft of talent and leadership" (Keyes and Teitcher, 1970).

Given the very propaganda value of the catchword of the *planner as an advocate* (and the fact that money was forthcoming under the *Model Cities Program* just as Davidoff had requested), it is not surprising to see that scores of programmes and agencies were created in due course. Urban Aid at M.I.T. and the "Urban Field Service" at Harvard roamed the well-trodden paths of urban sociologists and planners in and around Boston. These, and Davidoff's own group "Suburban Action" at New York, are probably best documented.

As with most highly topical, and, in this sense, political, papers, Davidoff's plea leaves some questions unanswered. As they appear in the follow-up literature, the questions fall into three categories.

1. What is the relationship between *advocacy planning* and the planning of public agencies ?
2. Who is the *client* of the planner as an advocate and what is his source of *legitimacy?*
3. What is the role of the advocacy planner, *expert adviser* or *politician?*

Davidoff's answer to the first question is that of an *interplay* between public planning and the pleading for special interests. Advocacy was to force planners into developing perspectives which they would generally not have considered. It would therefore improve the planning process in terms of the range of alternatives considered and the values and measurements adopted during evaluation.

Martin Rein (1969) in "Social planning: the search for legitimacy" also turns against an all-out emphasis on the advocacy element of Davidoff's argument. Yet he attends more to the *contradiction* between different concepts than he does to their subtle interplay. Others have questioned more intensely whether "comprehensive" planning and "pluralistic" advocacy planning could even coexist. Thus, Kaplan (1969) quotes Lindblom's paper on "The science of muddling through" (see pp. 151–69) claiming that comprehensive planning is not feasible. Keyes and Peattie (n.d.), in a research paper for the Economic Development Administration on "Citizen participation in the Model Cities", emphasize the "problem focus" of advocacy planning, and the disparagement of "comprehensiveness". Warren (1969), in a parallel study on the same topic, concludes that all planners are advocates, whether inside or outside the establishment. He sees the planner as a ". . . key actor in the essentially political process of inter-organizational decision-making", thus engaging in a type of ". . . mutual adjustment process which Lindblom claims is superior to central co-ordination and planning".

It is possible that comprehensive and advocacy planning build on two opposite models of society in which case there would be inherent conflict between the two kinds of planning. Hyman (1969), in his study of the planning process in the famous Boston Southend, appears to take this line identifying the "power elite" and the "pluralistic" model describing alternative planning styles associated with these models as centralized, comprehensive, and decentralized, action-oriented planning. It has been only very recently that models of society combining the features of both the power elite and pluralistic school such as the one presented by Etzioni in his "The Active Society" (1968) have trickled through to the planning literature (e.g. Chadwick, 1971).

The question of who is the client and what is the source of legitimacy for the advocate also remains unresolved. Davidoff has outlined a number of potential clients from political parties and organized city-wide interests to the *ad-hoc* protest organization on the level of urban neighbourhoods. As a matter of fact, advocacy planning is invariably associated with the plight of racial and ethnic minorities and the poor generally. The advocate planner becomes the promoter of radical principles of equality and participation.

Thus, he pleads not only for particular local groups—what Peattie calls "turfs"—but also for more abstract causes. Peattie of M.I.T., who has become one of the greatest authorities on advocacy planning (Peattie, 1968, 1969, 1970; Keyes and Peattie, n.d.), describes this in the case of her work with groups threatened by an urban motorway in Cambridge, Mass. Her intervention elevated their fight to the level of the more abstract issue of private versus public transport and thereby lost some of its legitimacy in form of a clearly identifiable client group.

But even where advocacy planners are keeping close to the ground, they are finding it difficult to identify their client and thus their presumed source of legitimacy. Peattie (1968) finds that, on close inspection, the community dissolves into various interest groups in turn, that many cleavages such as that between home-owners and tenants repeat themselves on the neighbourhood level, and that their client organization represents the more affluent, more stable, long-term residents of their community leaving the lowest income group and the transient population out in the cold: "In effect, advocacy planning miniaturizes but does not eliminate the problems of conflicting interests which inhere in the planning activities of city-wide agencies." In a later paper she even felt compelled to say that her planning group ". . . has come to see the notion of serving 'communities' as the same mirage as the traditional planner's idea of serving the 'general welfare' " (Peattie, 1970).

In this context, the third question of the role of the planner becomes pertinent. Peattie is under no illusion: "Even without administrative power, the advocate planner is a manipulator. The power to conceptualise is the power to manipulate" (Peattie, 1968).

The advocate planner can thus not help being elitist. He also becomes a self-appointed politician playing his own part in the drama of public life (Peattie, 1970). Yet, here, a sinister aspect of the lack of a meaningful community to relate to, and the consequent self-legitimation of the planner, is brought out by Gilbert and Eaton (1970). Their research highlights the role of activist-minorities in citizen participation, and the relative contentment of the ordinary residents with those conditions which are at issue. "In extreme cases", they conclude, "citizen activists have become a new generation of 'colonialists' ", and they surmise a coalition of activists and planners in their commitment to change in the ". . . interest of causes other than the welfare of the neighbourhood and/or the broader community".

Their conclusion points in the direction of reintroducing formal mechanisms of accountability to check the objectives of self-styled community representatives. Maybe the development has gone full circle from representative, "formal" democracy allied with the concept of bureaucracy to citizen involvement and advocacy planning and back again to the demand for accountability, though possibly on a different basis.

CREATIVE BUREAUCRACY?

One of the effects of having advocate planners operating in the environment of public bureaucracies, as Davidoff sees it, is that of making them more responsive and inventive. Grauhan outlines the alternative of making institutions themselves sources of *innovation*. Following certain of the ideas of Deutsch (1966), he wishes to make use of the potential for "political rationality" which processes of conflict have by creating within bureaucracies a plurality of centres of initiative.

Grauhan is representative of a whole generation of German scholars, not only in the planning field. Like many of his colleagues in the age-bracket of 30 to 40, he has spent some time in one of the distinguished universities of the United States. This generation reads and assimilates American and English works which gives them an edge over their English-speaking contemporaries, most of whom do not have similar access to German literature. There is a chance, therefore, that some new development may occur in German-speaking countries in the near future.

Also, the legal system much as the whole philosophical inheritance, not only of Germany but also other continental nations, requires scholars to think issues through much more thoroughly than is required from, in particular, their English colleagues. The legal nature of a land-use plan is one such issue to which Grauhan refers. With the distinction between a legislative and an administrative act being much more clear cut than in Britain, planners and legal theorists have had to spend more effort in analysing issues of a constitutional kind.

It is therefore not surprising to find in Grauhan's paper a mixture of German legal theory and American political science literature which is, furthermore, synthesized into proposals for new institutional forms of planning. Thus, even though acknowledging the necessity of "mutual adjustment" of various positions during the plan preparation phase, Grauhan does not go all the way along with Lindblom's *anti-planning* argument. Planning is still performed in the name of the whole of a local community, a region, or a state, and plans, once adopted, are still implemented by traditional, hierarchical forms of organization. But, the planning process itself is a political process, and planning institutions are structured after the model of political institutions.

The proposed interplay between planning organizations (upward and cross-flows of information, informal style, loose association between organizational entities) and implementing agency (downward flow of information and command, formal style, tight control and demarcation between spans of authority) is ingenious. Planning groups drawing from the membership of implementing agencies and otherwise collaborating with part-time citizen advisory boards—one is reminded of Nash and Durden's (1964) "task forces"—are surely a superb way of building "decision networks" which are now becoming recognized as important to the effective operation of planning (Institute for Operational Research, 1971), much in the same way as informal organizations make formal structures viable.

Grauhan's paper thus gives evidence of the way in which organization theory may be applied to planning. Taming the forces of benevolent bureaucracy and keeping it responsive to problems as they are on the ground, rather than in information files based on yesterday's assumptions, has namely come to be recognized as a major problem of our time (Schon, 1971). The Americans have gone their way of advocacy planning and are now finding it necessary to introduce an element of accountability into it. Grauhan presents the alternative of changing the structure of organizations engaged in making decisions about future patterns of life, a proposal much more relevant to the European planning environment which is still less turbulent than is the situation in American cities.

REFERENCES

Part IV

BAUER, R. A. (1968) "The study of policy formation: an introduction, *The Study of Policy Formation* (edited by BAUER, R. A. and GERGEN, K. J.), Collier–Macmillan, London.

BECKMAN, N. (1963) "Our federal system and urban development", *Journal of the American Institute of Planners*, Vol. 29, pp. 152–67.

BELLUSH, J. and HAUSKNECHT, M. (1966) "Entrepreneurs and urban renewal", *Journal of the American Institute of Planners*, Vol. 32, pp. 289–97.

CHADWICK, G. (1971) *A Systems View of Planning*, Pergamon Press, Oxford.

DALAND, R. T. and PARKER, J. A. (1962) "Roles of the planner in urban development", *Urban Growth Dynamics* (edited by CHAPIN, F. S. and WEISS, F. S.), Wiley, New York.

DEUTSCH, K. W. (1966) *The Nerves of Government—Models of Political Communication and Control*, 2nd ed., Macmillan, New York and London, 1966.

DYCKMAN, J. (1966) "Social planning, social planners, and planned society", *Journal of the American Institute of Planners*, Vol. 32, pp. 66–76.

ETZIONI, A. (1968) *The Active Society*, Collier–Macmillan, London.

FALUDI, A. (1970) "The planning environment and the meaning of 'planning' ", *Regional Studies*, Vol. 4, pp. 1–9.

FRIEDMANN, J. (1964) "Planning as innovation: the Chilean case, *Journal of the American Institute of Planners*, Vol. 32, pp. 194–204.

FRIEDMANN, J. (1967) "The institutional context", *Action Under Planning* (edited by GROSS, B. H.), McGraw-Hill, New York.

GAMBERG, H. (1966) "The professional and policy choices in middle-sized cities", *Journal of the American Institute of Planners*, Vol. 32, pp. 174–7.

GILBERT, N. and EATON, J. W. (1970) "Who speaks for the poor?", *Journal of the American Institute of Planners*, Vol. 36, pp. 411–16.

HARRINGTON, M. (1962) *The Other America: Poverty in the U.S.A.*, Macmillan, New York.

HYMANN, H. (1969) "Planning with citizens: two styles", *Journal of the American Institute of Planners*, Vol. 35, pp. 105–12.

INSTITUTE FOR OPERATIONAL RESEARCH (1971) *Beyond Local Government Reform: Some Prospects for Evolution in Public Policy Networks* (Conference Proceedings), Tavistock Institute, London.

JACOBSEN, G. A. and LIPMAN, M. H. (1937) *Political Science*, 4th ed., Barnes & Nable, New York, 1956.

KAHN, A. J. (1969) *Studies in Social Policy and Planning*, Russell Sage Foundation, New York.

KAPLAN, M. (1969) "Advocacy and the urban poor", *Journal of the American Institute of Planners*, Vol. 35, pp. 96–104.

KEYES, L. and PEATTIE, L. (n. d.) Research paper for the office of Economic Research of the Economic Development Administration, U.S. Department of Commerce, under Project No. OER. 228–G–68–14.

KEYES, L. C. and TEITCHER, E. (1970) "Limitations of advocacy planning: a view from the establishment", *Journal of the American Institute of Planners*, Vol. 36, pp. 225–6.

MEYERSON, M. and BANFIELD, E. (1955) *Politics Planning and the Public Interest*, Free Press, Glencoe.

NASH, P. H. and DURDEN, D. (1964) "A task force approach to replace the planning board", *Journal of the American Institute of Planners*, Vol. 30, pp. 10–12.

PEATTIE, L. R. (1968) "Reflections on advocacy planning", *Journal of the American Institute of Planners*, Vol. 34, pp. 80–88.

PEATTIE, L. R. (1969) "Teaching and learning for planners", *Journal of the American Institute of Planners*, Vol. 35, pp. 52–54.

PEATTIE, L. R. (1970) "Drama and advocacy planning", *Journal of the American Institute of Planners*, Vol. 36, pp. 405–10.

RABINOVITZ, F. F. (1969) *City Politics and Planning*, Atherton Press, New York.

REIN, M. (1969) "Social planning: the search for legitimacy", *Journal of the American Institute of Planners*, Vol. 35, pp. 233–44.

SCHON, D. (1971) *Beyond the Stable State*, Temple Smith, London.

WALKER, R. A. (1941) *The Planning Function in Urban Government*, University of Chicago Press, 2nd ed., 1950.

WARREN, R. L. (1969) "Model cities first round: Politics, planning, and participation", *Journal of the American Institute of Planners*, Vol. 35, pp. 245–52.

WEBER, M. (1948) "Politics as a vocation", *From Max Weber* (edited by GERTH, H. H. and MILLS, C. W.), Routledge & Kegan Paul, London.

What Makes Planners Plan?*

John W. Dyckman

THAT program for action in the 60's, the report of the *President's Commission on National Goals*, tells us that the number of classroom teachers will have to expand by almost one-third during the 1960's to take care of population growth. In round numbers, this would mean some 200,000 new teachers every year for ten years, to which must be added almost a half-million new college teachers in the same period.

Because the clients of city planning are communities, and not mere numbers of people, the demand for planners does not bear so close a relation to the expected population growth as does that for elementary school teachers. None the less, the same influences which are swelling the ranks of government personnel, and accelerating changes in population distribution and urban forms, can be expected to appreciably expand demand for community planners. The recruitment of these new professionals (most of whom, presumably, will seek entry in the AIP) is worthy of our present consideration.

Who is predisposed to become a planner? Perhaps in attempting to answer this question, the profession may not only locate major sources of recruits, but may in the process uncover some partially obscured aspects in its own bundle of motivations. Most planners are aware that there have been changes in the sources of recruitment in their profession. Many observers have marked the transition from the City Beautiful era of planning, in which the profession was dominated by the consultant architect or landscape architect, into the period of large municipal governmental staffs, manned by specialists of many kinds. There is, however, little empirical or analytical evidence on the composition of American city planning, or on its tasks.

* Reprinted by permission of the *Journal of the American Institute of Planners*, Vol. 27, May 1961.

One of the few empirical works, a student project conducted at the University of California by Paul Zucker, tends to confirm certain impressionistic views of the planning profession. Zucker obtained survey responses from 159 Bay Area planners, or about three-fourths of the total professionals in that region. His study finds a marked change in the training of planners over time, as represented by the undergraduate degree. The older respondents show a predominance of architecture and landscape architecture plus a category called "other" which includes the law, while the younger professionals show a strong pattern of majors in political science, economics, and sociology along with the traditional majors. The change in the percentage of the whole represented by these majors within age groups is marked.

In addition to confirming the rising role of the social sciences and political science in preparation for planning careers, Zucker's study also adds support to the prevailing impressions of the class biases of planners by characterizing most Bay Area planners as coming from "middle socialeconomic backgrounds". About three-fifths of the respondents gave the occupational status of fathers as "professional, proprietor, manager, or salesman". Holding age constant, Zucker found the occupational structure of the respondents' fathers to be very similar to that of a markedly middleclass community in the Bay Area.

The planning profession has been slow to digest the import of changes in its own body. Where city planning once shared the ethos of business and a rising professional aristocracy, it now finds itself sharing the outlook of the more crystallized professions, and even of the generic bureaucracies. Margy Meyerson has characterized the professional planning role as "predominantly universalistic, affectively neutral, collectivity-oriented and functionally specific, as well as achievement oriented". In nonsociological language, this means that the planner is a full-time professional in a field marked by technical standards of achievement for the evaluation of performance; operates in the absence of conventional profit motives, with the presumption that he will be sparing in the intrusion of his own values and will venerate "objectivity"; and is first and foremost a community servant who will put the common good above self-interest. Moreover, with the great growth of planning education in the university, a deepening role-sophistication has developed. As E. Hughes notes, professional education usually involves the replacement of stereotype images by more subtle, complex, and even ambiguous perceptions of the professional roles. That is, professional education reduces the dramatic oversimplification of role which exists in the popular image—the very image, in fact, which may have attracted the postulant in the first place.

If university-trained planners of the present generation are increasingly self-conscious about the practice of their profession, what do they see in that profession that attracts them? In the earlier days of American city planning, the existence of a challenging problem—the problem of growing urbanization, the despoliation of the landscape, and the absorption of the immigrants—was motive enough for those who perceived it. And the problem was self-selecting of its workers; only those imbued with civic concern, sensitive to the environment, and equipped with the awareness that something could be done about it, took upon themselves the task of city planning. The field can no longer hope to recruit enough people on this basis; and, besides, the tasks themselves are changed. It is no longer a field in which brave knights ride forward to slay the dragon of urban ugliness.

What roles do the new young graduates see for themselves in city planning? Nothing is really known about this, and city planning might provide an interesting profession for the kind of sociological study of occupation which has been so successful in the fields of medicine and law. Until then, however, we can only speculate on this score.

The challenge of charismatic leadership, the old urge to lead a strayed society out of the wilderness, is still strong in some young people, though it is undoubtedly less common than it was in a generation which experienced depression and war first hand. The opportunity to concretely "remake" the world is still present in city planning in a highly acceptable form. There is a great consensus in our society at the moment on the need for city planning, though the actual implementation of plans will undoubtedly lead to great value conflicts.

There is also opportunity for professional leadership in local government. City planning is one of the more attractive forms of government service— offering, as it does, an option to move in and out of government without loss of professional continuity and prestige. For those who want it, there appears to be substantial security. Indeed, as planning moves towards greater codification, licensing, etc., there is a distinct possibility that a higher proportion of entrants into the field will elect it on grounds that it offers a comfortable job sinecure. The old-time crusading planners will reckon this a real danger. Finally, there will no doubt be some young people, who like Fabians before them in England, will attempt to combine these two concerns.[1]

In fact, the distinction between the planner-crusader and the planner-public official may be overdrawn. As Dennis Brogan has pointed out, there is a strong current of the evangelical tradition in American politics. In the past, however, there has been a very sharp distinction between the practice of city planning whose evangelism is, after all, distinctly middle-class, civic-club salvation and the politics of American city government, which is dominated by working-class realists with a low regard for missionaries.

In this light, though the civic-beautification movement was challenge enough for the "doers" of its time, modern comprehensive planning in its more sophisticated professional form is likely to be a frustrating prospect. Banfield says "American cities . . . seldom make and never carry out comprehensive plans. Plan making is with us an idle exercise, for we neither agree upon the content of a 'public interest' that ought to override private ones nor permit the centralization of authority needed to carry a plan into effect if one were made."[2] If Banfield's appraisal were correct, city planning would scarcely be a field in which young men would march forth from school with real expectations of creating a world of their own making.

The expansion of planning budgets and staff, the abundance of federal aids, the growth and demand for and uses of information about the physical layout and land uses in the city, and the acceptability of "limited purpose" planning experts outside of government have all tended to obscure the great difficulties in making comprehensive plans for metropolitan areas reported by Banfield. Young men can find a place in the

---

[1] Though the Fabians have been called "prophets" they were in some respects more nearly evangelistic social engineers. For example, Sidney Webb had prepared a complete scheme for a "responsible" elected civil service, operating at a local governmental level. The Fabians were so preoccupied with the political importance of local government, of the role of the "expert" in civil service, that it is surprising that they had no theory of planning's role in running an economy or a society.

[2] "There is much talk of the need for metropolitan-area planning, but the talk can lead to nothing practical because there is no possibility of agreement on what the 'general interest' of such an area requires concretely (whether, for example, it requires keeping the Negroes concentrated in the central city or spreading them out in the suburbs) and because, anyway, there does not exist in any area a government that could carry such plans into effect."

planning profession without fear of being stranded when the ties of comprehensive planning programs go out. It is very likely that as many graduates as planning schools now produce annually could be absorbed indefinitely in one or another field of urban research, even if all general planning powers of city planning commissions were suspended at once.

But most professional planners did not enter the field for the purpose of studying the city. If they had such intentions, they would have been better served in many cases by matriculation in some program other than planning. Urban sociology, government and political science, economics, or history might have been better preparation. The planners, presumably, have been trained to practice the art of planning.

By temperament as well as training, moreover, the planners are for the most part not scientists. The practice of scientific pursuits requires a patient acceptance of the ordering of the universe which is far removed from the insistent urge to restructure and reshape. Newton is reported to have stated that in the course of his work "he felt like a child playing at the seashore, happy whenever he found a smoother pebble or a more beautiful sea shell than usual, while the great ocean of truth lay unexplored before him". Few planners have the disposition for this patient sifting of evidence, and even fewer have modern research techniques, with their elaborate operational procedures and mathematical language.

Neither scientist nor political-mover, the city planner is still no ornamental appendage of government. His forte is command over a commodity which, though rough and home-made, is still not accessible to most citizens. That commodity is a view of the future; not the future of a single enterprise, but of a whole complex system like the urban community. The planner is thus a purveyor of vital advice.

The occupational hazards of this role should be well known to would-be professionals. The advisor depends upon his acceptance as an expert by an audience. His very vulnerability on this side may keep him from the fullest exercise of an appropriate art of advice. A long-time student of public administration, Fritz Morstein Marx, recently published an article on "The Mind of the Career Man" in which he observed:

> All this is not entirely unnatural when the reputation of being an expert—rather than what he actually can do—is seen by the career man as his principal stock in trade. From such an angle, it will become emotionally necessary for him to spend more time showing himself right than exploring alternatives

that may be more helpful in moving toward the government's goals. Policy-makers who come to him with fresh ideas or administrative suggestions will find him resentful and defensive. Is it not he to whom all worthwhile insights would occur first? If pressure develops toward new approaches in meeting emerging administrative needs, the one thing policy-makers can be sure to hear from him is a story of obstacles and difficulties.

The planner, who in his earlier career history had to combat the image of the blue-sky dreamer, must also fight the tendency to slide into the defensive role of the critic. It is a difficult wire to walk.

Those who choose this profession in the face of these many disabilities, and who still elect to try for the greater role of helping communities to shape their future by sketching out alternatives and advising on realistic opportunities, are powerfully motivated men. If, as a recent biographer of Frank Lloyd Wright has claimed, it takes a certain arrogance to tackle the problems of space in all their grandeur, it can fairly be said that it takes a measure of determination no less fierce to tackle the problems of the future use of space by communities.

To sum up, the recruitment of planners, and the expectations of the beginning professionals, have shifted markedly over time with the matura-tion of the profession, and the alteration of opportunities for affecting the total form of communities. Once mesianic, the planner has become bureaucratic and conservative. Not politically powerful in most cases, the planner takes his rewards in professional prestige, for respect for his profession grows even as its threat to established forms diminishes.

Indeed, the prestige of the city planner may hinge on the remoteness of promised results, as with the clergy. Similar sources of strength are drawn upon by the "utopian" planners. But the prestige must be defended on occasion by walling-off the special operational role of the planner from the world of practical affairs. This segregation of operations is sometimes glorified as a rejection of "politics". (There is an analogy between the early civic reformer city planners and the disgruntled Athenian patricians who, in Aristophanes' *Birds*, wanted to escape from the demos-ruled city machine and go off to found an ideal city—"Cloud-cuckoo-town"—on Peisthetaerus' advice, "at the pole of the heavens above".) Furthermore, the obscurantism of some planning, so close to the priestly crafts of the ancients, is part of the common pact of the expert to refrain from telling "how he does it".

Though evidence on the origins of planners is slow in coming in, the

California planners at least seem to have been drawn from higher-income groups than one would expect to find in a corresponding group of clergy-men. Still, the city planner has much of the sense of "mission" of the clergy, and often much of the fundamentalism. Over time, this calling has become more and more protected, and more and more sustained by the approval of the group. In some states, legislation is called upon to legiti-matize the craft.

When the "high motives" of planning have been institutionalized, the rationalization of the profession will be complete. Appropriate, and safe, outlets will be prescribed for the enthusiasms of the neophyte planners. One wonders what misguided messianism might have been channelled into safe directions if professions like city planning had been established and institutionalized earlier. Erik Erikson, recalling the Kubizek account of *The Young Hitler I Knew*, tells us that

> Hitler wanted desperately to be a city planner; he walked around for days (and as if in a daze) rebuilding his home town of Linz. To rebuild, of course, he had to imagine the city destroyed, but no doubt he tried to be "construc-tive" on a vast, if almost delusional, scale. When he finally sent his plans for the opera house in Linz to a committee which paid no attention to them, he really broke with society. And would you believe it, in his very last days, after having destroyed Europe, having been cornered in his bunker, and having planned his self-liquidation, he put the last touches on his plans for the opera house in Linz, which he almost came to build.

City planning today could use a counter-cyclical dose of "constructivist" aspirations to offset its bureaucratic hardening. For, whatever the risk of its abuse, planning cannot do without this sense of mission. Without the deep personal conviction and commitment, the planner will be used as generations of civil servants have been used, and, as Julien Benda long ago warned that the intellectual "clercs" were prone to be used, as con-venient tools of the powerful.

The planners might be stayed from the error of inflicting ill-conceived enthusiasms on the public by adopting some of the traditional virtues of the scientist—his humility, tentativeness, self-criticism, and a sprinkling of his doubts. There is no need for planning to reduce all observation to calculation and to oppose reason to imagination; science itself is no longer so naïve. When the planner can clearly see that the consequences of a development will violate the goals of a community, it is his professional responsibility to point out this divergence, much as the atomic scientist may point out the consequences of a bomb. C. P. Snow has warned the latter that "It is the plain duty of scientists to explain this 'either or'. It is a duty which seems to me to come from the moral nature of the scientific activity itself." If planning cannot stake a claim as an equally "moral" activity it will fall increasingly short of attracting the critical young people it needs, for the critic is above all else a moralist.

REFERENCES

BANFIELD, EDWARD C. "The political implications o metropolitan growth", *Daedalus*, Winter 1961.

BROGAN, DENNIS. *Citizenship Today*. Chapel Hill: University of North Carolina Press, 1960.

BROWN, J. DOUGLAS. "Education for a learned profession", *The American Scientist*, September 1960.

ERIKSON, ERIK in *New Perspectives for Research in Juvenile Delinquency*, Helen L. Witmer (ed.), Washington: Department of Health, Education and Welfare, 1956.

HUGHES, EVERETT C. *Men and their Work*, Glencoe, Ill.: Free Press, 1958.

MARX, FRITZ MORSTEIN. "The mind of the career man", *Public Administration Review*, 16 September 1960.

MEYERSON, MARGY. "Characteristics of the community planner." Unpublished paper, Department of Sociology, Bryn Mawr College, 1954.

President's Commission on National Goals. *Goals for Americans*, New York: Prentice-Hall, 1960.

SNOW, C. P. "The moral un-neutrality of science." Address to the American Association for the Advancement of Science, New York, 27 December 1960.

ZUCKER, PAUL. "The characteristics of Bay Area planners." Unpublished student paper, University of California, Spring 1960.

The Planner as a Bureaucrat*

Norman Beckman

THIS column is motivated by the apparent attitude of many planners and other observers of the urban scene that: (a) little progress has been, or is likely to be made toward acceptance or implementation of sound urban planning; and (b) the cause of this failure to achieve rational, orderly urban development is "politics" and politicians—the elected officials that run our local governments. This distrust and dislike are often returned in kind. Indications that this malaise does exist are the sometimes high rate of reversals of staff planning and zoning recommendations; the extensive use of private consultants for public business rather than the building of strong institutional planning staffs in our local governments; and the high turnover and mobility rate of the planning profession.

A recent letter written by a local planner who was trying to form a panel to speak to an AIP chapter on the subject of professional and political obligations of the planning profession summarizes the situation. Expressing concern with the lack of effectiveness of planning programs in the Washington region, he observed that:

> Probably the best example I can give as food for thought is the fact that every planning director in the Washington metropolitan region has either resigned or has been replaced within the last 24 months. This indicates to me that there must exist a fairly wide gap in philosophy between political goals and planning goals.

In seeking solutions to the problem of improved planner–politician relationships, one could approach the subject in terms of improving public

* Reprinted by permission of the *Journal of the American Institute of Planners*, Vol. 30, November 1964.

relations techniques, identifying the local power structure, or improving the tools of the planning profession. The orientation used here, however, is that of public administration and the possible contribution of that academic and professional field to the problem at hand.

This column is addressed both to planners who are identified as politically controversial figures and to those who see themselves as planning technicians. In the long run, both may do harm to the causes and profession they serve—the former by his loss to the community in a change of administration or because he becomes "expendable", and the latter by the sterility of his efforts. I shall seek to examine the similarity of the roles of the politician and the planner and the conflict thereby engendered; the vulnerability of the planner if he challenges the elected official for community leadership; the unique capability of the planner to serve the chief executive, whether governor, county board, mayor, or manager; the special character of government employment and the place of the public servant in a responsible bureaucracy; and finally, some advice by experts on how to survive and be effective in the public sector.

In speaking of these problems, emphasis will be placed on certain fundamentals of our system of government that are often given lip service but not fully understood or applied in the particular situation. These fundamentals are: *one*, the dominant role of the politician in our governmental system; and *two*, the inevitable involvement of planners and other administrative generalists in the political process.

THE CASE OF CONFLICTING IDENTITIES

The public esteem of those who seek elected office, especially local office, is not always high. Neither, it should be noted, is the public esteem of the civil servant. Indeed the popular image of the politician is often heavily tinged with venality and hypocrisy, if not outright dishonesty. This is not an encouraging or healthy situation at a time when all levels of government are being called upon to provide expanded public services and play an increasingly influential role in our all lives. One can only speculate as to whether the attitude of the average planner is much different from that of the general population with respect to elected officials.

What are the traditional definitions of the function of a politician and political party? The role of politics has been defined as: *one*, coordinating diverse and antagonistic interests; and *two*, sublimating the private interests by furthering principles that merge them with the general interest. A useful working theory of politics defines the politician's role as that of a "broker–mediator". Under this approach, the typical party leader is a person concerned primarily in mediating, adjusting, and pulling views into sufficient harmony for action. Elected officials are assigned the difficult task of working toward decisions by bringing together the judgment of the expert and the "will of the people". Other roles of the party have been identified.[1] However, the broker–mediator theory seems to come closest to explaining the observable phenomenon of many interest groups, each seeking to influence action by government. Indeed, one of the rapidly growing industries of the National Capital area has been the opening of offices by interest-group associations.

No doubt many planners would favor having a planner for President just as businessmen, scientists, and economists, would like to see their profession represented in the office of Chief Executive. Perhaps some of the nostaligia and idealization surrounding the depression-born National Resources Planning Board is derived from the identification of the planning profession with the Presidency. (Technocracy was also in vogue about the same time.) A reassuring fact, however, is that none of the professions is likely to consider turning over our political leadership at the national level—or at the local level—to groups other than their own, except to politicians.[2]

One must keep in mind that the objective of a political party is to win elections and remain in office. Once the elected official obtains his position, his re-election is dependent upon how successfully he reconciles and integrates the many competing demands that we, as citizens and members of groups, place on him. A basic reason why our governmental system has been so durable is its capacity to meet many of the demands made by any one group in a manner that is consistent with the public interest. One of the major qualities of the successful politician is the ability to understand and adjust to these constant but ever changing demands. The competition in this occupation is keen, however, and the turnover rate is high—much

---

[1] See Neil A. McDonald, *The Study of Political Parties*, Garden City, New York: Doubleday & Company, Inc., 1955, pp. 8–36, for a useful summary of the literature on the functions of political parties.

[2] For a development of this thesis see Paul Appleby, *Policy and Administration*, University, Alabama: University of Alabama Press, 1949, p. 47.

higher than for the heads of even the largest private organizations. So much for the politician.

Now let us examine the role and function of the planner as described in a recent statement of the profession's roles and purposes and relate it to the above definitions of politician.

> As men who have specialized in the general, the truly effective city planners have functioned as catalysts for the developmental plans of the more specialized groups in government. By bringing representatives of public and private agencies together, they have helped to synthesize new amalgams that better reflect both the separate and the mutual goals of the various participants. Individual plans for components have been reframed to accord with criteria established by the plans for the next-larger systems of components that, in turn, conform to more comprehensive overviews of the future and of the community's objectives.[3]

Note the similarity of terms—"coordinate", "working harmony", "reconcile", "integrate", "public interest", "adjust", "synthesize", "next larger systems", "comprehensive overviews". Both the politician and the planner see themselves as responsible for integrating the independent development decisions with their attendant social and economic effects that are made in the community and for providing leadership in achieving the good life generally. Thus we are faced with a problem of conflicting identities. The conflict between some planners and some politicians arises because each believes that he is best fit—through training, experience, and institutional expectations—to serve the public as broker–mediator, coordinator, and goal-maker. *This conflict of identity can best be resolved, and the planner's effectiveness enhanced, if he is willing to accept the vital but more limited role that our system assigns to the public employee.*

In this role of assisting and serving the elected policy-maker, the tools of the planner's trade and his heritage of comprehensiveness give him a special competence, perhaps above all other public service professions. To quote further from the statement on the profession's roles:

> Improved data systems will permit planners continuously to meter the states of affairs of the various population groups, the economy, the municipal fisc, the physical plant, and other aspects of the city. Improved theory, describing and explaining the processes of city life and city growth, will permit us more

---

[3] Melvin M. Webber, "Comprehensive planning and social responsibility: toward an A.I.P. consensus on the profession's roles and purposes", *Journal of the American Institute of Planners*, Vol. XXIX (November 1963), pp. 236–7.

sensitively to identify those crucial points of public intervention that are appropriate to accomplishing specified objectives.[4]

Indeed, what is that *sine qua non* of the planner's profession, the land use map and the master plan, but an attempt to express a multitude of public and private decisions affecting a given political jurisdiction. Perhaps most important, "the city planner's realistic idealism, his orientation to the whole city, and his focus upon future conditions have placed him in a position of intellectual leadership",[5] in serving as key staff in the cause of effective political leadership.

It may be argued that the planner's bias toward the long-range and the politician's equal bias toward the immediate establishes a situation of continuing conflict. The politician faces frequent elections before an existent constituency, with a resultant need for short-range performance, while the planner may be more concerned about the provision of services in the still unpopulated areas of suburbia. But is concern with the broad geographic area, the interdependence of decisions, the future population, and the long-range interest inconsistent with providing answers to immediate issues? Until all basic questions concerning long-term development and goals—such as patterns of growth and industrial and residential character of the community—are dealt with, it is difficult to determine the most effective means of providing any given function. Surely the alternative of uncoordinated development, conflicting land uses, and resultant depreciation of property values and uneconomical public facilities, is not good politics.

The concern for "future conditions" is not unique to planners. Government exists because there is public concern for the long-term, for the citizen at large, and for the public interest. From agriculture to water resources, long-range planning is being carried on by competent professionals at all three levels of government. Perhaps the planner's main contribution is his concern for the inter-relatedness of more specialized long-term planning.

THE VULNERABILITY OF THE PLANNER

The planner is vulnerable in any competition with the politician.

---

[4] *Ibid.*
[5] *Ibid.*, p. 238.

Primarily this is because it is in the nature of his job to become deeply and inevitably involved in politics and the political process. In the field of government, every administrative action, from surly behavior of a licensing clerk to a health department decision to prohibit individual wells and septic tanks in an urban area, is weighed on a political scale. Those actions which benefit or hurt individuals produce a reading on that scale. It is difficult to anticipate what actions will be elevated to public attention. In my own community, a single zoning decision to permit construction of an apartment house along the Potomac resulted in the unseating of several members of the county board of supervisors. Planning agencies help to determine "who gets what, when, and how" and to do that means to function politically.

The commission form of organization and the professionalization of the occupation are presumably designed to "remove planning from politics". Yet the operating relationships of planning agencies with other local, state, and federal agencies and the effect on, and exposure to, large numbers of citizens inevitably means that the planner is politically involved and subject to political attack. Planning agencies, by having to operate on the cutting edge of politics and administration—concerned with the "obstetrics of public policy"—are especially vulnerable to such attack. The planner's main stock in trade are his professional skills, the merit of his ideas, and his ability and willingness to serve as a conduit for exchange of information with other governments and agencies.

The planner's place in the structure of local government differs from that of most other public employees. Instead of being held directly accountable to the elected executive, he is more commonly responsible to a lay or *ex-officio* planning commission.[6] Such boards have the inevitable effect of insulating the planner from the politician and the chief executive who most needs his help in moderating special interest demands. Too often, relatively independent commissions can operate to obscure public accountability, provide an excuse for delay, and produce a "lowest common denominator" kind of decision too early in the political decision-making process. The bulk of local planning activities today are executive or operational in nature and as such should be headed by a single executive. The use of boards

[6] On the subject, see the article by Peter H. Nash and Dennis Durden, "A task-force approach to replace the planning boards", *Journal of the American Institute of Planners*, Vol. XXX (February 1964), pp. 10–22.

and commissions to carry out local government planning activities might better be limited to the performance of certain quasi-legislative planning functions, such as zoning actions. The problems of regional planning agencies may be unique. Here the desire for representation by the various jurisdictions may require a board form, but this governing body should be chosen by, or made up of, responsible elected officials rather than by other subregional or local planning agencies.

Despite the facade of autonomy and independence behind which planning agencies seek to achieve the heavenly city of the twentieth century, it must constantly be kept in mind that planning agencies have almost no levers, no gifts, no grants, no weapons, no operating programs, no strong base of independent political support. It is, therefore, imperative to stick close to (and serve to the extent possible as key management staff) responsible officials who do have executive powers—the mayor, the county council, or the city manager.

The problem is especially acute for the metropolitan agency, since it has no single political jurisdictional counterpart. New Jersey's Department of Conservation and Economic Development properly advocates that area-wide planning agencies be headed by decision-makers:

> To create regional planning boards based solely upon the theory of impartial-disinterested citizen participation and to assign them the job of coping with area-wide long-range issues is to invite an unnecessary excursion beyond reality What regional planning needs is the participation of decision-makers. While this may or may not include participants other than elected officials, it must include the executive officials of those governments taking part in specific regional planning operations.[7]

Politicians, even lay planning commission members, are often only too glad to let planning staffs serve as advocates for new development proposals. If the public reaction (that is, interest group reaction) is adverse, well, it's back to the drafting board to devise a new formula for growth and redevelopment and perhaps to initiate efforts to recruit a new planning director. Getting very far ahead of commission members and elected officials is a dangerous game for any bureaucrat, especially a vulnerable one.

It is an occupational hazard of the professional public employee (and

---

[7] New Jersey State Department of Conservation and Economic Development, *The Setting for Regional Planning in New Jersey* (December 1961), p. 86.

planners perhaps are especially susceptible on this score) to become absolutely convinced not only of the rightness of his "plan", but that the plan, the zoning ordinance, and the zoning decision, is an end in itself. A public servant can never indulge that kind of faith without bad results. Much or the sense of frustration from which too many planners suffer springs from the expectation of immediate, measurable, and conclusive influence. He finds it hard to understand why responsible officials, and the public generally, do not do what he is satisfied is the best thing to do. He tends to forget that his is the more limited function of seeking to blend, to synthesize, and to adjust programs to the hopes and fears, likes and dislikes, of the politician he serves.

SURVIVAL IN A BUREAUCRACY

It is fundamental to our system of government that public employment "does not require partisans of a particular general outlook, whether Republican or Democrat, conservative, progressive, or socialist, but it does require specialists who know their job and will, therefore, *effectively execute the general rules decided upon by executive or legislative leadership in accordance with popular preferences*".[8]

Max Weber's idealized construct of bureaucratic organization still has validity today: (a) the head of the organization owes his authority and position to election; (b) the remaining staff under such authority are organized in a defined hierarchy of office; (c) they are selected on the basis of technical qualifications; (d) such an appointment constitutes a career, including promotion based on seniority and achievement as judged by superiors; (e) the person filling the office works entirely separately from ownership or the means of administration; (f) he is subject to strict and systematic discipline and control in the conduct of the office.

Large scale public and private organizations are similar—except in the important things. The public servant must remember that the character of *government* employment is different—first in its breadth of scope, impact, and consideration; second, in the public accountability to which he will be held; and third, in the political character of his work which requires

----

[8] Carl J. Friedrich, *Constitutional Government and Democracy*, Boston: Ginn & Co., 1950, p. 409. Italics added.

him to ask before making any decision: "Who is going to be mad? How mad? Who is going to be glad? How glad?"[9]

The planner, frustrated or disheartened by the decisions made by his superiors—elected or otherwise—must constantly remind himself that he serves in an official rather than a personal capacity. General Dawes, first Director of the United States Bureau of the Budget, explained how the system works: "If the President wants us to spread garbage around the White House, it is our job to figure out how to pile it deeply and uniformly at the least possible cost."

Not every one is built for the bureaucratic life, and for those planners whose "idealism" and "professionalism" make life in an institutional setting intolerable, perhaps the role of the academic, researcher, or technician is appropriate. However, the rest of the government bureaucracy will continue whether or not planners participate, and in the long-run, planners' contributions to administration will be best achieved by formal participation in the governmental hierarchy.

AN ILLUSTRATION: THE BUREAU OF THE BUDGET

Let us examine briefly the experience of a staff agency generally considered successful—the Bureau of the Budget. The Bureau has responsibility for developing the President's executive budget, for coordinating the executive branch legislative program, and for serving as an extension of the President to see that Presidential programs are supported by the often decentralized departments, agencies, and bureaus. How many of these politically charged personnel in the Bureau were replaced when Mr. Eisenhower took over from President Truman? Perhaps five. A similar number were affected when President Kennedy took over after eight years of Republican Administration. Indeed, the present Deputy Director has served at the directorate level under four Presidents. Several years ago he was given a present by Budget Bureau staff—a large seat cushion with a donkey on one side and an elephant on the other.

Let me summarize and paraphrase some of the orientation literature given to the new Bureau of the Budget employee, as it contains some clues to why the Bureau has had success in serving elected officials and affecting public policies indirectly. The advice is applicable elsewhere.

[9] Paul Appleby, quoted in Harlan Cleveland, "The case for bureaucracy", *New York Times Magazine*, 27 October 1963.

The employee has a difficult role to play. He must be humble, self-effacing, and quietly loyal. He will have little or no opportunity to use pronouns in the first person singular. He must be self-effacing because his role is institutional. He is a team player. His loyalty to the politician must be that of the disciplined soldier in combat who has been trained to know that while his commanding officer will protect him to the extent possible, he is nevertheless expendable, both as an individual and as part of a unit. This means that the staff member must develop his instinct for self-preservation to the highest possible point. He cannot afford to make many mistakes. The consequences to himself, his agency, and the elected official may be much too serious.

The administration to be served at any given time represents a point of view so far as public policy is concerned. The staff member's job is to understand this point of view and assist the public official in achieving his objectives. Above all, obstacles are not to be put in the way of the public official. What this comes down to is that every professional is expected to keep his personal notions about public policy in check. He should resist revealing strong attitudes which might raise doubt about his objectivity and, therefore, about his agency's goals. Proposals can often usefully be presented as a range of alternatives, the strengths and weaknesses of each (including the probable political ramifications) identified, and a staff preference stated.

Is this intellectually dishonest ? We are here to give public service to all the people. We do not have to compete for our jobs on a political basis. As Harlan Cleveland, Assistant Secretary of State, has recently noted, this does not mean the avoidance of controversy within the agency or the government generally or finding out what the boss thinks before you give him your opinion:

> The decisions that "work" are not produced by the pliant collaboration of yes-men, but by loud and cheerful argument among colleagues who know they are all trying to catch a glimpse of the same moon from different parts of the forest.
> The job of the top administrator is not primarily to make peace within his own organization. It is to tighten the web of tensions he deliberately creates weighing the options revealed by the arguments among his staff, and then to elicit the loyalty of these same people to the wider public interest as expressed in his decisions.[10]

[10] Harlan Cleveland, *op. cit.*

Planning agencies, like other institutional staff (the Bureau of the Budget, the city manager, the school superintendent), must be sensitive to shifts of public policy. A professional should be able to weather any political transition. Once the staff advisor has lost the confidence of his political superior his usefulness is finished. Those too closely identified with the ideals and aims of the previous administration must be expected to depart quietly, or not so quietly. This kind of adaptability is the hallmark of the professional bureaucrat at any level of government.

Even without a change of administration, bureaucrats must keep the way open for modification and adjustment. The ability to revoke or modify decisions on important issues becomes an important criterion of the successful administrator. The land use map has the unfortunate connotation of irrevocability, infallibility, and inviolateness. Emphasis should be on "the planning process" rather than on "the plan".

PLANNING IS THE ART OF THE POSSIBLE

Constant attention must be paid to problems and implications of implementation. No "unseen hand" will bring about orderly urban development. Action is needed to insure that urban expansion occurs in the "right areas". *The Year 2000 Plan* for the National Capital Region devotes 108 pages to proposals and three pages to implementation—one page for the District, one for the metro center, and one for the region. The *Wedges and Corridors* plan prepared by the Maryland National Capital Park and Planning Commission, designed to translate part of the *Year 2000* sketch plan into more detailed proposals, properly devotes almost half the report to zoning, tax policies, and controls to implement the plan.

Planning commission publications can no longer be limited to general development plans. They must also come up with sound proposals for governmental cooperation and restructuring where necessary to carry out carefully drawn plans. Planners today must not only be sewer, water, air pollution, highways, and recreation experts; they must also have legal, organizational, and economic competencies available to them. They must also be political pragmatists with a good public relations sense.

Chester Barnard, a long-time practitioner in public and private administration, has laid down four conditions that must be met before a proposal is accepted. These conditions may serve as a guide to making major land use proposals. The person receiving the proposal (the politician, the public) will accept it as authoritative if: (a) he can and does understand the communication; (b) he believes that it is not inconsistent with the purpose of the organization; (c) he believes it to be compatible with his personal interest as a whole; and (d) he is able mentally and physically to comply with it.[11]

Planners, above all others, cannot afford to be called dreamers or ivory tower types. To put out proposals that clearly have little chance of acceptance and accomplishment inevitably reduces the planner's always limited supply of public confidence and makes acceptance of subsequent proposals less likely, regardless of their merit.

Richard Neustadt, in his book *Presidential Power*, makes two observations of direct relevance to planners. First, the fact that the President issues an order does not necessarily mean that it will be carried out. Resistances all along the line can frustrate the President's wishes. Second, every defeat that a President suffers reduces the prestige and effectiveness of subsequent efforts, even in unrelated fields. If this is true for the Presidency, it is also true for lesser executive positions.

CONCLUSION

Influence on public policy is achieved within the bureaucracy through competence. Planners and other staff advisors have influence only as they can *persuade* their political superiors; their power is the power of the idea.

Given the high turnover rate of elected officials, continuity and accumulated experience are valuable assets to the bureaucracy. A number of small victories can be as important as a major victory. "As trifles make the sum of human things, so details make the substance of public affairs." To those discouraged by the failure to establish bold planning goals or to prompt resolute action to achieve these goals, perhaps the views of William James, given toward the end of his life, are appropriate. James commented that he was "done with great things and big things, great institutions and big success", and was rather "for those tiny, invisible, molecular moral forces that work from individual to individual, creeping through the crannies of

[11] Chester Barnard, *The Functions of the Executive*, Cambridge, Massachusetts: Harvard University Press, 1938, p. 165.

the world like so many soft rootlets, or like the capillary oozing of water, yet which, if you give them time, will rend the hardest monuments of men's pride".

Planners, like all professionals, are overly pessimistic about the status and recognition of their own field. The increasing reliance on planning requirements in federal grant-in-aid legislation, the availability of "701" and Community Renewal Program funds, the swelling membership rolls of the Institute, the expanding budgets for planning agencies, the emergence of the planner–development coordinator as a key staff advisor to a number of big city mayors—all indicate acceptance of the role of planning in the administration of the public business.

Planners in government are involved in the political process. If this conclusion appears to exalt planning, it must be remembered that in our system of government politics subordinates the public employee, grants responsibility and power to the politician, and vests ultimate authority in the voter.

Politics, Personality and Planning*

Francine F. Rabinovitz

In the more recently developed picture of urban politics, metropolitan areas are no longer viewed as political systems capable of purposeful action, but rather as composed of groups of political decision-makers who can coalesce for crises but whose influence is unequal to initiating or implementing solutions to long run problems generated by urban development.[1] An inevitable corollary is that planners and other experts cannot bring about changes in urban growth patterns simply by serving as staff aides to political executives. The structure of political influence being weak, it is the plans and programs of professionals which stimulate decision-making in otherwise static systems.[2] The normative issue of the right of the planner to "impose values" on the community aside, it appears that if metropolitan problems are to be dealt with, it is up to the planner and his professional cohorts to develop strategies which will include not only physical and social change but also the building of coalitions among the holders of influence in urban areas.

Can the planner adopt such a posture? The answer turns upon the ability of the planner to discover decision-making roles appropriate to

---

* Reprinted by permission of the *Public Administration Review*, March 1967.
[1] The weakening of the capacity to make public policy decisions is suggested in Edward Banfield, *Political Influence*, New York, 1961; Robert Dahl, *Who Governs?*, New Haven, 1962; Robert Wood, *1400 Governments*, Cambridge, 1960, and many others.
[2] This role is suggested in Robert C. Wood, "Urban regions: the challenges and achievements in public administration", *Planning 1962* (ASPO, 1962), and William Wheaton, "Integration at the urban level", *The Integration of Political Communities* (ed. P. Jacob and J. Toscano), Philadelphia, 1964.

the community in which he wishes to be an activist. The variability of community decision-making systems suggests a diversity of roles for those who wish to guide urban growth. A community with an elite political group may provide a hospitable environment for the planner as technical staff aid. In a community with a more competitive pattern of decision-making, the planner may be required to be a broker, arbitrating between opposed interests to build support for innovation. In a more fragmented system, where *ad hoc* coalitions form on particular issues but are rarely maintained, and it is easier to prevent action than sustain it, the planner may have to act as mobilizer of influence. He might first have to arouse those with interests in an issue and then coordinate these interests.[3]

But, roles for the exercise of influence are dependent variables. Success in playing a role rests on the ability to command resources adequate for the action desired, and on the capacity of the actor to commit himself to the kinds of actions required. Planners may wish to improve the urban environment. They may possess the resources for power necessary to exert influence. It may still be true, however, that their personal and professional needs and norms will not allow them to play the roles required.

One way to predict capacity to play required roles would be to ascertain how the personal and professional development experience of planners is likely to affect the acquisition of skills and values linked to roles. It is not proven what predisposes people to become urban planners nor how they are affected by the process of recruitment into the profession. In general as an individual becomes an active participant in his occupation, he is socialized to the norms of this community.[4] The degree to which the planner uses his resources to make planning effective thus depends in large

---

[3] This typology rests on the theory that not all communities need to be either pluralist or elitist but may range, in their decision-making structures, along a continuum. The whole might run from a very tight power pyramid to a community so loosely integrated as to be characterized by disarray and violence in its decision-making. Support for such a variable pattern hypothesis appears in Peter Rossi, "Power and community structure", *Midwest Journal of Political Science* (November 1960); Robert Agger, Daniel Goldrich, and Bert Swanson, *The Rules and the Ruled*, New York, 1964.

[4] This discussion follows Lucian Pye, "Political ideology and personal identity", *Political Decision Makers* (ed. D. Marvick), Glencoe, 1960; and Lucian Pye, *Politics, Personality and Nation Building: Burma's Search for Identity*, New Haven, 1962.

part on the incentive his profession's self image creates for him to play the appropriate roles.[5] In the case of the urban planner the skills required for discovering and formulating coalitions and maintaining alliances in all but the most cohesive systems are, to varying degrees, the skills of the politician. Thus, only if the profession's image includes the picture of the planner as rightfully a political actor will the planner attain both professional rewards and the completion of concrete programs.

THE NORMS OF THE PLANNING COMMUNITY

If planning were among the traditional professions, the mores conveyed to the planner through the channels of professional education and indoctrination would be the total content of practitioner socialization. However, while urban planning is referred to as a profession, it is actually an occupation in the process of attempting to become professionalized.[6]

The activity called planning has been accepted as desirable in many American cities, and recognized as requiring a high degree of technical skill developed through a period of professional training. Acceptance of the activity has, however, preceded recognition of the skill group required and has also preceded clear definition of the identifying marks of the skill group. Thus, planning has been aptly referred to as a function in search of an identity.[7]

The fact that the process of professionalization of planning is incomplete means that there are two sets of norms to which the practitioner is socialized. One describes the posture expected of the planner with respect to

[5] The role of occupational norms and goals in shaping practitioner performance is analyzed in Samuel Huntington, *The Soldier and the State*, Cambridge, 1957; Morris Janowitz, *The Professional Soldier*, Glencoe, 1960; William Kornhauser, *Scientists in Industry*, Berkeley, 1962; C. Wright Mills, *White Collar*, New York, 1956; C. P. Snow, *The Two Cultures and the Scientific Revolution*, New York, 1959.

[6] A detailed examination of the degree to which planning is a profession as well as the forces fostering and impeding the process and the role of the American Institute of Planners is contained in Harry Gold, "The process of professionalization in the occupation of urban planning" (unpublished doctoral dissertation, University of Michigan, 1965). Professionalization in planning is also discussed in Alan Altshuler, *The City Planning Process*, Ithaca, 1965, pp. 392–405. The characteristics of professionalization in general are analyzed in William Goode, "Community within a community", *American Sociological Review* (April 1957); Everett Hughes, *Men and their Work*, Glencoe, 1958; Alexander Carr-Saunders, *The Professions*, Oxford, 1933.

[7] "Planners thriving on urban renewal", *Business Week* (25 July 1964), p. 135.

technical competence, client relations, rules concerning advertising and actions in the community. The other relates to the search for a clearer professional identity, and describes not the job of the planner but the changes which must take place within the occupational system to promote the professionalization of planning.

Norm Relating to Technical Competence

In the first category, practitioner norms, the weight of pronouncements appears to be against a requirement that the planner take political postures, even though there is a growing respect for political success. The preferred role is one in which the professional planner does not go beyond technical and policy advice on use of community resources. He is neither a determiner of goals nor an implementer of programs. Ideally he provides existing decision makers with the means to reach community goals.[8]

Propagation of the idea that planning should be separated from politics began in an attempt to insulate it from the corruption of local politics in the early twentieth century. Now keeping the planner out of politics has taken on the force of an ethical endeavor. It is said that to assign to the planner the task of accomplishing social or economic reforms is to travel the road to authoritarianism.[9]

Planning educators appear to accept this role definition in so far as compliance can be inferred from the sparsity of courses in planning education which concentrate on problems of local political action. Very few empirical studies deal with the views of individual planning practitioners, so that it is difficult to judge whether the consensus attributed to officials of the professional association and theoreticians is shared by those in the field. One recent survey suggests that directors of planning agencies, while renouncing a wholly technical orientation for a more policy oriented stance,

[8] See John T. Howard, "City planning as a social movement, a governmental function and a technical profession", *Planning and the Urban Community* (ed. H. Perloff), Pittsburgh, 1960; John T. Howard, "The planner in a democratic society—a credo", *Journal of the American Institute of Planners* (Spring 1955); Seward Hiltner, "Planning as a profession", *ibid.* (November 1957).

[9] Henry Churchill, "Planning in a free society", *Journal of the American Institute of Planners* (Fall 1954).

follow the general pattern in rejecting the idea that planners are responsible for "selling" their proposals to city executives and legislators.[10]

There is also limited evidence that planners go into practice regarding political roles not only as unnecessary to truly professional planning but as inherently unprofessional. This hypothesis is suggested by answers to a survey conducted in a class of student planners in 1963 at the Massachusetts Institute of Technology. Responding on a scale to adjectives associated with the phrase "politicians are ———", 61 per cent stated they believed politicians to be "unprofessional" to a moderate or high degree.[11] Other responses expressed the conviction that what planning stands for is not what politicians maximize. Seventy-seven per cent of the group believed planning can and should be "rational"; at the same time 64 per cent believed that politicians are "irrational". While the students viewed planning as a social service, 76 per cent saw politicians as "selfish". Not one respondent believed politicians could be more than "slightly altruistic". Although 82 per cent of the group regarded itself as "liberal" and none saw themselves as "conservative", 72 per cent saw politicians as "conservative". There was even a tendency to think of politicians as necessarily opposite to what the individual student planner considered himself. Those who regarded themselves as non-liberals tended to regard politicians as more liberal than their colleagues whose self-image was liberal. Sixty-six per cent of those who felt they were "something-in-between" liberal and conservative identified politicians toward the liberal side of the scale.

The hypothesis that the planner not only has little professionally induced motivation to choose the more politicized roles but that the norms of the profession provide him with actual disincentives to do so is supported by

[10] Francine F. Rabinovitz and J. Stanley Pottinger, "Organization for local planning: the attitudes of directors", *Journal of the American Institute of Planners* XXXIII (January 1967).

[11] Francine Rabinovitz, "Hypotheses on the perceptions of student planners with regard to planning, politics, and political action", Cambridge (April 1963), typescript. It must be emphasized that this was a survey of a very small group, not randomly selected, and therefore can be considered valuable only in suggesting hypotheses, not in demonstrating relationships. It is interesting that of the remaining 39 per cent who did not believe politicians to be unprofessional to a high or moderate degree, 80 per cent were foreign students. It may be that the images of politics as "unprofessional" is culture bound, rather than common to planners. In the political culture of developing areas, for example, the image of the politicians may be more favorable than it has come to be in a culture where the stereotype of the "pol" is a city hall boss, not a charismatic leader.

observations of behavior made in case studies. Edward Banfield, describing the premises of city planning in a Chicago hospital dispute, noted that the planner, "following the usual professional practice", was likely to be insensitive to the need to include consideration of eliminating racial discrimination in his program calculations. "If it were expressly called to his attention", states Banfield, "he might even say that it is a 'political' factor which should not be allowed to influence the decision."[12] Abstracting from the results of a survey of 199 San Francisco Bay area planners, three-fourths of the total in the region, John Dyckman made a similar observation:

> . . . the prestige of the city planner may hinge on the remoteness of promised results, as with the clergy. But the prestige must be defended on occasion by walling off the special operational role of the planner from the world of practical affairs. This segregation of operations is glorified as a rejection of politics.[13]

Norms Relating to Professionalizing

The strain between the roles required for effective planning and the norms inculcated by the profession is intensified by the second area of practitioner socialization, the drive toward professionalization. There is, first, the traditional conflict between the concept of "professionalism" and the concept of "politics". Stephen Bailey has observed, with respect to educators, that:

> It is true of most professions that they attempt to justify their existence on the basis of high principle. In the language of American culture, "politics" and "self-seeking" are frequently synonyms. But "self-seeking" and "high principle" are antonyms. Only the naive would suggest that there is no self-seeking in the [professions]. But professions cannot exist without public support. If a profession wishes to gain that support, it surrounds itself with words and symbols that elicit public favor. That it feels constrained to do so is one of the moral wonders of the universe.[14]

To describe professional activities as "political" would place planners, as well as schoolmen, in a poor light in terms of the support building process. Thus the refusal to acknowledge the political nature of planning is in

---

[12] Edward Banfield, *Political Influence, op. cit.*, p. 330.
[13] John Dyckman, "What makes planners plan ?", *Journal of the American Institute of Planners* (May 1961), p. 166.
[14] Stephen Bailey *et al.*, *Schoolmen and Politics*, Syracuse, 1962, p. ix.

measure a politically astute posture for planners, as Bailey notes it is for schoolmen.

The arenas of action for schoolmen and planners are, however, quite different. The long heritage of "keeping politics out of education and education out of politics" succeeded in separating educational conflicts from other types of political battles, with the prominent exception of civil rights issues, at the local level. This is not true for planning. Although the myth of apolitical action remains, the success of planning is tied to the operation of the political system. In political systems too weak to support action, planners must have the knowledge and skill to marshall effective influence.

It is here that the second conflict with professionalization arises. The goal of effective planning imposes a series of strategies on planners which require increasingly heterogeneous skills as the political integration of the community decreases. But, professionalization is enhanced by the degree to which a profession can lay claim to a highly specialized set of techniques.[15] Thus while the thrust of professionalization along traditional lines leads planners to rivet their attention on narrowly defined skills, the task of politically effective planning calls for the opposite orientation. To ask the planner to seek political effectiveness is to ask his profession to require proficiency in skills which it cannot monopolize. The patterns of community decision-making may require the planner to have the verbal skill of a public relations man, the financial acumen of a banker, or the bargaining skills of a politician. Yet the more generalized the techniques of an occupation, the more difficult the achievement of professional recognition.

THE NEEDS OF THE PLANNER

A second aspect of the personality dimension is the correlation between individual needs and the postures required for politically effective planning. As Harold Lasswell suggested, people who participate in politics may do so to resolve personal rather than public problems. Political, economic,

[15] See Carr-Saunders, *The Professions op. cit.*, pp. 491–2; Paul Davidoff and Thomas Reiner, "A choice theory of planning", *Journal of the American Institute of Planners*, XXVIII (May 1962). Alan Altshuler, *The City Planning Process, op. cit.*, discusses another aspect of the enhancement of professionalization, the need for a set of ethical principles for the planning profession, maintaining that this lack is a greater impediment than the refinement of skills (pp. 397–401).

and social convictions form a pattern expressive of underlying personality traits.[16] The roles the planner in an urban community chooses to play may be a response to his personal needs, as well as to professional norms or to concrete problems.

Studies of the background and perceptions of planners are unfortunately few and contradictory. There is, however, some evidence that the anti-political bias identified in professional norms, perhaps strengthened by the strain between the requirements of the professionalization process and those of effective planning, are associated with personal needs "characteristic" of planners. John Dyckman has suggested that in the formative years of American city planning, the existence of a challenge was, according to the literature of the profession, the motivating force which brought those who perceived it to battle for the city beautiful. A process of self selection operated through which "only those imbued with civic concern, sensitive to the environment, and equipped with the awareness that something could be done about it, took upon themselves the task of city planning".[17] Today the city planner is no longer so daring. In a survey of the members of the American Institute of Planners concerning motives for entering the planning profession, the least popular alternative was that category designated "government and political motivation", i.e. "planning as a way to participate in community decision-making with regard to the public interest in physical land development".[18] Surveys of new graduates from planning programs at the University of California indicate that planners are primarily seeking security and professional status. There appears also to be a trend toward a higher proportion of entrants choosing planning on the grounds that it offers "a comfortable job sinecure".[19]

This motivation in turn limits the role planners play in urban decision making. In a study of political action and planning in six middle-sized cities, the author observed a marked similarity in attitude among planners

[16] Harold Lasswell, *Psychopathology and Politics*, Chicago, 1930; Erik Erikson, *Young Man Luther*, New York, 1958; Theodor Adorno *et al.*, *The Authoritarian Personality*, New York, 1950.

[17] John Dyckman, "What makes planners plan?", *op. cit.*, p. 165.

[18] Cited in Robert Daland and John Parker, "Roles of the planner in urban development", *Urban Growth Dynamics* (ed. F. S. Chapin, Jr. and S. Weiss), New York, 1962, p. 244.

[19] Cited in John Dyckman, "What makes planners plan", *op. cit.*

in several cities with regard to the subject of conflict. The planners generally favored methods which avoided controversy, regarding conflict as inimical to the proper work of planning. In one city this conviction took the form of avoidance of programs which seemed out of step with what the planners saw as established values. In another city the planner accepted the goals and means advocated by directly interested parties, avoiding personal involvement in any conflict among them. In both cases it was not clear that the values imposed were those of the majority of the community, or the majority of the ruling clique. They were the values of the most active. Participation in a conflict might not have cast the planners in the guise of philosopher king, but rather given representation to views not well articulated in the regular governmental establishment.

While it can be tentatively hypothesized that the needs of planners are related to the antipathy to conflict expressed in the profession, it is unclear what developmental processes underlie the need and link it to professional socialization. Analyses of social backgrounds normally work on the theory that people differing regularly in their social backgrounds may also differ regularly in various types of political behavior. It is possible to speculate on the question of whether those planners possessing similar political values have similar social backgrounds. Here again too little information is available to provide an answer. It is, however, interesting to note that in the M.I.T. survey, those who responded positively to three indices of politicization were distinguishable from those who reacted negatively on the basis of income level and undergraduate major. The "politicized" were defined as those who agreed with three statements in a series of ten. These statements were:

1. The planner should adopt a course of fashioning his plans and then building a coalition among diverse power centers to carry them out, rather than responding to the interests of participants.
2. The planner should be an open participant in the political process, staking his values in competition with others and openly striving to achieve his ends.
3. Power in a community is distributed among those who can best mobilize resources.

While 60 per cent of the "politicized" group reported family incomes over $12,000, 90 per cent of those disagreeing with the propositions reported incomes under $8000. While 60 per cent of the "politicized" respondents majored in subjects other than architecture, 69 per cent of the "non-politicized" were architecture majors before entering planning school.

THE IMPACT OF NEEDS AND NORMS

Does the manner in which planners are socialized leave them capable of adopting the complex role orientations required by diverse community decision-making patterns? The fragmentary evidence available suggests that the necessary perspectives are not instilled and, indeed, that the norms and needs of planners inhibit the attitudes required for effective implementation in today's urban political systems.

There is no doubt that further research is needed before the contributing hypotheses can be accepted. In the first place, there are a good many important links missing. To establish a negative psychic or social effect arising from the conflicting pressures of professionalization and political effectiveness, it would be necessary to know that practicing planners actually perceive the two sets of demands, are burdened by role conflicts, or have found ways to ignore or reduce them.

Not only is the information sparse, it also contains many unexplained factors. For example, the reasons expressed for entering the profession in the various existing studies do not seem entirely consistent. In the study of A.I.P. members, a majority of respondents said they entered the profession either "primarily as a way to improve the total environment of all citizens of the community" or because "planning seemed primarily the way to effect physically a more visually pleasing and aesthetically satisfying environment" rather than for the more personal motives suggested earlier by California planning students. Very few said they chose planning because "it combined the benefits of a profession sufficiently rewarding financially, of high status and great social utility". Does the low priority given to professional considerations as compared with design and social improvement motivations indicate that times have changed, or that practitioners have a different perception of their goals than planners now entering the field? To what extent were respondents in the first case influenced by a felt need to appear altruistic? If the motivation for entering the profession actually is not one of prestige or security, should we assume that prestige will be sacrificed if effectuation requires it?

There is also some question about the relationship between the search for professional identity and the more general anti-political bias present in professional norms. It is true that, traditionally, professions have been conceived of as highly specialized. While the planner has thus far also claimed a unique technical competence as the basis for professionalization, functional theories of planning are out of line with the claim, even before politicized roles are considered. There is a tendency, particularly among educators, to conceive of planning as a "generalist" rather than a "specialist" function. This view is related to the belief that if physical planning is a socially useful enterprise because the physical environment exerts influence on social behavior and psychology, plans should be treated as instrumental in the accomplishment of specific social and psychological goals.[20] Thus it is unclear what the impact of the conflict between the demands of effectuation and the demands of professionalization is on a profession which is without skill specialization for reasons not necessarily associated with politics at all. Does the generalist orientation implied by social roles reinforce the anti-political bias? Does it mean that planning will never become fully professionalized? Or does it suggest that urban planners will become professionalized in a different way?[21]

Although the addition of roles required for implementation may thus be only an adjunct to other conflicts between the skills needed by planners and the requirements of professionalization, it does appear that even if the resource potential of planners for exerting influence is substantial, their disposition to use these resources in the political arena is limited. It may be that the negative effects of contradictory personal and role requirements can be mediated by assigning different functions to different individuals. Students of voting behavior and communications have discovered that between formal organizations which broadcast messages and primary groups which receive, are "bridging groups" whose members serve as opinion leaders. In a parallel sense, planning may develop a series

[20] See, for example, Melvin Webber, "The prospects for policies planning", *The Urban Condition* (ed. Leonard Duhl), New York, 1963, pp. 325–8.

[21] Gold, *op. cit.*, suggests that planning belongs to a category of professions which will not conform to old models of professionalization. However, he hypothesizes that this class of occupations will use prestige goals to replace social control goals, such as legal registration and standardized skills. This emphasis might serve to increase, rather than to decrease, the conflict between the demands of professionalization and those of effectuation.

of actors within the profession who buffer potential role conflicts by translating technical work into political relationships in each community.[22] Or, planning may resort to a differentiation among functions by agency levels, each of which employs several planners who specialize in one portion of the total planning operation. On the higher levels this work might be more concerned with public relations and opinion molding than with technical specialties.[23]

At this point, another series of profound questions arises with respect to the desirable limits on political action by professionals, the advisability of giving planners very broad discretion and power to shape cities, and their capability to determine community goals democratically. However, while a decision to move toward functional specialization or a modification in professional attitudes toward politics will certainly raise new and difficult problems, the alternative to these changes is not pleasant to contemplate. For, if planners avoid the hard choices required, they may begin to find that as respect for their profession grows, its utility as a mechanism for effecting urban development is withering.

[22] See Bernard Berelson, P. F. Lazarsfeld and William McPhee, *Voting*, Chicago, 1954. It should be noted that Gold, *op. cit.*, points to some functional specialization already occurring in the planning profession. He suggests that agencies which have hired or promoted technicians from lower levels to the position of planning director have found the technicians unqualified to fill the roles required by the higher echelon. In consequence planning directors are often recruited from other professions. Daland and Parker also note that: "The director of planning will relegate his professional role to subordinates as the political innovation role expands", suggesting that top echelon positions now have different functions than that of other staff. "Roles of the planner in urban development", *Urban Growth Dynamics, op. cit.*, p. 219.

[23] John Friedmann, responding to an article by Alan Altshuler, has suggested a detailed organizational format according to this precept. He recommends the organization of planning into four branches—policy, program, design and land use —set up at the highest level of city administration as separate offices. See Alan Altshuler, "The goals of comprehensive planning", *Journal of the American Institute of Planners*, Vol. XXXI (August 1965); John Friedmann, "A response to Altshuler: comprehensive planning as a process", *ibid.*, pp. 195–7; and Altshuler, *The City Planning Process, op. cit.*, p. 351. Fascinating parallels to this suggestion for a two-step flow of authority, which converts conflicts pressing on one individual into separate, if still conflicting, roles in an institutionalized setting, are suggested in the literature on role conflict in people whose behavioral patterns are the result of traditional and Western interaction. See William J. Hanna and Judith L. Hanna, "The political structure of urban centered Africa communities", *The Politics of Urban Africa*, Chicago: Rand McNally, 1967.

Advocacy and Pluralism in Planning*

Paul Davidoff

THE present can become an epoch in which the dreams of the past for an enlightened and just democracy are turned into a reality. The massing of voices protesting racial discrimination have roused this nation to the need to rectify racial and other social injustices. The adoption by Congress of a host of welfare measures and the Supreme Court's specification of the meaning of equal protection by law both reveal the response to protest and open the way for the vast changes still required.

The just demand for political and social equality on the part of the Negro and the impoverished requires the public to establish the bases for a society affording equal opportunity to all citizens. The compelling need for intelligent planning, for specification of new social goals and the means for achieving them, is manifest. The society of the future will be an urban one, and city planners will help to give it shape and content.

The prospect for future planning is that of a practice which openly invites political and social values to be examined and debated. Acceptance of this position means rejection of prescriptions for planning which would have the planner act solely as a technician. It has been argued that technical studies to enlarge the information available to decision-makers must take precedence over statements of goals and ideals:

> We have suggested that, at least in part, the city planner is better advised to start from research into the functional aspects of cities than from his own estimation of the values which he is attempting to maximize. This suggestion

Author's note. The author wishes to thank Melvin M. Webber for his insightful criticism and Linda Davidoff for her many helpful suggestions and for her analysis of advocate planning. Special acknowledgment is made of the penetrating and brilliant social insights offered by the eminent legal scholar and practitioner, Michael Brodie, of the Philadelphia Bar.

* Reprinted by permission of the *Journal of the American Institute of Planners*, Vol. 31, November 1965.

springs from a conviction that at this juncture the implications of many planning decisions are poorly understood, and that no certain means are at hand by which values can be measured, ranked, and translated into the design of a metroplitan system.[1]

While acknowledging the need for humility and openness in the adoption of social goals, this statement amounts to an attempt to eliminate, or sharply reduce, the unique contribution planning can make: understanding the functional aspects of the city and recommending appropriate future action to improve the urban condition.

Another argument that attempts to reduce the importance of attitudes and values in planning and other policy sciences is that the major public questions are themselves matters of choice between technical methods of solution. Dahl and Lindblom put forth this position at the beginning of their important textbook, *Politics, Economics, and Welfare*.[2]

> In economic organization and reform, the "great issues" are no longer the great issues, if they ever were. It has become increasingly difficult for thoughtful men to find meaningful alternatives posed in the traditional choices between socialism and capitalism, planning and the free market, regulation and laissez faire, for they find their actual choices neither so simple nor so grand. Not so simple, because economic organization poses knotty problems that can only be solved by painstaking attention to technical details—how else, for example, can inflation be controlled? Nor so grand, because, at least in the Western world, most people neither can nor wish to experiment with the whole pattern of socioeconomic organization to attain goals more easily won. If for example, taxation will serve the purpose, why "abolish the wages system" to ameliorate income inequality?

These words were written in the early 1950s and express the spirit of that decade more than that of the 1960s. They suggest that the major battles have been fought. But the "great issues" in economic organization, those resolving around the central issue of the nature of distributive justice, have yet to be settled. The world is still in turmoil over the way in which the resources of nations are to be distributed. The justice of the present social allocation of wealth, knowledge, skill, and other social goods is clearly in debate. Solutions to questions about the share of wealth and other social commodities that should go to different classes cannot be technically derived; they must arise from social attitudes.

Appropriate planning action cannot be prescribed from a position of value

[1] Britton Harris, "Plan or projection", *Journal of the American Institute of Planners*, Vol. XXVI (November 1960), pp. 265–72.

[2] Robert Dahl and Charles Lindblom, *Politics, Economics, and Welfare*, New York: Harper & Brothers, 1953, p. 3.

neutrality, for prescriptions are based on desired objectives. One conclusion drawn from this assertion is that "values are inescapable elements of any rational decision-making process"[3] and that values held by the planner should be made clear. The implications of that conclusion for planning have been described elsewhere and will not be considered in this article.[4] Here I will say that the planner should do more than explicate the values under-lying his prescriptions for courses of action; he should affirm them; he should be an advocate for what he deems proper.

Determinations of what serves the public interest, in a society containing many diverse interest groups, are almost always of a highly contentious nature. In performing its role of prescribing courses of action leading to future desired states, the planning profession must engage itself thoroughly and openly in the contention surrounding political determination. More-over, planners should be able to engage in the political process as advocates of the interests both of government and of such other groups, organizations, or individuals who are concerned with proposing policies for the future development of the community.

The recommendation that city planners represent and plead the plans of many interest groups is founded upon the need to establish an effective urban democracy, one in which citizens may be able to play an active role in the process of deciding public policy. Appropriate policy in a demo-cracy is determined through a process of political debate. The right course of action is always a matter of choice, never of fact. In a bureaucratic age great care must be taken that choices remain in the area of public view and participation.

Urban politics, in an era of increasing government activity in planning and welfare, must balance the demands for ever-increasing central bureau-cratic control against the demands for increased concern for the unique requirements of local, specialized interests. The welfare of all and the welfare of minorities are both deserving of support; planning must be so structured and so practiced as to account for this unavoidable bifurcation of the public interest.

The idealized political process in a democracy serves the search for truth in much the same manner as due process in law. Fair notice and

---

[3] Paul Davidoff and Thomas Reiner, "A choice theory of planning", *Journal of the American Institute of Planners*, Vol. XXVIII (May 1962), pp. 103–15.
[4] *Ibid.*

hearings, production of supporting evidence, cross examination, reasoned decision are all means employed to arrive at relative truth: a just decision. Due process and two- (or more) party political contention both rely heavily upon strong advocacy by a professional. The advocate represents an individual, group or organization. He affirms their position in language understandable to his client and to the decision makers he seeks to convince.

If the planning process is to encourage democratic urban government then it must operate so as to include rather than exclude citizens from participating in the process. "Inclusion" means not only permitting the citizen to be heard. It also means that he be able to become well informed about the underlying reasons for planning proposals, and be able to respond to them in the technical language of professional planners.

A practice that has discouraged full participation by citizens in plan making in the past has been based on what might be called the "unitary plan". This is the idea that only one agency in a community should prepare a comprehensive plan; that agency is the city planning commission or department. Why is it that no other organization within a community prepares a plan? Why is only one agency concerned with establishing both general and specific goals for community development, and with proposing the strategies and costs required to effect the goals? Why are there not plural plans?

If the social, economic, and political ramifications of a plan are politically contentious, then why is it that those in opposition to the agency plan do not prepare one of their own? It is interesting to observe that "rational" theories of planning have called for consideration of alternative courses of action by planning agencies. As a matter of rationality it has been argued that all of the alternative choices open as means to the ends sought be examined.[5] But those, including myself, who have recommended agency consideration of alternatives have placed upon the agency planner the burden of inventing "a few representative alternatives".[6] The agency plan-

[5] See, for example, Martin Meyerson and Edward Banfield, *Politics, Planning and the Public Interest*, Glencoe: The Free Press, 1955, pp. 314 ff. The authors state "By a *rational* decision, we mean one made in the following manner: 1. the decision-maker considers all of the alternatives (courses of action) open to him; . . . 2. he identifies and evaluates all of the consequences which would follow from the adoption of each alternative; . . . 3. he selects that alternative the probable consequences of which would be preferable in terms of his most valued ends."

[6] Davidoff and Reiner, *op. cit.*

ner has been given the duty of constructing a model of the political spectrum, and charged with sorting out what he conceives to be worthy alternatives. This duty has placed too great a burden on the agency planner and has failed to provide for the formulation of alternatives by the interest groups who will eventually be effected by the completed plans.

Whereas in a large part of our national and local political practice contention is viewed as healthy, in city planning where a large proportion of the professionals are public employees, contentious criticism has not always been viewed as legitimate. Further, where only government prepares plans, and no minority plans are developed, pressure is often applied to bring all professionals to work for the ends espoused by a public agency. For example, last year a Federal official complained to a meeting of planning professors that the academic planners were not giving enough support to Federal programs. He assumed that every planner should be on the side of the Federal renewal program. Of course government administrators will seek to gain the support of professionals outside of government, but such support should not be expected as a matter of loyalty. In a democratic system opposition to a public agency should be just as normal and appropriate as support. The agency, despite the fact that it is concerned with planning, may be serving undesired ends.

In presenting a plea for plural planning I do not mean to minimize the importance of the obligation of the public planning agency. It must decide upon appropriate future courses of action for the community. But being isolated as the only plan maker in the community, public agencies as well as the public itself may have suffered from incomplete and shallow analysis of potential directions. Lively political dispute aided by plural plans could do much to improve the level of rationality in the process of preparing the public plan.

The advocacy of alternative plans by interest groups outside of government would stimulate city planning in a number of ways. First, it would serve as a means of better informing the public of the alternative choices open, *alternatives strongly supported by their proponents.* In current practice those few agencies which have portrayed alternatives have not been equally enthusiastic about each.[7] A standard reaction to rationalists'

---

[7] National Capital Planning Commission, *The Nation's Capital: a Policies Plan for the Year 2000*, Washington, D.C.: The Commission, 1961.

prescription for consideration of alternative courses of action has been "it can't be done; how can you expect planners to present alternatives which they don't approve?" The appropriate answer to that question has been that planners like lawyers may have a professional obligation to defend positions they oppose. However, in a system of plural planning, the public agency would be relieved of at least some of the burden of presenting alternatives. In plural planning the alternatives would be presented by interest groups differing with the public agency's plan. Such alternatives would represent the deep-seated convictions of their proponents and not just the mental exercises of rational planners seeking to portray the range of choice.

A second way in which advocacy and plural planning would improve planning practice would be in forcing the public agency to compete with other planning groups to win political support. In the absence of opposition or alternative plans presented by interest groups the public agencies have had little incentive to improve the quality of their work or the rate of production of plans. The political consumer has been offered a yes—no ballot in regard to the comprehensive plan; either the public agency's plan was to be adopted or no plan would be adopted.

A third improvement in planning practice which might follow from plural planning would be to force those who have been critical of "establishment" plans to produce superior plans, rather than only to carry out the very essential obligation of criticizing plans deemed improper.

THE PLANNER AS ADVOCATE

Where plural planning is practiced, advocacy becomes the means of professional support for competing claims about how the community should develop. Pluralism in support of political contention describes the process; advocacy describes the role performed by the professional in the process. Where unitary planning prevails, advocacy is not of paramount importance, for there is little or no competition for the plan prepared by the public agency. The concept of advocacy as taken from legal practice implies the opposition of at least two contending viewpoints in an adversary proceeding.

The legal advocate must plead for his own and his client's sense of legal propriety or justice. The planner as advocate would plead for his own and his client's view of the good society. The advocate planner would be more than a provider of information, an analyst of current trends, a simulator of future conditions, and a detailer of means. In addition to carrying out these necessary parts of planning, he would be a *proponent* of specific substantive solutions.

The advocate planner would be responsible to his client and would seek to express his client's views. This does not mean that the planner could not seek to persuade his client. In some situations persuasion might not be necessary, for the planner would have sought out an employer with whom he shared common views about desired social conditions and the means toward them. In fact one of the benefits of advocate planning is the possibility it creates for a planner to find employment with agencies holding values close to his own. Today the agency planner may be dismayed by the positions affirmed by his agency, but there may be no alternative employer.

The advocate planner would be above all a planner. He would be responsible to his client for preparing plans for all of the other elements comprising the planning process. Whether working for the public agency or for some private organization, the planner would have to prepare plans that take account of the arguments made in other plans. Thus the advocate's plan might have some of the characteristics of a legal brief. It would be a document presenting the facts and reasons for supporting one set of proposals, and facts and reasons indicating the inferiority of counter-proposals. The adversary nature of plural planning might, then, have the beneficial effect of upsetting the tradition of writing plan proposals in terminology which makes them appear self-evident.

A troublesome issue in contemporary planning is that of finding techniques for evaluating alternative plans. Technical devices such as cost-benefit analysis by themselves are of little assistance without the use of means for appraising the values underlying plans. Advocate planning, by making more apparent the values underlying plans, and by making definitions of social costs and benefits more explicit, should greatly assist the process of plan evaluation. Further, it would become clear (as it is not at present) that there are no neutral grounds for evaluating a plan; there are as many evaluative systems as there are value systems.

The adversary nature of plural planning might also have a good effect on the uses of information and research in planning. One of the tasks of the advocate planner in discussing the plans prepared in opposition to this would be to point out the nature of the bias underlying information presented in other plans. In this way, as critic of opposition plans, he would be performing a task similar to the legal technique of cross-examination. While painful to the planner whose bias is exposed (and no planner can be entirely free of bias) the net effect of confrontation between advocates of alternative plans would be more careful and precise research.

Not all the work of an advocate planner would be of an adversary nature. Much of it would be educational. The advocate would have the job of informing other groups, including public agencies, of the conditions, problems, and outlook of the group he represented. Another major educational job would be that of informing his clients of their rights under planning and renewal laws, about the general operations of city government, and of particular programs likely to affect them.

The advocate planner would devote much attention to assisting the client organization to clarify its ideas and to give expression to them. In order to make his client more powerful politically the advocate might also become engaged in expanding the size and scope of his client organization. But the advocate's most important function would be to carry out the planning process for the organization and to argue persuasively in favor of its planning proposals.

Advocacy in planning has already begun to emerge as planning and renewal affect the lives of more and more people. The critics of urban renewal[8] have forced response from the renewal agencies, and the ongoing debate[9] has stimulated needed self-evaluation by public agencies. Much work along the lines of advocate planning has already taken place, but little of it by professional planners. More often the work has been conducted by trained community organizers or by student groups. In at least one instance, however, a planner's professional aid led to the development

---

[8] The most important critical studies are: Jane Jacobs, *The Life and Death of Great American Cities*, New York: Random House, 1961; Martin Anderson, *The Federal Bulldozer*, Cambridge: M.I.T. Press, 1964; Herbert J. Gans, "The human implications of current redevelopment and relocation planning", *Journal of the American Institute of Planners*, Vol. XXV (February 1959), pp. 15–26.

[9] A recent example of heated debate appears in the following set of articles: Herbert J. Gans, "The failure of urban renewal," *Commentary*, Vol. 39 (April 1965), p. 29; George Raymond, "Controversy", 40 (July 1965), p. 72; and Herbert J. Gans, "Controversy", 40 (July 1965), p. 77.

of an alternative renewal approach, one which will result in the dislocation of far fewer families than originally contemplated.[10]

Pluralism and advocacy are means for stimulating consideration of future conditions by all groups in society. But there is one social group which at present is particularly in need of the assistance of planners. This group includes organizations representing low-income families. At a time when concern for the condition of the poor finds institutionalization in community action programs, it would be appropriate for planners concerned with such groups to find means to plan with them. The plans prepared for these groups would seek to combat poverty and would propose programs affording new and better opportunities to the members of the organization and to families similarly situated.[11]

The difficulty in providing adequate planning assistance to organizations representing low-income families may in part be overcome by funds allocated to local anti-poverty councils. But these councils are not the only representatives of the poor; other organizations exist and seek help. How can this type of assistance be financial? This question will be examined below, when attention is turned to the means for institutionalizing plural planning.

THE STRUCTURE OF PLANNING

Planning by Special Interest Groups

The local planning process typically includes one or more "citizens" organizations concerned with the nature of planning in the community. The Workable Program requirement for "citizen participation"[12] has enforced this tradition and brought it to most large communities. The difficulty with current citizen participation programs is that citizens are more often *reacting* to agency programs than *proposing* their concepts of appropriate goals and future action.

[10] Walter Thabit, *An Alternate Plan for Cooper Square*, New York: Walter Thabit, July 1961.

[11] The first conscious effort to employ the advocacy method was carried out by a graduate student of city planning as an independent research project. The author acted as both a participant and an observer of a local housing organization. See Linda Davidoff, "The bluffs: advocate planning", *Comment*, Dept. of City Planning, University of Pennsylvania (Spring 1965), p. 59.

[12] See Section 101(c) of the United States Housing Act of 1949, as amended.

The fact that citizens' organizations have not played a positive role in formulating plans is to some extent a result of both the enlarged role in society played by government bureaucracies and the historic weakness of municipal party politics. There is something very shameful to our society in the necessity to have organized "citizen participation". Such participation should be the norm in an enlightened democracy. The formalization of citizen participation as a required practice in localities is similar in many respects to totalitarian shows of loyalty to the state by citizen parades.

Will a private group interested in preparing a recommendation for community development be required to carry out its own survey and analysis of the community? The answer would depend upon the quality of the work prepared by the public agency, work which should be public information. In some instances the public agency may not have surveyed or analyzed aspects the private group thinks important; or the public agency's work may reveal strong biases unacceptable to the private group. In any event, the production of a useful plan proposal will require much information concerning the present and predicted conditions in the community. There will be some costs associated with gathering that information, even if it is taken from the public agency. The major cost involved in the preparation of a plan by a private agency would probably be the employment of one or more professional planners.

What organizations might be expected to engage in the plural planning process? The first type that comes to mind are the political parties; but this is clearly an aspirational thought. There is very little evidence that local political organizations have the interest, ability, or concern to establish well developed programs for their communities. Not all the fault, though, should be placed upon the professional politicians, for the registered members of political parties have not demanded very much, if anything, from them as agents.

Despite the unreality of the wish, the desirability for active participation in the process of planning by the political parties is strong. In an ideal situation local parties would establish political platforms which would contain master plans for community growth and both the majority and minority parties in the legislative branch of government would use such plans as one basis for appraising individual legislative proposals. Further, the local administration would use its planning agency to carry out the plans it proposed to the electorate. This dream will not turn to reality for a long time. In the interim other interest groups must be sought to fill the gap caused by the present inability of political organizations.

The second set of organizations which might be interested in preparing plans for community development are those that represent special interest groups having established views in regard to proper public policy. Such organizations as chambers of commerce, real estate boards, labor organizations, pro- and anti-civil rights groups, and anti-poverty councils come to mind. Groups of this nature have often played parts in the development of community plans, but only in a very few instances have they proposed their own plans.

It must be recognized that there is strong reason operating against commitment to a plan by these organizations. In fact it is the same reason that in part limits the interests of politicians and which limits the potential for planning in our society. The expressed commitment to a particular plan may make it difficult for groups to find means for accommodating their various interests. In other terms, it may be simpler for professionals, politicians, or lobbyists to make deals if they have not laid their cards on the table.

There is a third set of organizations that might be looked to as proponents of plans and to whom the foregoing comments might not apply. These are the *ad hoc* protest associations which may form in opposition to some proposed policy. An example of such a group is a neighborhood association formed to combat a renewal plan, a zoning change, or the proposed location of a public facility. Such organizations may seek to develop alternative plans, plans which would, if effected, better serve their interests.

From the point of view of effective and rational planning it might be desirable to commence plural planning at the level of city-wide organizations, but a more realistic view is that it will start at the neighborhood level. Certain advantages of this outcome should be noted. Mention was made earlier of tension in government between centralizing and decentralizing forces. The contention aroused by conflict between the central planning agency and the neigborhood organization may indeed be healthy, leading to clearer definition of welfare policies and their relation to the rights of individuals or minority groups.

Who will pay for plural planning ? Some organizations have the resources to sponsor the development of a plan. Many groups lack the means. The plight of the relatively indigent association seeking to propose a plan might be analogous to that of the indigent client in search of legal aid. If the idea of plural planning makes sense, then support may be found from foundations or from government. In the beginning it is more likely that some foundation might be willing to experiment with plural planning as a means of making city planning more effective and more democratic. Or the Federal Government might see plural planning, if carried out by local anti-poverty councils, as a strong means of generating local interest in community affairs.

Federal sponsorship of plural planning might be seen as a more effective tool for stimulating involvement of the citizen in the future of his community than are the present type of citizen participation programs. Federal support could only be expected if plural planning were seen, not as a means of combating renewal plans, but as an incentive to local renewal agencies to prepare better plans.

The Public Planning Agency

A major drawback to effective democratic planning practice is the continuation of that non-responsible vestigial institution, the planning commission. If it is agreed that the establishment of both general policies and implementation policies are questions affecting the public interest and that public interest questions should be decided in accord with established democratic practices for decision making, then it is indeed difficult to find convincing reasons for continuing to permit independent commissions to make planning decisions. At an earlier stage in planning the strong arguments of John T. Howard[13] and others in support of commissions may have been persuasive. But it is now more than a decade since Howard made his defence against Robert Walker's position favoring planning as a staff function under the mayor. With the increasing effect planning decisions have upon the lives of citizens the Walker proposal assumes great urgency.[14]

[13] John T. Howard, "In defense of planning commissions", *Journal of the American Institute of Planners*, Vol. XVII (Spring 1951).

[14] Robert Walker, *The Planning Function in Urban Government*, Chicago: University of Chicago Press, 1950. Walker drew the following conclusions from his examination of planning and planning commissions. "Another conclusion to be drawn from the existing composition of city planning boards is that they are not representative of the population as a whole" (p. 153). "In summary the writer is

Aside from important questions regarding the propriety of independent agencies which are far removed from public control determining public policy, the failure to place planning decision choices in the hands of elected officials has weakened the ability of professional planners to have their proposals effected. Separating planning from local politics has made it difficult for independent commissions to garner influential political support. The commissions are not responsible directly to the electorate and in turn the electorate is, at best, often indifferent to the planning commission.

During the last decade in many cities power to alter community development has slipped out of the hands of city planning commissions, assuming they ever held it, and has been transferred to development coordinators. This has weakened the professional planner. Perhaps planners unknowingly contributed to this by their refusal to take concerted action in opposition to the perpetuation of commissions.

Planning commissions are products of the conservative reform movement of the early part of this century. The movement was essentially antipopulist and pro-aristocracy. Politics was viewed as dirty business. The commissions are relics of a not-too-distant past when it was believed that if men of good will discussed a problem thoroughly, certainly the right solution would be forthcoming. We know today, and perhaps it was always known, that there are no right solutions. Proper policy is that which the decision-making unit declares to be proper.

Planning commissions are responsible to no constituency. The members

---

of the opinion that the claim that planning commissions are more objective than elected officials must be rejected" (p. 155). "From his observations the writer feels justified in saying that very seldom does a majority of any commission have any well-rounded understanding of the purposes and ramifications of planning" (p. 157). "In summary, then, it was found that the average commission member does not comprehend planning nor is he particularly interested even in the range of customary physical planning" (p. 158). "Looking at the planning commission at the present time, however, one is forced to conclude that despite some examples of successful operations, the unpaid board is not proving satisfactory as a planning agency" (p. 165). ". . . it is believed that the most fruitful line of development for the future would be replacement of these commissions by a department or bureau attached to the office of mayor or city manager. This department might be headed by a board or by a single director, but the members or the director would in any case hold office at the pleasure of the executive on the same basis as other department heads" (p. 177).

of the commissions, except for their chairman, are seldom known to the public. In general the individual members fail to expose their personal views about policy and prefer to immerse them in group decisions. If the members wrote concurring and dissenting opinions, then at least the commissions might stimulate thought about planning issues. It is difficult to comprehend why this aristocratic and undemocratic form of decision-making should be continued. The public planning function should be carried out in the executive or legislative office and perhaps in both. There has been some question about which of these branches of government would provide the best home, but there is much reason to believe that both branches would be made more cognizant of planning issues if they were each informed by their own planning staffs. To carry this division further, it would probably be advisable to establish minority and majority planning staffs in the legislative branch.

At the root of my last suggestion is the belief that there is or should be a Republican and Democratic way of viewing city development; that there should be conservative and liberal plans, plans to support the private market and plans to support greater government control. There are many possible roads for a community to travel and many plans should show them. Explication is required of many alternative futures presented by those sympathetic to the construction of each such future. As indicated earlier, such alternatives are not presented to the public now. Those few reports which do include alternative futures do not speak in terms of interest to the average citizen. They are filled with professional jargon and present sham alternatives. These plans have expressed technical land use alternatives rather than social, economic, or political value alternatives. Both the traditional unitary plans and the new ones that present technical alternatives have limited the public's exposure to the future states that might be achieved. Instead of arousing healthy political contention as diverse comprehensive plans might, these plans have deflated interest.

The independent planning commission and unitary plan practice certainly should not co-exist. Separately they dull the possibility for enlightened political debate; in combination they have made it yet more difficult. But when still another hoary concept of city planning is added to them, such debate becomes practically impossible. This third of a trinity of worn-out notions is that city planning should focus only upon the physical aspects of city development.

AN INCLUSIVE DEFINITION OF THE SCOPE
OF PLANNING

The view that equates physical planning with city planning is myopic. It may have had some historic justification, but it is clearly out of place at a time when it is necessary to integrate knowledge and techniques in order to wrestle effectively with the myriad of problems afflicting urban populations.

The city planning profession's historic concern with the physical environment has warped its ability to see physical structures and land as servants to those who use them.[15] Physical relations and conditions have no meaning or quality apart from the way they serve their users. But this is forgotten every time a physical condition is described as good or bad without relation to a specified group of users. High density, low density, green belts, mixed uses, cluster developments, centralized or decentralized business centers are per se neither good nor bad. They decide physical relations or conditions, but take on value only when seen in terms of their social, economic, psychological, physiological, or aesthetic effects upon different users.

---

[15] An excellent and complete study of the bias resulting from reliance upon physical or land use criteria appears in David Farbman, "A Description, Analysis and Critique of the Master Plan", an unpublished mimeographed study prepared for the Univ. of Pennsylvania's Institute for Urban Studies, 1959–60. After studying more than 100 master plans Farbman wrote:

"As a result of predominantly physical orientation of the planning profession many planners have fallen victims to a malaise which I suggest calling the 'Physical Bias'. This bias is not the physical orientation of the planner itself but is the result of it. . . . The physical bias is an attitude on the part of the planner which leads him to conceive of the principles and techniques of *his profession* as the key factors in determining the particular recommendations to be embodied in his plans. . . .

"The physically biased planner plans on the assumption (conviction) that the physical problems of a city can be solved within the framework of physical desiderata; in other words, that physical problems can be adequately stated, solved and remedied according to physical criteria and expertise. The physical bias produces both an inability and an unwillingness on the part of the planner to 'get behind' the physical recommendations of the plan, to isolate, examine or discuss more basic criteria. . . .

". . . There is room, then, in plan thinking, for physical principles, i.e. theories of structural inter-relationships of the physical city: but this is only a part of the story, for the structural impacts of the plan are only a part of the total impact. This total impact must be conceived as a web of physical, economic and social causes and effects" (pp. 22–26).

The profession's experience with renewal over the past decade has shown the high costs of exclusive concern with physical conditions. It has been found that the allocation of funds for removal of physical blight may not necessarily improve the over-all physical condition of a community and may engender such harsh social repercussions as to severely damage both social and economic institutions. Another example of the deficiencies of the physical bias is the assumption of city planners that they could deal with the capital budget as if the physical attributes of a facility could be understood apart from the philosophy and practice of the service conducted within the physical structure. This assumption is open to question. The size, shape, and location of a facility greatly interact with the purpose of the activity the facility houses. Clear examples of this can be seen in public education and in the provision of low cost housing. The racial and other socio-economic consequences of "physical decisions" such as location of schools and housing projects have been immense, but city planners, while acknowleding the existence of such consequences, have not sought or trained themselves to understand socio-economic problems, their causes or solutions.

The city-planning profession's limited scope has tended to bias strongly many of its recommendations toward perpetuation of existing social and economic practices. Here I am not opposing the outcomes, but the way in which they are developed. Relative ignorance of social and economic methods of analysis have caused planners to propose solutions in the absence of sufficient knowledge of the costs and benefits of proposals upon different sections of the population.

Large expenditures have been made on planning studies of regional transportation needs, for example, but these studies have been conducted in a manner suggesting that different social and economic classes of the population did not have different needs and different abilities to meet them. In the field of housing, to take another example, planners have been hesitant to question the consequences of locating public housing in slum areas. In the field of industrial development, planners have seldom examined the types of jobs the community needed; it has been assumed that one job was about as useful as another. But this may not be the case where a significant sector of the population finds it difficult to get employment.

"Who gets what, when, where, why, and how" are the basic political questions which need to be raised about every allocation of public resources.

The questions cannot be answered adequately if land use criteria are the sole or major standards for judgment.

The need to see an element of city development, land use, in broad perspective applies equally well to every other element, such as health, welfare, and recreation. The governing of a city requires an adequate plan for its future. Such a plan loses guiding force and rational basis to the degree that it deals with less than the whole that is of concern to the public.

The complications of the foregoing comments for the practice of city planning are these. First, state planning enabling legislation should be amended to permit planning departments to study and to prepare plans related to any area of public concern. Second, planning education must be redirected so as to provide channels of specialization in different parts of public planning and a core focussed upon the planning process. Third, the professional planning association should enlarge its scope so as to not exclude city planners not specializing in physical planning.

A year ago at the A.I.P. convention it was suggested that the A.I.P. Constitution be amended to permit city planning to enlarge its scope to all matters of public concern.[16] Members of the Institute in agreement with this proposal should seek to develop support for it at both the chapter and national level. The Constitution at present states that the Institute's "particular sphere of activity shall be the planning of the unified development of urban communities and their environs and of states, regions and the nation as *expressed through determination of the comprehensive arrangement of land and land occupancy and regulation thereof*".[17]

It is time that the A.I.P. delete the words in my italics from its Constitution. The planner limited to such concerns is not a city planner, he is a land planner or a physical planner. A city is its people, their practices, and their political, social, cultural and economic institutions as well as other things. The city planner must comprehend and deal with all these factors.

The new city planner will be concerned with physical planning, economic planning, and social planning. The scope of his work will be no wider than that presently demanded of a mayor or a city councilman. Thus,

---

[16] Paul Davidoff, "The role of the city planner in social planning", *Proceedings of the 1964 Annual Conference*, American Institute of Planners (Washington, D.C.: The Institute, 1964), pp. 125–31.

[17] Constitution of A.I.P., Article 11 "Purposes", in *A.I.P. Handbook & Roster—1965*, p. 8.

we cannot argue against an enlarged planning function on grounds that it is too large to handle. The mayor needs assistance; in particular he needs the assistance of a planner, one trained to examine needs and aspirations in terms of both short and long term perspectives. In observing the early stages of development of Community Action Programs, it is apparent that our cities are in desperate need of the type of assistance trained planners could offer. Our cities require for their social and economic programs the type of long range thought and information that have been brought forward in the realm of physical planning. Potential resources must be examined and priorities set.

What I have just proposed does not imply the termination of physical planning, but it does mean that physical planning be seen as part of city planning. Uninhibited by limitations on his work, the city planner will be able to add his expertise to the task of coordinating the operating and capital budgets and to the job of relating effects of each city program upon the others and upon the social, political, and economic resources of the community.

An expanded scope reaching all matters of public concern will make planning not only a more effective administrative tool of local government but it will also bring planning practice closer to the issues of real concern to the citizens. A system of plural city planning probably has a much greater chance for operational success where the focus is on live social and economic questions instead of rather esoteric issues relating to physical norms.

THE EDUCATION OF PLANNERS

Widening the scope of planning to include all areas of concern to government would suggest that city planners must possess a broader knowledge of the structure and forces affecting urban development. In general this would be true. But at present many city planners are specialists in only one or more of the functions of city government. Broadening the scope of planning would require some additional planners who specialize in one or more of the services entailed by the new focus.

A prime purpose of city planning is the coordination of many separate functions. This coordination calls for men holding general knowledge of the many elements comprising the urban community. Educating a man for performing the coordinative role is a difficult job, one not well satisfied by the present tradition of two years of graduate study. Training of urban planners with the skills called for in this article may require both longer graduate study and development of a liberal arts undergraduate program affording an opportunity for holistic understanding of both urban conditions and techniques for analyzing and solving urban problems.

The practice of plural planning requires educating planners who would be able to engage as professional advocates in the contentious work of forming social policy. The person able to do this would be one deeply committed to both the process of planning and to particular substantive ideas. Recognizing that ideological commitments will separate planners, there is tremendous need to train professionals who are competent to express their social objectives.

The great advances in analytic skills, demonstrated in the recent May issue of this *Journal* dedicated to techniques of simulating urban growth processes, portend a time when planners and the public will be better able to predict the consequences of proposed courses of action. But these advances will be of little social advantage if the proposals themselves do not have substance. The contemporary thoughts of planners about the nature of man in society are often mundane, unexciting or gimmicky. When asked to point out to students the planners who have a developed sense of history and philosophy concerning man's situation in the urban world one is hard put to come up with a name. Sometimes Goodman or Mumford might be mentioned. But planners seldom go deeper than acknowledging the goodness of green space and the soundness of proximity linked activities. We cope with the problems of the alienated man with a recommendation for reducing the time of the journey to work.

CONCLUSION

The urban community is a system comprised of inter-related elements, but little is known about how the elements do, will, or should interrelate. The type of knowledge required by the new comprehensive city planner demands that the planning profession be comprised of groups of men well versed in contemporary philosophy, social work, law, the social sciences, and civic design. Not every planner must be knowledgeable in all these areas, but each planner must have a deep understanding of one or more of these areas and he must be able to give persuasive expression to his understanding.

As a profession charged with making urban life more beautiful, exciting, and creative, and more just, we have had little to say. Our task is to train a future generation of planners to go well beyond us in its ability to prescribe the future urban life.

Notes on the Structure of Planning Administration

Rolf-Richard Grauhan*

FOLLOWING the classical doctrine of the separation of powers, the German Basic Law (*Grundgesetz*) defines administration as the function of the "executive power" (Article 20). The leading German textbook on administrative law accordingly defines administration as the function of "attending to matters by way of implementing them, which means to act purposively, i.e. following set goals, and hence adhering to a plan. In contradistinction to government, this is not in itself a goal-seeking activity, that is to say it is not planning, or the setting of directions, but is, rather, the pursuance of affairs in accordance with a set purpose."[1]

In this concept of the separation of powers, goal-setting and the planning function would fall to the parliamentary process, while the administrative implementation of programmes determined by parliament would devolve upon the "executive power". However, as everyone realizes, most of the Bills submitted to the legislature originate from the "executive power", which thus obviously engages in planning and to a considerable extent also in "goal-setting". Some people who wish to retain the concept of administration as implementation try to solve this dilemma by drawing a sharp distinction between political "government" and administration by conferring upon the government, and especially on its head with his responsibility for co-ordination,[2] the function of planning and goal-setting, a function for which "support by the legislature"[3] must be sought as well as its implementation by the administrative machine.

---

* Translated jointly by the author and editor and reprinted by permission of *Stadtbauwelt*, No. 22, 1969 (Zur Struktur der planenden Verwaltung).

[1] Hans J. Wolff, *Verwaltungsrecht*, Vol. I, 7th ed., Munich, 1968, p. 9.

[2] Cf. Wilhelm Hennis, *Richtlinienkompetenz und Regierungstechnik*, Tübingen, 1964.

[3] Hans J. Wolff, *op. cit.*, p. 74.

But in practice even this model has long been superseded: in particular contextuating decisions initiating new programmes need more and more extensive and well-planned preparation on part of the administration. One solution would be completely to ignore the concept of administration as "attending to matters by way of implementation" with no part in their planning. But there still exists a *structural* problem linked to the administrative function. The problem is highlighted in the following paper discussing three theses:

1. The structure of German administration, except where it is being performed by some form of private corporation, is modelled on the assumption of its function being that of executing predetermined programmes.
2. The introduction of the planning function into the administrative machine has been attempted by ways of adapting it to the structure of an administration geared towards implementation, thus distorting it.
3. To plan efficiently requires changes to the structure of administration with these changes following political principles, and resulting in a division of labour between political and administrative bodies which run in parallel.

I. THE STRUCTURAL MODEL OF ADMINISTRATION AS IMPLEMENTATION

The most outstanding characteristic of the existing administrative machine is its hierarchical structure. The existence of this administrative hierarchy is not surprising for those who are familiar with its historical origin as an instrument for establishing the sovereignty of territorial monarchs—an origin from which today's administrative structures derive almost without exception. Still, the perpetuation of this hierarchical structure of administration could not be explained without taking into account the fact that it allows for a rational division of labour and thus for passing policies successively down the line during their implementation.

The rationality of the bureaucratic–monolithic hierarchical structures for implementing predetermined programmes, allowing, as it does, for precision in conveying orders, has been recognized at least since Max

Weber's studies on bureaucracy.[4] But the concept of rationality which is at stake is a specific one, i.e. what on the one hand is, in Max Weber's terminology, called "formal" rationality with its aims of stability, reliability, calculability and universal formal applicability to all kinds of problems, etc.,[5] and, on the other, "purposive rationality" (*Zweckrationalität*) which accepts the ends of action as "given" and thus equates rationality with, in Simon's words, the selection of "effective means" to "reach designated ends".[6] According to this concept, the creation of new ends remains an open question residing in an undefined "political" realm of conflict between divergent goal concepts. Complementary to this is the view of administration as unpolitical and "purely technical" even where it serves wholly irrational political ends.

This very real possibility, for which historical evidence exists, apart, it appears that administrative rationality, in the sense of selecting effective means to obtain predetermined ends, is only feasible where a task may be subdivided and implemented deductively. This assumption underlies all those organizational charts which start from the highest level of the "chief executive" and work down to "main task groups", from there to "task groups", and finally to "tasks" allocated to individual administrators at the end of the line.[7] Coupled with this goes the assumption of administrative responsibilities being specified so strictly and deductively that any overlap must lead to confusion and inefficiency in implementing programmes.

The principle of specifying tasks deductively as one comes down the line assumes that problems may be handled simultaneously and, in principle, independently from each other. Though recognition of the existence of so-called "cross-cutting functions", has long modified this assumption, such recognition only concerns the "administration of administra-

---

[4] Max Weber, *Wirtschaft und Gesellschaft*, Studienausgabe Köln, Berlin, 1964, pp. 159 ff.; English Edition: *The Theory of Social and Economic Organization*, trans. by A. M. Henderson and Talcott Parsons, Oxford University Press, 1947.

[5] Max Weber, *op. cit.*, p. 164; reprinted in: Robert Merton *et al.*, *Reader in Bureaucracy*, Free Press, New York, 1952, p. 24.

[6] The quote is taken from Herbert Simon's first, Weberian ("maximizing"), model of rationality, in: *Administrative Behavior*, Free Press, New York, reprint from the 2nd ed. of 1957 (1966), p. 61.

[7] Cf. Reinhard Baadenhoop, "System der kommunalen Verwaltungsrationalisierung", in: *Handbuch der kommunalen Wissenschaft und Praxis* (ed. by Hans Peters), Vol. III, Heidelberg, 1959.

tion": organization, personnel, finance, thus leaving the principally hierarchical line-structure of the task-oriented sections of administration unchanged.

Max Weber has emphasized one other structural characteristic of administration as an executive organ: this type of rational-bureaucratic authority rests, as he says, "on the trust in the legality of established rules, and the legal authority of all who occupy positions of imperial control."[8] This means that coupled with the hierarchical form of the division of labour we have not only a hierarchical structure of controls, but also a hierarchy of norms. These descend layer by layer from the most general to the most concrete, thus circumscribing any administrative action of the administrator at the very end of the line so that there is only one decision for him to make, namely the correct one. Where, however, administrative decisions are unequivocally *determined* by the legal norms built into administrative programmes, there individual decisions can safely be made by individuals and there is no need for any social choice processes within administrative structures. The monocratic principle of individual responsibility, by its very nature, makes individual administrators personally responsible for implementing established programmes.

The structural model of administration as an executive power is therefore at variance with the notion of administrative discretion. Following the structural concept of the executive as safeguarding legality, German administrative courts have a tendency to reinterpret discretionary rules as norms and to assume that, even under conditions of uncertainty, they therefore predetermine administrative action in the sense of allowing only one correct solution.[9]

The hierarchical model of the executive function with its division of labour must therefore not be seen independently from the hierarchical model of a normative order. The latter operates on the presumption that immediate and binding guidelines for action may be deduced unequivocally from fundamental, unquestionable and hence always *certain* legal principles. We therefore have a model of the executive which consists of two elements

---

[8] Max Weber, *op. cit.*, p. 159.

[9] This is the opinion which prevails in legal practice and in the literature on legal and constitutional theory, cf. Ernst Forsthoff, *Lehrbuch des Verwaltungsrechts*, 9th ed., Munich and Berlin, 1966, p. 84, where further references may be found.

which are inextricably linked: the general norm and its application to individual cases which puts this norm into effect.

II. PHYSICAL PLANNING AND THE HIERARCHICAL MODEL OF THE EXECUTIVE

1. *Physical Planning and Executive Administration*

The discrepancy between this structural model on the one hand, and the problem of generating ends capable of being implemented in a situation of value conflict and in the face of uncertainty about the future on the other, is obvious. For quite a while the existing debate concerning administrative reform has already focused on ways of devising special organizational forms for planning.[10] But the intransigence with which the administrative hierarchy persists, despite the fact that it is justifiable only for the executive function, requires a more radical challenge of its premises than has yet been made.

Firstly, we must emphasize that administrative arrangements for coping with physical planning are to a large extent based on the deductive-hierarchical assumptions built into the executive model of administration. For instance, there has been a long judicial debate over whether a local land-use plan is a norm or an administrative act,[11] before the 1960 Federal Land Use Planning Act (*Bundesbaugesetz*) interpreted it as a norm adopted by the council of the local authority concerned and later implemented by granting, or refusing, planning permissions.

According to the concept of a hierarchy of norms as corresponding to the administrative hierarchy, the 1960 Federal Land Use Planning Act located the local land-use plan firmly within the framework of a hierarchy of state, regional and local plans which form a coherent pattern from the abstract to the concrete. Finally, the 1965 Federal Act on Physical Planning (*Bundesraumordnungsgesetz*) provided this edifice with a superstructure of some general planning goals directly linked to the immutable constitutional principles embodied in the Basic Law. This corresponds to a

[10] Cf. Eberhard Laux, *Planung als Führungsmittel der Verwaltung*, Vol. 5 of *Politik und Verwaltung*, Baden-Baden, 1967.

[11] Cf. "Der Plan als verwaltungsrechtliches Institut" in: *Veröffentlichungen der Vereinigung deutscher Staatsrechtslehrer*, Vol. 18, Berlin, 1970.

judicial concept of planning which reflects the continental urge for codification and which has been formulated by Joseph H. Kaiser: "Planning is the systematic design of a rational order based on all relevant available knowledge."[12] This rational order presents itself as a process of rendering fundamental general and comprehensive normative principles increasingly more concrete, just as Ernst Forsthoff comments: "With us, planning proceeds deductively."[13] This deductive concept of planning assumes the existence of a general and comprehensive plan at the top of the hierarchy which lends itself to being implemented deductively by lower-order and more detailed plans.

2. *Critique of the Executive Model*

(a) *Basic conflict.* The problem is that the more general a plan, the less substantive its content. To give an example, para. 2, section 1 of the 1965 Federal Act on Physical Planning lays down the goal of promoting the development of regions "with *healthy* living and working conditions and an economic, social and cultural *balance*" (my italics), and similarly a 30-year development plan for a city (i.e. Munich) establishes as a principle that "Within the built-up area, account must be taken of the mutual interdependence of employment and residential activities by balancing them against each other". Norms such as these become meaningful only whilst being implemented. But in conformity with the deductive model discussed above, implementation is considered only as putting into effect some basic principles, and fundamental discussion is therefore regarded as inappropriate on this level.[14] On the other hand, the thin mountain air of lofty planning principles does not exactly encourage clarifying discussions, and there is a tendency to include conflicting planning goals in a "declaration of basic principles":[15] e.g. the goal of urban growth following the radial model with mass transit lines converging on the centre is coupled with

[12] Joseph H. Kaiser, Planung I, *Recht und Politik der Planung in Wirtschaft und Gesellschaft*, Baden-Baden, 1965, Preface p. 7.

[13] In: "Der Plan als verwaltungsrechtliches Institut", *loc. cit.*, p. 183.

[14] Cf. for further information comparing the planning process in Munich and Boston: Rolf-Richard Grauhan, *Stadtplanung und Politik, Politische Vierteljahresschrift*, 1966, pp. 402 *et seq.*

[15] Cf. Gerd Albers, "Städtebau, Raumordnung und Politik", in: *Zeitschrift für Politik*, 1967, p. 171.

the goal of preserving its medieval urban core (Munich). Or, as in para. 2 of the 1965 Federal Act on Physical Planning, where it is stipulated that the growth of highly developed regions should be promoted in conjunction with an éven larger growth of developing regions.[16] But, where conflicts between goals exist at the top of the hierarchy, there "decisions" must be left to the level of so-called "implementation". This means that genuine political choice between alternative ends of action must be made on the level of ostensibly administrative "implementation" of planning principles. It also means that the whole hierarchical system of deduction with its idea of general norms being "implemented", and its allegedly well-defined filling in of frames and gaps turns out to be a myth.

(b) *The political character of "judicial" conflict resolution.* The deductive notion of planning is thus subject to the same criticism which Joseph Esser[17] has already levelled against the civil law element of continental legal systems which are also based on the premise of concrete decisions deriving logically from some general principles. Following the "interest-oriented school of legal theory",[18] Esser identifies conflict between those legal principles underlying the codificatory system of the law. These legal principles which are commonly seen as "axioms from which decisions may be deduced logically" he redefines as "problem-bound maxims in the sense of public policy". Their conflicting character follows from the "antithesis which exists between the basic goals of the law".[19] Because of this inherent conflict between legal principles with a bearing on particular cases, it transpires that concrete judicial decisions are *ex-post facto* rationalizations of *politically* selected solutions, the ostensibly logical deductions of such principles from the basic norms underlying a codificatory system notwithstanding.[20]

---

[16] Concerning this goal conflict: cf. Karl-Heinrich Hansmeyer, "Ziele und Träger regionaler Wirtschaftspolitik", in: *Beirträge zur Regionalpolitik* (ed. by Hans K. Schneider), Berlin, 1968, pp. 43 et seq.

[17] Josef Esser, *Grundsatz und Norm in der richterlichen Fortbildung des Privatrechts*, Tübingen, 1956.

[18] For further information on the school of "Interessenjurisprudenz", cf. the new edition of the works of Philipp Heck, in *Studien und Texte zur Theorie und Methodologie des Rechts*, Vol. II, Bad Homburg, 1968.

[19] Josef Esser, *op. cit.*, pp. 80 et seq.

[20] So explicitly, Josef Esser, *op. cit.*, p. 125.

The concept of logically deducing a code of practicable norms from basic legal principles, and of then solving concrete problems by subsuming them under these norms, which is the concept which Joseph H. Kaiser and others wish to retain for modern planning, reflects a specific institutional context: on the continent it coincides historically with the process by which judges have become independent from political interference. Judges were granted independence on the assumption that their decisions meant nothing more or less than the faithful "execution" of principles embodied in the law and that a judge himself was merely the "mouthpiece for the letter of the law".[21]

(c) *Planning decisions as conflict resolution.* In physical planning we find the same institutional context, but with the opposite intention: there is a tendency to conceive of physical planning as a hierarchical, deductive system, this tendency in turn resulting from the intention to keep it firmly within the institutional context of the ostensibly apolitical "executive" administration. Yet this intention is doomed to failure. Any plan providing a blueprint of the end-state of a project does, admittedly, complement administrative requirements for norms which are capable of being executed. Also, individual land-use plans, with their authoritative prescriptions of building lines and land-use categories, may be adopted as norms and executed administratively by the subsequent granting or refusing of planning permissions. But when physical planning extends its scope beyond land use plans to include structure, subregional and regional plans, then it becomes increasingly more complex and touches upon social and economic problems with their built-in conflicts. By seeking to influence the dynamics with which a variety of more or less *autonomous* decision-making units will develop, it soon becomes fraught with uncertainty and conflict. The conflicting nature of the guidelines for action couched in the form of "basic planning goals", and the necessity to resolve whatever conflict exists between them on various levels of implementation, are therefore not flaws in the planning process to be rectified but are rather inherent to the

---

[21] "La bouche qui prononçe les paroles de la loi" is a classical formula by Montesquieu, *De l'Esprit des Lois*, tome I, livre XI, chap. VI, Ed. Garnier, Paris, 1961, p. 171.

state of complexity which planning has to face in modern society—especially, although not exclusively, under capitalism.[22]

3. *The Political Rationality of Physical Planning*

When, however, the problems confronting physical planning arise from conflicting goals and uncertainty, then it becomes impossible to build on models of rationality which assume "designated ends". In solving the really difficult problems of physical planning, the judicial model of the "executive" is as inadequate as the "optimization models" of economics, which also build on the assumption of a consistent predetermined pay-off function. While the judicial model starts from the notion of a given set of laws within which planning must "find what is of right",[23] the optimizing models of economics build on designated ends which are never questioned.[24] But optimal solutions only exist in company with predetermined value criteria and, in the case of economics, the result is all too often an unquestioning preselection of the monetary criterion at the expense of other value scales.[25] Where, however, physical planning has to operate in a field of value concepts about which there is controversy not only between different social groups, but often also between so-called "experts" (one has only to remember the debate between proponents of low-density greenbelt towns and high density/high rise building giving a feeling of "urbanity") and where these value concepts, because of their future-orientation, are fraught with a considerable measure of uncertainty, there the potential form of rationality is not that described as purposive, with its dependency on predetermined goals, but that of the rationality of *choice*

---

[22] With respect to the problems of planning in metropolitan areas cf. Rolf-Richard Grauhan, "Die Symbiose von Stadt und Umland als politischer Prozess", in: *Probleme der Stadtentwicklung*, Loccumer Protokolle 18/1968, pp. 56 et seq.

[23] So: Joseph H. Kaiser, *op. cit.*, p. 23.

[24] The functional equivalent of the two models is discussed by Niklas Luhmann, *Theorie der Verwaltungswissenschaft*, Köln, 1966, p. 102.

[25] For a pertinent example, cf. Helmut Seidenfus, "Koordinationsprobleme und aktuelle Hemmnisse der Regionalpolitik, in: *Beiträge zur Regionalpolitik, loc. cit.*, pp. 126 et seq.

between alternative goals.[26] Physical planning therefore helps in rationalizing political choices between alternatives which result in further administrative action. Applying the concept of rationality, and consequently that of efficiency, to political choices requires one to abandon the idea of distinguishing it from irrationality by invoking the principle of contradiction; and, rather, to conceive of it, following the modern "open" decision models,[27] as a matter of the degree to which choices are conscious and informed by reason. The main characteristic of such a political choice is the necessity to choose between mutually incompatible goals and to accept political *responsibility* for *sacrificing*, wholly or in part, one or more of them; political *risk* results from the fact that such choices are based on incomplete information. Here, planning assumes the function of clarifying alternatives and of decreasing as far as possible the area of uncertainty. It assumes the character of a rational strategy[28] which is in principle open towards the future which, in the case of conflict, must be reconsidered, adapted to new situations and which must allow for reflection, even on goals, whenever new problems arise.

This result has far-reaching consequences for the planning process and the efficiency of those structures within which planning is performed.

---

[26] With respect to the concepts of "politics" and "rationality" underlying cf. Wolf-Dieter Narr, "Logik der Politikwissenschaft", in *Politikwissenschaft, Eine Einführung in ihre Probleme*, ed. by Dieter Senghaas and Gisela Kress, Frankfurt, 1969, pp. 21 et seq., and Hans Albert, *Traktat über kritische Vernunft*, Tübingen, 1968, p. 179. Recently, Rolf-Richard Grauhan and Wendelin Strubelt, "Political rationality—reconsidered", in *Policy Sciences*, Vol. 2 (1971), Elsevier, Amsterdam, pp. 249–70.

[27] The American literature on this subject, especially the works of Braybrooke/Lindblom and Alexis/Wilson, is critically discussed by Frieder Naschold, *Systemsteuerung*, Stuttgart, 1969, pp. 48 et seq.

[28] For the concept of planning as a rational strategy as distinguished from a (codificatory) plan as an instrument of management, cf. Hans-Joachim Arndt, "Der Plan als Organisationsfigur und die strategische Planung, in: *Politische Vierteljahresschrift*, 1968, pp. 184 et seq.

III. A STRUCTURAL MODEL OF PLANNING ADMINISTRATION

1. *Planning as a Political Process*

Conceiving of the task of planning as that of developing rational strategies for influencing future patterns of social and economic development where social conflict concerning goals and values is ubiquitous leads to a twofold division of the planning process: on the one hand, the phase when "possible futures"[29] are devised and analysed, that is during which alternative action programmes are developed, and on the other the phase of deliberation, and of choice between these alternatives. The planning process thus divides into a preparation and a decision phase[30] followed by a phase of "executing" the selected action programme. This being a *rational strategy* requiring continuous adaptation, the latter phase must incorporate an element of feedback so that goals and courses of action deriving from them may be re-examined and, where necessary, adapted.[31]

As has been shown above, in our political system, hierarchical administrative structures perform the "execution" of policies adequately. It is the institutional basis for the two phases of plan preparation and of choice which deserves more of our attention.

2. *The Structure of Choice*

(a) *Political bodies as institutions of choice.* As far as choice is concerned, it must firstly be remembered that there are institutions in our political system which are structured so as to rationalize choice processes. These are political bodies built on the principles of the protection of minorities, of providing the channels for the articulation of dissent, and of majority rule. The protection of minorities (or the right to form parliamentary factions) ensures that there are advocates for the many alternatives existing in any political choice situation and hence that each of these alternatives is elaborated during the choice process. The articulation of dissent (dissent, that is, from all views expressed within parliamentary bodies) strives to

[29] This expression coined by Olaf Helmer is used by Joseph H. Kaiser, *op. cit.*, p. 19.

[30] Also in this direction: Hans-Joachim Arndt, *loc. cit.*, p. 188.

[31] Cf., for example, the "optimal model" of policy-making devised by Yehezkel Dror, in *Public Policymaking Reexamined*, San Francisco, 1968, pp. 163 et seq.

ensure that the alternative action programmes under discussion are analysed for their inherent contradictions, that is that all the resulting costs
and benefits are identified and their pros and cons examined. Finally,
majority rule as an organizational principle aims to ensure that the outcome of this conflict represents the most convincing solution.[32]

But organizational design can do no more than optimize the *chances* for
the rational discharge of functions. In practice it is all too easy to miss these
chances. In planning it is imperative to mobilize the potential for conflict
and conflict resolution inherent to political bodies. But there are some very
real obstacles to this which have to be removed.

(b) *Existing obstacles.*

1. *Underestimation of conflict processes.* The first fact to be recognized
is that physical planning does not proceed according to the model of
purposive rationality: it does not assume its ends as given, and therefore
as not open to discussion. On the contrary, one of the functions of a
rational planning process is to identify and resolve conflicts over goals
and provide a basis for further action (goals being, in this case, something
more than high-flown phrases). The function of choosing between conflicting goals should therefore be carried out by bodies which are constitu-
tionally framed for exercising choice among alternatives. Because the
choices in planning relate to the future, there is always an element of *risk*
in the sense that they cannot be deduced from data currently available.
There must hence be an acceptance of political responsibility. Such
responsibility should be entrusted to those bodies which are elected directly
by the voters and are therefore directly responsible to them.

---

[32] The purposiveness of majority rule, protection of minorities and the articula-
tion of dissent for the rationality of choice was explicitly stressed by Karl W.
Deutsch, *The Nerves of Government*, 2nd ed., New York, 1965, pp. 254 et seq.
Further indications with respect to the rational implications of a social choice
process for the choice among incompatible alternatives are given by Edward C.
Banfield, *Political Influence*, Glencoe, 1961, pp. 326 et seq., and Charles E. Lind-
blom, *The Intelligence of Democracy*, New York, 1965, p. 172 and passim. As far as
I know, the first hint toward rational effects of an opposition within the ranks of
bureaucracy itself were given by Norton E. Long in his article of 1956: "Public
policy and administration: the goals of rationality and responsibility", reprinted in:
Claude E. Hawley and Ruth Weintraub (eds.), *Administrative Questions and Political
Answers*, New York, 1966, p. 63.

2. *Tendency towards a reduction of political bodies.* The federal structure of the Federal Republic and the institution of local autonomy result in a considerable variety of parliamentary bodies at three—and if the districts are included four—spatial scales. Each of these has certain planning powers and each of these powers represents a separate area of political responsibility. This fragmentation has been criticized from the point of view of the efficiency of physical planning, and more centralization of powers and responsibilities has been mooted. Such an argument could only be convincing if physical planning worked within an hierarchical-deductive goal-system determining programmes for smaller territorial units on the basis of fundamental goals designated for the territory as a whole. As has been pointed out, this presumption cannot be made realistically. Even if one conceived of a hierarchy of physical plans, descending from the most embracing to the smallest territorial units, one must take into account that in the process the basic planning goals will regroup into new sets of conflicting goals requiring the assumption of political responsibility for their resolution.[33]

The proliferation of centres of responsibility resulting from federalism and local autonomy should, rather, be seen as an advantage of our political organization. It allows political conflict processes to occur at the different implemental levels on which programmes must be chosen, and hence fosters rationality and democratic responsibility in physical planning. This political structure also helps to remind us that the goals of physical planning for the territory as a whole simply cannot be taken for granted, but must be adapted together with and against planning decisions made by smaller units during a feedback process. In turn decisions by these smaller units cannot be postponed until a consistent plan for the territory as a whole has been worked out. Herein lies the logic of the so-called "principle of counter-current" (*Gegenstromprinzip*) which requires central and local plans to be "mutually" coordinated, and which has been incorporated in para. 4, section 5, of the Federal Act on Physical Planning. This principle has often been unduly criticized and misinterpreted when viewed from the standpoint of a hierarchical-deductive planning system.

---

[33] More detailed information in: Rolf-Richard Grauhan, *Die Symbiose von Stadt und Umland als politischer Prozess, loc. cit.*

3. *Parliaments as legitimizing bodies*. However, the function of choosing
between alternative programmes is one which our parliaments only rarely
fulfil. Parliaments are seen instead as bodies which legitimize policy
decisions made by the chief executive of either central or local government.[34]
This concept arises from a traditional view of politics which is still unaware
of the possibility of devising "possible futures", and which therefore either
ignores the need for a political process to define conflicts existing between
alternative planning proposals, or orients itself towards an idealized model
of British democracy assuming a fairly regular change of office between
political parties pursuing alternative policies.

These considerations demonstrate the need for viewing the present
scope of planning firmly within the framework of the total political system.
A system which assumes regular change of government and opposition
party implies that the main conflict over policy issues occurs during election campaigns. The winning majority party therefore has a clear mandate
for the "implementation" of its programme, this having been tested
during the campaign and then selected by the electorate. However, such an
assumption cannot be made about the German political system. Firstly,
party platforms are not formulated at all precisely, nor are they themselves
free from inherent goal conflicts. Secondly, the structure of the three-party
system shows considerable areas of overlap and of ambiguity of value
positions as regards practical problem areas.[35]

But even on the assumption that a perpetual alternation of government
and opposition party does bring forward into the election campaign some
of the essential debate concerning action programmes, the whole range of
choices which have to be made continuously during the planning process
is never predetermined unequivocally, nor do all the requisite structural
provisions for choice processes exist. In order to win "a broad majority"
election programmes furthermore show the tendency to harmonize conflicting goals formally so that political choice processes during the phase of
implementation become inevitable. Those who really care about the

---

[34] This model is discussed at length in: Rolf-Richard Grauhan, *Modelle politischer Verwaltungsführung*, Konstanz, 1969, pp. 13 et seq.

[35] For example, left-wing of C.D.U. and S.P.D. vs. F.D.P. in questions of social
policy; F.D.P. and S.P.D. vs. C.D.U./C.S.U. in issues of educational policy;
right-wing of C.D.U./C.S.U. and F.D.P. vs. S.P.D. in issues of economic policy.

openness and democratic control of the planning process should therefore urge political bodies to realize their potential for a rational pursuit of conflict, instead of leaving this potential untapped by submitting their members to party discipline and to three-line whips to make them follow the policies laid down by the head of the political executive.

4. *Parliaments as ratification organs.* However, what political bodies like parliaments lack most in fulfilling their function of choice is knowledge of the concrete alternatives which originate in the administrative machine. It is common practice among heads of the political executive on the federal level, as well as on the level of the state and of the local authorities, to present only *one* programme alternative which the legislature can subsequently either ratify or reject without knowing the whole range of choice available. The traditional interpretation of the responsibility of the head of the political executive "for establishing policy guidelines" (*Richtlinienkompetenz*) has the same effect, much as do those standing orders of collegiate forms of governmental bodies (central as well as local) which rule that submissions to the legislature have to be made "unanimously."[36] Even in systems of local government which confer the responsibility for setting policy guidelines upon the council, the prevailing opinion is "that once co-ordination of departmental points of view has taken place [i.e. once alternatives have been eliminated—R.R.G.] the chief executive officer must present *the* administrative proposal to the council and convince it of its quality"[37] (emphasis mine).

It is a very recent phenomenon that the administrative heads of local authorities begin to show awareness of the fact that the function of preparing decisions, especially in policy areas such as urban development, is that of "restoring to the politician what is his essential role by ways of good and careful analyses and presentation of alternatives".[38] But

[36] Cf., for example, p. 28 of the standing order of the Federal Cabinet.

[37] For example, Verbandsdirektor Ahrens of the Grossraum-Hannover-Verband, in "Sachverstand und Verantwortung", 34. Staatswissenschaftlicher Fortbildungskurs Speyer, *Schriftenreihe der Hochschule für Verwaltungswissenschaft*, Vol. 30, Berlin, 1966, p. 147.

[38] For example, Oberstadtdirektor Neuffer, Hannover, in: *Der Sachverständige in der Politik, Loccumer Protokolle*, Vol. 21 (1967), p. 27. Similarly, Oberbürgermeister Vogel, München, according to: *Süddeutsche Zeitung*, 27 March 1969, p. 13.

this process of preparing alternatives for political choices requires a restructuring of administrative machines which have been framed primarily for the implementation of predetermined alternatives.

3. *Structure of the Preparation Phase*

There are three structural conditions for the plan preparation phase: (1) the creation of centres of initiative from which the impetus for preparing alternatives comes; (2) the provisions for the articulation of conflict within the administrative machine leading to an elaboration and clarification of existing alternatives which are then submitted to the political body making its final choice; and (3) structural provisions for feedback within the process of the executive administration.

(a) *Centres of initiative.* Where the modern planning function is no longer seen as that of designing one blueprint from which detailed plans may be derived during the implementation process, where therefore planning is seen as a continuous process, during which even general planning goals may be reconsidered in the light of what actually occurs, there it becomes evident that the number of those centres of initiative from whence the impetus for new planning proposals could arise should increase. One of the important centres of initiative would still be the head of government who, by virtue of his holding a political appointment, has received a mandate for taking initiatives, and whose position at the interface between the arguments going on within political bodies and within the administrative machine would create favourable conditions for fulfilling this role.[39] But if the total capacity for taking initiatives were monopolized by the head of government, and if the other participants in the planning process were to rely on him in fulfilling this function, the efficiency of the total system would suffer. This applies to factions in the political body as much as to the potential for the administrative machine taking initiatives of its own. In order to make full use of the latter, the hierarchical principle with its downward flow of information ought to be abandoned. Recognition of this

[39] Cf. for further details: Rolf-Richard Grauhan, "Der Oberbürgermeister als Verwaltungschef", in: *Politische Vierteljahresschrift*, 1965, pp. 310 et seq.

requirement has resulted in the current discussion concerning "staff management" in administration.[40]

However, it would not be conducive to the efficiency of the plan preparation phase to concentrate it entirely within isolated staffs whilst leaving the administrative hierarchy intact. Such a solution might lead both to severe problems in obtaining information by the staffs as well as to inadequacies in the process of feedback from the executive administration. It would lead to a greater increase in the number of centres of initiative if one were to opt for a solution which, while not involving the establishment of permanent staff units, created staffs with a (possibly changing) membership of people who have shown personal initiative and from which the team leaders for *ad hoc* planning groups might be drawn. Here one immediately encounters the problem of the administrative "generalist" and an accompanying problem of vocational training for administrators. Current efforts to reform the educational system for the administrative services point in this direction.[41]

But even this change would not satisfactorily solve the problem of who takes the initiative. Further possibilities must be discussed in conjunction with the process of articulating conflict within the administrative machine.

(b) *Articulation of conflict.* The necessity for abandoning the hierarchical principle is most obvious in that part of the preparation phase concerned with elaborating and presenting alternative choices to political bodies. During this phase, the downward flow of information must be replaced by an upward flow whose information content is not, as frequently occurs in hierarchies of command, increasingly dissipated when decisions are eliminated by superiors during progress up the line. This principle of a division of tasks descending into individual responsibilities must be substituted by that of social co-operation in information processing, which compounds all the information provided by individual specialists until workable propositions are reached. As far as the preparation phase is concerned, the monocratic principle of separating responsibilities is then

---

[40] Cf. Eberhard Laux, *op. cit.*, p. 33.

[41] Fritz W. Scharpf, "Pläne für ein Verwaltungsstudium an der Universität Konstanz, with comments by Roman Schnur and Werner Thieme, in: *Die Öffentliche Verwaltung*, 1969, pp. 395 et seq.

replaced by committee work which is already practised informally in a variety of administrative working parties and task groups.

These informal working procedures must be developed so that eventually the preparing planning committees are also firmly entrusted with the function of preparing and presenting alternatives, thus enabling representative bodies to make political choices. The principles underlying the organization of representative bodies which seek to improve upon the elaboration and comparative evaluation of alternative courses of action, that is the protection of minorities, and the right of dissent, must therefore likewise underly the structure of preparatory committees in the administration. Only the principle of majority rule does not apply, because it is not the function of planning administration to make decisions, but rather to prepare for decisions made by the legislature.[42] This task of preparing alternatives is facilitated by modern planning techniques such as systems analysis and by the availability of electronic data-processing systems which, when fully developed, would allow accumulated data to be regrouped quite rapidly, depending on alternative value positions. Organizational structure and planning techniques must thus combine to defeat the ideology of the "one correct solution" which, given the complexity of modern planning problems, in practice suppresses the conflicting character of relevant value principles, and prevents clarification of all those possibilities for action which exist in reality.

Since it must be the task of administrative bodies to prepare choices made by political bodies by presenting alternatives, any model of planning administration requires the development of lateral parliamentary controls. One existing example, though one which is very much open to improvement, is the institution of the "Verwaltungsbeirat" in the Bavarian system of local government: the "Verwaltungsbeirat" is a councillor attached to a certain administrative department who is kept informed of what is happening and whose consent to, or disapproval of, administrative proposals must then be conveyed to the political body as a whole. But the full use of this instrument is hampered by the relatively small amount of time which these honorary officers can afford to spend, so that once more the question arises whether large city councils inundated with business can much longer afford to have honorary members.

[42] For further discussion cf. Rolf-Richard Grauhan, "Modelle politischer Verwaltungsführung," *loc. cit.,* pp. 23 et seq.

Taking these considerations of the structure of planning administration as a preparatory body to its logical conclusion, one must concede that it cannot be the exclusive domain of the majority party. The structure of the preparation phase must reflect the complexity of actual choices to be made. In order to increase the rationality of choice, existing problems must also be evaluated in terms of value criteria affecting minority groups. The establishment of parliamentary counter-bureaucracies to achieve this has been discussed for some time. But, quite independently from this proposal, the preparation phase within the administrative machine must become more accessible to members of political bodies, because it is *their* choices which it has to prepare. The model of planning administration must therefore include immediate access for members of political bodies, even for those of the opposition party, to the administrative bodies engaged in plan preparation.

(c) *Feedback from the executive administration.* One may conceive of a whole range of models for the structure of those bodies engaged in plan preparation, and it will be necessary to experiment with these. For example, it remains to be seen whether the institutionalization of the right of dissent and of the protection of minorities, in the sense of forming factions, will suffice to make administrative bodies prepare alternative courses of action, or whether one has to think in terms of establishing competing planning groups. My own experience of the readiness of professional planners to engage in discussion points in the first direction.

A further problem is that of the interdependence of different planning groups working on different planning problems. Usually, at least two types coexist: the *ad hoc* planning group set up to solve a specific problem, and the permanent body engaged in plan preparation. *Ad hoc* planning groups will usually be initiated by the head of government or administration, or by a parliamentary group; but executive departments should also be allowed to initiate project groups to follow up possibilites or programme initiatives originating from those engaged in implementation. This power should run in parallel with the right to ask for the collaboration of staff planners during implementation. Thus the adaptation of innovative ideas to the experiences gathered during implementation, and vice versa, would be established at the outset.

In matters of ongoing plan preparation, one would envisage a system of ascending bodies engaged in plan preparation and constantly overlapping with the descending executive hierarchy which guarantees feedback between planning and implementation. At first glance, this concept seems confusing, but in fact it is very simple: on all levels of the administrative hierarchy, subordinate staff are subject to the orders of their superiors in executive matters—but in matters of preparation, they form a committee in which the principles of dissent and the protection of minority rights operate. This ensures that even those proposals which do not find approval higher up must be submitted to a political choice process. Lateral political controls as discussed above, a new system of promotion independent of the immediate superior's assessment, the introduction of assessments of superiors by their subordinates, and legitimate ways of resorting to the public[43] could support the operation of such a system from the wings.

The dual principle itself is not new. Once it is recognized that the planning function pervades the whole administrative machine, the dual principle would mean devising its organization according to the model of an institution, for which this double function of preparing and implementing policies has long since been acknowledged: for example, the federal and Länder cabinet ministers are subordinate to the chancellor or to the prime ministers of the Länder where these lay down "policy guidelines" for the ministers to "execute" in their respective administrative departments. But in the preparation of political programmes, they act as a committee of equals in which the head of government acts as a chairman and has only a casting vote.

Reflecting on the structure of the plan preparation phase in physical planning thus takes one back to first political principles, and cannot do otherwise. Of necessity, complex processes of physical planning operate in a field of conflicting values and, because of their orientation to the future, in an area of uncertainty; and they are therefore eminently *political* processes. Consequently the structures in which physical planning must take place have to follow organizational principles which are themselves political.

---

[43] This point is discussed by Rolf-Richard Grauhan, "Die Planende Verwaltung zwischen Leistungsprinzip und Öffentlichkeit, in *Mitteilungen der Deutschen Akademie für Städtebau and Landesplanung*, Vol. 14 (1970), pp. 22 et seq.

PART V

POSITIVE THEORIES OF PLANNING

Introduction

A *positive theory of planning* treats its subject-matter as a researchable phenomenon: it assumes that planning shows enough constancy to warrant the formulation, in the long run, of *general laws*, which, ideally at least, would explain its recurring aspects and allow making predictions about planning. Such general laws of planning might also be transformed into *prescriptions* concerning improvements to the institutions and the style of planning based on valid knowledge. For the positive theorist of planning, understanding and improvement are clearly and logically interrelated.[1]

The orientation of a positive theory of planning is towards precision of concepts and measurements. Invariably, however, the degree of exactitude for which positive theorists of planning are aiming by far exceeds that of available research findings. Their work therefore consists mainly of more or less elaborate schemes—semantic structures, as Dror (1968) says—some tentative findings and suggestions for (sometimes vast) research programmes.

On the methodological front, the authors represented in this section may be described as "collectivists": terms which they are using such as "planning environment", "planning units" and "planning style" are "collective terms" (Kaplan, 1964). Such terms describe planners and their clients engaging in planning as if their joint actions added up to the behaviour of some higher-order entity. Assumptions like this are widely made in the social sciences, and in particular in organization theory.

---

[1] What is perhaps sometimes less evident to him is how his conceptual framework is influenced by his own normative theory of planning. See the comment on Dror's paper on p. 319.

> Organizations make decisions. They make decisions in the same sense in which individuals make decisions: The organization as a whole behaves as though there existed a central co-ordination and control system capable of directing the behavior of the members of the organization sufficiently to allow the meaningful imputation of purpose to the total system (Cyert and March, 1959).

These assumptions are, however, not universally shared, neither in the social sciences, where "methodological individualism" poses an alternative, nor in planning theory where Davidoff and Reiner have, for instance, gone as far as denying that general laws explaining planning behaviour could be formulated (see p. 8).

Other possible reservations concern the actual *usefulness* of positive theories of planning. All writers in this field demand *more research* before the promised prescription for better planning can be obtained. But will not too much effort be spent on refinement of schemes, and too little on the thorny business of *prescription*? Will findings still be relevant to the problems of the day once they become obtainable? These are questions which, so far, the positive theorists of planning have failed to answer conclusively.

Studies in this field are few and far between. One of the more extensive ones is that by Daland and Parker (1962) using the sociological concept of *role*. Faludi (1970, 1971) defines three *dimensions for the analysis of planning behaviour* and attempts to combine these with the concept of a planning environment introduced by Friedmann in his work discussed later in this introduction. Mann (1964), in a paper otherwise concerned with the community power literature and its relevance for planning, speculates on the possibility of *"general laws" of community decision behaviour* invoking findings and suggestions by Rossi. Rabinovitz (1969) refers to some factors quoted by Mann making for certain of the features of the "pattern of influence" prevailing in a community and relates optimal *planning styles* to those.

In the first paper included in this selection Dror takes the most explicitly "behavioural" approach, concentrating entirely on defining the component elements of planning as the units of analysis of his phenomenon under study. His procedure is, first, to review definitions of planning, then to put forward his own definition based on these, from there to analyse his definition into its elements, and finally to suggest four main "facets" of planning. Each of these is broken down further into secondary and tertiary facets. Lastly, Dror gives some thought to the formidable problems of measuring each of these. He suggests that only such measurements can lead to actual systematic study—though even his conceptual analysis alone seems to be capable of improving intuitive understanding of planning which is, in my opinion, almost as important as research findings based on his framework would be. Trying to define measurable "facets" forces him to be so precise that his framework becomes more refined and at the same time more comprehensive than most writers have achieved to date. Research findings may be unobtainable for a long time to come, yet the clarity of his paper is an immediate benefit.

On the other hand, his paper constitutes a vast research programme which he himself has not fulfilled. In his later book, *Public Policymaking Reexamined*, he still complains about lack of systematic research and feels compelled to proceed on the basis of intuitive understanding.

There are a few other points which one has to make about his paper. One is that the way in which he derives the four primary facets from the elements of the definition of planning is not made explicit, nor is it clear for that matter why Dror's definition should be superior to those which he quotes.

The second point is a general one about conceptual schemes: Dror gives the impression that his scheme is *value-free*, a neutral frame for looking at the facts. But surely there must be an assumption underlying it, the selection of definitions quoted, and the range of "facets" included? Such assumptions amount to elements of a *normative theory of planning* to which Dror admits only briefly in his introduction, and only as if it was a truism, postulating that man can and ought consciously to shape his future. But the ideological debate about planning from which he wishes to emancipate its empirical study still turns on precisely this issue, as the section on comprehensive planning demonstrates. It is by no means a foregone conclusion that man ought to engage in planning his collective future. At least as far as collective planning is concerned, some normative models —notably those proposed by the "pluralistic" school—state precisely the opposite.

Despite these comments the paper constitutes an important contribution to a positive theory of planning. The facets are intuitively appealing as major determinants of planning behaviour, though little systematic evidence is available to support such a judgement. This is with the exception of the *planning environment* which has been singled out for discussion by Friedmann.

Simon (1956) and Schutzenberger (1954) have used the concept of a planning environment in developing an abstract model of planning behaviour. Usually, though, to introduce the concept of a planning environment is a concomitant of a behavioural approach. Planning, instead of being an abstract, normative concept, becomes a dependent variable, dependent that is on the environment of decision-making, an approach which has been taken in organization theory some time before it became prominent in planning (Haire, 1959), largely due to the writing of Friedmann.

Friedmann, like Dror, emphasizes the usefulness of any conceptual framework for the comparative study of planning, and the benefit to be derived from it in terms of predicting planning styles and prescribing strategies for improving planning. Indeed, his paper on "The institutional context" (1967) aims explicitly at establishing a framework for cross-national research for which he draws from his varied experience in Venezuela (Friedmann, 1965) and Chile (Friedmann, 1964, 1969).

Friedmann grants empirical validity to Simon's (March and Simon, 1958) and Lindblom's observations concerning the limitations on human problem-solving capacity, but asks simultaneously whether these are absolute or relative limitations, a question discussed extensively in Part III. The hypothesis is that of a variable "planning style", meaning amongst other things degrees of "boundedness", to introduce one of Simon's concepts. The social context of decisions is identified as one of the factors determining this planning style and thus the extent of boundedness of planning. This social context of decisions, or the decision-making environment, has entered the literature as the "planning environment".

On the basis of his work on the concept of the planning environment, Friedmann has offered his own conceptual framework which forms part of this section. This paper reflects once more the range of interests and experiences of its author which spans planning in Third World countries as well as the United States. He rejects both a purely normative approach, as well as the mere description of planning ventures, as contributing next to nothing to the growth of verifiable knowledge concerning planning and demonstrates how *empirical hypotheses* may be derived from a conceptual framework aiming at providing the elements of a positive theory of planning.

The final paper in this selection also aims at building a framework for the behavioural study of planning. It includes the planning environment as one of the variables, but it also attempts to synthesize a good deal more of the mainly social science literature in the field of planning theory, drawing on many of the works referred to earlier on in this reader. Unlike Dror, but like Friedmann, Bolan's concern is also not purely formal (i.e. he is not oriented solely towards outlining what a positive theory of planning would be like) but also substantive: he puts forward specific, *testable hypotheses*. It is furthermore synthetic in the sense of linking two fields with each other which have been separated for a while: the substantive problem which planning deals with, and the planning process, thus pointing the way for a theory of planning taking the systematic variations of "issue attributes" into account and thereby promising to bridge the gap between theory *of* planning and theory *in* planning referred to in Part I.

As with all the other authors contributing to this section, Bolan is basically optimistic. Though he admits to the problems of operationalizing his concepts, and of obtaining research findings, he is confident that this could be done in principle. Yet, to date, the greatest benefit derived from his paper is again clarity of his conceptual framework, which is an immediate result, independent of any additional effort spent.

REFERENCES

Part V

CYERT, R. M. and MARCH, J. G. (1959) "A behavioral theory of organizational objectives", *Modern Organization Theory* (edited by HAIRE, M.), John Wiley, New York.

DALAND, R. T. and PARKER, J. A. (1962) "Roles of the planner in urban development", *Urban Growth Dynamics* (edited by CHAPIN F. S. and WEISS, F. S.), John Wiley, New York.

DROR, Y. (1968) *Public Policymaking Reexamined*, Chandler, Pennsylvania.

FALUDI, A. (1970) "The planning environment and the meaning of 'planning' ", *Regional Studies*, Vol. 4, pp. 1–9.

FALUDI, A. (1971) "Towards a three-dimensional model of planning behaviour", *Environment and Planning*, Vol. 3, pp. 253–66.

FRIEDMANN, J. (1964) "Planning as innovation: The Chilean case", *Journal of the American Institute of Planners*, Vol. 32, pp. 194–204.

FRIEDMANN, J. (1965) *Venezuela: From Doctrine to Dialogue*, Syracuse University Press, Syracuse.

FRIEDMANN, J. (1969) *Urban and Regional Development in Chile*, Ford Foundation, Chile.

HAIRE, M. (1959) Introduction, *Modern Organization Theory* (edited by HAIRE, M.), John Wiley, New York.

KAPLAN, A. (1964) *The Conduct of Inquiry: Methodology for Behavioral Science*, Chandler, Pennsylvania.

MANN, L. D. (1964) "Studies in community decision-making", *Journal of the American Institute of Planners*, Vol. 30, pp. 58–65.

MARCH, T. G. and SIMON, H. A. (1958) *Organizations*, John Wiley, New York.

RABINOVITZ, F. F. (1969) *City Politics and Planning*, Altherton Press, New York.

SCHÜTZENBERGER, M. P. (1954) "A tentative classification of goal-seeking behaviours", *Journal of Mental Science*, Vol. 100, pp. 97–102, and in *Systems Thinking* (edited by EMERY, F. E.), Penguin, Harmondsworth, 1969.

SIMON, H. A. (1956) "Rational choice and the structure of the environment", *Psychological Review*, Vol. 63, pp. 129–38, and *Systems Thinking* (edited by EMERY, F. E.), Penguin, Harmondsworth, 1969.

The Planning Process: A Facet Design*[1]

Yehezkel Dror

INTRODUCTION

A close perusal of the large and growing literature dealing with different kinds of planning shows a transfer of the focus of attention from ideological discourses on the desirability of planning to examination of substantive problems associated with the planning process, such as its nature, the phases of planning, conditions for successful planning, planning techniques, etc. This change of emphasis in discussions on planning goes hand-in-hand with recognition of the basic nature of planning as a methodology of rational thought and action, rather than a blueprint for one or another definite course of action.

Emancipation of the concept of "planning" from any ideological annotations or connotations other than a belief in the ability of *homo sapiens* to engage to some extent in the shaping of his future and a belief in the desirability of his doing so is an essential prerequisite for scientific examination of planning as a basic social-administrative process; but in order to be able to approach the study of planning in a really scientific and systematic way, we need first of all a much closer and more refined examination of its components and elements than is generally found in the literature dealing with it. In fact, it is very interesting to note that, despite the growing number of articles and books dealing with planning on one level or another, only a few efforts have been made to develop a systematic approach to the study of planning as an administrative process. Even authors well known

* Reprinted by permission of the *International Review of Administrative Sciences*, Vol. 29, 1963.
[1] First published in the *International Review of Administrative Sciences*, Vol. 29, No. 1 (1963) pp. 46–58. Reprinted in Yehezkel Dror, *Ventures in Policy Sciences*, New York: American Elsevier, and Amsterdam: Elsevier, 1971.

for their original contributions to the administrative sciences have often failed to deal adequately with the planning phase of institutional action. A more systematic approach to the study of planning, utilizing more refined concepts and more advanced research designs and methods, is urgently needed, if we want our knowledge of this basic and often crucial phase of organizational action to be in line with the progress being made in other areas of administrative sciences; if we want to advance the study of planning as a part of policy sciences; and if we want knowledge to contribute to the improvement of the rapidly spreading practice of planning.

In this paper an effort is made to deal with one of the first phases of a systematic study of planning, namely, a preliminary concept analysis—or, to use a more technical term, facet design—trying to identify the main factors and variables composing and shaping the planning process. We will first explain and justify the methodological rationale and objective of this paper and discuss briefly its significance for the study of planning as a part of policy sciences; then we will define our subject matter and proceed to the presentation of the various primary and secondary facets of planning; finally, we will point out some lines for empirical research, based on the facet design and directed at various problems of planning identified with the help of the facet design.

METHODOLOGY[2]

The concept of facet design, as first developed by Louis Guttman[3] and as applied to the study of various phenomena,[4] is based on R. A. Fisher's

[2] I am indebted to Professor Louis Guttman for his important help and suggestions concerning the methodological aspects of this paper.

[3] Louis Guttman, "An outline of some new methodology for social research", *Public Opinion Quarterly*, Vol. 18 (1954), 395–404; Louis Guttman, "What lies ahead for factor analysis", *Educational and Psychological Measurement*, Vol. 18 (1958), pp. 497–515; Louis Guttman, "Introduction to facet design and analysis", *Proceedings of the Fifteenth International Congress of Psychology*, Brussels, 1957 (1959), pp. 130–2; Louis Guttman, "A structural theory for intergroup beliefs and action", *American Sociological Review*, Vol. 25, No. 3 (June 1959), pp. 318–28. Currently, Professor Guttman is working on more sophisticated methods of nonmetric measurement, which may provide more advanced designs for the study of planning.

[4] Uriel G. Foa, "The foreman–worker interaction: a research design", *Sociometry*, Vol. 18, No. 3 (August 1955), pp. 226–44; Uriel G. Foa and Louis Guttman, *Facet Design and Analysis of Data on Personality and Attitudes related to Human Organization*, Jerusalem: Israel Institute of Applied Social Research, 1960.

approach to the design of experiments and tries to systematize the construction of a semantic structure which identifies the different elements and variables of which the phenomenon to be studied is composed and by which it is shaped.

A short citation from the paper by Louis Guttman in which the concept of "facet" was first proposed will serve to clarify the general methodological significance of this concept:

> Perhaps the most practical way of defining the concept is in most general terms. Consider a set of A of any elements a_1, a_2 . . ., and a set B of any elements b_1, b_2 . . . Let C be the *direct product*[5] of A and B: $C = A \times B$. That is, a typical element of C, say c, is a pair of elements $c = (a_j, b_k)$, one coming from A and the other from B. If A has m elements and B has n elements, then C has mn elements. We shall say that C is a two-faceted set, and that A and B are facets of C. A facet, then, is a *set* of elements. In general, C may be the direct product of any number of facets, not just two.
>
> Facet theory is useful for designing the *universes of content* of research projects. This aspect of the theory is part of *facet design*. Facet design may also refer to the population, P, being studied. The facet formula for a project can always be written in the general form: $P \times C = R$, where R is the set of possible responses of results.[6]

Application of the methodology of facet design to the study of the planning process is not easy because of the very complexity of the planning process, which results in a complex and multifaceted set, in which each facet in turn is the product of a large number of secondary facets, which in turn are the product of various tertiary facets which can be analyzed in terms of different subsets, and so on. Nevertheless, if the study of planning is to progress beyond impressionistic images or generalizations based on limited experience, it is essential that an effort be made to identify the main elements of planning, that is, that a preliminary facet design of planning should be constructed.

Construction of a facet design is but a first, though very important, step which should, if possible, be followed by construction of a statistical or quasi-statistical structure designed for empirical research. While some of the primary and secondary facets to be presented in this paper form a simplex[7]—the primary facets being ordered in a simple order pattern from

---

[5] Not to be confused with the "logical" product or the "intersection" of two sets.

[6] Guttman, "An outline of new methodology", *op. cit.* [in footnote 3].

[7] Louis Guttman, "A new approach to factor analysis: the radex", in Paul F. Lazarsfeld (ed.), *Mathematical Thinking in the Social Sciences*, New York: Free Press, 1954, pp. 258–348.

more external to more internal ones and the secondary facets being partly ordered from more simple ones to more complex and comprehensive ones —it may be necessary at a later stage to try to construct more complex structures for empiric research of planning.

In its present, rather amorphous form, the facet design of planning to be presented in this paper is intended to serve more as stimuli for directing thought toward basic problems than as a ready-made apparatus which can be directly applied to empiric investigations.[8] Nevertheless, even in its present form, the facet design should be of help for comparative study of planning instances, and should serve as a checklist of factors to be considered and dealt with in any investigation of planning and in any attempt to set up, improve, or analyze planning processes.

An additional remark must be made here on the relation between our facet design of planning and various "models of planning" and other discussions of some of the issues involved in the planning process found in modern literature on decisionmaking, statistical decisions, theory of games, etc. Nearly all these models and discussions, insofar as they are relevant to our subject, deal with the sequential phases of rational action, providing various schemes or sequences which are designed to lead to rational outputs. If for some purposes some of these models can be regarded as parts of blueprints of an ideal flow-chart for the planning process, then our facet design should be viewed as dealing with the environment and structure, or, to use a technical term, *space* within which the planning process takes place. Thus, we are dealing here with one part of a general theory of the planning process from the point of view of policy sciences.

THE CONCEPT OF PLANNING

Any effort to deal in a methodologically sound way with so elusive a phenomenon as planning must be anteceded by a more or less exact delimitation of the area of investigation, that is, a definition of planning. While the validity of the definition is by its very nature limited to our world of discourse and adjusted to the purposes we have in mind, the definition should be in line with the more commonly accepted uses and meanings of

---

[8] This paper can also be regarded as trying to apply the "facet" concept to a decision process as an experiment designed to test the usefulness of this methodological tool for policy sciences in general.

the verbal referent *planning*, to avoid unnecessary communication difficulties. Simultaneously, our definition must be wide enough to include planning processes taking place in different contexts and sharp enough to distinguish between planning and other related processes.

A short examination of some commonly used definitions will facilitate preparation of our own definition. Even leaving out of consideration definitions explicitly dealing with a limited area of planning—such as physical planning, economic planning, regional planning, etc.—we are faced with a wealth of definitions, only a few of which can be quoted here. We will select our quotations so as to illustrate the main basic approaches to the definition of the concept "planning".

One school of thought emphasizes the nature of planning as decisions concerning future action, as illustrated by the following definitions:

> Planung ist die geistige Vor-Formung eines Organismus, Organs oder eines Funktionsablaufs.[9] (Planning is the mental preformation of an organism, an organ, or a process-flow).
> Speaking generally, planning is deciding in advance what is to be done; that is, a plan is a projected course of action.[10]
> Planning . . . is the working out in broad outline the things that need to be done and the methods for doing them to accomplish the purpose set for the enterprise.[11]

Another school of thought regards rationality and the utilization of knowledge as characterizing planning:

> Planning is an organized effort to utilize social intelligence in the determination of national policies. It is based upon fundamental facts regarding resources, carefully assembled and thoroughly analyzed; upon a look around at the various factors which must be brought together in order to avoid clashing of policies or lack of unity in general direction; upon a look forward and a look backward. Considering our resources and trends as carefully as possible, planners look forward to the determination of the long-time policies.[12]

---

[9] Karl Stefanie-Allmayer, *Allgemeine Organisationslehre*, Vienna: Humboldt Verlag, 1950, p. 136.

[10] William H. Newman, *Administrative Action*, New York: Pitman Publishing Corp., 1958, p. 15.

[11] Luther Gulick, *Notes on the Theory of Organization, Papers on the Science of Administration*, New York: Institute of Public Administration, 1937, p. 13.

[12] Charles E. Merriam, "The National Resources Planning Board", in G. B. Galloway (ed.), *Planning for America*, New York: Henry Holt & Co., 1941, p. 486.

Planning consists in the systematic, continuous, forward-looking application of the best intelligence available to programmes of common affairs in the public field. . . . Planning is a continuous process, and necessitates the constant reexamination of trends, tendencies, policies, in order to adapt and adjust governmental policies with the least possible friction and loss. . . . Planning is not an end, but a means, a means for better use for what we have, a means for emancipation of millions of personalities now fettered, for enrichment of human life. . . .[13]

Planning is one of the functions of the manager, and, as such, involves the selection, from among alternatives, of enterprise objectives, policies, procedures, and programmes. It is thus decisionmaking affecting the future course of an enterprise. . . . Planning is thus an intellectual process, the conscious determination of courses of action, the basing of decisions on purpose, facts, and considered estimates.[14]

. . . Planning is more and more regarded as equivalent to rational social action, that is, as a social process for reaching a rational decision.[15]

Of special interest in this connection may be a similar definition by a Soviet economist:

By "Planning" we mean the fullest and most rational utilization of all work and of all the material resources of the community, in the light of a scientific forecast of the trends of economic development and with strict observance of the laws of social development.[16]

Some of the quoted definitions already include the evaluative element of being directed at the "social good". This element becomes predominant in some other definitions of planning:

Planning is the means by which the discipline of Science applied to human affairs will enable man to incarnate his purposes. It is the inevitable link between means and ends. Moreover, it is in itself an inspiring ideal. For once it is realized that there is no natural harmony of nature, no Divine or other purpose hidden beneath the flux and chaos of present planlessness, it becomes immoral to let poverty, ignorance, pestilence, and war continue if they can be obliterated by a plan. Although there is some disagreement as to the nature and desirable limits of planning, students of administration are all "planners".[17]

[13] National Resources Planning Board, *A Report on National Planning and Public Works*, 1934, pp. 83–84.

[14] Harold Koontz and Cyril O'Donnel, "The nature and purpose of planning", in David W. Ewing, *Long-range Planning for Management*, New York: Harper & Row, revised edition, 1964, pp. 21, 22.

[15] Robert A. Dahl. "The politics of planning", *International Social Science Journal*, Vol. 11, No. 3 (1959), p. 340.

[16] Ch. Touretzki, "Regional planning of the national economy in the U.S.S.R. and its bearing on regionalism", *International Social Science Journal*, Vol. 11, No. 3 (1959), p. 380.

[17] Dwight Waldo, *The Administrative State*, New York: Ronald Press Co., 1948, p. 67.

Planning is an activity by which man in society endeavours to gain mastery over himself and to shape his collective future by power of his reason. . . . Planning is nothing more than a certain manner of arriving at decisions and action, the intention of which is to promote the social good of a society undergoing rapid changes.[18]

Some other students of public administration have tried to present more elaborate definitions of planning, composed of various elements:

Planning . . . is that activity that concerns itself with proposals for the future, with the evaluation of alternative proposals, and with the methods by which these processes may be achieved. Planning is rational, adaptive thought applied to the future and to matters over which the planners or the administrative organizations with which they are associated have some degree of control.[19]

Planning is essentially a means of improving decisions and is therefore a prerequisite to action. It seeks to answer two vital questions: What is the purpose of an agency or a program, and what are the best means of achieving that purpose? However, policy, organization, and the social environment are in a constant state of flux. This means that planning must be continuous and dynamic; it must anticipate change. Very broadly, administrative planning must consider political ends and the appropriate ways of achieving them. It must design effective operating procedures and provide supervisory techniques which will ensure that what has been planned is in fact being achieved. In the process, planning touches upon every aspect of management, including decisionmaking, budgeting, coordination, communications, and problems of structure. Planning, in a word, is management.[20]

Taking into account this variety of definitions, it is not surprising that some authors get weary of the whole business and despair of any attempt at formulating a generally valid definition of planning:

Planning is a word of many meanings. To some it means a blueprint for the future; to others it means only foresight, and action with the forward policies of the government for regulation of the economy as a whole. To some it means government responsibility to take whatever action is necessary to ensure that the economic system operates efficiently, to others it means only that the government should correlate whatever functions it undertakes toward desired overall objectives.[21]

[18] John Friedmann, "Introduction" (to series of articles on The Study and Practice of Planning), *International Social Science Journal*, Vol. 11, No. 3 (1959), pp. 327–9.

[19] Herbert A. Simon, Donald W. Smithburg, and Victor A. Thompson, *Public Administration*, New York: Alfred A. Knopf, Inc., 1950, pp. 423–4.

[20] John M. Pfiffner and R. Vance Presthus, *Public Administration*, New York: Ronald Press Co., 1953, p. 83.

[21] Emmette S. Redford, *Administration of National Economic Control*, New York: Macmillan Co., 1952, p. 18.

We could go on and quote a large number of additional and more recent definitions of planning; or we could choose to subject the various definitions to critical examination, showing that most of them are of limited validity, include irrelevant elements, or are unsatisfactory in some other respect. But it seems that there is a better way to achieve our objective of clarifying the concept of planning as used in our paper, namely, presentation of our own definition of planning. As will be easily discerned, our definition relies on some of the quoted ones, covers most of the elements included in them, but is constructed in a different way designed to meet the needs of the study of planning.

It seems to me that for the purposes of the improvement of planning,[22] planning can usefully be defined as follows:

> Planning is the process of preparing a set of decisions for action in the future, directed at achieving goals by preferable means.

This definition includes seven different elements. A short discussion of each of these elements in turn will clarify the meaning and implications of the proposed definitions and will introduce some of the concepts of which the facet design of planning is to be composed.

1. *Planning is the process.* Planning is a process, that is, a continuous activity taking place within a unit and requiring some input of resources and energy in order to be sustained. Planning as a process must be distinguished from a "plan". A plan can be defined as "a set of decisions for action in the future" and can be arrived at either through planning, or through some other—rational or irrational—methods of decisionmaking.

2. *Of preparing.* Planning is substantially—and, in most cases, also formally and legally—a process of *preparing* a set of decisions to be approved and executed by some other organs. Even if the same unit combines planning functions with authority to approve and execute, these are distinct, though interdependent, processes which must be kept analytically separate.

3. *A set.* It is very important to emphasize the difference between planning and decisionmaking and policymaking in general. While planning is a kind of decisionmaking and policymaking, its specific characteristic in this

---

[22] The dependence of the definition's validity and utility on the world of discourse within which it is to be used must be borne in mind.

respect is its dealing with a set of decisions, that is a matrix of interdependent and sequential series of systematically related decisions.

4. *Of decisions for action.* Planning is primarily directed at action and not at other objectives, such as pure knowledge, development of the planners, and so on. Planning does in fact have various secondary results, such as executive development, better decisionmaking on other issues, training in teamwork, etc., but as long as those results are only secondary objectives, the planning function is not impaired. It is true that often a planning activity is engaged in as a device to mobilize support, improve public relations, and so on. If this is the case, the process is not "planning" in its full sense and the actual process in such cases will deviate in most respects from the characteristics and phases of the "pure-type" planning process as defined by us, which is essentially *action* or *execution*-oriented.

5. *In the future.* Nearly all definitions recognize that planning is directed toward the future. This is perhaps the most important characteristic of planning, introducing the elements of prediction and uncertainty and conditioning all aspects, problems, and features of planning.[23]

6. *Directed at achieving goals.* The planning process cannot operate unless it has more or less defined goals to the achievement of which its recommendations for action in the future are directed. This does not mean that the planning process begins to operate with clearly defined objectives. Rather, in most cases, the first phase of the planning process consists in the formulation of operational planning objectives on the basis of rather ambiguous and undefined goals set before the planning process by some other, in most cases "policy", processes.

[23] Friedmann, *op. cit.* [in footnote 18], p. 334, gives an interesting list of planning characteristics resulting from the futuristic orientation of planning: "(1) It places a limit upon the time period over which projections into the future can be made without loss of practical significance for present decisions. (2) It establishes the necessity for continuing planning analysis and assessment throughout the planning period and the constant reevaluation and adjustment of means to ends. (3) It suggests the use of expectational calculus in connection with statements about the future. (4) It argues for adoption of a system of framework or structural planning. (5) It forces the careful consideration of flexibility in planning where the degree of flexibility introduced into a solution must be proportionate to the degree of uncertainty about future events. It is through an approach such as this that reason can come to terms with uncertainty."

7. *By preferable means.* The very nature of planning, as a process for rational shaping of the future according to our desires, depends on the means-ends relationship, which is basic to the planning process. The planning process is directed at suggesting the preferable means for achieving our goals, that is, at selecting on the basis of rational processes— including, for example, collection of information, utilization of knowledge, and systematic and integrative data processing—the preferable means for achieving the desired goals. The basic problem of planning methods, procedures, and techniques is the provision of ways for identification of these preferable means with a feasible input of resources.

It is on these elements of the definition our facet design of planning is based.

THE FACETS OF PLANNING

Following the concept of facet, as developed by Louis Guttman, we will now present the primary facets and secondary facets of planning.

The four primary facets of planning appear to be the following:

Primary facet A: The general environment of the planning process.
Primary facet B: The subject matter of the planning process.
Primary facet C: The planning unit.
Primary facet D: The form of the plan to be arrived at.

Each primary facet is the product of a number of secondary facets, which in turn are the product of a series of tertiary facets, and so on. We will now proceed to an examination of these various facets and secondary facets and some of their subsets. To concretize our presentation, a few observations on the relative significance of the various elements of the facet design and some of their characteristics will be introduced from time to time, which will point out some examples of possible lines for empiric investigation utilizing the tools provided by the facet design.

PRIMARY FACET A: THE GENERAL ENVIRONMENT OF THE PLANNING PROCESS

One of the more interesting characteristics of planning is its bi-directional relation with its environment. On the one hand, the planning activity is shaped and conditioned by various environmental factors; on the other hand, planning is in many cases directed at that environment, trying to shape it to a greater or lesser extent. While, therefore, the environment is not a fully independent variable, it nevertheless is at any point in time relatively fixed and is one of the primary facets shaping the planning process.

The main secondary facets of the general environment are these:

A_1. The basic environmental factors which constitute the physical, demographic, ecologic, social, cultural, geophysical, geoeconomic, etc., phenomena which are the general background against which the planning process takes place.

A_2. The resources in manpower, knowledge, capital, etc., which are potentially available for the planning process and for eventual plan execution.

A_3. Various values, power groups, and ideologies which limit the alternatives to be considered by the planning processes, in terms of methods that can be used for plan execution (e.g. force), of conditions that are required for recruiting the necessary support for the planning process, of the actual resources that will be put at the disposal of plan execution, and the like. Neglect by the planners of these limitations results in utopian, non-realistic planning.

A_4. The terms of reference within which the planning process is to take place, including general goals set for the planning process; contextual goals, that is, values and institutions which should not be impaired;[24] basic directives concerning some aspects of the working methods to be used during the planning process, such as giving an opportunity to interested persons to have a hearing; and so on.

It is these environmental elements which constitute the basic framework within which the planning process takes place and which also determine, or at least influence, directly and indirectly, the form of most of the other facets.

---

[24] "Contextual ends are represented by social values and traditions that do not in themselves, constitute the immediate objectives of planning, but are sufficiently vital to make their preservation socially worth while." Friedmann, *op. cit.* [in footnote 18], p. 330.

PRIMARY FACET B: THE SUBJECT MATTER OF THE PLANNING PROCESS

The subject matter of the planning process is the product of at least nine different secondary facets:

B_1. The structural relation between the subject matter and the planning unit.

B_2. The degree to which the subject matter is predetermined or elastic.

B_3. The degree of penetration.

B_4. The significance of the subject matter of the planning process.

B_5. The orientation of the subject matter toward the planning process.

B_6. The extent to which the subject matter has already been subjected to planning.

B_7. The scope of the activity subjected to planning.

B_8. The demographic territorial area related with the subject matter of the planning process.

B_9. The time span.

Let us examine these secondary facets more closely, one by one:[25]

B_1. *The structural relation between the subject matter and the planning unit.* The structural relation between the subject matter of the planning process and the planning unit can take either of three forms, which constitute the subset of this secondary facet:

(*a*) The subject matter is structurally identical with the planning unit or a part of it, for example, planning the future staffing of the planning unit or planning the work program of the planning unit.

(*b*) The subject matter belongs to an organizational structure of which the planning unit is itself a part, for instance, the personnel department planning the executive development scheme for the enterprise.

[25] Compare this list with the "dimensions of planning" suggested by LeBreton and Henning: complexity, significance, comprehensiveness, time, specificity, completeness, flexibility, frequency, confidential nature, formality, authorization, ease of implementation, ease of control. See Preston P. LeBreton and D. A. Henning, *Planning Theory*, Englewood Cliffs, N.J.: Prentice-Hall, 1961, pp. 22–56.

(c) The subject matter does not belong to an organizational structure of which the planning is itself a part, for example, a central planning agency preparing a master plan for a town or an economic development plan for a region or state.

While these distinctions are, at least, partly relative ones, depending on the strictness or looseness of the organizational structure which serves as a frame of reference for the analysis (e.g. one can regard a whole society as a kind of loose organizational structure), they help in pointing out the basic difference between so-called organizational planning, which is more "inner directed," and various kinds of "outer directed" planning.

B_2. *The degree to which the subject matter is predetermined or elastic.* There is a big difference between various planning instances in the extent to which the subject matter of the planning process is clearly delimited and defined when submitted to the planning unit or is left for the planning unit to determine and to change from time to time. In general, it seems that planning units—driven by their *bona fide* sense of mission, their belief in their own expert knowledge, and their empire-building drives—have a tendency to try to overcome even rigorously predetermined definitions of their subject matter, and to enlarge the scope of activities subjected to their planning.

B_3. *The degree of penetration.* Planning can penetrate more or less into its subject matter, trying to deal with all the elements and aspects of the subject matter or aiming only at its main directions and central factors. This is an important dimension for comparative study of planning, because even if identical activities are subjected to planning, entirely different degrees of penetration may be aimed at.

B_4. *The significance of the subject matter of the planning process.* Depending on the subject matter of the planning process, the (public or private) character of the planning unit and of the organization to which it belongs, and the socio-political-ideological environment, the significance of the subject matter of a certain planning process will be viewed mainly from the angle of the organization engaging in the planning activity, from the angle of various political-economic-social interests, from a "public interest" angle, or from the angle of various combinations of these different points of view.

From these different points of view, the subject matter of a planning process can be of high or low significance, either objectively (in the sense of the impact of the subject matter of the planning process on other areas of activity) or subjectively (in the sense of the importance of the subject matter of the planning process according to various cognitions, values, or ideologies).

B_5. *The orientation of the subject matter toward the planning process.* Depending on various tertiary facets, the persons and institutions related with different subject matters can have a more passive or active and more positive or negative orientation toward the planning process (and the planning unit—these two are closely related in the public image). A moot point, in urgent need of research, is what orientation of the subject matter toward the planning process provides better results in terms of the quality of the planning process; it seems that often the planning process and, even more so, the plan execution process need a lot of active, positive support to be successfully maintained.

B_6. *The extent to which the subject matter has already been subjected to planning.* Prior subjection of the subject matter to planning does not only influence its orientation toward the present planning process, but creates various expectations, traditions, and factors which are of much importance in shaping the future planning processes. In this respect, there are significant differences between various planning instances dealing with subject matters (or even an identical subject matter) subjected to more or less prior planning.

B_7. *The scope of the activity subjected to planning.* Planning always deals with a delimited subject matter, which is defined in terms of functions, territorial units, or some other characteristics. Total planning, that is, planning including within its subject matter all extrapersonal and interpersonal (and perhaps even intrapersonal) activities, is unimaginable outside of a fantastic counter-Utopia. The limitations of the human mind, the limitations of resources and the many competing alternative uses for them, the limits on the maximum integrating capacity of organizations, and the existence of strong opposition to planning of certain subject matters—all these limit planning at any given time to a selected, relatively small number of subject matters. On the other hand, recognition of the interdependence of various aspects of activity, especially under conditions of rapid change (e.g. rapidly developing societies, rapidly growing enterprises), is one of the more important reasons for enlarging the scope of activities subjected to planning, leading in the direction of a comprehensive planning approach.

B_8. *The demographic territorial area related with the subject matter of the planning process.* The relation between planning and demographic territorial area is a rather complex one, which has at least three distinct, though closely interrelated, possible aspects. Since all human activity takes place in space time, by its very nature planning must, and does, take into account this fact, and delimits its scope within these dimensions. Even in the few cases where the subject matter of planning is not defined in demographic territorial terms (e.g. *all economic activities*), the fact that all material phenomena are distributed in space will make it convenient, and even inevitable, to use some demographic-territorial subdivision as units for delegated planning purposes.

To this general consideration on the inherent role of space in human thought and activity, a second aspect of the relation between area and planning must be added—the specific importance of demographic territorial units in social affairs. Beginning with the nearly instinctive, emotional attachment of an individual to his place of birth, and going through all levels of social institutions, the special role of territory in social life is always apparent (though, in the future, it may decrease very much).

A third aspect of the relation between demographic territorial area and planning has its roots in the fact that one of the most important functions of every society is adjustment to its territory. Such adjustment is brought about to some extent by changing the physical environment and making the territory fit the needs of the society. In the field of planning this aim is reflected in the many planning activities having as their subject matter certain aspects of what we call territory. Such "earthbound" fields include landscaping, resources conservation, flood control, urban redevelopment, and many more. The present pollution and environmental concerns belong to this aspect.

In all these cases, the relation between demographic territorial area and planning poses two problems, the solutions of which have to be reconciled somehow. First, the *technical-optimum* area for dealing with the subject matter of the planning activity must be defined; and second, this technical-optimum area must be reconciled with the existing demographic territorial units of social action and the limited freedom of the planning unit.

The best possible compromise between the two sets of areas will yield the *social-technical-preferable* demographic territorial areas for the designed planning activity.[26]

B_9. *The time span.* Each planning process deals with a certain, though not necessarily exactly predetermined, time span. The selection of the preferable time span for each planning activity depends on various factors, including, for example, the natural cycle of the subject matter of planning, the acute need for interference to change an unbearable situation, limitations on our ability to predict the future, our evaluation of present versus future needs, and the desire that planning should serve as a guide to present actions.

We shall now proceed to the two remaining primary facets of planning, which are of a somewhat more limited nature but exert a tremendous influence on the planning process.

---

[26] It is incorrect to regard the technical-optimal area as the "desirable" area of action which is "distorted" by the "unfortunate" existence of nations, states, local units, etc. We have already mentioned the psychological importance for human happiness of emotional attachment to territories and the inevitablity, till basic social institutions change, of territorial units of social action and their role in planning. Here it should be emphasized that these existing demographic territorial units of social action have to play a significant role in planning: the most important initiators are those who can mobilize loyalty, resources, and support. The planner cannot and must not neglect these human and moral facts in favor of a quasi-mechanical "social engineering" approach.

PRIMARY FACET C: THE PLANNING UNIT

The characteristics of the planning unit are the product of seven secondary facets:

C_1. *The basic nature of the planning unit.* Planning, as defined by us, can take place on the level of individuals and on the level of various institutions, such as a family, a tribal council, and the like. A special case of institutional planning which is of highest contemporary importance and which includes most socially significant planning processes, is planning in and by bureaucratic structures. It is this kind of planning, which is particularly related to policymaking, at which our facet design is mainly directed.

Because of the underdeveloped state of neurology and individual psychology, we know nearly nothing on the factors conditioning and shaping planning on the individual level. This is all the more regrettable because, after all, organizational planning is also done by individuals, and more knowledge on planning on the individual level may well contribute much to the understanding and improvement of the organizational planning process.

C_2. *Primary or delegated planning units.* Delegated planning is planning which constitutes plan execution from the point of view of another planning unit; primary planning is planning not as part of any higher-level plan. In general, delegated planning will be more detailed, will be for a shorter time span, and will deal with a smaller subject matter.

The importance of this distinction can be illustrated by applying it to a concrete issue, for example, the preferable subject matter of city planning, Some authors[27] relied on the precedent of large-scope city planning in the United States during the big depression, including economic and social spheres of social activity, to justify a similar large subject matter for city planning at later periods. But it seems that much of the enlarged scope of city planning at that period was delegated planning, part of a national plan to relieve unemployment and rehabilitate the economy. Therefore, what happened then is not directly relevant to the problem whether, in the

---

[27] For example, cf. Robert A. Walker, *The Planning Function in Urban Government,* Chicago: University of Chicago Press, 1950.

absence of national planning of some subject matters, cities should deal with them through primary planning.

C_3. *Status.* The status of the planning unit (including the status of the institution and of the planners as individual role bearers) influences the resources which can be mobilized for the planning process, the extent to which limitations on alternatives and similar externally determined limits imposed on the planning process can be overcome, and so on. In other words, the status of the planning unit is closely correlated, though not identical, with its power, which is an important factor in the implementation strategy of planning.[28]

C_4. *Values, information, and character of the planning unit.* The planning process in all its phases entails constant judgments involving the value systems, the information, and the character of the decisionmakers—the planning unit as a collection of individuals and the planning unit as an institution. This is a factor of tremendous importance, having significant implications for the selection of planners, their education and their control, and for the design of planning units.

C_5. *Resources and means.* The resources in manpower, knowledge, equipment, time, etc., at the disposal of the planning unit and the planners are other important factors which have a definite influence on the planning process and must therefore be carefully considered.

C_6. *Work systems, procedures, and methods.* The systems, methods, and procedures of work in the planning unit determine the detailed form of the planning process. The more important systems, procedures, and methods deal with information gathering, data processing, and decisionmaking. The introduction of electronic data-processing equipment, while much increasing the possibilities of planning, introduces serious complexities into work systems, work methods, and procedures and makes even more essential careful attention to consciously and rationally established explicit systems,

---

[28] The policy of planning is still a sadly neglected subject. With the exception of single case studies on concrete planning instances and planning institutions and a few general studies dealing with some relationships between macro-planning and political regimes, only very little is known on this critically important subject.

procedures, and methods through which the planning process is channelized. Even more important is the emergence of policy sciences, which provides novel designs for planning—designs which require radical changes in contemporary planning patterns.

C_7. *Organizational structure.* Last, but not least, the organizational structure of the planning unit (already mentioned in a different context) raises difficult problems, especially concerning the distribution of functions between specialized overhead planning function and the ordinary line units in charge of day-to-day operations in regard to specific subject matters. In both small- and large-scale, inner- and outer-directed planning, the organizational issues are most complex and the solutions adopted determine to a considerable degree the form taken by the planning process, and its success or failure in fulfilling its tasks. As yet, despite some recent literature on the subject, the organizational problems of planning are among the most neglected subjects—in the study of planning, in organization theory, and in policy sciences as a whole.

PRIMARY FACET D: THE FORM OF THE PLAN TO BE ARRIVED AT

D_1. *The realism of the plan.* We have already mentioned cases of planning directed at political advantages, public relations, training objectives, and the like. In these cases, it is not always necessary to arrive at the final phase of the planning process, that is, preparation of a plan; and even if a plan is prepared, it is often on purpose utopian in nature. Leaving such cases of "quasi-planning" aside, there is a legitimate span of more or less realism aimed at in the preparation of a plan. Indeed, a certain utopian element may be essential for gaining the necessary support and may be fully compatible with a realistic approach to planning and with successful plan realization. In any case, the degree of realism of the plan to be arrived at is an important subfacet influencing the entire tone of the planning process.

D_2. *The form of the plan.* The subset of this secondary facet includes various forms of plans: fixed-time plans, such as five-year or seven-year plans; contingency plans, to be executed at a given occurrence which might or might not happen at an unknown point in the future, such as most military operation plans; master plans, showing a blueprint of a desired state of affairs without setting down a fixed timetable for its achievements, such as many town plans; budgetary plans, constructed in terms of monetary units; work plans, constructed in terms of technical specification, drawings, etc.; and more.

The modern tendency seems to be in the direction of composite plans, including long-range and short-range timetables, financial and physical breakdown, contingency and predetermined elements, and so on. It seems that the more complex and large-scale the subject matter of the planning process is, the more multiform and complex the plan has to be.

D_3. *Degree of details.* The plan to be arrived at can be more or less detailed. In general, the larger the time span to be covered by the plan, the more the plan will include general frameworks and directions, leaving details for later or delegated planning.

A related element of the subset is, will the plan be single-alternative, providing one direction of action, or multialternative, providing different directions, for later selection (in the light of developments) of the preferable one ?

CONCLUSIONS

Returning to the concept of facet as used in this paper, we can regard planning (P) as the product (in the mathematical sense of *cartesian product*)[29] of primary facets A, B, C, and D.

In other words, generally speaking,

Planning = (general environment) × (subject matter) × (planning unit) × (form of plan), or P = A × B × C × D.

Each primary facet in turn is the product of a number of secondary facets, namely:

$$A = A_1 \times A_2 \times A_3 \times A_4$$
$$B = B_1 \times B_2 \times B_3 \times B_4 \times B_5 \times B_6 \times B_7 \times B_8 \times B_9$$
$$C = C_1 \times C_2 \times C_3 \times C_4 \times C_5 \times C_6 \times C_7$$
$$D = D_1 \times D_2 \times D_3 \times D_4$$

We have thus twenty-four secondary facets of planning, each one of

[29] Guttman, "An outline of some new methodology", *op. cit.* [in footnote 3], p. 1.

which—even if not regarded as the product of a series of tertiary facets —can take different forms. Thus, we have:

$$A_{1a}, A_{1b}, A_{1c} \ldots D_{4a}, D_{4b}, D_{4c}, \ldots D_{4n}.$$

The forms of some of the secondary facets (e.g. the time span) can be expressed in metric units; others can be expressed in transitive but not fully comparable units (e.g. the secondary facet "significance"); still others can only be expressed by rough qualitative terms (e.g. most of the secondary facets related to the form of the plan to be arrived at). Following further elaboration of various classifications of the form of the various secondary facets, the basic problems are reached: Which combinations of forms do in fact appear in real planning instances? What combinations give, under various conditions, the best results? Why?

In other words we would like to know for which values of $a_{11}, a_{2j}, \ldots d_{4n}$, planning ($p = a \times b \times c \times d$) can exist in reality, and given the values of some of the secondary facets—which values for the non-predetermined secondary facets will maximize the quality[30] of the planning process (qp).

Available experience and impressionistic data provide some guidelines to these problems. Thus, we would not expect long-range planning of a large-scope subject matter to go with very detailed plans and a high degree of penetration; we would not expect planning to succeed if the planners lack certain qualifications; and so on. But available material, based as it is on limited experience and subjectivistic impressions, does not permit many conclusions beyond such rather obvious and partly semantic ones. Only systematic empirical study, utilizing the best available research designs and methodologies, can perhaps provide us with valid and reliable answers to these and other problems and provide a sound basis for the study of the planning process and its improvement as part of policy sciences.[31]

---

[30] On the problem of evaluation of quality, see Yehezkel Dror, *Public Policy-making Reexamined*, San Francisco: Chandler, 1968, part 2.

[31] On the concept of policy sciences and its relevance to planning, see Yehezkel Dror, *Design for Policy Sciences*, New York: American Elsevier, and Amsterdam: Elsevier, 1971, and Yehezkel Dror, *Ventures in Policy Sciences: Concepts and Applications*, New York: American Elsevier, and Amsterdam: Elsevier, 1971.

A Conceptual Model for the Analysis of Planning Behavior

John Friedmann

UNTIL a few years ago, discussions of planning were restricted to consideration of an abstract model of perfect rationality in social decision-making.[1] In use, however, this model turned out to be unsatisfactory. As a theoretical model, it failed to lead to fruitful hypotheses and, because of its logical rigidity, it was incapable of substantial modification. As a normative model it failed because rationality in real life is always "bounded" so that the recipes for planning that could be drawn from the model were frequently inapplicable.[2]

With the recent upsurge of interest in national planning, however, social scientists have begun to study the actual workings of the planning process. Some students are focusing on the substantive contents of national plans and on the propriety of the strategies adopted; others are doing research on the administrative machinery evolved; still others are curious about how planning got started in particular societies and how the first plans came

* Reprinted by permission from *Administrative Science Quarterly*, Vol. 12, No. 2, September 1967.

[1] A concise description of this model will be found in Edward Banfield's "Note on conceptual scheme" in Martin Meyerson and Edward C. Banfield (eds.), *Politics, Planning and the Public Interest: The Case of Public Housing in Chicago*, Glencoe, Ill.: The Free Press, 1955, pp. 303–30. In a more sophisticated version, this model also underlies much of Jan Tinbergen's influential work, *Economic Policy: Principles and Design*, Amsterdam: North Holland, 1964. For a critique of classical decision theory, see Charles Lindblom, *The Intelligence of Democracy*, New York: The Free Press, 1965.

[2] On the concept of "bounded rationality", see James G. March and Herbert A. Simon, *Organizations*, New York: John Wiley, 1958, pp. 203–10.

to be made.[3] But where the earlier theorists erred in ignoring planning practice, the new empiricists are leaning too much in the other direction: they simply look at activities called planning and describe what they see.

Although this is leading to the collection of much information, it is also giving rise to unwitting distortions when basic preconceptions have not been made explicit. Simple descriptions of something as ephemeral as national planning is scarcely even of historical value, and certainly does not add significantly to *verifiable* knowledge, which alone is capable of serving as a sound foundation for a theory of planning.[4] The importance of these studies lies primarily in their fresh approach, which has brought the study of planning within the scope of empirical social research.

The present paper is an attempt to create that minimum of conceptual order which is necessary for a scientifically more disciplined study of planning.[5] There are various ways of defining planning.[6] Here planning will be considered as the *guidance of change within a social system.*[7] Specifically, this means a process of self-guidance that may involve *promoting*

---

[3] Recent examples include Everett E. Hagen, *Planning Economic Development*, Homewood, Ill.: Richard D. Irwin, 1963; John and Anne-Marie Hackett, *Economic Planning in France*, Cambridge, Mass.: Harvard University, 1963; chapters on the Netherlands, France and Japan in Bert G. Hickman (ed.), *Quantitative Planning of Economic Policy*, Washington: Brookings Institution, 1965; Albert Waterston, *Development Planning: Lessons of Experience*, Baltimore: Johns Hopkins University, 1965; and the several volumes in the National Planning Series published by Syracuse University Press under the general editorship of Bertram M. Gross.

[4] Planning theory was formerly little more than an exercise in the logic of rational decision-making; its reformulation on an empirical basis will involve extensive work in the description and explanation of planning phenomena and in generalizations derived from these data.

[5] A study complementary to the present one and fundamental for any serious research into planning is Bertram M. Gross, "The managers of national economic change", in Roscoe C. Martin (ed.), *Public Administration and Democracy: Essays in Honor of Paul H. Appleby*, Syracuse: Syracuse University, 1965.

[6] For some frequently used definitions of planning, see Yehezkel Dror, "The planning process: a facet design", *International Review of Administrative Sciences*, Vol. 24 (1963), pp. 1–13.

[7] This definition is in line with, if somewhat more general than, Bertram M. Gross' definition of planning as the "processes whereby national governments try to carry out responsibilities for the guidance of significant economic change". See his "National planning: findings and fallacies", *Public Administration Review*, Vol. 25 (1965), p. 264.

differential growth of subsystem components (sectors), *activating the transformation of system structures* (political, economic, social), and *maintaining system boundaries* during the course of change.[8] Accordingly, the idea of planning involves a confrontation of expected with intended performance, the application of controls to accomplish the intention when expectations are not met, the observation of possible variances from the prescribed path of change, and the repetition of this cycle each time significant variations are perceived.[9]

To this view of planning as a self-guidance system, a still more general conception may be added that will lead directly into the structure of the model. Planning may be simply regarded as reason acting on a network of ongoing activities through the intervention of certain decision structures and processes. The emphasis here is on intervention and, hence, on *planning for change*. This intervention is made on the basis of an intellectual effort or, more simply, of thought. "Introducing" planning, then, means specifically the introduction of ways and means for using technical intelligence to bring about changes that otherwise would not occur.

This is fundamental in my view. Society is a going concern. The ongoing stream of life does not wait for planners to give it direction. Planners must act upon social and economic processes with the fragile instrument of their minds (amplified by whatever practical means they may command) to guide society towards desired objectives. A comprehensive model of planning must, therefore, include forms of thought as an important category for analysis.

THE MODEL

The model proposed here for the analysis of planning behavior has three general characteristics (see Fig. 1). First, it is valid only for what is here called planning for change. Other forms of planning may be

---

[8] The distinction between self-guidance systems and those in which guidance is imposed by agents external to the system is of theoretical and practical importance, but will not be pursued further in this paper.

[9] This description of the logic of planning coincides with Neil W. Chamberlain's model as developed in his *Private and Public Planning*, New York: McGraw-Hill, 1965, especially chap. 7.

identified, such as operations research, but these are not included. Second, it is an attempt to distinguish among different forms of planning for change and to show the relationships among them. Third, the model is intended as an aid to empirical research. On the basis of the actual findings, it will almost certainly need to be refined, modified, and expanded. Specifically absent from the model are the institutional forms of planning and explicit recognition of the time dimension in which planning processes occur.

Forms of planning. A convenient way for entering the model is to consider the two major forms of planning for change. The criterion for distinguishing between them is the relative autonomy of planning units in the making of decisions. Under *developmental planning*, there is a high degree of autonomy with respect to the setting of ends and the choice of means; under *adaptive planning*, most decisions are heavily contingent on the actions of others external to the planning system. In practice, of course, most planning decisions are made along the continuum between complete autonomy and complete dependency, and the behavior of planning systems will differ according to the distribution of decision functions between the two extremes. For instance, planning for urban development at the level of the city will usually be more adaptive than developmental: to a great extent, it will need to respond or adapt to external forces, such as shifts in the locational preferences of national industries, which the municipality cannot significantly influence through its own actions. In planning for national development, on the other hand, the public authorities are able to control a larger number of the variables relevant to its own objectives, so that the nation is much more independent than any of its municipalities. Even among nations, however, there may be differences in the degree of dependency on external forces; and a small, weak nation such as Haiti has to plan more adaptively with respect to international conditions—if it is planning at all—than the city of Sao Paulo with respect to Brazil.

What are the main differences in the expected behavior between developmental and adaptive planning?

Adaptive planning. In adaptive planning there will be a tendency to push decisions upwards to centers of developmental planning where the parameters for choice at lower levels may be changed. In attempting this,

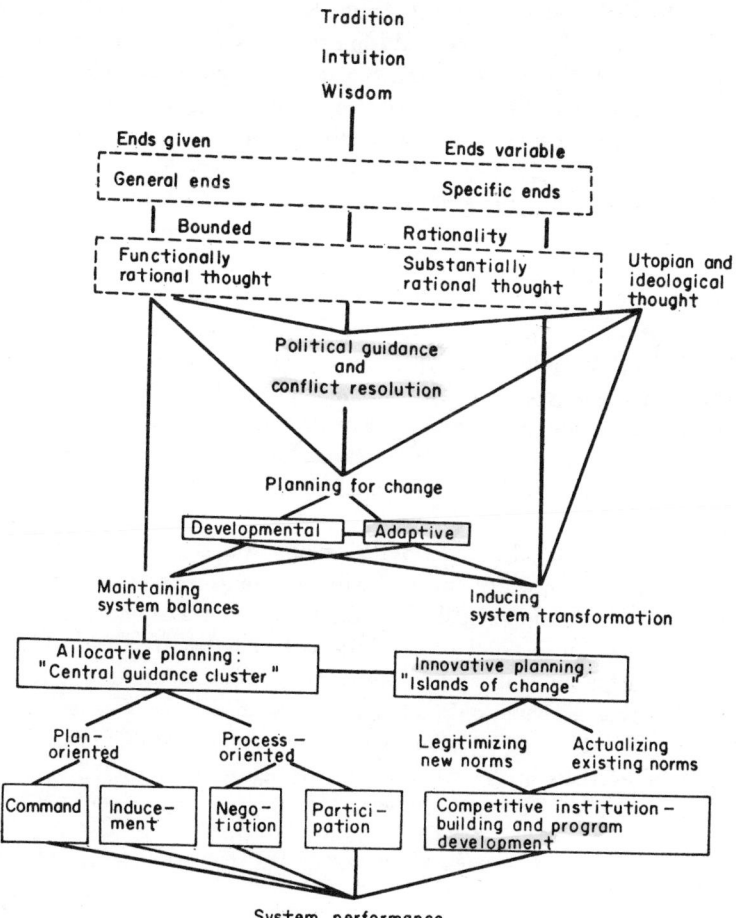

Fig. 1.

lower-level planning systems will generally rely on political manipulation to achieve their ends. So that negotiations with the central authorities may be conducted with equal technical competence, however, counterplanning may be added to political action. Since, on the government's side, any bargaining in a complex advanced economic system is usually done by qualified technical experts, the contending parties must enter negotiations at least as well prepared.[10]

At the same time, the gradual recognition of interdependence within the system may lead the separate, partisan interests—each engaged in a measure of adaptive planning—to discover a common or public interest. Such an interest, as the work of the Bureau of Economic Research, the Brookings Institution, the Committee for Economic Development, and the National Planning Association in the United States clearly demonstrates, will lead partisan interests gradually in the direction of quasi-governmental policy planning, although the interests they nominally represent are private. Thus, on the technical side at least, adaptive planning may become fused with developmental planning, that is, sub-system with system planning.

Finally, adaptive planning is typically opportunistic. For instance, one reason for the frequently noted instability of long-term capital improvement programs for municipalities in the United States is that cities cannot afford to lose the federal or state financial aid that frequently plays a decisive part in municipal public works. Since funds from external sources often become available only upon short notice, are tied to specific performance criteria, and normally require matching contributions, significant modifications in the program are frequently made to accommodate the emergence of sudden opportunities for external financing.[11] Similarly,

[10] A typical example of counterplanning is the large number of national planning agencies that were set up in Latin America when it became known that the Alliance for Progress would make financial aid contingent on the preparation of national plans. In order to deal with the international agencies in Washington, a country had to send economists who could negotiate for aid on the basis of a logical program for development. This program was then compared to the Alliance's own planning for Latin America, whether by the Committee of Nine, the Agency for International Development, or the Interamerican Development Bank. In many Latin American countries today, national planning is primarily a means of obtaining international assistance rather than a means of guiding the use of resources within the country.

[11] W. H. Brown and C. E. Gilbert, *Planning Municipal Investment. A Case Study of Philadelphia*, Philadelphia: University of Pennsylvania, 1961, chap. 8.

so-called national planning is often related to the availability of funds and the requirements of international sources, as for example, the sudden creation of national planning agencies in Latin America in response to a call for national plans as a basis for Alliance for Progress assistance. These plans closely reflect what each country believes will, at a given time, be the most persuasive program for obtaining funds from the Alliance; they are not necessarily related to the priorities of domestic needs.

Different degrees of autonomy and dependency in decision-making tend to be mirrored in a hierarchy of planning authorities which stand in more or less systematic technical and political relation to one another, each level having its appropriate function and decision power. Since each higher level is capable of changing some of the relevant conditions for decisions at all lower levels, and since every change of this sort represents some change of policy, policy planning tends to be emphasized at higher decision levels and programming—the detailed specification of investments in volume, time, and place—at lower levels. Or, put in another way, developmental planning tends to shade off into policy making, adaptive planning into programming. In fact, however, the two become mixed in varying proportion, according to the point on the autonomy-dependency continuum where planning occurs.

Developmental planning. In developmental planning, the role of political institutions for guidance and conflict resolution becomes obviously crucial; for it is here that the basic policy decisions are made and that the clashing interests of adaptive planners must be resolved. Developmental planning is not only a technical, but also, and to a large degree, a political function. The relationship between planning and politics is therefore a crucial one.[12]

First, an effective decision process almost always involves both experts and politicians (or policy-makers) simultaneously in close interdependency.

---

[12] For excellent discussions of the relation of planning to politics, see Alan Altshuler, *The City Planning Process: A Political Analysis*, Ithaca: Cornell University, 1966. At the national level, one of the best accounts will be found in the forthcoming study by Robert T. Daland, *Brazilian Planning: A Study of Development Politics and Administration*, Chapel Hill: University of North Carolina, February 1966, mimeographed.

No politician who values the services of an expert can afford consistently to disregard his judgment, nor will any expert desiring influence, systematically oppose the wishes of his employer. Therefore every decision will be influenced by political interests in varying degrees and, at the same time, it must satisfy some technical criteria. Once a decision is made, it becomes exceedingly difficult to separate the contributions made by each group, for it represents a synthesis of political and expert judgment. Failure to achieve this synthesis will mean that the plans are not carried out or that policies adopted, being exclusively political, will be inadequate or inappropriate.[13]

Second, successful planning in its more technical aspects must meet certain needs internal to the political process itself. Although these uses of planning are not usually made explicit, they are nevertheless real. They may include: (1) symbolic representation of progress, modernity, and so on; (2) mobilization of external resources; (3) redistribution of the relative influence or weight of participants in a diffused power structure (for example, strengthening the role of the Presidency, of technicians, of the industrial sector, and so forth); (4) helping to build a national consensus on fundamental values; (5) stimulating an acceptance of development; and (6) encouraging counterplanning.[14]

For example, in his recent study on planning in Tanzania, Anthony Rweyemamu writes:

> In a new nation like Tanzania, a national plan is a major, albeit incomplete, substitute for the goods which were promised explicitly or implicitly during the struggle for independence. Insofar as it is indicative of a future of abundance, a national plan serves as a unifying agent of an otherwise loose and fragile society. . . . Therefore, even if the economic and social goals are not completely realized, a plan is successful to the extent to which it serves to mobilize the people's energies, bring about national integration and a measure of political consensus.[15]

[13] Józef Pajestka, "Dialogue between planning experts and policy makers in the process of plan formulation", paper presented to the International Group for Studies in National Planning, 15–22 November 1966, Caracas, Venezuela.

[14] These and other functions are discussed in J. Friedmann, *Venezuela: From Doctrine to Dialogue*, Syracuse: Syracuse University, 1965. For corroborative evidence, see Robert T. Daland, *op. cit.*, chap. 6.

[15] Quoted in Bertram M. Gross' preface to Fred G. Burke, *Tanganyika: Pre-planning*, Syracuse: Syracuse University, 1965, pp. 19–20.

These varied uses of planning are frequently not only more important than the explicit purposes for which planning is undertaken (more rapid growth, greater efficiency, better coordination) but also inconsistent with these purposes. It is evident that they will also define the respective roles of experts and politicians and help to shape the institutional framework of planning.

In any system, there are large areas of indifference where political behavior is possible without planned intervention. The relative influence of a technical planning function in guiding social and economic change will depend chiefly on five variables: (1) the clarity of system objectives, (2) the extent of consensus about them, (3) the relative importance that politicians attach to them, (4) the degree of variance relative to objectives expected in the performance of the system, and (5) the extent to which a technical (as contrasted with a purely political) approach is believed capable of making system performance conform to these objectives. Technical planning, therefore, moves temporarily into the foreground whenever goals are clear, widely held, and deemed to be important; whenever in such a situation system performance is believed to depart significantly from the norm; and whenever, given all of these conditions, expert judgment coupled with a variety of control mechanisms is held to be more effective than political manipulation. Where these conditions do not occur, planning is likely to be reduced to a vestigal function only.

Relation of kinds of thinking to planning. All political and planning activities are in varying degree influenced by different kinds of thinking that may be classified as rational or extra-rational. Rational thought can be further considered as bounded or nonbounded. And bounded rationality may be considered as functionally or substantially rational. Far from being superfluous categories for the analysis of planning, these kinds of thinking are decisive in influencing both the prevailing styles of planning and the actual behavior of planners.

Bounded rationality. This refers to the fact that thought and consequent action intended to be rational are contingent on environmental conditions —the social context of planning—which represent the medium in and through which planning decisions are made.[16] This environment for decision is often discussed in terms of so-called obstacles to planning, but it seems preferable to speak of it simply as the specific set of structural conditions under which planning must occur.[17] In discussing planning in Italy, Joseph LaPalombara underlines the critical importance of the decision environment. He writes:

> No one with even the most cursory knowledge of the Italian bureaucracy could seriously hold that, within its present structure, it is able to support state intervention in the economic sphere, much less to direct and to co-ordinate economic planning on a national scale.[18]

But, in fact, the limitations of bureaucracy are only one aspect of the decision environment, which is more adequately described in categories such as the following:

1. The number and diversity of organized interest groups and their power to influence decisions.
2. The degree to which political opposition is tolerated or accepted, and the role assigned to it.
3. The dependence of the economic system on private enterprise, and the characteristics of enterprise (size, monopoly, and others) and of entrepreneurial behavior.
4. The efficiency of the relevant information systems: their capacity, load, reliability, promptness, secrecy, etc.
5. The structure of bureaucratic institutions and their performance.
6. The educational level of the population and size of the university-educated elite.
7. The availability of relevant information and its reliability.
8. The predictability of change within the system and of external changes that will affect its performance.

[16] Reference to "adaptive" rationality is made in J. Friedmann, "The institutional context", in Bertram M. Gross (ed.), *Action Under Planning*, New York: McGraw-Hill, 1966, chap. 2. The equivalent concept of *bounded* rationality was introduced into the literature by Herbert Simon (see footnote 2). The importance of "context" for planning has also been stressed by Fred W. Riggs, *The Ecology of Development*, Comparative Administration Group, American Society for Public Administration, *Occasional Papers*, Bloomington, Indiana, 1964.

[17] Albert Waterston, *op. cit.*, chap. 8.

[18] Joseph LaPalombara, *Italy: The Politics of Planning*, Syracuse: Syracuse University, 1966, p. 106.

In short, to be "bounded" means that a decision can be no more rational than the conditions under which it is made; the most that planners can hope for is the most rational decision *under the circumstances.* "Until administrative improvements are clearly foreseeable," writes Albert Waterston, "planners must prepare plans which take account of administrative capacity. This means, among other things, that complex forms of planning must be avoided when a country's administration is not ready for them."[19] The author might have broadened this statement to include all conditions that provide the social context for decisions and action.

The concept of bounded rationality suggests the possibility of identifying a number of discrete planning styles which result from the adaptation of the institutional forms and procedures of planning to relatively stable characteristics of their institutional environment. These environments and the forms of planning adapted to them can both be reduced to a few general types. The study of planning styles would therefore be helpful in formulating hypotheses for the comparative study of planning behavior.

It is useful to distinguish two basic forms of bounded rationality:

Functionally rational thought is rational with respect to the means only; the ends are assumed by the planner to be given and may be more or less rational or even, according to certain criteria, irrational.[20] The ends must remain fairly stable, however, because the decision must appear rational not only before but also *after* implementation. As a rule, the more general the objective, the more stable it will tend to be. It may therefore be concluded that functional rationality in planning is found chiefly in connection with stable, general ends that are applicable to the system as a whole or at least to major portions of it. For example, the general ends of national economic development usually include such values as growth, more equitable income distribution, and full employment. These ends undergo relatively little change through time; but at the same time, they point only in a general direction. Functionally rational thought will try to guide the evolution of the system in this direction.

Substantially rational thought is rational with respect to both the ends and means of action. But this clearly implies the possibility of altering the

---

[19] Albert Waterston, *op. cit.,* p. 292.
[20] This is Karl Mannheim's terminology for describing the two forms of rationality, in *Man and Society in an Age of Reconstruction,* New York: Harcourt, Brace, 1949, pp. 51–60.

ends during the action as a result of changing circumstances or new information. One would, therefore, expect to meet with frequent modifications of the ends. Since only specific ends are capable of being modified in this way, it is permissible to posit a strong correlation between substantial rationality and variable ends.

In any planning system, both forms of rationality will usually occur: functional rationality with respect to system ends and substantial rationality with respect to more specific, subsystem ends; that is, one would expect to find stability in the general direction of the planning effort and adaptability in detailed planning. For example, lengthy conferences operate on what might be called "daily blueprints", that is, frequent revisions of the detailed schedule to accommodate unforeseen events, yet the main purposes of the conference will usually remain the same, although the course towards them may be tortuous and seemingly anarchic.

Nonbounded rationality. The nonbounded form of reason, free from temporal constraints may be called *utopian and ideological thought.* In such thinking there is a picture of an ideal social order, often in considerable detail, and almost always as a final state existing in a perfect equilibrium outside of historical time. The images of perfect communism and perfect capitalism are such utopias, as are the corporate state, national socialism and participant democracy.

Utopian and ideological thought may be considered rational in two senses. Its constructions are not only logical and coherent; they are also concrete representations of abstract social values such as equality, freedom, and social justice, and it is primarily these qualities that make this kind of thinking so often persuasive.[21] Forms of planning are often historical precipitates of utopian and ideological thought. Agricultural planning in the United States, for instance, can be illuminated by analyzing it against a background of Jeffersonian democratic thought; national planning in Spanish-speaking Latin America needs to be viewed in the light of the philosophy of the corporate state; and Indian planning still reflects the influence of Gandhi's social philosophy. What is still more significant is that many of the internal conflicts that rage about specific planning proposals turn precisely on philosophical issues such as these rather than on

[21] Martin Meyerson, "Utopian traditions and the planning of cities", *Daedalus* (Winter 1961), pp. 180–93. The influence of utopian thought on economic planning has barely been recognized, however, and merits a full study.

more pragmatic problems. The outcomes of these conflicts are usually decisive in setting the direction of development for an entire sector or even the whole nation.[22]

Extra-rational thought. The category of extra-rational thought includes what may be loosely called *tradition, intuition,* and *wisdom.* These forms of thought are not derived from coherent, logical structures, nor based on specific technical expertise. They are, however, the source of most political decisions and, therefore, play an exceptionally large part in planning processes. It must be admitted, however, that recently there has been a steady diminution of the role of extra-rational thought in public decision-making. Measurement and calculations are driving intuition and wisdom into more and more exclusive spheres, whereas the rapidity of change renders tradition meaningless as a source of decisions oriented towards the future. The result appears to be a weakening of the political elements in planning accompanied by a strengthening of the role of the technician. How this trend should be assessed is not yet clear.

Allocative planning is the assigning of resource increments among competing uses. Typically, this is the task of national planning institutions and, for many people, it is the only task with which planning should be properly concerned. Four characteristics of allocative planning help to define it.

1. *Comprehensiveness.* Allocative planning must be comprehensive with respect to at least the following: (a) the interdependence among all of the explicitly stated objectives of the system (or subsystem), (b) the interdependence in the use of all available resources of the system (or subsystem), and (c) the influence of all external variables on the setting of intermediate targets.[23]

Comprehensiveness has become a preoccupation with allocative planners. They believe that their special contribution to social decision-making derives mainly from their ability to manipulate a comprehensive set of variables and objectives and to acquire, as a result, a point of view that

---

[22] John H. Kautsky (ed.), *Political Change in Underdeveloped Countries: Nationalism and Communism,* New York: John Wiley, 1962. See also J. Friedmann, "Intellectuals in developing societies", *Kyklos,* Vol. 13 (1960), pp. 513–44.

[23] Jan Tinbergen, *op. cit., passim.*

necessarily coincides with the interests of the system (or subsystem) as a whole, that is, with the public interest. Their close association with executive power reinforces this conception of themselves. Thus, far from being mere experts, neutral with respect to values, allocative planners will often defend a set of value propositions as essential to the survival and well-being of the system (or subsystem). Since the concept of a public interest is difficult to maintain, however, especially in pluralistic or in nonintegrated societies, the powers of allocative planning are often resented by groups whose partial concerns are threatened by an insistence on public values arrived at independently of any political process.

2. *System-wide balances.* The optimality criterion, the basic norm for allocative planning, requires a balance among the variable components of the planning system. The model with which allocative planners customarily work is necessarily in equilibrium. Thus, planned investment must not exceed the capacity to invest; total imports must not exceed projected exports; employment gains must not be less than the increase of the labor force; electric energy production must meet projected power consumption. It is a question of determining the right magnitudes as the targets of the economic system. Accompanying a set of carefully worked out quantitative targets, is usually a text suggesting changes in existing policies that are thought necessary for their achievement.

3. *Synthesis.* Neither comprehensiveness nor systematic balance can be obtained without the aid of one or more synthetic models of the economy. These models allow study of the functioning of the system under quasi-experimental conditions as different conditions are considered and their implications are observed. The most common models include national economic accounts, input–output matrices, simulation models, and econometric policy models.[24] These models are abstracted from the institutional and legal framework of the economic system and from the persons through whom the system works.

4. *Functional rationality.* Allocative planning is an attempt to be functionally rational in that the objectives of the system are supposed to be

[24] See Bert G. Hickmann, *op. cit.*, for a discussion of the current planning models.

determined externally through a political process that does not significantly involve the planners themselves. Planning, therefore, appears as only a working out of the implications for public policy of norms established independently. As a well-known economist has recently explained it:

> The tendency now is to abandon the effort to determine through economic analysis, what is the best form of economic organization or the "best" set of economic policies, and to accept goals established through the political process and stated by governments—full employment, price stability, more rapid economic growth, elimination of pockets of poverty or distressed areas, and the like. For the most part, such goals seem reasonable to economists, but by starting their analysis at the point where government policy is already determined, they avoid value judgments of their own. They may point out inconsistencies among goals, or worry about such new dilemmas as rising cost of living and increasing unemployment side by side, but choice between goals is left to the government, as is the establishment of priorities. Usually some set of measures for achieving goals—once priorities are established—can be suggested, even if there remains doubt as to whether they constitute the best possible set of measures.[25]

The impossibility of remaining uninfluenced by values has already been pointed out. Nevertheless, by shifting the major burden of choice among values to the political process, allocative planning can appear as an activity intended in large measure to be functionally rational and thus, presumably, objective.

Implementation. The institutions charged with implementation of the plans must remain constantly aware of the need to carry out the policies and advance towards the targets of the models. Implementation, however, is not an independent step taken subsequent to plan making: *the kind of implementing mechanism adopted will itself influence the character of the plan and the way it is formulated.* The formulation and implementation of plans are closely interdependent processes, so that the choice of one will in large measure also determine the second. For this reason, allocative planning will be either *plan-oriented* or *process-oriented.*[26]

In Italy, where central planning has not yet advanced very far, the question of the appropriate mechanisms for plan implementation, and

[25] Benjamin Higgins, "An economist's view", in H. M. Phillips (ed.), *Social Aspects of Economic Development in Latin America*, UNESCO, 1963, p. 247.
[26] The best current discussion of problems of planning implementation is that of Bertram M. Gross, "Activating national plans", in his *Action Under Planning, op. cit.* The terminology adopted in the present paper, however, differs from that of Gross.

consequently for the whole structure of the planning system, is basic to the present controversy there. According to LaPalombara,

> The question of control is a critical one. Is planning to be by "inducement" or "indication", as some Italians claim, or is it to have "compulsive" dimensions? If the latter, will compulsion apply only to the public sector or will it be extended to the private sector as well? If planning is to be compulsory or obligatory for the public sector, what instruments will the government utilize to enforce private-sector adherence to the plan? Will the plan encompass the whole economy or will it be limited to only particularly important sectors? These are merely a few of the questions. Although the 1965 plan provides some tentative answers, many of them remain unclear.[27]

The production of a blueprint and adherence to its basic structure of goals may be viewed so essential by the political leadership of a country that maximum use will be made of the available powers of command and inducement in the endeavor to carry out the plan. In *command planning*, sanctions are applied to compel adherence to clearly formulated objectives and targets. The plan itself may have legal force or may be promulgated in a series of executive decrees in order to obtain specific results.[28] For Jean Maynaud, for instance,

> A plan is not a plan unless it is central and global, involving specific objectives, and directly inserted in the existing socio-economic context even if it anticipates some social change. . . . Public authorities must make a strong effort to assure that the results of planning will be close to what is predicted. This suggests that some compulsion is essential, even in places like Italy, where it appears that the forces of the free market have created rapid economic expansion.[29]

Inducement is a weaker form of activation in that its effects are not, as a rule, experienced as coercion. It arranges the decision environment of others in such a way that one kind of decision will tend to be preferred over possible alternative decisions. Typical instruments of inducement are special lines of credit, interest manipulation, subsidies, exchange-rate policies, tax exemptions, and preferential import tariffs.

[27] Joseph LaPalombara, *op. cit.*, p. 103.
[28] The concept of command planning has been suggested by Peter Wiles in his brilliant analysis of *The Political Economy of Communism*, Cambridge, Mass.: Harvard University, 1962. See also his "Economic activation, economic planning, and the social order", in the aforementioned volume edited by Bertram M. Gross, as well as Zygmunt Bauman, "The limitations of 'perfect planning' ", in the same volume.
[29] Joseph LaPalombara, *op. cit.*, p. 104.

Both command and inducement are clearly plan-oriented in that the plan will tend to be regarded as a serious long-term commitment in which changes can be made, but not made easily. However, where the performance of subsystems is important for the attainment of system-wide goals (where the carrying out of the plan depends, for instance, on the actions of the private sector), and the imposition of sanctions or indirect controls is impracticable, allocative planners will tend to stress *process* over plan. In this case, the participation of all the principal interests will be enlisted in the formulation of the plan itself. This has come to be known, following the recent French experience, as indicative planning.[30] And, according to LaPalombara, "The very fact that planning procedures will include pluralistic participation undercuts the idea of compulsion."[31]

Both strong and weak forms of process-oriented planning are encountered. The strong form makes extensive use of bargaining; planning appears, therefore, as a process of continuous *negotiation*, with central government agencies among the list of main protagonists. According to Neil W. Chamberlain,

> There are few policies which are so "technical", so independent of people's reactions, that they can be instituted without question. Most matters of any consequence involve discussion and compromise. The views of those on whom the functioning of the system depends cannot be wholly ignored unless the system is prepared to part with their services—in which case it must come to terms with their replacements.
>
> A system of bargains among people must be contrived, and it presumably can be contrived more or less efficiently from the viewpoint of achieving the objectives of the system—that is, with varying degrees of sacrifice of system objectives to subsystem (individual) goals.[32]

The weaker form of process-oriented planning depends for its implementation on nothing more persuasive than the participation of key actors in the planning process, those who will be charged with implementation. There is but a minimum of negotiation, and the plan document itself will come to be regarded as less important than the possible benefits resulting from a joint consideration of targets, policies, and instruments. These benefits include establishing a diaologue among contending sectors,

---

[30] John and Anne-Marie Hackett, *op. cit.*, for a comprehensive account of French planning.

[31] Joseph LaPalombara, *op. cit.*, p. 104.

[32] Neil W. Chamberlain, *op. cit.*, pp. 7 and 8.

creating a wider awareness of national problems, providing the main economic actors with a common information base, encouraging socially more responsible decision-making, reducing uncertainty in the calculation of sectoral investment programs, and so on.

In the pure case, process-oriented planning would probably not need to have a plan at all except as an informal discussion document which would register the temporary consensus of all the parties involved. But the pure case of process-oriented planning is rare; usually it will be found strongly mixed with a command and inducement, so that a formally adopted plan may have some substance, after all.

Hagen and White in their appreciation of French experience, write:

> On approval of the plan, comprehensive and vigorous intervention by the government began to see that the targets were attained. Or rather, the intervention under the preceding plans continued. French planning, M. Pierre Massé, the present director of the *Commissariat au Plan* has said, is "more than indicative and less than imperative". The phrases are correct, but how much more than indicative, even though also much less than imperative, is the actual process! In M. Massé's delicate Gallic phraseology in another place, "the heart of the matter is that French planning is active; it . . . regulates the stimuli and aids at the disposal of the public departments in such a manner that the objectives assigned to the private sector are achieved."[33]

Choice of kind of planning. Which kind of planning predominates will depend on the nature of the decision environment and the urgency of the problems to be solved. Allocative planning can occur under either developmental or adaptive planning. In adaptive planning, planners will be chiefly concerned with predicting the behavior of external variables and with adjusting the available policy instruments in order to maintain the system in some sort of equilibrium under the impact of changes which may impinge upon the subsystem (for example, national economic plans are not yet drawn up so as to optimize development potentials concurrently at national and local levels; the local impact of national plans is, therefore, determined largely by chance). The actual scope for allocative planning under these conditions is quite limited, since adaptations are made to external conditions, special opportunities are seized, and decisions are made about what are probably matters of only secondary importance to the community and, hence, are politically more vulnerable.[34]

[33] Everett E. Hagen and Stephanie F. T. White, *Great Britain: Quiet Revolution in Planning*, Syracuse: Syracuse University, 1966, p. 105.
[34] W. H. Brown, Jr. and C. E. Gilbert, *op. cit.*

Under developmental planning, allocative planners perform a quite different role, although they continue to build models or set targets. Their functions in this case can be best understood with reference to innovative planning.

Innovative planning. This appears as a form of social action intended to produce major changes in an existing social system. According to Neil W. Chamberlain, it creates "wholly new categories of activity, usually large in scale, so that they cannot be reached by increments of present activity, but only by initiating a new line of activity which eventually leads to the conceived result".[35] Unlike allocative planning, it is not *preliminary* to action but a fusion or synthesis of plan-making and plan-implementing activities within an organizational frame. Four characteristics help to distinguish innovative from allocative planning.[36]

1. Innovative planning seeks to introduce and *legitimize new social objectives.* Its central attention is, therefore, on the main points of leverage that will accomplish this task. By concentrating on only a few variables, innovative planners inevitably ignore large parts of the total value spectrum of the society into which the innovation is to be introduced. At the same time, only the most general consequences are considered, with attention to those which relate to expected structural changes in the system. The emphasis, therefore, is on the guidance of change through a selective repatterning of the influences on social action rather than on the multiple consequences of alternative allocations.

2. Innovative planning is also concerned with *translating general value propositions into new institutional arrangements and concrete action programs.* This difficult task usually falls upon a creative minority, which is basically dissatisfied with the existing situation. The organization of these groups, their self-articulation, and their functioning—until they themselves become subject to inevitable routinization—may all be thought of as part of the process of innovative planning.

For example, Bertram Gross referring to what he calls an "institutionalized capacity to build other institutions", writes in his introduction to Robert Shafer's treatment of Mexican planning:

[35] Neil W. Chamberlain, *op. cit.*, p. 175.
[36] This form of planning is discussed more fully in J. Friedmann, "Planning for innovation: the Chilean case", *Journal of the American Institute of Planners*, Vol. 32 (June 1966), pp. 194–203.

A new institutional infrastructure was needed. To build it in small pieces, however disconnected, seemed infinitely superior to the piling up of a vast hierarchical bureaucracy in a small number of ministries. It provided more upward career channels for people with ability and ambition. By placing scarce eggs in many baskets, there was more room for trial and error, more protection against failure. Promotion of new institutions took precedence over their coordination.

This kind of institution building has a pulse rate of its own. The more successful it is in getting things done, the more problems the new institutions create. This leads to increasing pressure to pull things together a little more tightly. . . . But then the effort to get important things done leads once again to new spurts of decentralized institution building. Central promotion of decentralized institutions once again races ahead of central coordination.[37]

3. From this it follows that innovative planners are public entrepreneurs who are likely to have more interest in *mobilizing resources* than in their optimal allocation among competing uses. They will seek to redirect financial and human resources to those areas which promise to lead to significant changes in the system. In contrast to allocative planners who strive for equal marginal returns, innovative planners seek to obtain the largest amount of resources for their projects, even if this should mean weakening the purposes of competing organizations. Innovative planners are only peripherally concerned with these other purposes; by weakening other parts of the system, they may even gain a temporary advantage for themselves and facilitate the process of transformation.

4. Innovative planners propose to guide the process of change and the consequent adjustments within the system through the feedback of information regarding the actual consequences of innovation, in contrast to allocative planners, whose main endeavor is accurately to predict the chain of consequences resulting from incremental policies and then to adapt these policies to the prospective changes. To state the difference more succinctly: innovative planners are not, as a rule, interested in gradually modifying existing policies to conform to expected results. Innovative planners are more limited in focusing mainly on the immediate and narrowly defined results of the proposed innovation, and more ambitious in advancing a major project and laboring diligently to introduce it into society. Modifications of this project will tend to occur only as a result of political compromise in the course of getting it accepted and the

[37] Bertram M. Gross, "The dynamics of competitive planning", preface to Robert J. Shafer, *Mexico: Mutual Adjustment Planning*, National Planning Series No. 4, Syracuse: Syracuse University, 1966, p. xix.

actual consequences of the policy in operation that suggest the desirability of changes in its original form. In place of experiments *in vitro* (through the manipulation of econometric models), innovative planners prefer the device of pilot schemes, where the utility of an idea can be observed in action.

Innovative planning is especially prevalent in rapidly changing social systems. It is, in fact, a method for coping with problems that arise under conditions of rapid change, and it will tend to disrupt existing balances. There is much still to be learned about the different ways that major changes are introduced into an established society or how new social systems emerge. But it is certain that equal progress cannot be made on all fronts simultaneously. Rather, the image that comes to mind is that of successive waves and wavelets of innovation spreading outwards from a number of unrelated focal points, or innovating institutions, from Clarence Thurber's "islands of development".[38] Since it is difficult to sustain innovation at any of these points over prolonged periods, there may be frequent shifts of emphasis in innovation, one wave succeeding another, but in a different direction. It is even more difficult to succeed in establishing effective organizational linkages among institutions engaged in innovative planning, although clearly where a massive effort for change is intended, this is a necessary condition for the successful transformation of the system.

The strategic problem is to identify the critical points for system transformation and to activate innovative planning at these points. But if a system is already undergoing rapid change, the importance of this strategic problem decreases sharply; for the system generates change automatically. It is engaged in what Akzin and Dror call "high-pressure" planning. Speaking of Israeli experience, they write:

> The high rate of unpredicted change and the central social roles of government activities impose a fast pace of operation upon the civil service. Although nearly all ministries are overloaded with pressing day-to-day problems, energetic senior civil servants continue to launch relatively large numbers of new projects and activities. The constant pressure of issues necessarily lessens systematic long-range thinking and encourages a problem-by-problem manner of decision-making.[39]

[38] Clarence E. Thurber, "Islands of development: a political and social approach to development administration in Latin America", paper presented to the National Conference of the Comparative Administration Group, 17 April 1966.

[39] Benjamin Akzin and Yehezkel Dror, *Israel: High Pressure Planning*, Syracuse: Syracuse University, 1966, p. 17.

But this pragmatic approach, they say, "is frequently the optimal master strategy. For many problems in the economic, social, political, and technological fields, no applicable knowledge is available. Rather than be misled by theories and recommendations based on quite different circumstances, it is wiser to proceed pragmatically."[40]

Under high-pressure planning, detailed target achievement is not possible. The general ends will remain fairly stable and give rise to efforts of allocative planners to keep the system in balance and generally moving in the desired direction. But specific ends may be frequently revised in the light of changing conditions and a constant reevaluation of the action. Innovative planning thus appears as a concrete form of substantial rationality.

Innovative planning is typically uncoordinated and competitive, and this is yet another reason why target achievement is, in any functional sense, unattainable. The top leaders of the Israeli government, writes Bertram Gross,

> have deliberately nourished the institution-building, empire-constructing, resource-grabbing expansionism of organizations in all sectors of society, including science and education as well as the trade union movement, political parties, and private business. This has meant the promotion of sectoral (or facet) planning. The result has been more and more high-pressure planning and implementation by competitive institutions. Under such circumstances clear-cut coordination by command of central authorities has been neither feasible, essential, nor desirable.[41]

Role of allocative planners in innovative planning. But not all systems find themselves already engulfed in a process of rapid internal transformation. Allocative planning is sometimes advanced as a means of generating more rapid changes, especially in the economic field. Dissident young engineers and economists, eager to transform traditional stagnation into dynamic industrial systems, regard the creation of central planning agencies as in itself a major act of innovative planning. For them a central planning agency represents a "permanent institutionalized symbol of the Government's sustained commitment" to the goal of rapid economic growth.[42]

But in their enthusiasm, they may forget that their comprehensive econometric models accommodate discontinuous change only with

[40] *Ibid.*, pp. 16–17.
[41] In the preface to Akzin and Dror, *op. cit.*, pp. 26–27.
[42] Bertram M. Gross in his preface to Robert J. Shafer, *op. cit.*, p. 13.

difficulty. The more allocative planning relies on such models, the more conservative is it likely to be. Detailed awareness of interrelations tends to make experts cautious and hesitant to prescribe radical solutions. Allocative planners, then, confront essentially two choices; either to remain satisfied with the *symbol* they have created and to move gradually towards the bureaucratization of the planning function—but, at the same time, to forfeit ambitious goals, or to risk the seeming anarchy of rapid change, consciously using allocative planning for compelling and inducing maximum efforts in key areas and for endeavoring to maintain only a reduced number of strategic balances throughout the system. In the second case, allocative planners will not only resort increasingly to command as a form of implementation, but will encourage large-scale innovative planning to carry out major elements of the plan or to respond to new problems that are generated by rapid change.

In this vitally important interrelationship between allocative and innovative planning, the role of allocative planners is to develop new kinds of leadership, to channel resources to priority areas or points of change, to facilitate communication among the highly competitive innovative organizations, to search for areas of agreement, to help resolve interinstitutional conflicts especially with regard to the use of limited resources, and to encourage organizational links among the many "islands of development". Over time, and as the pace of change slows down, allocative planning tends to replace innovation in the management not only of organizations but also in the social system as a whole.

In general, then, we may conclude, first, that innovative planning is needed to accomplish a major—as compared to only a marginal—reallocation of resources. New institutions and new programs are needed if money is to be spent in radically different ways. The second conclusion concerns the process of translating abstract values into specific projects and programmed activities (goal reduction). Contrary to the belief of some theorists, this is not inherently a logical process but one that requires institutional innovation.

CONCLUSION

The model suggested furnishes a skeleton for the analysis of planning. But why carry out such an analysis in the first place? What may be gained from an analysis of planning behavior?

First, *empirical findings may be incorporated into a positive theory of guided system change*. Many of the elements of such a theory already exist; what has been lacking up to now is a preliminary theoretical framework for ordering the available data and for supplementing them with studies that will ask theoretically relevant questions and begin to test promising hypotheses. In this paper, some of the hypotheses suggested are:

1. Under adaptive planning, there will be a tendency to push decisions upward towards centers of developmental decision-making where the conditions for choice at lower levels may be changed.
2. The formulation and implementation of plans are closely interdependent processes, so that the choice of one will in large measure also determine the second.
3. General, system-wide objectives are modified less frequently than more specific subsystem objectives.
4. Innovative planning is typically uncoordinated and competitive.

Second, *empirical findings will permit a systematic analysis of planning pathologies*. What leads to the breakdown of guided system change? Under what conditions and for what reasons does planning cease to be effective? The reasons may include such variables as the failure of planning to adapt itself optimally to its decision environment, the resilience of this environment to change, conflicting relations between experts and policy-makers, failure to achieve an optimal distribution of planning functions according to their position on the dependency-autonomy continuum, neglect of either innovative or allocative planning functions, rigidity in planner's attitudes and procedures, and inappropriate mix between plan-oriented and process-oriented forms of implementation.

Third, *empirical findings may serve as a basis for formulating a prescriptive planning theory*. In the light of positive theory and a systematic knowledge of planning pathologies, a normative theory of planning may be formulated that should be superior to existing formulations. Such a theory will have to be expressed as a function of the decision environment of planning.

On the basis of these several purposes, the model raises important questions that can serve as a useful starting point for any research into planning behavior:

1. What is the role of political institutions in goal formulation, policy making, and conflict resolution under different planning systems? (The

analysis will have to specify not only the social context of planning but also whether planning is developmental or adaptive, and the relations between allocative and innovative planning.)

2. What is the relation of planning institutions and processes to their social context? Can typical planning styles be identified, especially in relation to the mix of implementation procedures? What is the relative importance of allocative and innovative planning under different environmental conditions?

3. What are the political uses served by planning under different systems and how do these uses influence planning behavior?

4. What is the influence of utopian and ideological thought on the formulation, implementation, and substance of planning decisions?

5. What are the dynamic relations between developmental and adaptive planning under different environmental conditions? Under what circumstances does counterplanning appear, and how are the resulting conflicts resolved? Does something like a public or common interest arise from a system in which counterplanning is prevalent? How are planning functions distributed along a centralization-decentralization continuum, and what are their relations horizontally at each level as well as vertically among a hierarchy of ordered centers?

6. What is the relation of policy-makers (or politicians) to experts (or technicians) under different planning systems? How does this relationship influence the effectiveness of planning? Does planning lead inevitably to a "depolitization" of major developmental issues?

7. What is the relation of allocative to innovative planning? What are the roles of either type of planning in guiding system change?

8. What are the relations of competitive innovative planning units to each other? What conditions are conducive to greater coordination among them, and which may be claimed to represent "obstacles to change"?

9. What are the self-images of planners in contrast to the images of planners held by others, and how do these images affect behavior?

Perhaps a philosophical postscript will be permitted. If planning is accepted as the attempted intervention of reason in history, then it is clear that such intervention cannot be immediate and direct, but must be filtered through a series of complex structures and processes to be effective. A definitely anti-heroic picture of reason emerges. It is not the great mind that intervenes, but a multitude of individual actors, each playing his role in a collective process that he does not fully comprehend because he is involved in it himself and lacks perspective. Reason, therefore, to the extent that it operates on society, is a "collective representation" in Durkheim's sense, whose functioning is contingent on structures and forces which are independent of itself.

Community Decision Behavior: The Culture of Planning*

Richard S. Bolan

THOUGH planning has never operated in a vacuum, the scope of today's urban problems seems to impose special demands for awareness of the complex decision web in which the planner must function. The community decision arena could be considered the "culture" of planning, since its rules, customs, and actors determine the fate of community planning proposals. Understanding the nature of this cultural envelope will help in determining appropriate strategies and techniques for planning and intervention. One way to extend understanding is through comparative examination of recently begun behavioral studies focused on this area.

Previous investigation of the character of urban decision-making has been limited in a number of respects. Research has tended to proceed from relatively narrow viewpoints with major attention paid to idiosyncratic case studies often carried on with self-prophetic methods.[1] Examination of prior efforts shows strict respect for the limiting boundaries of disciplinary tradition. Little attention has been given to exploring the potential contributions of a rich variety of relevant social science disciplines. Perhaps most important, past research has been preoccupied with the concepts of power and influence and has failed to examine an equally interesting aspect of decision-making—the quality and effects of the

---

* Reprinted by permission of the *Journal of the American Institute of Planners*, Vol. 35, September 1969.
[1] See Lawrence D. Mann, "Studies in community decision-making", *Journal of the American Institute of Planners*, Vol. XXX (February 1964), pp. 58–65.

decisions themselves and the planning process that contributed to such decisions.[2]

A corollary question relates to the efficacy of the planning process in urban government. Recent writings suggest that "rational" planning procedures bear little relation to the governing of cities: the time horizons and issues that have preoccupied planners are largely irrelevant and local urban governments are so disorganized, fragmented, dispersed, and incompetent that no injection of "rational" planning (even when relevant) can survive such a political culture.

This paper attempts to formulate a conceptual framework for describing and understanding the relationships between planning and decision-making in urban government. Variables of the framework are identified and interaction between them is suggested by a series of interrelated hypotheses developed on the basis of past work in the field. Ultimately, following extensive empirical observation and testing, such a framework should prove useful in extending the theory and "state of the art" of urban planning in the sense that future planning practice might be more specifically adapted to the sociopolitical culture in which it operates. What is sought is not a normative or ethical theory as to how urban government or urban planning *should be*, but rather a system for describing how urban government planning and decision-making *do occur* and how they are influenced by the environmental and social structure that surrounds urban government. The approach, in short, is behavioral in nature.

THE GENERAL FRAMEWORK

To begin, a classical model of rationality is described. Then this simplified rational model is adapted to succeeding levels of complexity to make

---

[2] The comments of Norton Long are appropriate to this outlook: "The question 'Who Governs?' has proved in the end rather less interesting than expected. In a sense it has been a blind alley arising from the obsession with when can it be shown that 'A' has power over 'B' and the understandable desire to refute the social science fiction of C. Wright Mills and Floyd Hunter. . . . This could lead to looking at the process of governing and its consequences rather than at the consequences of the specific acts of prestigious personages with top roles in the system." From "Political science and the city", Leo F. Schnore and Henry Fagin (eds.), *Urban Research and Policy Planning*, Beverly Hills, California: Sage Publications, 1967, p. 252.

it more realistic. For an individual, the classical model may be viewed as a series of steps.

1. The individual, in adapting to his environment, continually scans his surroundings and seeks to modify those parts that impinge on him in some fashion—offering either limitations or opportunities with respect to his needs or gratifications. He evaluates his environment in relation to a value set he has acquired from prior experience and cultural or social traditions.
2. After determining circumstances he seeks to modify (either to overcome a hardship or seize an opportunity), he establishes goals to be achieved.
3. From this, he designs as many alternative methods of achieving his goals as time and resources permit.
4. A full and complete set of probable consequences is predicted for each alternative means.
5. Each alternative means is evaluated to determine which method maximally accomplishes the desired goals with minimum cost or effort.
6. On the above basis, a method of goal achievement is selected and acted upon.
7. Over time each such rational process becomes a part of the individual's experiential makeup. Thus, either implicitly or explicitly, there tends to be a reevaluation of a past decision as a guide to the next.

This is, of course, an idealized sequence. Individuals seldom have the time or resources to carry out each step in fullest measure. Seldom is information wholly adequate; explicit specification of goals is often lacking; only a few alternative sets of means and ends can usually be considered; the ability to predict all possible consequences is highly restricted; meaningful evaluation for optimizing is difficult; and prior decisions often serve as constraints on the decision at hand. Thus, rationality, at best, is an imperfect process for the individual.[3]

For a community of individuals seeking to make collective, or public, decisions the process is even more complex. However, many of the same

[3] See, Herbert Simon, *Administrative Behavior*, New York: The Free Press, 1965, chaps. 3–5.

elements are present. An intelligence system scans and evaluates circumstances and conditions in the community. This system must also have a capacity to set goals and plot schemes for achieving goals. It must have integrative mechanisms to handle conflicting demands and balance allocations of limited resources. It must possess some capacity to select among alternatives and take action. Thus, the *process steps* of rationality are similar whether an individual or a community is involved in decision-making.[4]

Multiplicity of participation and involvement introduces other dimensions as well. The presence of many actors creates the potential for specialization of *process roles*. Some persons, for example, excel at the identification of problems and opportunities; others perform publicist or popularizer roles; and others are brokers in the exchange of power and influence. How skillfully each actor plays his role, his ability to marshall and manipulate resources, his ability to enlist other individuals to play other roles, and the influences of motivation and self-interest have a bearing on the decision process and influence decision outcomes.[5]

In addition, the *decision field* has substantial impact on community decision-making, and the ability to make and implement social plans and programs. The term *decision field* is meant to describe organizational and institutional arrangements prevailing in a given community and their influence in structuring roles of actors and determining complexity of problem-solving arrangements. It is affected by the character and nature of structural differentiation in the community. Thus, functional specialization, social differentiation, and degree and character of leadership and hierarchical structure all have a bearing on the outcomes of urban planning decisions. Moreover, internal characteristics of the specific decision units

[4] Martin Meyerson and Edward Banfield, *Politics, Planning, and the Public Interest*, Glencoe, Illinois: The Free Press, 1955, pp. 312–22; David Braybrook and Charles Lindblom, *A Strategy of Decision*, New York: The Free Press, 1963, pp. 37–41; John Friedmann, "The institutional context" in Bertram Gross (ed.), *Action Under Planning*, New York: McGraw-Hill, Inc., 1967, p. 34.

[5] Roscoe Martin, Frank Munger *et al.*, *Decisions in Syracuse*, Bloomington: Indiana University Press, 1961, pp. 311–12; Ronald L. Nuttall, Erwin Scheuch, and Chad Gordon. "The structure of influence" in Terry N. Clark (ed.), *Community Structure and Decision-Making*, San Francisco: Chandler Publishing Co., 1968; and William A. Gamson, "Reputation and resources in community politics", *American Journal of Sociology*, Vol. LXXII, No. 2 (September 1966), pp. 121–31.

Initial Premises
Process Steps
I. Structuring and defining ideas as proposals
II. Identifying the properties of alternatives
III. Structuring the decision field
IV. Engaging in the overt decision-making processes
V. Carrying out the consequences of decision process

↓

Independent Variable Sets Influencing Decision Outcomes	
Variable Set 1. Process Roles	**Variable Set 3. Planning and Action Strategies**
a. Process role specialties b. Process role measures Actor motivation Actor opportunity Actor skills	a. Planning strategies Relation to decision focus Method strategies Content variables b. Action strategies Reallocation of resources Institutional change Client change
Variable Set 2. Decision Field Characteristics	**Variable Set 4. Issue Attributes**
a. Sociopolitical environment Formal structure Informal structure General polity structure b. Decision unit character Source of power Accountability Group dynamics Group role	a. Ideological stress b. Distribution of effects c. Flexibility d. Action focus e. Predictability and risk f. Communicability

↓

Dependent Variable
Decision Outcomes

FIG. 1. Diagram of the conceptual scheme for community decision-making.

375

that ultimately vote on a given issue will also play a large role in determining decision outcomes.[6]

Similarly, *strategies of planning and intervention* have a substantial influence on the nature of community decision-making. These are the factors of prime concern to the planner. It is important to learn, for example, the degree to which one may exercise technical discretion in methods of solving problems and the relationship of those methods to the community decision-making process and structure.[7]

Finally, *the character and origin of issues* or problems that a community undertakes to solve, have a bearing on the nature of the decision-making process. Issues that create substantial ideological tension, that have significant and widespread impacts of costs and benefits, that suggest substantial changes in the distribution of power or wealth, or that entail high levels of risk are generally debated with greater intensity and over longer periods of time than are issues that are more incremental or of lesser consequence.[8]

These, then, are the basic variable sets: (1) *process steps*; (2) *process roles*; (3) *a decision field* in which the decision-making process takes place; (4) *planning and intervention strategies*; and (5) *issue attributes*. The interaction of these basic sets of variables would seem to influence the character and quality of decision outcomes (see Fig. 1).[9]

Any community, resolving an issue, regardless of its nature, must go through the decision process steps in order to reach a decision and undertake action.[10] A general outline of this process is: (a) structuring and defining ideas as proposals; (b) identifying alternatives; (c) structuring the decision field; (d) engaging in social decision-making transactions; and

[6] See *ibid.*; Clark (ed.), *Community Structure and Decision-making*, chaps. 1–5; and Roland Warren, "The interorganizational field as focus for investigation", *Administrative Science Quarterly*, Vol. XII, No. 3 (December 1967), pp. 397–403.

[7] *Ibid.*; Friedmann, "The institutional context", pp. 31–41.

[8] Richard S. Bolan, "Emerging views of planning", *Journal of the American Institute of Planners*, Vol. XXXIII (July 1967), pp. 233–45.

[9] The model is somewhat similar to that of Robert Alford in "Comparative study of urban politics" in Schnore and Fagin (eds.), *Urban Research and Policy Planning*. Those classes of variables that he labels "structure" and "culture" are viewed here as a part of the general classes of variables of the decision field. The "situation" variables would be included here as part of the plan and action systems. See pp. 264–71.

[10] These process steps are adapted from the process model described in Nuttall, Scheuch, and Gordon, "The structure of influence", pp. 351–2.

Process Step I. Structuring and Defining Ideas as Proposals

a. Recognition of discrepancy between desirable and current conditions.
b. Identification of the case as potentially actionable.
c. Formulation of possible and realizable solution(s).

Process Step II. Identifying the Properties of Alternatives

a. Inherent merits of alternative solution(s) as identified by experts.
b. The values held by individual actors.
c. The anticipated effect on the resources of the individual actors and the collectivity.[b]
d. The presumed effect on the position or status of individual actors in the social structure of the collectivity.[b]
e. The presumed availability of social support for alternative courses of action.[b]

Process Step III. Structuring the Decision Field

a. Identification of potential support and opposition.
b. Initial solicitation of support.
c. Initial negotiation informally offering the exchange of positive and negative sanctions.
d. Planning strategy for overt decision-making.
e. Organizing the necessary personnel and their resources.

Process Step IV. Engaging in the Overt Decision-making Process (Possibly repeated at several levels or in other systems)

a. Acknowledgement of overt commitment and responsibility.
b. Involving the relevant audiences including manipulation of meanings.
c. Exchange of support and sanctions (including procedural and administrative facilitation or block).
d. Final negotiation.
e. Situated contingent action, committing the collectivity to course of conduct.
f. Legitimation.

Process Step V. Carrying Out the Consequences of Decision Process

a. Implementation by designated persons or organizations.
b. Final application of positive or negative sanctions (pay-off).
c. Appraisal of actors and power relations.
d. Appraisal of action and consequences.[b]
e. Reappraisal of program.[b]
f. Regeneration of process steps (if necessary as a result of appraisals).[b]

FIG. 2. Initial premises: outline of process steps.[a]

[a] See Reference 29 at end of article.
[b] Considered optional items, desirable and important to decision outcomes, but may be omitted. All other steps, it is assumed, must be taken if decision-making is to run its course from beginning to end.

(e) carrying out the consequences of the process. Figure 2 provides a detailed listing of the process steps. These steps are virtually identical to those in the classical concept of rationality with specific adaptations for group decision-making. Significant differences first appear after proposals and alternatives have been inserted into the system. Predicting consequences and calculating optima yield to a primary emphasis on managing and manuevering the social processes intrinsic to collective decision-making.

To one degree or another, it is assumed for the purposes of the conceptual scheme that most, if not all, of these steps must be undertaken if an urban government is to make any public policy decision. They chart the course of the process in the same manner that innings chart the course of a baseball game—although clearly in less rigid fashion. They are consequently viewed as the initial premises of the framework.

Variable Set 1: The Properties of Process Roles

Shown in Figure 1 are the major properties of process roles that actors play to carry out the process steps. The general impact of role relationships is that decision outcomes reflect the values, goals, and interests of those actors who possess the most resources, occupy a favorable position in the decision-making structure, possess the best skills in negotiating decision outcomes, and have the capacity for developing the best tactics and modes of influencing behavior.

The first major characteristic of role-playing deals with the nature of role specialization. As suggested by one recent research effort, a multitude of role specialties have been observed.[11] The listing of these key specialties for the purposes of this framework is as follows:

Major Process Roles

Critic	Social-Emotional Expert	Negotiator
Initiator	Strategist	Propagandist
Planner	Organizer	Symbolic Leader
Technical Expert	Spokesman, Advocate	Enforcer
Investigator; Analyst	Mediator, Arbitrator	Evaluator

[11] Nuttall *et al., op. cit.*

There are many dimensions to actors' participation and skills. These involve a complete range of factors including expertise, friendship patterns, and the time and resources available to any actor in the light of competing matters requiring his attention. The specific hypothesis linking role and decision outcomes states:

An actor's ability to influence decision outcomes in a manner favorable to his own interests increases when the following attributes are present:

1. *Motivation.* The actor desires to participate because of needs for achievement, socialization, or status;
2. *Opportunity.* The actor has time, money, and situational factors that permit or require him to participate;
3. *Skills.* The actor possesses some or all of the following skill attributes:
   (a) high intelligence;
   (b) extensive experience in community decision-making activities;
   (c) good interpersonal competence (warm, personal, well-liked);
   (d) good communications competence (speaks and writes well, makes effective use of symbols and media);
   (e) extensive knowledge of issue under discussion;
   (f) specific knowledge of contextual matters bearing on issue (legal background, legislative background, regulations, history, and the like); and
   (g) wide network of socioprofessional contacts.[12]

Variable Set 2: Decision Field Characteristics

The literature on the manner in which the decision-making environment affects decision outcomes agrees on many basic points.

[12] See, R. F. Bales, *Interaction Process Analysis: A Method for the Study of Small Groups*, Cambridge, Mass.: Addison-Wesley Press, 1950; John M. Pfiffner and Robert Presthus, *Public Administration*, 5th ed., New York: The Ronald Press Company, 1967, chap. 5; Robert Presthus, "Authority in organization", *Public Administration Review*, Vol. XX (Spring 1960), pp. 86–92; Ralph M. Stogdill, "Personal factors associated with leadership; a survey of the literature", *Journal of Psychology*, Vol. XXV (January 1948), pp. 60–66; Peter M. Blau and W. Richard Scott, *Formal Organizations*, San Francisco: Chandler Publishing Company, 1962, pp. 87–130; James W. Julian, Edwin P. Hollander, and C. Robert Regula, "Endorsement of the group spokesman as a function of his source of authority, competence and success", *Journal of Personality and Social Psychology*, Vol. XI (January 1969), pp. 42–49; and various authors, "Personality and politics: theoretical and methodological issues", *The Journal of Social Issues*, Vol. XXIV, No. 3 (July 1968).

Conclusions from this literature lend themselves to further synthesis. Two basic sets of factors, and corresponding sets of hypotheses describing their probable influences are identified below and in Fig. 3. A distinction between characteristics of the decision *environment* and characteristics of the decision *unit* is recognized. Evidence suggests the decision environment may influence a decision unit in a variety of ways. To the extent that a

Decision environment characteristics	Tending toward action	Tending toward inaction
Formal-legal structure	Focused decision center	Dispersed decision centers (22)[a]
	Highly competent bureaucracy	Incompetent or lacking bureaucracy (24)
	Articulated hierarchy	No hierarchy (8)
Informal structure	Strong party machine	Nonpartisan (3, 14)
	Elite or interest group dominance	Amorphous (32)
Characteristics of polity	Homogenous	Heterogeneous (8,32)
	Crystallized	Noncrystallized (8,32)
	Tradition-free	Tradition-laden (24)
	Striving	Prosperous or settled (24)
Decision unit characteristics		
Source of power	Appointed body	Elected body (16,30)
Accountability	Large clientele	Small or specialized clientele (18)
	Long term of office	Short term of office (18)
Group dynamics	Socially cohesive	Socially heterogenous (6)
	Significant reward-punishment schema	Insignificant reward-punishment schema (3)
	High status	Low status
	High functional role differentiation	Little or no role differentiation
Group role	Focused	Comprehensive

Fig. 3. Hypotheses on the impact of the decision field on decision outcomes.

[a] Numerals refer to references at end of article.

decision unit has identity, status, and independent power source, it will also be subject to independent internal forces.

(a) *Decision environment characteristics.* Decision environment variables that effect decision outcomes include the following:

The formal-legal structure has been well noted in the literature as being influential in urban decision-making. Generally, a highly focused and centralized decision center is more likely to produce action on a given proposal than a dispersed structure of many autonomous decision centers. Moreover, as Friedmann[13] has pointed out, a highly competent and stable bureaucracy is more likely to produce positive influences on decision outcomes than those environments where bureaucracy is lacking or is relatively incompetent. A corollary hypothesis would be a structure with a highly articulated and respected hierarchy is more likely to produce positive action than a structure with no hierarchy.

The informal structure has been extensively described by many who have contributed to the body of political decision-making case studies of recent years. As Banfield[14] and Munger[15] point out, a community possessing a strong party mechanism is more likely to act on a proposal than a community which is nonpartisan (the party organization provides an informal mechanism for centralization). Moreover, the existence of strong private interest groups that dominate local politics means such groups will tend to influence decisions (in ways which coincide with their interests) much more than in circumstances where private interests are apathetic or dispersed. In short, as suggested by Clark,[16] communities with relatively strong integrative mechanisms for reconciling social stratification will tend to have a greater capacity for purposeful decision-making.

Finally, the characteristics of the polity have a strong influence on decision outcomes for the public agenda. As Rossi[17] has pointed out, homogeneous communities tend to easily decide on goals and means to achieve

[13] Friedmann. "The institutional context", chap. 2, p. 41.

[14] Edward C. Banfield, *Political Influence*, New York: The Free Press, 1965, p. 237.

[15] Martin, Munger *et al.*, *Decisions in Syracuse*, p. 46.

[16] Clark (ed.), *Community Structure and Decision-making*, chap. 2.

[17] Peter H. Rossi, "Power and community structure", in Edward C. Banfield (ed.), *Urban Government: A Reader in Administration and Politics*, New York: The Free Press, 1961, pp. 418–19.

them. Heterogeneous communities, where values and goals are numerous and usually conflicting, will find decision-making relatively difficult. Rossi also makes a distinction between a "crystallized" community and a "non-crystallized" community. In the former, cleavages in values and public opinion tend to coincide with economic and class structure. Where this is true and where one class has clear political dominance over others, that class tends to dominate decision outcomes. A non-crystallized community (or a crystallized community in perfect political balance) tends to lead to indecision and inaction.

As Friedmann[18] has suggested, a populace relatively free of long-standing traditions (such as urban areas on the U.S. west coast) is more prone to action than a mature, settled, and tradition-laden community. A corollary hypothesis would suggest that a striving community is more likely to take positive action on issues and proposals than a prosperous or settled community. This hypothesis is clearly related to the degree to which a populace is aroused and concerned about the public agenda.

(b) *Decision unit characteristics.* As previously indicated, governmental decision-making is a function unlikely to be delegated to a single individual. The most usual circumstance is decision-making by groups of individuals. These groups may be relatively unorganized in any formal sense and brought together on a purely ad hoc basis. Conversely, they may be long-standing, highly organized units of government (such as a legislative body) with internal characteristics of their own, set traditions of procedure, and well defined social mores. Some of the factors that would be influential are listed in Fig. 3 and suggest the following hypotheses.

Of importance is the source of power for the decision-making unit. The more stable and unthreatened the decision unit, the more likely it is to take positive action on proposals. Thus, an appointed body whose accountability is somewhat obscure is more prone to action than an elected body whose mandate is continually challenged at the polls. Accountability itself has an influence. One might expect a decision-making unit with a large clientele and a long term of office to be more prone to positive action than a decision-making group with a specialized clientele and a short term of office (the upper house of a legislative versus the lower house, for example).

[18] Friedmann, "The institutional context", chap. 2, p. 40.

Internal dynamics greatly influence group actions.[19] Socially cohesive bodies are more prone to take action on issues within the group's value preference field than are socially heterogeneous groups. This arises because of the pressures for conformity within such groups. For example, a legislative body, such as an upper house, whose members represent significantly large and heterogenous populations and hold long terms of office, becomes a socially cohesive organization. Consequently, it is more prone to positive outcomes than a legislative body whose members represent a wide variety of small populations and hold short terms of office.

Within groups where rewards and punishments are significant, one would anticipate a strong incentive for action. Conversely, if rewards and punishments are insignificant, one expects a stronger force for inaction. This suggests that the reward and punishment system represents a set of highly sensitive pressures on the behavior of group members.

Internal role differentiation might also tend to produce positive action. Examples of this are the highly structured committees of legislative body (such as the Congress) whose individual members become specialists in the committee's work. The committee itself becomes a kind of interest group or spokesman for those who share the specialty. With strong role differentiation, the recommendations of the smaller group (the committee) tend to dominate and sway the actions of the larger group.

Finally, the group role as seen by the group tends to influence its behavior. A group (such as a regulatory body) that sees its role as highly specialized and focused within a carefully circumscribed arena of action is more likely to act positively on proposals (which fall within that sphere of action) than a group that has a broader, more comprehensive area of responsibility (such as a legislative body).

Variable Set 3: Planning and Intervention Strategies

It is hypothesized that generally, the manner and degree to which a public issue is seen and understood will influence the decision outcome.

[19] Dorwin Cartwright and Ronald Lippitt, "Group dynamics and the individual", in Warren Bennis, Kenneth Benne, and Robert Chin (eds.), *The Planning of Change*, New York: Holt, Rinehart, and Winston, 1961, pp. 269–72; S. E. Seashore, "Group cohesiveness in the industrial group" (Institute for Social Research, University of Michigan, Ann Arbor, 1954); and Leon Festinger, Stanley Schachter, and Kurt Back, *Social Pressures in Informal Groups*, New York: Harpers, 1950.

The amount of information brought to bear, the way it is introduced, and the actors involved in presenting information affect the kinds of decisions that might be expected. The detailed variables and their related hypotheses are outlined below and in Fig. 4.

(a) *Planning strategies.* Three general variables influence planning strategies as outlined in an earlier paper.[20] The first is the strategic variable of planning *position* in which attachment to a power center is hypothesized to be more influential in guiding or directing public decision-making than independent and advisory planning bodies. A second factor is planning *method* where it is hypothesized that problem-solving of an incremental or opportunistic character is more likely to guide or direct public action than comprehensive classical methods of planning that place great stress on identifying and quantifying interdependencies and related complexities among a variety of systems. The third variable influencing planning strategies is planning *content*. It is hypothesized that planning which deals with the immediate, focuses on means, and deals only with highly selective and narrowly strategic information is more likely to guide or direct action than planning which looks to a long-term time horizon, is goal oriented, and focuses on comprehensive and complex systems of information. Most planners undoubtedly wish that these hypotheses could be proved incorrect, and determining the conditions under which they might be proven wrong is a key object of further research.

(b) *Action strategies.* Three variables are at work here much in keeping with the action strategies recently outlined by Rein.[21] These strategies include: (1) efforts to reallocate the distribution of resource; (2) efforts to change individual or societal behavior; and (3) efforts to change institutions and organizations within society. The guiding hypothesis is that action strategies which little disturb the status quo are more likely to be adopted by a political system. This would mean efforts to bring about social change that maintain the existing distribution of resources and/or the present structure of institutions and organizations would more likely be accepted

[20] Bolan, "Emerging views of planning", pp. 237–43.
[21] Martin Rein, "Social science and the elimination of poverty", *Journal of the American Institute of Planners*, Vol. XXXIII (May 1967), pp. 146–63.

Planning strategies	Tending to guide or direct action	Tending to minimum effect on action
Positive variable	Attachment to power center	Independent and advisory (3,15,23,24)[a]
Method variables	Ad hoc opportunism Problem-solving	Comprehensive (24) Classical focus on inter-dependencies (7,18)
	Incremental	
Content variables	Immediate time horizon Means oriented Selected and focused information	Long-term time horizon (24) Goal oriented (7) Comprehensive informa-tion system (7)
Action or intervention strategies	Efforts to maintain distribution of resources	Efforts to reallocate distribution of resources (31)
	Efforts to change or modify individual behavior	Efforts to change or modify societal behavior (31)
	Efforts to bring about change with existing institutions and organizations	Efforts to alter existing institutions and organizations (31)

Fig. 4. Hypotheses on the impact of planning strategies on decision outcomes.

[a] Numerals refer to references at end of article.

than those that seek major reallocation of wealth or power. Similarly, programs that are designed to change individual circumstances (such as social security) tend more toward action than programs that attempt massive changes in aggregate societal behavior (such as prohibition).

Variable Set 4: Characteristics of Public Issues

The general hypothesis relating to how public agenda characteristics influence decision outcomes is that positive action can usually be expected in any decision system where proposals are easily predictable in their consequences; are easily accomplished (both economically and administratively); and generally lie within a social value or preference field. What this means in specific terms lies in the influences of six basic variables affecting decision outcomes, shown schematically in Fig. 5.

	Tending toward action	Tending toward inaction
	Nonideological	Highly ideological (7,13,23)[a]
	Limited distribution of costs and benefits; limited scope	Wide distribution of costs and benefits; wide scope (7)
Agenda Characteristics	Flexible over time	Irreversible; inflexible over time (7)
	Single focus for action programming	Dispersed focus for action programming (24)
	Consequences easily predictable	Consequences highly uncertain (1)
	Features of issue easily communicable	Features of issue abstract and complex (10)

FIG. 5. Hypotheses on the impact of the nature of the public agenda on decision outcomes.
[a]Numerals refer to references at end of article.

The ideological content of a proposal for change will influence the decision outcome. If there is little conflict over basic values implicit in a proposal, then it is hypothesized that there will be a greater tendency toward positive action. However, should a proposal seriously conflict with widely held values, then there will be a tendency toward rejection. If, for example, an urban government proposes to acquire all land and buildings by eminent domain and thereby eliminate private property within its borders, there would most likely be vigorous resistance in virtually all urban areas in the United States. In essence, communities are not likely to easily cut off widely held social values.

The second variable relates to distribution and scope of cost and benefits that are likely to occur if action is taken on a given proposal. This involves not only how many people are influenced by the proposal but how much they are influenced. Generally speaking, proposals involving wide and broad distribution and a substantial measure of intensity of costs and benefits are usually rejected in the political process. Proposals involving only limited costs and benefits as well as limited intensity are more likely to be accepted. More simply: political systems will tend to reject a proposal that costs a lot of people a lot of money and accept one that costs a few people a little money.

The third variable is the flexibility of action intrinsic to a proposal. If a proposal is irreversible or inflexible over time, it is more likely to be rejected than a proposal that can later be changed if proven inappropriate or in need of modification. Urban expressways provide an example of irreversible decisions, while a new educational program is an example of a decision that may be easily changed or adjusted in the light of later experience.

The fourth variable deals with the problem of programming action. If carrying out the proposal involves a great deal of coordination among a large number of dispersed and autonomous groups, it is more likely to be resisted and eventually rejected (largely because of uncertainty that will actually be carried out as proposed). Even if adopted, it may easily be subverted in implementation. Proposals that concentrate or focus action within a single agency or a relatively few individuals and involve few external coordination problems will more likely be adopted.

Dealing with uncertainty clearly affects the decision-making process. This is true not only in political systems but in other more tightly controlled, group circumstances as well. Where risks are high and consequences uncertain there is hesitancy to act. If on the other hand, consequences are easily predictable and risks minimized (and all other factors are favorable), positive decisions are readily reached.

Finally, ease of communication is a key variable. Issues that are abstract and require sophisticated powers of conceptual reasoning are less likely to be communicated well (and are thus rejected) than issues that can be clearly perceived and understood by the actors who will have to deal with them. This is an important variable that is easily overlooked. Difficulty in communication can be equally, if not more, detrimental to decision-making than lack of communication. A recent seminar at Boston College brought together a number of protagonists involved in an issue which generated one of the major riots in the ghetto of an eastern city (Newark,

New Jersey) in the summer of 1967. Observing these actors was like observing those in the movie *Rashoman*. Each perceived and interpreted the same set of facts and circumstances in an entirely different way.

CULTURAL DYNAMICS

In any given governmental planning-decision-making environment, individual hypotheses are presumably exerting individual influences on decision outcomes. In addition, it could be expected that one might find interactions (and collinearity) between independent variables. Moreover, such interactions could occur at various levels. For example, an agenda item that is nonideological, predictable, inexpensive, and easy to accomplish may still be rejected because of interactions arising from particular interest group resistance. Moreover, interaction may occur on three different "vertical" levels with (1) formal public pronouncements and positions taken at formal ceremonies required by law (hearings, legislative sessions, and so on); (2) informal group activities (such as partisan caucuses); and (3) independent activities of individual actors. In addition, "horizontal" influences may be present in which a given agenda item may be linked to another simultaneously occurring agenda item. This linking could occur in a variety of ways such as a "technical" linkage (one issue is related to another in some logical, substantive way) or a purely "political" linkage (such as log rolling—"You vote for my bill, and I'll vote for yours").

An additional complication in the dynamics of the structure occurs when more than one decision unit must act on a given agenda item. This provision is frequently built into federal grant-in-aid programs to insure coordination; for example, a prerequisite for a water or sewer grant is approval of the local project by a metropolitan planning agency. In this instance, the process flow in Fig. 1 would take on additional complicating elements; namely the addition of more decision units—some at different levels of government, with different functions, different traditions and styles of operation, and different internal social attributes.

One can, in fact, envision for complex issues an entire network of decision units including some completely outside the community. Thus, for a given issue in a particular urban area, one would find a variety of circumstances with respect to issue attributes, planning and action strategies, and internal and external environmental pressures.

Another important dimension is the possibility of feedback throughout the system. For example, generation of issues has been suggested to occur through sources both internal and external to the system.[22] Thus, an issue might be generated by planners and strategists, by actors within the decision field, or by actors within the general polity. Issues may be redefined or reformulated and consequently regenerated through the system before actual decisions are reached. Issues may experience unfavorable outcomes (inaction) at first and later be reintroduced with resulting favorable actions.

IMPLICATIONS AND CONCLUSIONS

This description of the conceptual framework of the culture of urban planning is, at best, a preliminary and tentative one in which many of the variables require more precise definition. It is also clear that development of objective measurement scales for each of the variables is an immediate and formidable task. Specific relationships between variables are not as yet seen precisely. The design of empirical research and analysis will be equally complex and demanding.

If, however, in advance of extensive empirical testing, the conceptual scheme can be imagined to reasonably reflect reality, it seems possible to formulate a number of potential implications for the urban planner if he is to adapt his theory and practice to the framework.

Process versus Substance

The framework suggests very strongly the delicate nature of the relationship and balance between the substance and process of planning. It reinforces the notion that one cannot be emphasized at the expense of the other. The planner who approaches the cultural framework with technical expertise alone soon finds others' perception of his role quite narrow and his operating arena and impact highly circumscribed. He may be viewed as effective but only on certain restricted issues. On the other hand, focusing on process alone limits the planner to symbolic emotional support roles and unduly hampers his capacity for professional judgment as to feasibility of means and ends in any given problem

[22] Bolan, "Emerging views of planning", pp. 236–7.

situation. The framework points up the need for a planning function in the community fully capable of effectively coping with both in proper degree and balance.

Impact on the Substance of Planning

The substance of planning is clearly affected by the scheme in quite serious ways. If the hypotheses in any way reflect actual tendencies, the thrust of such effects pushes toward developing a balance between short-run and long-run vistas, between selective and comprehensive prescription, and toward a deeper understanding of the importance of incremental decision-making and negotiated conflict resolution. Since planning attempts to deal with rather profound policy matters for the urban community, it should come as no surprise that it has all the attributes of a legislative process even if in an administrative, or even purely informal, context.

Thus, our concepts of optimality, our focus on an abstract welfare function, and our concern for an illusory greater good (or "public interest") is brought into serious question by the framework. Planning is being challenged more and more, not on its service to an overall public, but rather on the differential and distributional aspects of its results affecting particular publics. Who actually pays and who actually benefits from community development programs are usually the crucial problems facing the decision-making apparatus of the urban community. Aggregate measures of this arouse only academic interest. Too often, in the past, the beneficiaries of a program have been an entirely different group than the group paying the price. We are generally unable to arrive at some means of restoring equity because, in our preoccupation with an overall public interest, we have failed to fully explore and understand these distributional effects.

Reconciliation of conflicting goals, values, interests, and even drastically different concepts of discounting the future is an intrinsic part of planned social change. Thus, analytical techniques emphasizing the concepts of marginality and differential incidence become paramount to the planner's kit of methodological tools. These will likely provide greater utility and relevance in the social transactions of a real-world planning process. The concept of suboptimality proved highly advantageous in the technological setting of the Department of Defense; in the social-cultural framework envisioned here it would seem essential if the wide and complex array of publics in the urban community are to find any mechanism at all for decision-making.

Authority for Planning

The conceptual scheme strongly suggests traditional notions of position and power as bases of authority and leadership cannot be divorced from less formal mechanisms for legitimating authority and exercising power.[23] With the multitude of roles and the complex array of skill dimensions, an urban planner is usually faced with an inability to assume all speaking parts in the play. Even assuming he had the skills, he would likely find it impracticable to assemble the necessary resources. Thus, he is inevitably faced with the problem of *coordinating* and *motivating* others in their participation in the decision-making process.

With relatively few exceptions, the American urban community has so fragmented and dispersed authority that the proponent of any program or plan is forced into informal arrangements for exercising leadership and influencing decision-making. It helps to be in a position of authority if this can be arranged, but it is still no guarantee of success. Thus, skill in inducing motivation, in coordinating other's actions, and in building concensus in a contextually appropriate coalition (without recourse to coercion) is demanded of those who wish to see a proposal through to a favorable decision outcome.

This clearly is a massive task, as anyone who is attempting to direct a Community Action Program or Model Cities effort can attest. It seems to have best chance for success when the planner enjoys a wide range of social acceptability and is generally identified with the community's dominant norms and values.[24] The conceptual scheme described here would also seem to suggest that the proposal itself cannot be too far removed from the norms and values of the relevant community.

Training of Planners

Finally, the conceptual framework seems to suggest training orientations

---

[23] Pfiffner and Presthus, *Public Administration*, chap. 5.
[24] Presthus, "Authority in organizations".

in the education of planners quite different from those found in the traditional city planning curriculum. On the one hand, more sophisticated techniques in such areas as operations research, development of heuristic models, and other emerging planning tools still provide an essential element of planning training but with a new focus on subsystem analysis and new research into problems of incidence and differential effects of city-building activities. On the other hand, however, quite unlike the methods of architectural design, the development of social designs emphasizes training in interpersonal skills, social interaction theory, group dynamics, political theory, communications theory, and community organization. It suggests more effort at structured and supervised field or "intern" experiences in actual social decision-making settings.

In short, many of the educational thrusts suggested in a recent *Journal* article by Brooks and Stegman[25] are reinforced in our examination of the cultural setting. The Brooks and Stegman argument, however, suggests these educational reorientations *because* of the issues of the day. The conceptual scheme presented here implies these kinds of educational reforms are essential *regardless* of the issues of the day. This lack has contributed to many past failures when planning had no significant impact on urban policy-making.

Finally, to paraphrase Roscoe Pound, city planning, like law, is judged by its results, not by its logical processes. But results and logical processes are inextricably linked by the social milieu in which both are operating. The conceptual scheme presented here is an effort to develop a more detailed and useful understanding of these relationships. Built in are the mechanisms for beginning to examine and test alternative strategies and methods of urban planning with explicit recognition of process steps, process roles, and environmental and social climate influences. Even beyond this, however, it is hoped that the framework can provide a forward step in explanatory power in a highly complex area of human behavior that exerts crucial influences in restricting or expanding opportunities to develop better urban communities.

---

[25] Michael P. Brooks and Michael A. Stegman, "Urban social policy, race, and the education of planners", *Journal of the American Institute of Planners*, Vol. XXXIV (September 1968), pp. 275–86.

REFERENCES

Books

ALAN ALTSHULER. *The City Planning Process: A Political Analysis*, Ithaca, New York: Cornell University Press, 1965.

ROBERT F. BALES. *Interaction Process Analysis: A Method for the Study of Small Groups*, Cambridge, Massachusetts: Addison-Wesley Press, 1950.

EDWARD C. BANFIELD. *Political Influence*, New York: Free Press, 1961.

EDWARD C. BANFIELD (ed.). *Urban Government: A Reader in Administration and Politics*, New York: Free Press, 1961.

PETER M. BLAU and W. RICHARD SCOTT. *Formal Organizations*, San Francisco: Chandler Publishing Co., 1962.

WARREN BENNIS, KENNETH BENNE and ROBERT CHIN (eds.). *The Planning of Change*, New York: Holt, Rinehart & Winston, 1961.

DAVID BRAYBROOKE and CHARLES LINDBLOM. *A Strategy of Decision*, New York: The Free Press, 1963.

TERRY N. CLARKE (ed.). *Community Structure and Decision-making: Comparative Analysis*, San Francisco: Chandler Publishing Co., 1968.

ROBERT A. DAHL. *Who Governs*, New Haven: Yale University Press, 1961.

HENRY FAGIN and LEO F. SCHNORE (eds.). *Urban Research and Policy Planning*, Urban Affairs Annual Reviews, Vol. 1, Beverley Hills, California: Sage Publications, Inc., 1967.

LEON FESTINGER, STANLEY SCHACHTER and KURT BACK. *Social Pressures in Informal Groups*, New York: Harpers, 1950.

BERTRAM M. GROSS. *Action Under Planning*, New York: McGraw-Hill, 1967.

PETER MARRIS and MARTIN REIN. *The Dilemmas of Social Reform*, New York: Atherton Press, 1967.

ROSCOE MARTIN, FRANK MUNGER *et al*. *Decisions in Syracuse*, Bloomington: University of Indiana Press, 1961.

MARTIN MEYERSON and EDWARD BANFIELD. *Politics, Planning and the Public Interest*, Glencoe: The Free Press, 1955.

JOHN M. PFIFFNER and ROBERT PRESTHUS. *Public Administration*, 5th ed., New York: The Ronald Press Company, 1967.

HERBERT SIMON. *Administrative Behavior*, 2nd ed., New York: Macmillan Co., 1961.

AARON WILDAVSKY. *The Politics of the Budgetary Process*, Boston: Little, Brown & Co., 1964.

Articles

ROBERT ALFORD. "The comparative study of urban politics" in Fagin and Schnore (see Books).

RICHARD S. BOLAN. "Emerging views of planning", *Journal of the American Institute of Planners*, Vol. XXXIII (July 1967), pp. 233–45.

MICHAEL P. BROOKS and MICHAEL A. STEGMAN. "Urban social policy, race and the education of planners", *Journal of the American Institute of Planners*, Vol. XXXIV (September 1968), pp. 275–86.

ROBERT A. DAHL. "The politics of planning", *International Social Science Journal*, Vol. XI, No. 3 (1959).

JOHN FRIEDMANN. "The study and practice of planning", *International Social Science Journal*, Vol. XI, No. 3 (1959).

JOHN FRIEDMANN. "The institutional context", in Gross (see Books).

WILLIAM A. GAMSON. "Reputation and resources in community politics", *American Journal of Sociology*, Vol. LXXII (September 1966), pp. 121–31.

JAMES W. JULIAN, EDWIN P. HOLLANDER, and C. ROBERT REGULA, "Endorsement of the group spokesman as a function of his source of authority, competence and success", *Journal of Personality and Social Psychology*, Vol. XI (January 1969), pp. 42–49.

NORTON LONG. "Political science and the city", in Fagin and Schnore (see Books).

LAWRENCE D. MANN. "Studies in community decision-making", *Journal of the American Institute of Planners*, Vol. XXX (February 1964), pp. 58–65.

RONALD L. NUTTALL, ERWIN SCHEUCH and CHAD GORDON. "On the structure of influence" in Terry N. Clarke (see Books).

ROBERT PRESTHUS. "Authority in organizations", *Public Administration Review*, Vol. XX (Spring 1960), pp. 86–92.

MARTIN REIN. "Social science and the elimination of poverty", *Journal of the American Institute of Planners*, Vol. XXXIII, No. 3 (May 1967), pp. 146–63.

PETER ROSSI. "Power and community structure", in Banfield (see Books).

RALPH M. STOGDILL. "Personal factors associated with leadership: a survey of the literature", *Journal of Psychology*, Vol. XXV (January 1948), pp. 60–66.

ROLAND L. WARREN. "The interorganizational field as a focus for investigation", *Administrative Science Quarterly*, Vol. XII, No. 3 (December 1967), pp. 396–419.

Various authors. "Personality and politics: theoretical and methodological issues", *The Journal of Social Issues*, Vol. XXIV, No. 3 (July 1968).

BIOGRAPHICAL NOTES

ALTSHULER, Alan. Secretary of Transportation and Construction, Commonwealth of Massachusetts, formerly Professor of Political Science at M.I.T.

Major publications include: *The City Planning Process: A Political Analysis*, Cornell University Press, 1966; *The Politics of the Federal Bureaucracy*, Dodd, Mead & Co., 1968; *Locating the Intercity Freeway*, Inter-University Case Program, Bobbs-Merrill Co., 1965; "The role of transport in metropolitan life", in Barton-Aschman Associates, *Guidelines for New Systems of Urban Transportation*, Chicago, 1968; "Transit subsidies: by whom, for whom? The values of urban transportation policy", *Transportation and Community Values*, 1969.

BANFIELD, Edward C. William R. Kenan, Jr. Professor at the University of Pennsylvania.

Major publications include: *Government Project*, The Free Press of Glencoe, 1955; *The Moral Basis of a Backward Society*, The Free Press of Glencoe, 1958; *Political Influence*, The Free Press of Glencoe, 1961; *Big City Politics*, Random House, 1965; *The Unheavenly City*, Little Broom & Co. 1970; *Politics, Planning and the Public Interest* (with Martin Meyerson), The Free Press of Glencoe, 1955; *Government and Housing in Metropolitan Areas* (with Marton Grodzns), Rand McNally, 1958; *City Politics* (with James Q. Wilson), Harvard University Press, 1963; *Boston: The Job Ahead* (with Martin Meyerson), Harvard University Press, 1966; *Urban Government* (ed.), The Free Press of Glencoe, 1961, revised edition 1969.

BECKMAN, N. Deputy Director, Congressional Research Service, Library of Congress, Washington D.C.

Major publications include: "Federal long-range planning", *Journal of the American Institute of Planners*, 1960; "Our federal system and urban development", *Journal of the American Institute of Planners*, 1963.

N. Beckman has reviewed federal and state legislation for the *Journal of the American Institute of Planners* for several years and was previously with the Department of Housing and Urban Development, the Advisory Commission on Intergovernmental Relations, and the Bureau of the Budget.

BOLAN, Richard S. Associate Professor and Chairman Community Organization and Social Planning, Boston College Graduate School of Social Work; Editor, *Journal of the American Institute of Planners*.

Major publications include: "Emerging views of planning", *Journal of the American Institute of Planners*, 1967; "The social relations of the planners", *Journal of the American Institute of Planners*, 1971; "Educating the urban planner: an expert on experts", *Planning*, 1971, American Society of Planning Officials, 1971.

DAVIDOFF, Paul. Director of the Suburban Action Institute and a member of the faculty of Princeton University, formerly Professor and Director of the Urban Planning Program at Hunter College.

Major publications include: "A choice theory of planning (with Thomas A. Reiner), *Journal of the American Institute of Planners*, 1962; "School integration, a reply", *Journal of the American Institute of Planners*, 1964; "The new city planning", *Journal of the American Institute of Planners*, 1965; "The role of the city planner in social planning", *Proceedings of the American Institute of Planners*, 1964; "Advocacy and pluralism in planning", *Journal of the American Institute of Planners*, 1965; "Integrated integration", *Integrated Education*, 1966; "The educational park in the community", *Education Parks*, Washington, 1967; "Democratic planning", *Perspecta Magazine*, Yale University, 1967; "A rebuilt ghetto does not a model city make", *Planning*, 1967; *Normative Planning, Planning for Diversity and Choice*, Sandford Anderson (ed.), M.I.T. Press, 1968; "Social Welfare Planning" (co-author), *Principles and Practice of Urban Planning*, International City Managers Association, 1968; *A Housing Program for New York State* (with Neil N. Gold and Harry Schwartz), New York, 1968; "Suburban action: advocate planning for an open society", *Journal of the American Institute of Planners*, 1970; "Opening the suburbs: toward inclusionary land use controls", *Syracuse Law Review* (with Linda Davidoff), 1971; "The suburbs must open their gates", *New York Times Magazine* (with Linda Davidoff and Neil N. Gold), 1971.

DROR, Yehezkel. Head, Public Administration Division, Department of Political Science, The Hebrew University of Jerusalem.

Major publications include: *Israel: High Pressure Planning* (with Benjamin Akzin), Syracuse University Press, 1966; *Public Policymaking Reexamined*, Chandler, 1968; *Design for Policy Sciences*, Elsevier, 1971; *Ventures in Policy Sciences: Concepts and Applications*, Elsevier, 1971; *Crazy States: A Counter-conventional Strategic Problem*, Heath Lexington, 1971.

DYCKMAN, John W. Professor of City and Regional Planning, University of California, Berkeley.

Major publications include: *Capital Requirements for Urban Development and Renewal*, McGraw-Hill, 1961; *The Changing Uses of the City, The Future Metropolis*, L. Rodwin (ed.), Braziller, 1961; "Planning and decision theory", *Journal of the American Institute of Planners*, 1961; "Some conditions of civic order in an urbanized world", *Daedalus*, Summer 1966; "Changing normative styles in urban studies", *Public Administration Review*, 1971.

ETZIONI, Amitai. Professor of Sociology, Columbia University, and Director, Center for Policy Research.

Major publications include: *A Comparative Analysis of Complex Organizations*, Free Press, 1961; *Political Unification*, Holt, Rinehart & Winston, 1965; *The Active Society*, Free Press, 1968.

FOLEY, Donald L. Professor of City Planning and of Architecture, University of California, Berkeley.

Major publications include: *Neighbors or Urbanites?*, 1952; *The Suburbanization of Administrative Offices in the San Francisco Bay Area*, 1957; *Controlling London's Growth: Planning the Great Wen 1940–1960*, University of California Press, 1963; co-author, *Explorations into Urban Structure*, University of Pennsylvania Press, 1964; co-author, *Characteristics of Metropolitan Growth in California*, 2 volumes, 1965–6; *Governing the London Region: Reorganization and Planning in the 1960's*, University of California Press, 1972.

FRIEDMANN, John. Professor of Planning and Head, Urban Planning Program, School of Architecture and Urban Planning, University of California at Los Angeles.

Major publications include: "Introduction to the study and practice of planning", *International Social Science Journal*, 1959; "Cities in social transition", *Comparative Studies in Society and History*, 1961; "Regional planning as a field of study", *Journal of the American Institute of Planners*, 1963; "Regional planning in post-industrial society", *Journal of the American Institute of Planners*, 1964; *Regional Development and Planning* (with W. Alonso), M.I.T. Press, 1964; *Venezuela: From Doctrine to Dialogue*, Syracuse University Press, 1965; *Regional Development Policy. A Case Study of Venezuela*, M.I.T. Press, 1966; "Planning as a vocation", *Plan Canada*, 1966; "Planning as innovation: the Chilean experience", *Journal of the American Institute of Planners*, 1966; "The institutional context", in *Action Under Planning*, edited by Bertram Gross, McGraw-Hill, 1967; "A conceptual model for the analysis of planning behavior", *Administrative Science Quarterly*, 1967; "Regional planning and nation-building: an agenda for international research", *Economic Development and Cultural Change*, 1967; "Education for regional planning in developing countries", *Regional Studies*, 1968; "A strategy of deliberate urbanization", *Journal of the American Institute of Planners*, 1968; "An information model of urbanization", *Urban Affairs Quarterly*, 1969; "Notes on societal action", *Journal of the American Institute of Planners*, 1969; "Intention and reality: the American planner overseas", *Journal of the American Institute of Planners*, 1969; *Urban and Regional Development in Chile: A Case Study of Innovative Planning*, The Ford Foundation Urban and Regional Development Advisory Program in Chile, 1969; "The future of comprehensive planning: a critique", *Public Administration Review*, 1971; *Transactive Planning: A Theory of Societal Guidance*, Doubleday and Anchor Books, Publication 1972; *Urbanization and National Development*, Sage Publications, Publication 1972.

GLASS, Ruth, Director, Centre for Urban Studies, University College London.

Major publications include: *Watling: A Social Survey*, 1939; *Middlesbrough: The Social Background of a Plan*, 1947; *Urban Sociology in Britain: A Trend Report*, 1955; *Newcomers: The West Indians in London*, 1960; *London, Aspects of Change* (ed.), 1964; *London's Housing Needs* (with John Westergaard), 1965; *Housing in Camden*, 1969.

GRAUHAN, Rolf-Richard. Professor of Political Science, University of Bremen.

Major publications include: *Modelle politischer Verwaltungsführung*, Konstanz, 1969; *Politische Verwaltung*, Freiburg, 1970; *Grosstadtpolitik* (ed.), 1972.

LINDBLOM, Charles E. Professor of Economics and Political Science, Yale University.

Major publications include: *Unions and Capitalism*, Yale University Press, 1949; *Politics, Economics and Welfare* (with Robert A. Dahl), Harper & Brothers, 1953; *A Strategy of Decision* (with David Braybrooke), Free Press, 1963; *The Intelligence of Democracy*, Free Press, 1965; *The Policy-making Process*, Englewood Cliffs, Prentice-Hall, 1968.

MEYERSON, Martin. President, University of Pennsylvania, formerly Professor at the Graduate School of Design at Harvard University.

Major publications include: *Politics, Planning and the Public Interest: The Case of Public Housing in Chicago* (with Edward C. Banfield), The Free Press of Glencoe, 1955; "Metropolis in ferment", *Annals of the American Academy of Political and Social Science*, 1957; "Utopian traditions and the planning of cities", *Daedalus*, Winter 1960; co-author, *Housing, People and Cities*, McGraw-Hill, 1962; *Boston: The Job Ahead* (with Edward C. Banfield), Harvard University Press, 1966; "Urban policy: reforming reform", *Daedalus*, Fall 1968.

RABINOVITZ, Francine F. Associate Professor of Political Science, University of California, Los Angeles.

Major publications include: Co-author, *Urban Government for Greater Stockholm*, New York, 1968; *City Politics and Planning*, New York 1970; co-editor, *Latin American Urban Research*, Beverly Hills, 1971; co-author, *On the City's Rim: Politics and Policy in Suburbia*, Lexington, Mass., 1972.

REINER, Thomas A. Associate Professor of Regional Science, University of Pennsylvania.

Major publications include: "Soviet city planning" (with Robert J. Osborn), *Journal of the American Institute of Planners*, 1962; *The Place of the Ideal Community in Urban Planning*, University of Pennsylvania Press, 1963; "Client analysis and the planning of public programs" (with Janet S. Reiner and Everett Reimer), *Journal of the American Institute of Planners*, 1963; "Sub-national and national planning: decision criteria", *Papers, Regional Science Association*, 1965; Review Article: "Urban Poverty" (with Janet S. Reiner), *Journal of the American Institute of Planners*, 1965; "The planner as value technician" *Taming Metropolis*, Eldridge, H. W. (ed.), 1967; "Regional science" (with Walter Isard), *Encyclopedia of the Social Sciences*, 1968; *The Crosstown Controversy: A Case Study* (with Robert Sugerman), 1970; "A multiple goals framework for regional planning, *Papers, Regional Science Association*, 1971.

ROBINSON, Ira M. Professor and Chairman, Graduate Program in Urban and Regional Planning, University of Southern California.

Major publications include: *Decision-making in Urban Planning: An Introduction to New Methodologies*, Sage Publications Inc., Beverly Hills, California 1972; co-author, "Amenity resources for urban living" in *The Quality of the Urban Environment*, Harvey S. Perloff (ed.), Resources for the Future Inc. and Johns Hopkins Press, 1969; co-author, "Goals and objectives in civil comprehensive planning", *Town Planning Review*, 1969; "Beyond the middle-range planning bridge", *Journal of the American Institute of Planners*, 1965; co-author, "A simulation model for renewal programming", *Journal of the American Institute of Planners*, 1965; Foreword to *The Planned Non-permanent Community* by V. S. Parker (Northern Co-ordination and Research Center, Department of Northern Affairs and National Resources, Ottawa), 1963; "The Peace River Region" in *Regional and Resource Planning in Canada*, edited by Ralph R. Krueger *et al.*, Holt, Rinehart & Winston, Toronto, 1963; New Industrial Towns on Canada's Resource Frontier (Research Paper No. 4, Department of Geography, The University of Chicago, 1962).

Professor Robinson has participated in the Arthur D. Little, Inc., Study for the San Francisco Community Renewal Program and in the American-Yugoslav Project in Regional and Urban Planning at Ljubljana, Yugoslavia.

WEBBER, Melvin M. Professor of City Planning and Director of the Institute of Urban and Regional Development, University of California, Berkeley.

Major publications include: Co-author, *The Urban Place and the Nonplace Realm, Explorations into Urban Structure*, 1964; "The role of intelligence systems in urban systems planning", *Journal of the American Institute of Planners*, 1965; "Planning in an environment of change: I. Beyond the industrial age; II. Permissive planning, *Town Planning Review*, 1968 and 1969; co-author, *The Social Context of Transport Planning*, 1969; *Alternative Styles for Citizen Participation in Transport Planning*, 1971.

URBAN AND REGIONAL PLANNING SERIES

Other Titles in the Series